THE DRAMA OF SOCIAL LIFE

THE DRAMA OF SOCIAL LIFE

Essays in Post-Modern Social Psychology

T. R. Young

Transaction Publishers
New Brunswick (U.S.A.) and London (U.K.)

Library of Congress Catalog Number: 89–4594
ISBN: 0–88738–202–9
Printed in the United States of America

Library of Congress Cataloging-in-Publication Data

Young, T. R.
   The drama of social life : essays in critical social psychology /
T. R. Young.
     p. cm.
   Bibliography: p.
   Includes index.
   ISBN 0–88738–202–9
   1. Social interaction. 2. Social psychology. 3. Microsociology.
4. Drama—Psychological aspects. I. Title.
   [DNLM: 1. Interpersonal Relations. 2. Psychology, Social. HM
251 Y77d]
HM291.Y68   1989
302—dc20
DNLM/DLC
                                 89–4594
                                 CIP

This book is about how drama fits into
the runs of everyday life. It is about
the drama of love, and death, and work,
and sports. Above all it is about religion—
how people fit themselves together in
the drama of life. Linda Bowman fit me
into her life at a time when the drama of
death all but extinguished my spirit. It is
to Linda that I dedicate this book. I regret
to say that Linda loved the theatre more than
she could love me. Still, I owe her much.

T.R.Y.

Contents

Acknowledgments

I would like to express my appreciation to Norm Denzin and the Society for the Study of Symbolic Interaction for permission to reprint "Hard Times and Hard Tomatoes: Symbolic Interaction Theory in a Mass Society," from the *Proceedings of the Society for the Study of Symbolic Interaction*. The editors of the *New England Sociologist* were kind enough to allow use of "The Typifications of Christ: Political and Social Uses of the Jesus Symbol," from its special issue of *Religion: The Cutting Edge*. The chapter "The Sociology of Sport" is reprinted with permission from the editors of *Sociological Perspectives*. The centerpiece of this book is "The Dramaturgical Society" coauthored with Garth Massey, an article published in *Qualitative Sociology*. Transaction Publishers itself holds the copyright to the chapter "The Politics of Sociology." The other chapters are unpublished but some were circulated in limited edition by the Red Feather Institute in its Transforming Sociology series.

John Welsh has worked and shaped my thinking on critical dimensions in dramaturgical analysis for the past seven years. He is the author of a series of articles too long neglected in the discipline. Welsh has read and critiqued every article I have written in the area as well. Our ideas and works are too much entwined easily to sort out. To John I owe much that is in this book.

Garth Massey has been a colleague, friend, and coauthor for almost fifteen years. His contribution to the essay on the dramaturgical society is substantial. It is no great tragedy that he turned his attention away from social psychology in the past ten years; an analysis of the problems of socialist development is far too important to the twenty-first century to discount in any calculus of scholarly endeavor. I do miss his wide-ranging knowledge and the added dimensions he brought to this work, however.

Much of the work on the structure of self in this collection of essays was written against Louis Zurcher—yet written for him. Zurcher wrote his book

The Mutable Self in an effort to stimulate discussion and debate. In private correspondence, Lou said that he was interested in the renewal of social psychology and that he was very pleased that I had responded to his book with my article "The Structure of Self in Mass Society: Against Zurcher"—that it was his idea that lively debate would renew social psychology. A most gracious and useful rejoinder from a good and decent human being. He is sorely missed in the politics and policies of social—and I mean social—psychology.

Valerie Malhotra has contributed greatly to my understanding of the works of Kenneth Burke and has added her great scholarship to this volume.

My wife, Dorothy (d. 1981), gave me unstinted support and love over most of the years of this work. I loved her greatly and miss her sorely yet today. My second wife, Nancy Maxson, helped me to think about the Buddhist structure of self and how it differs greatly from yet resonates with the kind of authentic self we would like to see develop in a good and decent society.

I am greatly indebted to those in England who work in the area of cultural Marxism. They helped me to get to know the literature and the research in that field when I was on sabbatical at the University of Exeter. Barry Turner of the sociology department at Exeter was most helpful to my work.

The Red Feather Institute has continued to support my research and work over the past twenty years.

Larry Reynolds, Alice Littlefield, and the sociology-anthropology faculty at Central Michigan University gave me safe harbor in a time of troubles. With this book, I give my thanks to all of these good people.

A Great University

In our Ivy cover'd towers
In our magic meeting hours
we are met to concoct brews;
Images of Greatness from the muse
of art and craft and small deceit;
all the stuff with which to cheat:
and the Legislature bemuse
from the drink that doth enthuse.

We are met to conjure truth;
we are meant to abjure ruth;
we are sent to fashion's booth
where we gauge the tiger's tooth.

In our secret silent places,
we conspire to polish faces
of the college leaving traces
of our schemes in public places.

We have raced around the world
we have chased some plans to curl
your hair and set your teeth on
edge; mayhap make you seethe on
with rage at what this group can do
and the depths which we will stoop to.

Plan the First requires that we
empty out the faculty;
Cut the budget for the books,
hire some lawyers for our crooks;
and the journal subs all stop:
when it comes to new instructors
buy the cheapest of the crop.

Sell on plastic cards of credit
Make the classes predit
ery; dump out econ, psych and hist
ory; cut out anthropology.
Even if a little drastic,
profits will be satisfactory.

Plan the B requires that we
define anew the 'un'versity':
Its the image . . . not content
that will help us pay the rent.

From the ads for sex and pop
we will take our cue and stop
the caffeine and the swizzle
so our un-versity will sizzle.

Onto Business we shall yield
the great escrucheon of our shield,
sell out Thebes and sell out Rome
fetch us MBAs to clone.

When the business brigades
find a school and invades,
first they modernize the college
so poetry yields to useful knowledge.

Hire the teams to win us fame,
build a palace for their game:
baseball, football, basketweaving;
hide the secrets, leave off grieving,
what care we who does the thieving.

With the aid of giant computers,
sell to business all our tutors.

Professors back from secret missions,
having sold their eruditions,
take a certain healthy pride
in prising out what's inside
that can be used to make us buy
even if we weep and die.

Encamped upon the college plain
a million technicians have to train
themselves within computer software
better yet to engineer
the market, votes, and the mindware
of the Brave New World they bear.

Instructors with sarcastic tongue
search among the freshman forces
for the kids who love the courses
upon which the jobs are hung
that pay the wages; pay the moppets,
help a business extract fat profits.

Lonely scholars, clipping fast
for the corporations crass;
that such scholarship well funded,
ensure their interests well fended;
and the public carefully replundered.

Intellectual marines,
clipping up the magazines,
where, behind the copy dwell
all the science they can sell.

This the image we must hide
for it shames us deep inside.
And find an image with less trouble
to parade before the gull'ble.

Thus does end our quest for
arts and science yet we gain more
monies in our coffer
for these empty images we offer.

—Inspired by and dedicated to
W. H. Auden, March 2, 1989.

Introduction

The Postmodern Idea

There is little more mystifying and yet so simple as the idea of the post-modern. It is a great nuisance to the ordinary reader that such terms are used, since they are so far removed from ordinary language conventions yet are important to an understanding of the era in which we now live. Since all the essays in this book are oriented to the postmodern psychology and morality that suffuses everyday behavior, the informed lay person must take some time to learn what is at issue in the use of the term.

The modern era began about 1500 with the beginnings of systematic thinking that we now call science. "Modern" thought assumed an intercon-nected set of universal laws governing the scientific method. With the work of Sir Isaac Newton, it was assumed, falsely, that there was perfect order in the universe and that men of genius could unscramble the complex codes of nature much as Crick and Watson unlocked the riddle of the genetic code with their work on the double helix. This era lasted until the nineteenth century, yielding to the ideas and assumptions of postmodernity.

Most thinking people still live in the "modern" epoch. They believe in the unchangeable regularities; eternal patterns of life that have been the product of two centuries of science. Some people—inconoclasts, rebels, philosophers of science, or simply those who are hurt by existing social arrangements—challenge this idea. They think that much if not all of na-

1

ture and society can be created anew, that there are no eternal, unchanging ways to be human or to "do" nature. A most disconcerting thought, yet having much support and promise in its more positive modes. In its negative modes, postmodern thought is bleak, cynical, nihilistic, and downright destructive of all that is valuable to the human project. It is important that the lay person who wants to be part of the knowledge process grasp the major arguments of both modernist and postmodernist thought.

A great many people, probably most people in the world today, live in a premodern world; one in which there is mystery, magic, the inscrutable will of God, or the whimsical caprice of gods. Preoccupied with the ordinary routines of physical survival or the extraordinary business of profit and loss, such persons make little effort to enter into the lively discourse of science and philosophy. Yet much is at stake for them and their children. One day they must take the time.

Beginnings of Modern Thought

For most of human history, the knowledge process centered around the effort to understand the will of God. The idea was that it was safer to find and to obey the will of God than to act in ignorance of it. The long centuries of human thinking came to be vested in religious mystics and teachers who somehow came into contact with God and could convey His will to ordinary people. Prayer, psychogens, dance, danger, meditation, or revelation were pathways to that kind of knowledge. Most people still center their quest for knowledge around priestly persons and around a quest for the holy.

The very beginnings of modern science and logic came with Aristotle, Zeno, Plato, and Pythagoras. Rather than the majesty of the gods, the early philosophers saw majesty in the perfection of logic, mathematics, astronomy, and later physical science. A whole new knowledge industry opened up. By the turn of the twentieth century, A. D. White would write a book about the history of the warfare between science and theology in Christendom—and declare science the winner.

The bounty of science was impressive—still is. Predictions of the arrival of comets, knowledge of the tides, revelations of the inner workings of the atom, discovery of the four forces of nature, harnessing of nuclear power, development of electronics, biochemistry, genetic surgery, and cloning seem to establish the triumph of the scientific revolution. Yet there was room for doubt.

Most of the doubt came in the politics of social protest. The early founders of sociology, psychology, economics, and political science were convinced that social relations had the same kind of iron laws that physical reality revealed, and that the task of the enlightened social scientist was to reveal those laws of the psyche and of the social order so that the human project could be advanced. A noble idea rewarded by the Nobel prize.

A first principle of social life to tumble was the idea of unilateral evolution toward higher, better forms of social life. Many sociologists and anthropologists thought, falsely, that each society went through stages of social evolution until they became *modern* societies. A lot of people still believe in the idea of progress. The problem was to identify the best social arrangements. No one could agree. The Germans tended to think Aryan culture was superior; the Chinese tended to believe that Chinese culture was at the top of the evolutionary ladder as did the Japanese, while Americans were convinced that America was the best of all possible societies. Those who stepped back a bit saw that science was another name for ethnocentrism and personal advantage.

A second iron-bound law that was challenged was in gender roles and relations. Early feminists argued that the eternal, natural laws of patriarchy were neither eternal nor natural. Those laws were the result of some ugly gender politics that gave men the right to exploit women, beat, rape, and discard them while men benefitted from their domestic and sexual services. Social science became another word for alienated gender relations.

Minority groups learned that their ways of life were inferior in this scaling of social life. Many minority persons challenged the assumptions of the majority to their pain and injury. Vast wars of colonial imperialism were justified, in part, by the belief that modernization would benefit the "savages" of Africa, Asia, and the Americas.

The iron-bound dogmas of the Muslim, Jewish, and Christian theodicies were challenged by atheists and by more thoughtful theologians alike. The teachings of the gentle Buddha found their way into American and European consciousness by those who brought back more than trophies and souvenirs from empire. The idea that Christ could speak to and could be heard in the voices of the poor infused liberation theology. The idea that women had something of value to offer Christianity other than cleaning and polishing or tending floral displays inspired another, feminist theology. The idea that human sexuality had more than one permitted form found a persistent voice in the gay liberation theology. All these are packed into a postmodern understanding of religion; an understanding that challenges the rigid logic of White Anglo males with their linear, authoritarian views of God and justice.

Carol Gilligan challenged the assumptions of Kohlberg, Piaget, and others who work the field of moral development. She thought there was a higher morality in human affairs than the simple application of universal principles of justice; that women and the way women thought was more congenial to the human project than the principled behavior of stage five or stage six moral character. For Gilligan, people were more important than principles. A simple but postmodern view.

In the art world, the impressionists, the abstractionists, and the cubists offered a postmodern form of art. Line, form, and perspective were not the essentials of good art as the modern mentality would claim. It is the spirit of a scene or a subject that is captured by the artist; not the form. The camera and the printing press could produce exact copies of nature; artists could do more; they could capture the essence of the subject.

In the meantime, James Joyce, e.e. cummings, John dos Passos, Gertrude Stein, John Steinbeck, and others were developing new literary styles. In the world of literary criticism, Raymond Williams at Cambridge was insisting that there was not an eternally valid set of principles by which good writing or good poetry could be judged.

The classic music of Bach, Beethoven, and Mozart might come close to mathematical precision in the beauty and elegance of their musical phrases but there was jazz to challenge that perfection. Gershwin, Ellington, Coltrane, Miles Davis, Teddy Wilson on the piano and Lady Day Holiday pushed modern musical theory aside. Out of the pain and anguish of everyday life in the modern world, they brought doubt and rebellion. Then came the Beatles.

The poetry of William Blake set forth a postmodern critique of religion with his famous essay on the oneness of religion, his essay on the origins of religions, and his more famous poems.

All Religions Are One. The voice of one crying in the wilderness.
The Argument. While the true method of knowledge is experience, the true method of understanding experience is poetic genius.
Principle 1. To be truly human, one must employ one's poetic genius. The forms of all things are derived from that poetic genius that the ancients called Spirit, Angel, or Demon.
Principle 2. As all human beings are alike in outward form, so (and with the same infinite variety) all are alike in poetic genius.
Principle 3. Humans think, write, or speak from the heart, that they intend as truth. Thus all sects of religious philosophy derive from the infinite variety of the poetic genius of truthful but differing humans.
Principle 4. None, by traveling over known lands can find the unknown. Therefore, no person could know more than the common experience of all. But having access to the common experience, a universal poetic genius emerges that is accessible to all.
Principle 5. The religions of all nations are derived from each nation's different use of poetic genius—which is everywhere called the spirit of prophesy.
Principle 6. The Jewish and Christian Testaments are an original derivation from poetic genius. This is necessary from the limitations of perception, the limitations of bodily sensation.

Principle 7. As all humans are alike (though infinitely varied), so all religions, and, as all similars, have one source: The true source is true human, the poetic genius.

The Marriage of Heaven and Hell

The Ancient Poets animated all objects with their genius,
Calling them by lovely names and adorning them with wondrous
property; woods, rivers, streams, mountains, lakes, cities,
nations . . . whatever their senses could perceive.

And particularly they studied each city and country
giving each a deity appropriate to its nature;
'til a system was formed . . . which some took advantage
and enslaved the common man by separating the deity from its
object: thus began the priesthood.

Choosing the forms of worship from poetic tales.
And at length they pronounced that Gods had order'd such things.

Thus men forgot that All deities reside in the human breast.

The Tyger

Tyger, tyger, burning bright
in the forests of the Night,
What immortal hand or eye
Could frame thy fearful symmetry?

In what distant deeps or skies
Burnt the fire of thine eyes?
On what wings dare he aspire?
What the hand dare seize the fire?

And what shoulder, and what art,
could twist the sinews of thy heart?
And when thy heart began to beat,
What dread hand and what dread feet?

Where the Hammer, where the chain?
And what furnace forged thy brain?
What the anvil? What dread grasp
dare your deadly terrors clasp?

When the stars threw down their spears
and water'd heaven with their tears,
Did he smile his work to see?
Did he who made the lamb make thee?

Tyger, tyger burning bright
in the forests of the night,
what immortal hand or eye
dare frame thy fearful majesty?

—William Blake

In the formal propositional form of his arguments, Blake uses the idea of deductive reasoning. In the concept of those arguments, Blake goes far beyond postmodern critique based on observation, rational thinking, and systematic organization of principles, far beyond that to a transmodern view that poetic genius and prophesy are sources of human understanding that surpass rational thinking. In the passage above, Blake links the source of God—and social order—in the human heart rather than in the reasoning mind. In the poem that follows, above, Blake casts doubt on the coherence of a world designed by a rational supreme being. Thus Blake adopts and transcends the modern critique and presents himself as one of the first postmodern thinkers in Western thought while writing in the eighteenth century. He leaped over an entire age that still informs most work in the philosophy of knowledge and science.

Physical Science

In the world of physical science as well, the assumptions of a knowable, general theory of physics was set askew by Heisenberg and his idea that not everything is knowable, not everything is measurable. The new physics turned certainty into probability while probability lost its certainty at subatomic levels of physical reality. Even physical reality slipped away in the uncertain realm of wave/particles that were neither matter nor merely energy.

In the world of biology, the curious case of the skunk cabbage served to undermine the principles of genetics and physiology. The plant had one shape in Alaska and another, quite different form, in Ohio. It turned out that a rose is not a rose is not, after all, a rose. Roseness (and skunk cabbageness) is a dialectically variable function of genetics and environment. There is no such thing as the ideal rose, the ideal oak tree, nor the ideal skunk cabbage. Our whole notion of what is normal and abnormal is destroyed by such dialectics.

Postmodern thought receives its scientific cachet from Chaos Theory if such thought needs a science or a theory to endorse it. In the past twenty years, the work in chaos research has revealed quite a different world from that of the modern world-view. In place of order, perfection, and normality, chaos is the rule. There are tiny pockets of order and determinacy but they are exceptions to the rule and are bought at great expense in energy and control from the more flexible and unpredictable environment (Gleick, 1987).

Chaos theory is just one of the many manifestations of the transition from modern ways of understanding (and responding to) the world of nature and culture toward postmodern ways of acting, thinking, and believing. If the modern world was born out of the success of science and technology in the Eighteenth Century; postmodern responses came out of the curious reluctance of women, colonial peasants, workers, artists, poets, and architects, as well as young scientists to accept the fixed order and eternal laws of modern science that froze existing relationships in society and in nature for all eternity.

There is now anticolonialism; feminism; black liberation; postmodern architecture (from whence the term first came); postmodern art; postmodern morality (which is to say, very chaotic at best); postmodern music; postmodern poetry; and postmodern physics, which is full of quarks, color, and charm. A postmodern sociology is developing, while such a criminology has yet to be born.

In modern science and in modern criminology, order was desired; finding mathematical paths and mathematical equations was the task of the graduate student and the task of the research scientist. No one wanted findings that were unstable or correlations that were weak. A simple unified theory of behavior subsumed by structural-functional models was preferred. Chaos and indeterminacy were signs of failure—signs of poor scholarship and weak intelligence. In post-modern science and in postmodern criminology, such disorder becomes the arena in which one must work. If we want order, now we must ask ourselves, what kind of order do we want; there are no unchanging structures in science or society after which we must strive. Freedom is no longer acceptance of the inevitable.

Above all, modernism requires the idea of the ideal, the idea of the normal, as well as an explanation for the abnormal. The monumental advantage of postmodern ideas is that there is no ideal in the abstract from which existing reality is but a pale and imperfect shadow. There is only infinite variety; each variation equally normal, equally natural to every other variation.

In such an unstable, uncertain world there is much to trouble one, much to enliven one. There is the absence of all laws, rules, norms, principles, and coherent connections between the runs of human behavior as between the regularities in the physical world. This indeterminacy and openness of social reality has much promise and many problems. At its best, postmodern thought is enlivening and enabling. At its worst, it is ugly, vicious, solipsistic, and self-serving. Its best is to be found in the poetry of Arnold:

Empedocles on Mt. Etna

Is it so small a thing
to have enjoyed the sun
to have lived light in the Spring
to have loved; to have thought,
to have done;
To have advanced true friends
and beat down baffling foes

That we must feign a bliss
of doubtful future date
and, while we dream on this,
lose all our present state
and relegate to worlds yet distant
our repose?

But thou, because thou hear'st
men scoff at heaven and fate,
because the gods thou fear'st
fail to make blest thy present state
Tremblest, and will not dare to trust
the joys that are!

I say, Fear not. Life still
leaves human effort scope.
Nurse no extravagant hope;
Because thou must not dream, thou
need'st not then despair!

—Matthew Arnold

The worst of the postmodern critique is to be found in a bourgeois liberalism that holds that any human good or service should be freely available as long as a market exists for it: drugs, child pornography, prostitution, agricultural chemicals, as well as hand guns. We find the postmodern spirit at its worst in Sid Vicious and the Sex Pistols; in Abby Hoffman and his apology for theft; in William Buckley and his apology for predatory capitalism.

Yet one should not lightly discard the Sex Pistols, Johnny Rotten, and the punk movement. They are trying to tell us something in a language made necessary by our preoccupation with premodern ideas of heaven and hell as with our "modern" ideas of the natural and the normal. If painters, authors, singers, and poets scream at us, it is because we cannot hear, we will not listen to more reasoned and reasonable critique. We create the Sid Vicious characters in the same instant we create and enforce our ideas of nature and normalcy. We could have listened to A. E. Housman, lonely and afraid in a world he never made, but failing that, we now hear Johnny Rotten. Both are equally spokespersons for the postmodern spirit.

In the chapters in this book, I want to carry the postmodern critique into the realm of dramaturgy; into just-pretend and never-was. I want to show all the negativity there is to be found in the sustained effort to colonize desire within the empire of market economics. I want to join with Blake and Arnold to advance a different fate for desire and for poetic genius than singing commercials for soap, beer, or packaged political candidates. I want to amplify, in the mind of the reader, the vast potential of magic and make-believe for authentically human endeavor—in religion, sport, politics, and even in economics.

Central to this postmodern critique is the concept of dramaturgy and dramaturgical analysis, best set forth perhaps by Erving Goffman in his many essays on human behavior. Most informed lay persons have heard of Goffman, Burke, and Duncan if not of Ewen or Welsh. For those who have not, what follows is a quick sketch of dramaturgical analysis and its issues.

I intend to go beyond a description and application of dramaturgical analysis to show the reader its historical sources and social psychological effects. In our peculiar language system, this effort is called "structural analysis" or "macroanalysis" as contrasted to a focus on real living, striving, crafting human behavior or microanalysis. Both are essential to the emancipatory impulse, to the postmodern spirit.

Dramaturgical Analysis

In the attempt to understand the character and processes of social life, social psychologists necessarily utilize the conceptual framework with which they are socialized. One of the more useful frameworks with which to comprehend, describe, communicate, and transform the character and processes of social life is dramaturgy: the analytic perspective that social life resembles theater or, more accurately, drama.

Dramaturgy, as a perspective on social life, has existed for centuries. The well-known quote from the mournful character Jacques in Shakespeare's *As You Like It* presents the best-known and least theoretical understanding of the dramaturgical perspective:

All the world's a stage
And all the men and women merely players:
They have their exits and their entrances;
And one man in his time plays many parts.

The literary critic Kenneth Burke began to develop a "dramatistic" model of human behavior in his early writings in the 1930s. Burke maintained in his book *Permanence and Change* (1935) that human beings are active communicators who express themselves and relate to others much in the same way actors do when playing roles on a stage. In concert with the symbolic interaction theories of George Herbert Mead and Charles Horton Cooley, Burke insisted that mechanistic models of human behavior were inadequate since they eschewed any notion that humans act with any purpose or attribute any subjective meaning to their objective behavior.

For two decades, Burke's insights from *Permanence and Change* and the later works, *A Grammar of Motives* (1945) and *A Rhetoric of Motives* (1950), remained outside of mainstream social thought. But with the writings of Hugh D. Duncan (1953; 1962; 1968; 1969) and especially Erving Goffman (1956–59; 1961a) the notion that society could be studied as drama began to make inroads into sociology and social psychology. It was then that dramaturgical sociology was born and its imperative to study society as drama was taken seriously by students of the social world.

Goffman began his work on dramaturgy with *The Presentation of Self in Everyday Life* (1959). In this book he examined the ways in which a person gauged the responses of his/her behavior and altered it to create the kind of impression that s/he wanted an audience to take as an authentic representation of a mood, a social identity, or a social occasion. With minimal props, the actor can make these moods, social occasions, or a character in a performance sufficiently convincing to initiate a self-fulling prophesy of a given form of social reality.

The early works of Goffman were especially helpful in formalizing the dramaturgical model for American sociology, but they were critically important because they demonstrated that humans often separated their subjective intention from their objective behavior. They gave off impressions of motives far different from those they had in mind. The Dale Carnegie school of acting friendly for nonfriendly purpose received formal statement in the works of Goffman.

So, while dramaturgical sociology was born out of the intellectual milieu of Burke's dramatism and Mead's symbolic interactionism, it went beyond both in its basic understanding of human behavior to help the student of social psychology understand the dynamics of cynical, manipulative, insincere, and fraudulent interaction. This was at a time when orthodox social-psychological analysis, especially symbolic interactional theory, stressed consensus, mutuality, and shared symbolic worlds.

There had always been fraud, deceit, duplicity, and dissembling in human behavior but it was in a particular kind of society that such behavior—dramaturgical behavior—became a way of life warranting its own special model of analysis. Dramaturgical analysis in the style of Erving Goffman arose in a mass, exploitive, conflict-ridden society; one in which each person was an unknown stranger to each other person, each pursuing separate goals to greater or lesser degree exclusive of each other.

In such a society, the central assumption of symbolic interaction theory that communicating people attempt to create a *shared* symbolic world does not hold. Doctors, lawyers, furniture salespersons, politicians, clerks, bosses, employees, welfare applicants, police officers, auto repair mechanics—all lived in their own private world of meaning while trying to give off the dramaturgical impression of mutuality of purpose.

For most people in the most important realms of life, a transparent world built of faith, belief, and innocent trust can still be assumed without thought of betrayal. In family life, among friends, among those who help each other, in the church and around the playground, shared meaning and mutuality of purpose could be assumed without jeopardy. There were, to be sure, the occasional husband or wife who did treason to the marriage vows, the unreliable cousin who had to be watched, the persistent liar who was known as such in the town but, as a *way of life* for millions of people through the long hours of the day, dramaturgical behavior—acting, staging the appearance of commitment to the social frame at hand—was inconceivable.

The ancient tactics of social control gave way to scientific tactics. Workers, students, wives, minorities, political dissenters, have been controlled throughout human history by overlapping structures of domination: the social power of significant others; the economic power of elites; the moral power of the church; and the physical power of the state converged to control and thus pattern human behavior in ways that reproduced the ancient structures of gender, racial, class, age, and authoritarian domination.

Such tactics do not work in a mass society. There are no significant others in the supermarkets of life. The use of moral power to persuade people to buy computers, cars, or pharmaceuticals is limited. The use of physical power to rid a factory of strikers declined after the Flint strike of 1937. The use of economic power to shape the behavior of unknown others is still widely used. However, in a profit-oriented marketplace or in a cost-conscious bureaucracy, economic incentives are used to influence strategically placed union leaders rather than workers en masse; to influence selected government officials rather than citizens generally.

So, as you will see, a new technology of social control developed to replace the traditional forms of social power. Psychology in its perverted form joined with mass electronics as well as the tactics of theatre to manage the minds; to create the selves; to order the society where before mind, self and society had been the collective product of persons mutually open.

For many orthodox social psychologists of the 1950s and 1960s, dramaturgical analysis was itself a fraud and a perverse distortion of social reality. In the well-ordered world of the academic living in a well-ordered, middle-class family, dealing with motivated students and working among colleagues known too well for deception to last long, such an analysis was inappropriate. But that world changed after World War II as psychology joined with marketing and management to create the postmodern world of mind, money, and mass managers.

For many other, mostly young, sociologists during the 1950s and 1960s, the dramaturgical analysis of Goffman came as a breath of fresh air. Just as American sociology was becoming more abstract and mathematical, more depoliticized, more impersonal and more removed from the everyday forms of human behavior, dramaturgy spoke clearly about the everyday behaviors of humans in difficult situations.

While Talcott Parsons, Robert Merton, and Wilbert Moore spoke in the dry, dusty, opaque language of formal theory, dramaturgy used a lively and comprehensible language. Lundberg, Dodd, and Blalock tried to convert the richness of social life to the bleakness of rational numbers. Then too, the rise of orthodox dramaturgical analysis must be understood in part in the political and social context of American society at the time. For American sociologists during the 1950s and 1960s it was risky to speak in a tone and with terms that exhibited a concern with oppression, conflict, social justice, and social reform.

Only those theoretical models that were sufficiently depoliticized or remote from the context of the lived experiences of humans could be safely advanced within the universities. Dramaturgy was not remote from human experience but, with the exception of Goffman's *Asylums*, it was sufficiently depoliticized. Consequently, in addition to the model's intuitive validity, dramaturgy was appealing to those who were turned off by the irrelevance of structural-functionalism, who were suspicious of the sunshine and sweetness of traditional symbolic interactionism, yet were politically cautious.

Since the middle of the 1950s and the early 1960s dramaturgical analysts have produced an impressive stockpile of interesting and important studies of human behavior in a wide range of social locales. Certainly, by the mid-1980s, dramaturgy has been established as an important theoretical framework in mainstream social inquiry.

If the writings of Burke, Duncan, and Goffman were emancipatory in that the use of the dramatic model meant that humans acted with purpose as against the idea that objective structures shaped human behavior, these writings also demonstrated that humans could and did hide their purposes from others as they acted and, in so doing, managed and manipulated the behavior of others. Not only did dramaturgy have humanistic and emancipatory dimensions, it had repressive dimensions as well.

As it became clear that dramaturgical analysis contained dehumanizing implications for humans and their social behavior, many sociologists and social psychologists reacted with a knee-jerk negativism, rejecting dramaturgical analysis completely as a mere justification of con artistry.

This book, taken as a whole, appreciates the duality in dramaturgical analysis but, rather than reject the model as devoid of empirical or political value, seeks to organize many of the questions that have been raised about dramaturgy with the goal of improving it as a perspective on society and human behavior and locating dramaturgy within the context of advanced monopoly capitalism.

The chapters contained within are meant to help develop a critical dramaturgical analysis. The specific meaning of the term *critical dramaturgy* and how it is similar and dissimilar to orthodox dramaturgical analysis is developed in these chapters but for the present it signifies (1) a concern with the changing social conditions under which dramaturgy arises as an adequate model of human behavior and (2) a concern for the ways in which human drama, very broadly defined, can be used to augment, rather than distort or destroy, human social existence.

Such are the concerns of this book. Their realization requires a rethinking of the old concepts, issues, and topics previously identified as salient to dramaturgical analysis: an extension of dramaturgy to encompass new issues and topics that previously have been defined outside the scope of interest of dramaturgical analysis as well as an inclusion of the insights of classical and contemporary social theorists excluded by orthodox dramaturgical analysis.

Similarly, the core theoretical problems of orthodox dramaturgical analysis, such as the problematic nature of meaning and communication, the estrangement between subjective meaning and overt act, the problems included in self-presentation and role performance, and the dehumanizing dimensions of dramatic actions, are rethought and transformed.

These chapters attempt to restore to dramaturgical analysis its sociology and its history ignored by Goffman and a second generation of those who work the field. These essays explore and include new topics salient to a critically transformed dramaturgical analysis that have been excluded hitherto. They relate the dramaturgy of social life to the structural contradictions of advanced capitalism, to the problems of maintaining the legitimacy of the capitalist state, to the problems of political opposition and social revolution, to the problems of self-presentation and reality construction in family work, school and market relations, as well as to the problems of massified forms of communication which mystify and distort knowledge of the social world.

It is imperative to add the insights of writers whose views have not yet been included if dramaturgical analysis is to deal with the issues surrounding its empirical adequacy and political meaning. Consequently, many of the concepts and insights of Goffman, Mead, Cooley, and Duncan have been subjected to scrutiny with the insights of Marx, Weber, Marcuse, Habermas, Lukács, and Gramsci. One of the major contributions of this work is the melding of dramaturgical analysis and critical social theory achieved by each of the chapters included herein.

While it retains the traditional symbolic interactionist ideas that human action is bound to group interactions, that consciousness is shaped by symbolic activity, it rejects the mystifications, trivialities, and political limitations of traditional social psychology. As a new dramaturgical analysis it accepts and retains the tragic chronicles of the world of spoiled identities, total institutions, cynical and alienated role performances, infinitely mutable self-presentations, and fraudulently staged encounters.

I argue for the transformation of dramaturgical sociology and for the transformation of the society it describes. *The Drama of Social Life* says, "Yes, this is the way things are, but they can be different." These fraudulent, alientated, distorted relationships can be changed and it is to the nature of the social formation where we must turn our attention if we want to change them. Drama can be put to better uses than those of the profit needs of capital, the legitimacy needs of the state, or the private needs of the alienated individual.

The dramaturgical analysis developed here is not safe, sanitary, nor value-neutral. It speaks directly to the fear, anguish, blood, and fire of the real social world. It speaks against social structures of domination that produce the cynicism, tragedy, and violence that call forth the behavior exhibited and endured by the actors in the Goffmanesque social world. It speaks against the collaboration of social science with this distorted social world. It speaks against careerist aims, opportunism, and liberal reforms advanced by social psychologists. It speaks against a dramaturgical social psychology managed by psychiatrists, police, and social workers that survives and profits off the social anguish produced by capitalist and bureaucratic social forms.

Critical dramaturgy not only describes and analyzes the alienated relations that produce alienated social dramas, but also speaks to change them to forms more responsive to human rationality, human rights, and human potential. The political task of critical dramaturgy is to expedite the replacement of the fraudulent, conniving, exploitive, privatized dramaturgy so ably described by Goffman by an enlivening, caring, entrancing, and redeeming dramaturgy.

The knowledge content and models of sociology and of social psychology cannot be neutral; the only question is whose politics are to be served: those of privilege and power or those of emancipation and social justice. Certainly, dramaturgical analysis has contributed to the former but it has the potential to contribute to the latter in a systematic and effective way. Consequently, within these pages the reader will find a general approach that contains not only intellect but passion, not only scholarship but political commitment.

I offer a preview of how a thoroughly radicalized, thoroughly politicized, emancipatory dramaturgical analysis can be made to enhance social relationships and the human project rather than betray them in politics, sport, religion, social science, and in society generally. In so doing, I offer a vision of a postmodern philosophy of life that resonates with the poetic genius of Blake, the prosocial praxis of Marx, the strong democracy of Bernard Barber, and the wholeness of mind of the feminists.

For us, the individual
on the stage serves a social function
not his relationship to God
But his relationship to society
Stands center stage.
Where he appears, he represents
Class conflict and struggle.

—*Erich Maria Remarque*

Part I

The Politics of Social Psychology

Introduction

In this first section, there are three essays that contribute to the political struggle to reunite social science and morality. In a postmodern social psychology, the task is more than the simple description and reporting of the processes by which a soul and a self emerge. It is also a task to map the context in which self and interaction succeed or fail. It is a task to help clarify the conditions under which a strong and competent self system arises and is sustained in an open and supportive society. To do social psychology in a postmodern mode is to be openly, frankly, passionately committed. Out of that passion comes not a search for the iron laws of society and self-development but rather a quest for the myriad permutations of social organization that permit an infinite variety of self-patterns to emerge within the simple structures of praxis: sociality, intentionality, creativity, and rationality. In the postmodern world, social psychology cannot be neutral or value-free; it must have a politics. The only interesting question becomes what shape that politics? One answer is offered here.

The first essay, "Hard Times and Hard Tomatoes," was presented at the Annual Meeting of the Society for the Study of Symbolic Interaction. Norman Denzin, then president of SSSI, was kind enough to invite me to help the members of the society understand why most of the major assumptions of Symbolic Interactional Theory could not be met in mass society: school, marketplace, shop, factory, church, or sports field. I was only too happy to oblige.

I suggested to the forty or fifty interactionists assembled there that we must no longer assume undistorted processes of symbolic interaction, of selfhood, of communication, of the significant other or the looking-glass process. Rather we must work assiduously as praxical scientists to help create a world in which symbols elicit the same meaning in the self as in the other. We must work to reveal the structural obstacles to the self process.

We must rewrite the textbooks that assume that interaction in mass society has the same result as interaction in a praxis society.

The second article, drafted first, but a special case in the larger study of the sociology of knowledge, follows with an appreciation and defense of Goffman from his many detractors. If Goffman describes a sociology of fraud, one need not subscribe to it. Even if Goffman is a partisan on behalf of dramaturgy used in the service of fraud, still less can we reject his observations. We can look at them and ask after their truth value; we can ask whether such a state of affairs is congenial to the human process. We can work to put dramaturgy to better uses in the creation of self and society. The second part of the article proposes that a more aggressive methodology is essential to meet the information needs of an authentically democratic and transparent society. Under conditions of conflict, the polite and cooperative stance taken by social psychologists in a society marked by sincerity, honesty, and mutuality does not answer the research process nor does it answer to the trust accorded social science when we are given time, resources, and social honor in return for our work.

The third article sets forth the theoretical and practical characteristics of an informationally rich and interactionally rich society—one at the opposite end of the sociology of fraud that now provides the raw data for an alienated dramaturgical society. These three articles, together, set the tone and the mood for a wide-ranging critique and call for a radical, emancipatory, participatory social psychology in the postmodern mode.

1

Hard Times and Hard Tomatoes

This is the land of lost Content
I see it shining plain
The Happy Highways were I went
and Cannot go again.

—*A. E. Housman*

The Plight of Symbolic Interaction Theory in an
Interactionally Deficient Society

Symbolic Interaction Theory has always been the heart and soul of American sociology. Other theoretical approaches have focused on disembodied statistical aggregates, impersonal macroprocesses, the raging, changing flow of class struggle, and on the surgical interplay of demographic categories. Most sociology is concerned with the correlation of variables, with measures of dispersion and of association of disembodied fragments of social activity. Symbolic interaction theory has focused on real thinking—intending, trying, failing, loving, hurting human beings.

Symbolic interactionists have brought us understanding of how men change into gynecologists when examining women in order to strip the interactional matrix of its sexual potential and thus facilitate the diagnostic process. Symbolic interactionists have taught us how three-year-old children come to be human beings, come to reflect on and chastise their own behavior and that of others as the social self—the me—arises.

Interactionists have shown us how a young boy, within a process of symbolic activity, becomes a young woman. Interactionists have informed us of how police officers work their beat, how they count some things as crime and others not. We have been shown how cottagers hold outsiders at a distance and how, sometimes, they bring them into a closed world of meaning.

21

We have watched, through the analytic eyes of symbolic interactionists, how mental patients maintain the dignity of a whole person in the face of the degradation routines of the mental hospital, how prisoners maintain a rich underlife in the most lifeless prisons, and how adults distance themselves from the child's world of the merry-go-round. We have seen Purdy parade himself as a meteorologist before unknown and unknowing others. We have seen the secret places of trade and commerce in the asylum. We have observed the moral career of a whole person being turned and tossed by the official routines of hospital staff.

Symbolic interaction research opened up the social organization of homosexual life, of barroom behavior, of the microdynamics of the classroom as well as the structure of action at funerals, weddings, courts martial, and in the framing of the holy. The constitution of Halloween as well as the social nature of God has been made visible. We know that it is as possible to believe in the reality of God as to believe in Detroit, the NAACP, or the notion of a mother—all are, equally, human constructs and, as long as human beings organize their behavior as if there really is a God or a Detroit or an NAACP, there really are those things.

Symbolic Interaction Theory as a discipline has provided us with a conceptual scheme and a wide variety of methods by which we can unravel the most mysterious process of all—how human worlds of thought and action are created by distinctly human creatures. It is a wondrous accomplishment.

We learned that mind, self, and society are trine-born—that there is no such thing, ontologically, as the separate individual in its social form. The notion of a mother is nonsensical without the child defined as such and the woman acting as such within a larger set of constructed human activity. We have been taught to explore the structure of self and the social identities which are inculcated into the self system and which, ceteris paribus, mediate human behavior in situationally appropriate ways within symbolically constituted worlds. We have learned that our very consciousness is shaped within the web of human affiliations.

Our perceptions of physical reality and our interpretations of social events are collective efforts. Language and symbols do not hang disembodied in time and space with predetermined meaning—despite what dictionaries tell us. Space, time, mass, volume, pressure, temperature, velocity, density, gravity, and magnetism may, just may, be human constructs as well—artifices of human interest and imagination. People, together, create the meaning of a thing. People, together, construct and deconstruct the meaning of whole historical epochs.

Out of the nineteenth century had come the understanding that social reality was a human construct—that social forms and processes were not ontologically prior to the actions and intentions of intending people. The belief that social forms were set eternally by the hand of a creator slowly was displaced by the belief that social forms were the product of countless trials and failures of countless tribes and families.

The idea that Western social forms were the highest point in an upward spiral of social evolution lingers, in most societies, to the present moment, but now we know that there are thousands of equally adequate but differing ways to build social relations dawned slowly on a few scholars—mostly anthropologists. Still the innocent of the world believe that whatever social system into which they are born is the best of all those myriad forms.

Along with many other doubters, Marx set in motion a vigorous line of enquiry into the social sources of human alienation, into the processes of false consciousness, mystification, and the ideological hegemony of ruling elites. It was a blasphemous thought that existing social forms were the source of much mischief and pain rather than the last final perfect child of the gods or of evolutionary processes.

In the famous Paris Manuscripts of 1844, Marx spoke of the intimate relationship between human intention and social reality. One's relationship to the means of production tended to define and limit one's ways of acting, thinking, and feeling. For Marx, the structures of domination—race, class, gender, and authority—distorted the knowledge process. The solution to human alienation was not an ever more perfect approximation to the will of a god.

For Marx, the solution to human alienation was collective human control over the social relationships which people built and experienced. But, in Marxian terms, the relationships people created varied greatly in their capacity to promote human welfare. Under some conditions of social organization, the social life worlds created by humans turned back against them as alien forces. Feudalism, slavery, and capitalism were economic formations in which many people labored and a few benefitted. Primitive communism lay in the dim prehistory of human beings.

These social worlds were, mercifully for Marx, eradicated by capitalism and with them, the idiocy of rural life. Either the means of production were inadequate or the relations of production were oppressive in those four formations. Through revolution, people could build a just society, a praxis society. In a praxis society, human beings—*species beings*—could create themselves collectively as full and competent agents of their own destiny. Not as rugged individuals, apart from the main, but rather as collaborators in that wondrous endeavor. Human beings would create law, religion, politics, and morality but, this time, they would benefit from those creations rather than be made each year more miserable.

Marx became midwife to the dawn of posthistory, an epoch in which human beings would be creative, rational, self-determining, and sociable—

in dialectic fashion. Today the vision of Marx inspires much of the movement toward a praxis society in the most oppressed parts of the globe. Joined with the ancient wisdom of Christ's liberation theology, Marxism is a powerful catalyst for progressive change in the Christian part of the Third World.

The operative question became how to make the revolution toward a praxis society. For Marx, good theory and good practice was the answer. Ideas and material resources joined together would help give humans ever more control over the social forms in which they must live out their lives.

The revolutionaries taught us that social reality was not fixed for all time nor was it divinely established by the gods as the proper way for human beings to organize themselves into human groups. Social reality was a human creation; it was made by humans and it could be changed by humans.

The quest for the laws of society became, for radical researchers, the quest for a liberating knowledge process in which human beings could, in undistorted communication, create a public sphere in which dialogue and moral power replaced coercion and economic power in shaping the symbolic interaction process. Out of all this came an awful realization and an awful responsibility. Humans had lost their innocence and were now responsible for the good and evil of their world. That was the political implication for all those who reflected on the knowledge process. Such an understanding takes the locus of human morality out of the individual and places it in the complex interaction between mind, self, and society where it properly belongs.

No longer may we speak of the moral development of the child in isolation from others but rather of the morality of symbolic social life worlds involving significant others, peers, orders, commands, role sets, social occasions, social institutions, as well as social values.

The social location of morality is in the dialectic relationship between individual and society—not in the single individual, its psyche, its self structure, or its small, wee voice of conscience.

Some would say that, still, one is responsible and one acts in bad faith when one follows orders, but such an assertion ignores the brutal realities of power and wealth; ignores the need for trust, faith, and belief; it ignores the trine-born nature of mind, self, and society.

Such a placement of credit or onus for the good and evil individuals do, exculpates the good and evil of the larger symbolic environment shaped more by some than by others: more by bosses than employees; more by males than by females; more by bureaucratic elites than by the masses they manage and manipulate. In this world, physical and economic power distort the reciprocity of interaction, the mutuality of the knowledge process, the sharing of the symbol.

Out of the late-nineteenth-century social science, especially anthropology, came the growing realization that there was an infinite variety of ways to be human—and less than human. Out of the early twentieth century came the archangels of symbolic interactional theory: Mead, Cooley, Thomas, Lewin, Blumer, and dozens of others. They revealed to a generation of eager students the magical process by which people came to intersubjective understanding, defined a social occasion, reified it, and fulfilled the prophesy of its reality in their consequent activities.

But symbolic interaction theory arose in simpler times, more innocent times, more congenial times. Today Symbolic Interaction theory has fallen upon hard times. It developed in a world in which people tried with considerable success to share in the creation of a cooperative symbolic environment with but little in the way of practiced deceit and scientifically informed fraud. With the growth of social psychology came the human power to polish or to obscure the looking-glass process by which we, jointly, shape our own behavior.

In the mid-century, a Lucifer came bringing the reality-creating activity of human beings into a new and different light. Goffman, in a series of ground-breaking studies, showed us the dark underside of symbolic interaction. Mead and Cooley had stressed the cooperative, transparent, honest aspects of shared lifeworld creation, but Goffman showed us the cynical, managed, fraudulent parts of it.

Many of us did not like the Goffmanian message. The early book reviews of Goffman were indignant that someone might disparage and discredit the wonderful reality-creating, the Promethean part of every person. We wanted a world in which Mead was the apt theorist, not Goffman.

But as we looked more closely at more and more of politics, sports, religion, of the marketplace and its sales tactics, we began to take Goffman's view more seriously. Even in the university we could see the stagings of greatness, pretensions of student service, of academic excellence, of public agency behind which lay much fraud.

The modern university remains a sexist, racist, elitist knowledge process shaped more by the interests of business and the job market than by the ideals of the humanities, arts, and value-full social sciences. Even today, football coaches are paid more than are people in the fine arts, since they help create the dramaturgical semblance of greatness. Those in the fine arts only make the times great, not the image of the university.

When we looked at the use of social psychology in politics, business, and industry, and even in counseling, we found a discipline on the make selling its wares to whomever had the price to pay. Did you want to create false needs for overpriced goods? Simple—just call in the social psychologists. They could tell you of the vulnerabilities of the individual, of the mechanisms by which people came to trust, believe, and act.

Did you want to garner votes without taking a stand on issues? Easy—just call in the pollsters, the demographers, the depth psychologists, and the dramaturgical experts from Hollywood. They would guarantee political office at a price. Did you want a new personal image that would inspire respect and trust apart from personal merit? No problem—just hire a consultant. They will dress you, coach you, manage you, and sell you to an innocent, believing, trusting public.

A whole new industry arose using the combined technologies of social science, electronics data management, and electronics communications media together with the art and craft of theatre, cinema, and song. The best writers, the best singers, the best actors, the best directors, the best artists, the best social scientists signed on to the sociology of fraud.

Out of the dynamics of privatized individualism, the accumulation of wealth, the impetus of consumerism, the rise of market science, and the betrayal of social psychology to these crude beasts marching to Bedlam, arose the dramaturgical society informed more by the forces of fraud than by joy, delight, surprise, and invention.

Public relations, advertising, and industrial psychology became multibillion dollar endeavors. Advertising alone had revenues over $110 billion in 1989. We now know what rough beast, its time come round, was born at Bethlehem; it was the *dramaturgical society* and it was born on Madison Avenue out of Hollywood. Nowhere were the technologies of the dramaturgical society deployed more adroitly than in the election of Richard Nixon, who staged a convincing performance before a believing mass that he was indeed something called a president which matched in adequate ways the prophecy in the American Constitution. Later, the revelations of Watergate made visible the backstage activities in which Nixon used scripts, assigned actors to read parts, edited out scenes which brought no applause, directed his bit players in the FBI, the CIA, the IRS, and the Justice Department, and used other stage props to bring forth the convincing impression of honest agency. Nixon tried to turn America into a political Disneyland and, barely, failed. Now comes Reagan with more success.

For most people, most of the time, in their everyday life and among themselves, the assumptions of symbolic interaction about the shared meaning of a symbol, about the inclusive boundaries of a social occasion, about the rights of those present to share in the shaping of a symbolic universe— these and more assumptions are fully met.

People had lied before, but lying then was a handicraft, a cottage industry. People had joined in teams to swindle before, but that was petit bourgois fraud compared to the fully automated, electronically based, expertly managed fraud of the large-scale organization.

For most people today, most of the time, the innocence of trust, the readiness of belief, the transparency of action fully justifies the faith one has in friendships, family, classroom, church, and sociability occasions. Most of the time for most people, Mead is the better theorist than either Marx or Goffman.

But in important ways which affect the wages, the welfare, and the fate of human beings, both Marx and Goffman were right—dead right. The sociology of fraud trumps the sociology of faith. Moral power and social power are betrayed to the economic power of the rich and powerful by the mind managers, the administrative scientists, the social psychologists of the marketplace.

In a mass society, in a class-ridden society, in a racist society, in a sexist society, in a bureaucratically organized society, the structural conditions for fraud abound. The motives of profit, privatized power, racial preference, gender privilege, and of religious fervor all move us toward a sociology of fraud.

The midline between reality and make-believe is deliberately obscured by those engaged in the management of mass audiences for the private profit of their clients. Even nation-states hire PR people to polish up their image and to hide the ugliness of their politics. The Union of South Africa, the military dictatorships in Latin America, the authoritarian regimes in Asia— all hire professional dramatists to freshen their hoar leprosy to our April day.

For most of history, most people created their social life worlds using voice, body, clothing, and behavioral sets. These information flow media were inalienable. Under his breath, down on his knees, Galileo would still mutter that the *world* turns—not the sun. Workers on the dock in England could use a different voice to express their contempt at their working conditions at the morning lineup—they farted in the general direction of the boss. The king of Denmark proudly wore the star of David on his arm as a protest against the Nazi power.

Today, the media are more readily wrested from the symbol-using creature we call human. The media are mass media. They are owned by unknown others serving unknown purposes. They need not be but they are.

In elitist societies, the public media are appropriated by the rich or powerful to control the symbolic interaction process, and thus controlling, divert it from the human project.

We could use the vast trillions of dollars our labor creates to fashion interactively rich and informationally rich electronically based communication systems. We could fashion the strong democratic politics Bernard Barber so wisely urges. We could develop the environmentally sound economic system in which the authentic needs of human beings could join with the authentic needs for community. We could recapture the world of play and pretend to the antic joy of love and life. All these things we could do with an interactionally rich electronics.

These same technologies now underwrite the false needs of the compulsive consumer. They underwrite the ugly politics of the Right wing; they underwrite the nasty military maneuvers in Central America. Human beings have lost their voice to the owners and operators of the mass media, and these entrepreneurs sell the media to the highest bidder. In these times, the highest bidder is the multinational corporation, whose goals are not participation but profit and management.

Given all these profound changes of technology and technique in the twentieth century, symbolic interaction theorists no longer have the luxury to work solely out of the consensus model of social interaction. As we go into the twenty-first century, we must increasingly be on the watch for conflict relations mediated and magnified by this new technology of electronic fraud. Today the data for interactional research come as much from the electronic ministries and from the electronically based Right-wing political action groups as from the structure of action between friends and family.

The use of fraudulent reality processes in the Iran-Contra scandal are an especially rich vein to work for symbolic interactionists today. The Reagan administration used the mass electronic media to label the thugs in Honduras "freedom fighters." The Reagan team hid their ugly dealings in the dark, out of sight of the public whose trust they betrayed. They used the secret police to build whole social realms and to fund them outside the Constitution and outside the Congress. The self-fulfilling prophecy of the American Constitution is subverted by the close and secret worlds created by the Poindexters, McFarlanes, Secords, and Norths who wait upon their masters.

The old assumptions of symbolic interaction, emerging out of the well-ordered life of middle-class America no longer suffice for the discipline. We now find hard tomatoes in our symbolic supermarket—tasteless, artificially colored and designed to last until some innocent customer, still believing in the "tomatoeness" of life buys it and consumes it.

As we move into the twenty-first century, those who are part of the body of symbolic interaction theory have a new task. Since symbolic interaction theory is the heart and soul of American sociology, our task is to bring forth a new generation of researchers, analysts, teachers, and activists.

We must join Marx, Marcuse, Habermas, Gramsci, and E. P. Thompson to the syllabi of interactional theory along with Mead, Cooley, Blumer, Stone, and Goffman. We must integrate the vast research of the cultural Marxists with the extensive research capacity of American social psychology. We must learn from the cultural Marxists in England, Germany, France, Yugoslavia, Italy, and Australia. We must master that literature and make it available to our students, to our colleagues, and to the more general public as warning and pathway to social justice.

We must focus upon the sociology of fraud which makes mock of the assumptions of the old symbolic interaction theorists. We must generate a new, subsidiary theory of human behavior setting forth the systematic distortions of the interactional process. We must produce a new, radical generation of symbolic interactionists as we move into the twenty-first century. We must not allow the second half of the twentieth century to be the precursor of the twenty-first. We need an epistemic break from our more innocent understandings of the symbolic world in which we must, each willy nilly, live out our days.

As we are human beings and honor that estate, we must act ethically to make visible the processes and practices of fraud in the creation of social life worlds which conserve and expand the ancient wrongs of race, class, bureaucracy, and national pride. We must show that the politics of America in the world capitalist system do not serve the human intersts in freedom, dignity, democracy, justice, and cooperative exchange as the Reagan administration falsely prophesied, but rather serves the interests of some 500 transnational corporations, 300 of which are based, for a while, in the United States. We must begin to speak of systematically distorted prophesies rather than self-fulfilling prophesies in our work.

As we are charged with the task of being impartial and truthful social scientists, we must make visible the vast fraud in the marketplace, in the electronic ministry, in the production of commodity sports, in the massification, technicization, and depoliticization of the university, as well as the creation of the living dead in the factories, schools, offices, mines, and fields of America by the management scientists of modern corporate industry.

Let us help build a world in which the assumptions of symbolic interaction theory as we learned them in all our innocence might once again be valid, might once again be used to build a social life world by human beings in which trust, belief, faith, and innocence are not betrayed to a class elite, a bureaucratic elite, a party elite, or an intellectual elite.

Let us join American symbolic interaction theory with critical theory, phenomenology, semiotics, sociolinguistics, and dramaturgical analysis to create an emancipatory social psychology that empowers rather than manages, enlivens rather than objectifies, transcends rather than freezes existing structures of power and privilege.

There is much to do. Let us set our hearts and souls to do it as long as we shall live, and let us begin right after the picnic. You can be Lenin and I will be Marx. It should be grand sport.

Origins of the "Hard Times" Essay. In the last years of his life, Gregory Stone chaired a session at the Midwest Sociological Society (MSS) in which he called for a rapprochement between symbolic interaction theory and critical theory. I had not heard of critical theory so I hurried to the library upon my return from the MSS meetings that year. Over the next five years, I read Marcuse, Gramsci, Horkheimer, Wellmar, Habermas, and other Europeans in the sociology of knowledge; names I had not known in graduate school at Michigan or Colorado. On my next sabbatical, I spent a year in England getting to know the modern expressions of critical theory in London, Glasgow, Birmingham, and Oxford. This essay is a product of those years and the lectures I have prepared since—and a result of the inspiration from Stone.

2

The Politics of Sociology: Gouldner, Goffman, and Garfinkel

What rough beast,
Its time come round at last
Marches toward Bethlehem to be born?

—William Butler Yeats

In *The Coming Crisis of Western Sociology*, Gouldner (1970) analyzes the contributions of Goffman and Garfinkel and exposes their technical and political meanings to professional scrutiny. This exercise in the politics of sociology has as its objective the extrication of the liberative potential from contemporary sociology. Gouldner insists that judgment of theorists in sociology should not be limited to "autonomous" technical criteria inasmuch as this limitation requires us to be "moral cretins" in our technical roles.

Gouldner is very perceptive in his technical analysis of Garfinkel and Goffman and extremely helpful to our understanding of their political meaning. However, Goffman and Garfinkel have more to offer to conflict theory and to reflexive sociology than Gouldner's analysis permits; both men embody perspectives that supplement and complement those of Gouldner.

Gouldner makes several telling points in his judgment of Goffman; I shall summarize and respond to each of the more important ones. By and large, I agree with Gouldner in his interpretation of Goffman's technical points of meaning but disagree with his interpretation of some of the political points of meaning of Goffman. Later in this paper, I shall provide an analysis of the meaning of Garfinkel to the politics of methodology.

Political Meaning of Goffman

The first technical point Gouldner (p. 379) makes about Goffman is that Goffman's approach to sociology is taken without a "metaphysics of hierarchy." By that he means that the points of view of psychiatrists, salesmen, professors, and police have no prior claim on the loyalty of the sociologist than do the points of view of the patient, the customer, the student, or the criminal. This is a valid technical judgment. Goffman neither celebrates the priest nor castigates the prostitute.

However, the question of the political meaning of this new perspective is unanswered because of two ambiguities that are intrinsic to it. One aspect of the ambiguity is its avoidance of the question of whether the existing stratification system is therapeutic, economic, educative, redemptive, or whatever—or whether another stratification or none at all is preferable. A second aspect of the ambiguity derives from the fact that by failing to sustain the point of view of the official hierarchy, Goffman appears to be "against those advantaged by it."

The ambiguity can be resolved by any one of at least three political acts by radical sociologists: (1) interpreting Goffman as being against the stratification system; (2) using Goffman as a point of departure to raise and settle the question "should the stratification system in these social arenas be dismantled or some other policy preferred in the matter of the psychiatrist and the patient?" or (3) searching in Goffman's work for specific instances where he condemns stratification mechanisms in implicit terms.

The second point raised by Gouldner (p. 379) regarding Goffman's technical meanings is that Goffman's focus on copresence dwells on the immediate and episodic. This is a valid statement. Gouldner's political analysis is that such a focus ignores the permanent and hostile features of society; that such a focus places the onus on indivuduals as "gamesmen" rather than on society as fostering gamesmanship. Goffman's model of the human being is a person who accepts and "works" this dehumanized system rather than rebels against it or rises above it in Rousseauian modes.

But it is Goffmanian analysis that permits Gouldner and others to understand the world as it has come to be and to begin to take political action to transform it. By making the analysis, Goffman provides sociologists with the basic ingredient for that reflexivity that Gouldner urges upon us with such fervor (pp. 488–500).

The political danger of Goffman on this point is that his analysis will be helpful to gamesmen. However, the writing of Gouldner now preempts Goffman from being helpful to gamesmen. New sociologists, having read Gouldner and understanding Goffman, are not likely to celebrate the human model as an ideal. More importantly, they now have the insight, from

Gouldner, to focus on the social conditions that underwrite the management of team front as well as the episodic merchandising of self to anonymous others.

McGinniss's *The Selling of the President* (1968), for instance, is a condemnation of the politics of "impression management." Student protest can be understood as a demand on the part of students that society and the university live up to the earlier moral codes that were lately traded off for tact and image. The typical university has more people assigned to managing and packaging students than to teaching them ethics.

While students are attacking the impression management norms of faculty, counselors, deans, dormitory cadres, placement officers, alumni, and trustees by presenting nonnegotiable demands backed by moral claims, second-generation dramaturgists in the 1960s used tactics of a living theater of the absurd to attack the court system, the political system, the draft system, the university, and the military. Both groups have accepted the idea of a different script for reality from that engineered by academic and political functionaries. As in these cases, the Goffmanian perspective can be put to use in ways not discussed by Gouldner to sustain a radical relation between the sociologist and the social forms in which he deals.

The third technical observation on Goffman by Gouldner (p. 379) is that in Goffman's social world, "tact" replaces moral codes as the major constraint of behavior among anonymous others. Because individuals in a mass society must deal with unknown others, they must deal in safe supplies and must project acceptable and dehumanizing images. One must not make one's moral code visible for fear of losing a customer, offending a voter, or getting a "bad" grade. In academia as in business, one must not challenge the morality of another for fear of losing support when one's own morality is called into question.

The political consequence of this reading of Goffman is that we have, taking Goffman and Gouldner together, lost our innocence on the point about tact versus morality. We now must face the question of the place of morality in mass society. Gouldner has stressed the importance of morality as a source of tensions as well as a barrier to the location of alternative and perhaps more important sources of adaptation, innovation, and rebellion in society.

We now must examine questions centering around the conditions that tact imposes on social behavior; for example, tact may be dangerous because it avoids conflict. In the research setting realms of data and realms of meaning may be lost to the researcher who, constrained by tact, avoids pressing the demand for information. I shall return to this point later.

Rather than to castigate Goffman for his view of life as theater, Gouldner should praise him for the political act of legitimizing the view that all social reality is staged. Shakespeare said it earlier and better than Goffman did, but Shakespeare was "only" a playwright while Goffman is "really" a sociologist and, therefore, to be taken seriously.

The political payoff is that we understand that all social reality requires, in part, a script, actors, front, front-stage, impressions given off, audiences, rehearsals, editing, body idiom, ethos, involvement norms, clearance norms, relevance rules, conventions for boundary closure, disengagement moves, and so on. We understand that the script for reality can be changed, and new, more human forms of reality may take the stage given adequate political means for choosing between scripts.

Dramaturgical activities are supportive of the sociology of fraud when they are used to abort a creative dialectic. In the ordinary run of social events, images and visions are crucial to the self-fulfilling cycle of prophesy and performance. Fraud exists when performance bears no correspondence to the implied prophesy.

In the political struggle for control over the education of Black children, a dramaturgical sociology may be helpful. There are bits of evidence that Black children in the ghetto, being less contaminated by the eye-thinking and linearity of middle-class educators, have adopted a dramaturgical world in which they can function best. Marcella Saunders, a teacher at Jefferson High School in Los Angeles, has had some success in teaching history and math to Black students by having them deal in studio scripts rather than listen to straight lectures.

Mark Rudd, when a student activist at Columbia, made the transition from old-style agitation—pamphlets, meetings, and issues—to guerrilla theater, and he has consolidated this means of activism among the first generation to be reared in a fully developed dramaturgical society.

Jacob Moreno has experimented with psychodrama as a therapeutic tool, and sociodrama has begun to move into areas other than medicine as a mode of experience. Abbie Hoffman has been identified as a New World Shakespeare by virtue of his applications of dramaturgy to the political arena. The point is to understand and to use Goffman as a starting point; he is too valuable to the liberation of sociology to be used merely as a horrible example of the apolitical sociologist.

Gouldner's point (p. 380) about the type of theater Goffman chooses to focus on is important. Goffman focuses on neoclassic theater, wherein the actors deal in images, rather than on living theater or guerrilla theater, where actors deal in politics, authenticity, and passion. But we cannot fault Goffman too much on that score; these are recent developments. Had living theater or guerrilla theater been available as grist to Goffman's analytic mill, his book might well have been entitled "The Generation of Passion in Everyday Life." Had Goffman been Black, he might well have written a treatise about the Black Muslims or the Black Panthers entitled "The Repair of Damaged Identities."

If it is possible to fault the credentials of Goffman in political terms, the best place to start is with the point made by Gouldner that Goffman has failed to explain why some selves (the flimsiest ones) are presented and some (the most authentic ones) are held in abeyance. Still less does Goffman clarify the manner in which power and wealth affect the capacity to project self in terms of variety and adequacy.

Gouldner (p. 381) provides the answers to these questions in the same section where he discusses the political value of Goffman. In a society where people have few real choices, they often mobilize their resources to support images, pets, and sports. Goffman and Gouldner together provide us with some real choices. As sociologists, we can accept the responsibility for analyzing and constructing a social world based on values that transcend impression management.

We have the choice to reject a sociology that is handmaiden to a managerial ethic. In class, in university life, in the community, we can speak as citizen-scientists rather than as merely citizens. We need not protect the fraudulent image of the scientist as value-free and uninvolved in creating the conditions of repression where on every hand scientists are the paid mercenaries of a managed society.

Every piece of foreign policy, every bit of fraudulent advertising, every piece of military weaponry, every bit of testing, every act of consultation made by us as scientist is also made by us as citizen even as we deny it. We should not pretend to be apart from so much sorrow. We polish our image and protect our budget by such fraud. We have a choice in part because Goffman obliterated the false boundaries between worlds of pretend and words of reality.

When Gouldner (p. 384) treats Goffman as a partisan of the sociology of fraud, I must protest. I have always read Goffman as a Puck in the camp of the sociology of fraud rather than as an apostle for it. I think Gouldner permits himself the luxury of unreflective naiveté when he implies that loyalty, sincerity, gratitude, friendship, and love are destroyed when a sociologist examines the handlings of another in the attempt to display these sentiments. Goffman exposes the commercial uses of these sentiments, which, I agree, are vital to a sense of community and should not be used for Gesellschaft purposes.

When I read Goffman's (1959:4) treatment of Purdy, I read it with pain and sympathy on Purdy's behalf because Purdy lives in a world where devious handlings of self are necessary, and he is seldom called to account for this pathetic behavior. I read Goffman's *Presentation of Self* as an indictment of the sociology of fraud rather than an apology and encouragement to play the game. I read his *Asylums* as a savage and profound assault on the official image of total institutions.

I think we should assume that those who read Goffman have a sociological perspective, and it is somewhat redundant to point out that conning behavior is symptomatic of a poorly organized social world.

There is evidence that Goffman takes this poorly organized world as a tacit assumption, because in *Behavior in Public Places* (chapter 14 dealing with the significance of situational improprieties) he places the onus on the community, social establishments, social relations, and on the structure of face engagements for the incapacity of persons to sustain involvement. Goffman instructs us in graphic terms that "symptoms" are acts of silent rhetoric by which a person communicates the anguish, hostility, alienation, and rage that the social situation elicits from him.

The response of sociologists to Goffman should focus on the political significance of his works at the time they were published. As a radical political activist in the late fifties and through the sixties, Goffman liberated a generation of sociologists from their naïve partisanship on behalf of the establishments they examined. Goffman gave us a perspective from which we could become disenchanted with the images of society projected by administrators, managers, politicians, and by those alienated from such a world.

That Gouldner is the more important sociologist to radical sociology at this stage there can be little doubt, but we need both Goffman and Gouldner for technical and political reasons. I reject any part of an analyses that interprets the political meaning of Goffman as hostile to radical endeavor. He is vital to it.

If a person has reservations about Goffman's purity as a practicing radical sociologist, s/he should read the last sentence in chapter 14 of Goffman's *Behavior in Public Places* (1963b:24), where he says there are more psychologically sound reasons for walking away from social encounters than are dreamt of by those who are always loyal to society. Also worth reading is Goffman's introduction to *Asylums*, in which he openly presents himself as a partisan of the patient's situation and offers to repair the imbalance caused by a one-sided literature.

If a person doubts Goffman's essential morality, s/he might do well to read the conclusion to *Presentation of Self* (1959:251) in which he states that we " . . . come now to the basic dialectic: that individuals qua performers are not concerned with the moral issue of realizing standards of life but with the amoral issue of engineering a convincing impression that these standards are realized."

Goffman should be read as a radical sociologist; he will open radical vistas impossible to come by when reading him as apolitical. No event, no word, no person—including Goffman—has meaning apart from the context in which they appear. We construct the meaning of Goffman when we adopt a perspective with which to view his work. It is both valid and essential to the radical perspective to read Goffman's works as a producing mine of radical insights.

From Conflict Theory to Conflict Methodology

Gouldner (1970:50) makes it clear that one political result of survey methodology is that it provides the technical basis for a police state. The dynamics of the greater part of contemporary methodology, based as that methodology is on tact, consensus, cooperation, persuasion, and establishment sponsorship, are compatible with a managed society—managed on behalf of the large-scale organizations of business, government, military, industry, finance, and education.

With reference to ethnomethodology and the political meaning of Garfinkel, Gouldner's analysis is incomplete. It can be completed by understanding that: (1) ethnomethodology is a special case of conflict methodology; (2) a conflict methodology is vital to a conflict theoretical approach; and (3) a methodology that stands in overt hostile contrast to its subject produces dimensions of scientific enterprise closed off by traditional methodologies.

This chapter serves as a starting point from which a person can understand the epistemological advantages accruing from a conflict methodology. In the pursuit of insight, understanding, validity, and other ways of "knowing," these epistemological advantages include additional dimensions of meaning, additional sources of data, as well as dimensions of dedication lost to the "impartial" researcher.

Conflict methodology restores the political dimension to an engaged sociology—one which has been reduced to the production of technical knowledge and separated from the use of human reason,

conflict methodology may be defined as comprising those techniques by which information is obtained from and introduced into systems under conditions of hostile contrast.

In the everyday language of social events, hostile contrast means that some companies, unions, banks, businesses, and schools withhold information from other sectors of the general public which, if available, would advance the latter's interests. Hostile contrast also means that sometimes business, government, military, mass media, and educational organizations introduce information to the general public that leads to behavior inimical to the latter's good health and welfare.

There are a variety of modes in which one may be in overt hostile contrast to the subject of study. They range from the gentle and small-gauge activities of ethnomethodologists such as Garfinkel to the bestial and brutal experiments in prisons, asylums, and concentration camps—experiments in human degradation, sensory deprivation, physical pain, and inquisition by means of electroshock therapy, chemotherapy, or rehabilitation—all of which provide valid scientific data hostile to the human project.

The Heisenberg uncertainty principle states that by studying a field the field is changed. In its sociological expression the principle is known as the Hawthorne Effect. The dominant schools of research methodology in American sociology view it as a cardinal sin of science to deliberately provoke the operation of the Heisenberg principle. With the aim of research neutrality, unobtrusive measures, open questions, nonintrusive participation, and one-way observation are greatly valued.

To achieve neutrality in research, contemporary methodologies advocate the appearance of consensus. Hostility and disgust toward a respondent, subject, or client are suppressed if such human responses arise in the breast of the "objective" consensus methodologist. If attitudes of distrust, animosity, or anger arise as a result of the researcher's activities, s/he disguises these feelings and puts quite another face of meaning on the research, as in the case of studies of fascist attitudes in South Carolina or studies of homosexual space in the *Tea Room Trade*.

If the findings of the study are inimical to the interest of the subject, consensual methodology requires the implication of hostile contrast to be hidden. If the findings are available only to those who are in hostile contrast to the subject, the canons of "objectivity," "value neutrality," and "freedom of speech" become disclaimers behind which a researcher can fashion the image of innocence. At the same time, the hostility and partiality of the use of the findings produce a covert conflict relation between researchers and researched as was the case in many studies of minority problems.

Ethnomethodology, as Garfinkel practiced it, requires one to poke, probe, provoke, and puncture the social system to make visible its chief characteristics. The principle of consensus, under an ethnomethodological view, is a political obstacle to a more complete understanding of the nature of the social system. Thus, an ethnomethodologist might assign students the task of testing the trust of a relationship to obtain a full understanding of the importance of naïve trust in sustaining social relations. That importance is never visible in research procedures available to consensus methodologists.

Trust is a highly important social-psychological component of a wide range of social systems and is a part of that which is taken for granted. The taken-for-granted aspects of trust mean that it is seldom visible. An unobtrusive observer with a limited repertoire of research techniques would scarcely notice a crucial element of these social systems. Unless one were the subject of the response to a breach of trust, one could not know the meaning of that response. Both parties to the conflict arising from a challenge to trust know the meaning of the response far better than a neutral observer could possibly know it. The more we stand in hostile contrast to naïve trust, the more we understand its vital role in the construction of social systems.

Halfway between the trivial things that Garfinkelians do and the horrible things that Nazis or the CIA do that comprise the content of conflict methodology is the law suit. As Sax (1971:53–62) has demonstrated, the law suit produces information and clarifies positions that would otherwise be hidden from public view by what he calls the "Insider Perspective."

The insider perspective produces a surrender of the public trust on the part of public agencies in that decisions must balance off all constraints, pressures, and influences among conflicting constituencies and thus the insider cannot make decisions hostile to the interests of the most powerful of the agencies' constituents. One must never put the budget of the bureau in jeopardy by one's rulings.

In the concrete cases discussed by Sax, administrative officers in the Department of the Interior, the Bureau of Public Roads, the United States Army Corps of Engineers, the Bureau of Sport Fisheries and Wildlife, and the Fish and Wildlife Service practiced the decision-making strategy of "suboptimization." This practice resulted in the abrogation of the United States policy on matters of conservation by the very agencies established to oversee conservation and guard the environment.

A law suit supervised by a competent attorney is an adversary procedure by virtue of which suboptimization need not obtain. The point is crucial. It is through conflict in the adversary procedure that information otherwise unavailable is obtained. The adversary position also permits a person to insist that policy be implemented in spite of the interests of some constituents to the contrary.

Sax (1971:108–24) outlines the advantages accruing from adoption of an adversary procedure. He provides insight on the advantage of a trained researcher's acting as adversary in ferreting out information on behalf of his client through such legal instruments as the hearing, the rules of discovery, the interrogatory, the injunction, the court order, and public record laws. He emphasizes that a request for information by a private person can be ignored by administrators of governmental or private organizations but a court order for documents cannot readily be discounted.

As a methodology for the acquisition of relevant, timely, accurate information on the operations of a business or a state agency, the law suit is often superior to questionnaires, interviews, content analysis, and other tactics of consensus and cooperation. As a methodology, the law suit has conflict, partisanship, subjectivity, and hostile intent to damage the interest of the object of one's research. *Law is an essential tool in the epistemological arsenal of the morally informed social scientist.*

The canons of consensual methodology are as fully compatible with conservative politics as are the canons of structural functionalism. Consensus methodology respects the false peace of a well-institutionalized system of class exploitation, gender oppression, racial privilege, and bureaucratic power. Conflict methodology takes direct aim at these when used to advance the human interest for praxis and for a praxis society.

The canons of conflict methodology may be put to a variety of political uses, one of which is radical, emancipatory social change. Radical sociology cannot limit itself to the research procedures of conservative scientists; to limit itself would be unscientific as well as self-defeating. The experience of the liberal camp in sociology well demonstrates the last point. Liberal sociologists are far too concerned with tact and consensus to be effective in dealing with the establishment on any terms save those permitted by sponsors.

We must understand that a conflict theoretical approach requires a conflict methodology and that a conflict methodology produces more accurate, continuing, relevant, and reliable information under some conditions of social organization than tactful, safe, consensual, and contemporary methodology does. We must understand that Garfinkel and, to a lesser extent, Goffman embody the tactics of conflict methodology. These two are unimportant to emancipatory science except that they have, in their own small way, challenged the basic assumptions of American social science.

Goffman challenges the assumptions of Symbolic Interaction Theory that the social life world created by intending human beings is a shared, transparent symbolic universe. Garfinkel serves to challenge the assumptions of research methodology that the best data are generated under conditions of consensus and honest disclosure. To tell the truth in a circle of liars does not produce good data; good theory requires good data.

Western sociology has been stripped of its radical potential by several generations of conservative and liberal practitioners of the art. The works of Marx, Horkheimer, Marcuse, Gramsci, and E. P. Thompson did not make the journey from Europe to the United States as did the works of

Spencer, Durkheim, and Comte—only part of Weber's work did. The lack shows. In such a depoliticized sociology, Goffman has helped us to sustain an underlife of radical consciousness in Western sociology.

In the twenty-first century, American sociology will have to accommodate itself to the limitations it has imposed upon itself in the effort to establish and to fund itself in the American economic and political context. When social science comes of age, it will not look past the dramaturgical distortions of the knowledge process in everyday life. It will not limit its arsenal of research rules to practices that respect the existing structures of domination and thereby reproduce them all the while claiming to be a true science—a way of knowing. I can scarcely imagine a more distorted knowledge process nor imagine a more distorted knowledge product than the one we presently call American sociology.

Decalogue for the Successful Sociologist

Thou shalt live above thy means
with credit cards of golds and greens.
And pay these off, if in time,
you learn to live and love this Rhyme:

Thou shalt be on friendly terms
with the Gods of corporate firms.
Nor will thou speak with such
who write their articles for its prose:
Nor, above all, make love with those
Who think too much.

Thou shalt not have Gods, you see
unless they help get publicity free,
To the poor give time and thought
preferably for a handsome fee.

Thou shalt not do questionnaires
or quizzes upon world affairs:
if they offend a powerful audience,
nor give any talks. Thou shalt lie and sit
with statisticians, but not commit
a social science.

Thou shalt do as Business pleases;
thou shalt write thy master's thesis
upon Japanese Economies.

A version of this essay appeared in the *American Sociologist*, November 1971. Reprinted by permission.

Thou shalt find some sex that teases
all to want to to peruse,
all who find it good to use
functional criminologies.

Thou shalt worship those researches which
tend to make the richer rich
or pacify truculent minorities.

At Christmas time, you can't be rude
so send out cards by all means;
but edit first your mailing list to include
Chairs and Heads and college Deans.

If thou must choose between the classes,
don't take chances; chose the one which best advances
your career and your finances.

When you send off compositions
send them off to new Transactions
or if you try the old newspapers
check them first for circulations

Join all the best Associations
infiltrate the most viable professions;
Thou shalt entertain, of course,
those who head Committees first.

If, from this list of skills promotive,
You work hard and are assertive,
I guarantee that you play the game
or have, at least, a famous name.

And splash your name around the bog
when you are a famous frog;
and strut around the day livelong
to croak your name among the throng!

One would suppose that Albert, Emily and old Auden
might most strenuously object to the fraud in
this most helpful of verse;
but they, God knows, have done far worse
to keep their fame from the public purse.
Now who knows or even cares what they wrote in.

Fame, friends, Fame is the stuff to drink
for sociologists whom it hurts to think:
and fame does more than Reagan can
to bend the truth and ruin the land.

—Inspired by W. H. Auden and
dedicated to Bernie Meltzer.

3

The Structure of Democratic Communications

Speak truth to each other.

—Unitarian Creed

Introduction

It is trite to say that the media in the last part of the twentieth century have failed the democratic project. Yet in these times, the electronic media, the print media, as well as the personal media are oriented to projects other than the informationally rich and interactionally rich environment so necessary to authentically democratic engagement.

If Symbolic Interaction theory helps us understand anything, it helps us know that an undistorted structure of communications is essential to a well-constructed social life world. Here social psychology and the public media intersect. Here we can learn how an adequate media industry can help fashion an adequate public sphere and thus advance the human project.

Of the 25,000 or so media outlets in the United States—book publishers, newspapers, television stations, radio stations, motion picture and billboard companies—most are part of twenty-six media conglomerates, themselves often part of larger conglomerates. Almost all are for-profit enterprises, and thus must work and print within the logic of capitalism.

It is not a conspiracy that such media push an elitist politics with elitist policies. The people who run the media accept and benefit from the sanitized politics with which we are burdened. In the short run—their lifetime at least—such undemocratic politics pay off handsomely.

That others than newspeople or politicians bear the costs of distorted politics; that the poor absorb the price of tax policy; of housing policy; of health care policy; of debt policy; of educational policy—that others pay the price of elitist politics is of small concern to those for whom the system works well and is made to work so well by media people.

There is another way for the media to work, for those who manage the media to act. The media could be reorganized to create a *public sphere;* the media could be oriented to develop public opinion rather than mass, alienated, uninformed opinion. The media could help realize the human project instead of parasitizing upon it.

Communication, Culture, and Alienation

The central premise here is that all sources of human alienation reside in concretely existing social relations. A solution to human alienation requires radical transformation of those social relations. This view stands against more ancient and more accepted Buddhist and Christian understandings that alienation is inevitable or that it involves a separation from God.

The Hegelian view that alienation arises from a failure to know fully the nature and richness of objective social and physical reality is, as Marx noted, part of but not all of a theory of alienation. A fully human and humane theory of alienation postulates the necessity of an active human participation in the creation of social reality. In more focused terms, the solution to human alienation requires both understanding and undertaking. The point is not to study the social world in various ways but to change it, and that requires a special kind of communication where symbolic worlds are concerned.

The conditions that make social psychology possible—or impossible—in a society are most relevant to the forms and degree of alienation. In societies where mind, self, and society cannot be trine-born; in societies where the self-fulfilling prophesy is engineered unilaterally by hirelings; in societies where there are no significant others, only impersonal functionaries; in a world where symbols are turned inside out to make the tyrant a freedom fighter and the freedom fighter an enemy—in such a society, the basic conditions for social psychology are lacking.

A second grounding premise is that social life worlds exist as a result of human activity. The human activity central to the constitution of social life is shared, intentional, constrained, patterned symbolic interaction. Any social form that excludes people, in part or in whole, from shared participation in that symbolic activity that generates social life thereby alienates people to the same degree from the human process.

Essential to active participation in the construction of social reality are the media with which a symbolic universe might be shared. Only in the last century have the media been so alienated from the social process. There is nothing in nature which requires that radio, television, cinema, theatre, or other electronic media be designed and deployed to exclude people from politics, religion, market, or university. The control needs of capitalist and bureaucratic structures dictate the media's shape, content, and accessibility.

Constructing Reality

In all human history, there are four major language systems used to create social relations, including family, work, communal, political, and religious relations. These four include the voice, the body and its positions, cosmetics and clothing, as well as complex runs of behavior. These four language systems are the media that people in history have developed to define/call forth religious occasions, work relations, state institutions, as well as whole networks of health, play, and schooling relations.

There are a number of variables one can control in those sounded plosives we call voice that give us an amazingly wide range of sounds with which we can create the most subtle and complex forms of social life. Frequency, volume, meter, timbre, tone, pace, slope, and timing all provide a multitrillion information bit inventory which we could, in an unalienated situation, use to create the most wondrous varieties of play, art, science, song, therapy, or love.

In conjunction with the languages of face, hands, and posture we can say things never before said; if and only if we have the opportunity to participate in symbolic activity. Those structures of media that limit language dimensions also limit the human project. With our body talk, we can say clearly whose turn it is to speak or who is excluded from the symbolic process—all can be signaled by a turn of the head, a wave of the hand or a curl of the lip.

There is also much that may be said with cosmetics and clothing: what we are doing, who we are, how we feel; whether this is a funeral or a formal dinner, a rehearsal or that which is seriously meant. In New Guinea, tattoos are the gateway between body and the spirit world. Body decorations constitute a third medium with which the solid reality of social occasions can be fashioned. We dress, put on make-up, wear flowers, and apply perfume in order to tell another person that s/he is special to our life.

A complex series of activities enacted by an individual or a group can be read out just as a book or a song can be interpreted. The dance is one such line of physical activity with which meaning is constituted and can come to be shared. Ballet and mime can tell engrossing stories about sexual need, gender relations, political conflict, or religious agony. Societies around the world use dance to call forth their gods. Psychiatrists learn to read the cycles of neurotic behavior that tell of the sources of human anguish besetting us.

In interactionally rich social occasions, these media can be used to create social self, social status, social institutions, and whole societies. In interactionally barren situations people are struck dumb, are bored and boring— They lose whatever potential they have to be or become human. They act as dispirited objects; characters out of the novels of Ionesco, Kafka, Kesey, or Camus, out of the paintings of Daumier or Hooker, out of the music of the Clash or the Sex Pistols.

For such persons, the assumptions of a stringent physical or psychological determinism may obtain. On the other hand, when people have a secure and democratic relationship to the means to produce meaning, to produce knowledge and wisdom, to produce joy and delight, they are able to act in ways not possible in the simple models of cause and effect, prediction and probability, necessity and need which are said to model the lives of animals.

While it is possible to still the voice, to restrict body decorations, to tame the body, or to limit the kinds of behavior in which people engage, nevertheless it is not easy to alienate people from their own symbolic systems. It is much easier to alienate people from mechanical or electronic media.

In modern times, new media have been developed that may complement or supplant those media over which one has personal control. Voice, clothing, body, and behavior can be eliminated as language media. With the advent of movable type, electronic technology, photography and cinema, laser and microprocessor technology, it is possible to so organize media as to still the human voice. Radios can be built to permit only a one-way flow of information. Access to television can give the capitalist and the state functionary control over the symbolic process. Alienation from the means to produce human culture is now possible in ways never before imagined.

Clothing and cosmetics can be eliminated as symbolic systems. Students, workers, soldiers, and prisoners can be made to wear uniforms which effectively limit the information potential of costume. The body can be disciplined in the classroom or in the office to say nothing; to mean nothing. Soldiers are made to stand at attention thus muting their body language.

The cycles of behavior through which one lives out one's hopes and/or anxieties can be lost in the impersonality of work and religion. Routines and lockstep in the factory and office can destroy the creativity and intimacy of behavioral sequences. In mass society, the very tools of thought and talk can be alienated from people's bodies.

Language systems can be organized to create a rich information and interactional field within which the uniquely human labor of reality constitution may transpire or the media may be organized to exclude, restrict, or to produce patterned activity in nonhuman modalities.

It is a subversion of the language to call these preprogrammed, mindless, thoughtless behavior forms "social" or "human" behavior . . . they are neither.

Whether such activity is in fact human activity, or whether human activity is merely economic/political activity stripped of its human character is an empirical question. Not all patterned activity of Homo sapiens is human—not at all.

The way in which information systems are organized determines whether distinctly *social* life worlds emerge. For that to happen, personal and shared control of the medium is necessary whether it is a single piece of clothing or an entire television network. Only through democratically organized media is human life in its fullest potential possible.

In this historical epoch, the solution to alienation centers around the question of who controls the computer, the camera, the receiver, or the microphone, in a word, the knowledge process. In other times control of land, capital, the work process, the ballot, and of the surplus value produced was centrally important to an understanding of alienation in human terms.

In the past, alienation centered around exploitation—the alienation of property, wealth, and material resources from those who produced them. Even in the worst of times voice, body, and clothing were individually owned and used. The same cannot be said of the media in mass and class-bound society. For much of the world exploitation in economic relations continues to be the central source of alienation; of poverty, despair, powerless rage, and hopelessness.

More is needed than material wealth to end alienation. That lesson is clear in the rich capitalist countries and is beginning to be clearly established in developing socialist countries. Material resources are the beginning but not the end of a solution to human alienation.

> Some could gaze and not be sick
> But I could never learn the trick.
>
> There's this to say for guile and guise
> They often bring their own surprise.
>
> It often takes a little while
> for one to learn of guise and guile
>
> and what one learns, it's sad to say
> the tricksters often have their way.
>
> —adapted from A. E. Housman

Interactionally Distorted Communication

In advanced capitalist societies there are five major power relationships that systematically distort communication. The private/noncollective control over the news media tends to reinforce these structures of domination.

While distortions of the knowledge process vary from society to society and take special forms in military dictatorships or in bureaucratically organized socialist nations, the major sources of distorted communication include class privilege, gender preference, racial discrimination, age grade exclusion, and a division of labor that awards authority to a relatively few and mandates compliance to a large majority.

In the classroom, everything from textbooks to intelligence tests is written from a White, male, middle-class point of view. The histories of women, minorities, workers, peasants, and rebels are lost to the knowledge process.

Class and Interaction

In class-organized societies it is entirely possible for a few thousand people to own the electronic and mechanical means to produce meaning. In the United States, Australia, Britain, France, Germany, and other capitalist countries, the trend is toward concentration of ownership of newspapers, television stations, radio, and computer-based information systems. These systems are organized for the mass diffusion of messages on behalf of corporate or state elites rather than for democratic communication.

In the United States media, socialist failures are magnified by privately owned media and socialist successes are passed over. At the same time, capitalist successes are proclaimed in the news, in the classroom, and in the cinema. The failings of capitalist systems are attributed to individual failings, racial inferiorities, or to greedy workers, lazy welfare mothers, and to the odd psychopath. Anyone who listens to William Buckley will despair at the distortion of the knowledge process in politics and economics.

Apart from a few university lectures that enrich the knowledge process, a few magazines and journals that repair the damage to human understanding, a few movies and plays that enlarge our views of what is possible—there are few media that give a fair and balanced analysis of differing social life worlds.

The mass format of electronic and print media is not only interactively distorted but also informationally poor. A democratic communication system must be both interactively and informationally rich.

Over half the nations in the world use torture, terror, and murder to still political dissent. Eight countries in Latin America use murder squads. The United States is party to the attempt to distort political communication in that part of the Third World from which its corporations get profits, raw materials, and cheap labor.

The call by the Unaligned Nations for a new international information order is justified by the increasing political and economic inequality between nations in the two hemispheres. The response on the part of the twenty rich capitalist countries to this plea for more egalitarian access to the electronic spectrum falls on deaf ears; The United States and other countries insist, in the name of freedom of information, on the right to shape the cultural process in Third World countries on behalf of the structure of international capital.

In the factory, store, shop, and office, the structure of class relations systematically distorts communication. Workers, having sold their labor power to the employer, also sell their voice. What may be said, to whom one may talk, in what kinds of words one may express thoughts, and how often one may speak—all these are part of the package sold to the employer when one takes wages and salary.

Montgomery Ward's forbids its employees from talking to each other about personal life; McDonald's insists that its counter people say exactly the same thing to every customer in every city. All corporations forbid their employees from warning the public about the criminal activity in which the corporation is involved. Employees must learn to speak in the disjointed, impersonal language of business, science, or mathematics. Class relations suborn both personal and mass media to the task of producing and concentrating wealth.

Gender Politics and Interaction

Gender relations also distort communication prossibilities. When men talk, people listen; when women talk, people do not listen. In politics, in church, in academia, in family, and at work, what women say and do is not valued as much as what men say and do. Apart from the substantive content of the message, apart from its merit or congency, what women as a category, say, carries less weight than what men say.

The structure of gender preference gives males access to offices from which they can speak and are able to enforce their directives. The exclusion of women from strategic positions in society excludes them from the symbolic interactional process by which policies affecting their bodies, their children, their jobs, and their health are created.

When women do work for wages, their status in the family knowledge constitutive process improves and their control over the meaning process is better but still not equitable. The data of gender discrimination in professional occupations, science, art, music, math, and politics clearly say that women do not have full access to the vocal, print, or electronic symbol systems used in most societies to create social reality.

In the family, the politics of marriage all too often produce women who are diminished by the decision-making process. The male makes unilateral decisions that affect the family, and the woman is to accept such decisions passively. In contemporary society, women become very uncomfortable with such politics. They try to circumvent them, absorb this pathology in their body and spirit, or, all else failing, seek divorce only to go to another relationship in which such alienated politics is reproduced.

Racism and Interaction

The severity of distortions in access, use, and response to symbolic activity of Black, Chicano, or Asian people is great and continues in even the most liberal capitalist societies. The struggles of Black people to recapture their own institutions and cultural processes in America are well known. From the earliest days of the nation, brutal and systematic efforts to exclude Blacks from political, religious, and academic participation and to exploit them in economic life are well documented.

The exclusion of minorities from school, church, public office, and social space is but a device to render them voiceless in a racist world. The shooting, lynching, bombing, beating, and burning of minorities in South Africa, Palestine, Uganda, or Guatemala—all work to still the voices of protest and social policy.

The same distortion of communication is to be found among age-grades. Such distorted patterns of communication are treated as normative. The unilateral origins of symbols, the one-sided compliance in linguistic activity, the variation in authority—all are treated as normal and functional to the social process. That democratic forms of communication could be used with young people or with the elderly is seldom a topic of political discussion.

Women, Blacks, workers, and senior citizens in the United States have all assembled some moral, economic, and legal power with which to retain and recapture control over the communication process, the knowledge process, and the political process, but their successes must not be overestimated. However, since the advent of the accumulation crisis in the United States, the Reagan administration has worked assiduously to subvert civil and economic gains made in earlier gender, class, and racial struggles.

Bureaucracy and Interaction

The rules of bureaucracy are all designed to control the flow of information in such a way as to amplify the voice of the bureaucratic elite and to diminish that of the student, the patient, the soldier, or the consumer. The work of Erving Goffman on the rules and rights governing those in total institutions offers graphic evidence of such interactionally meager social forms.

In the corporation, information about its crimes, pathologies, and petty oppressions are covered up by the public relations people and refreshed once again to the April day. PR people try to filter out negative information about their clients and try to disseminate positive information—mostly false or misleading about their clients and the products of the client.

The rules of the classroom are designed to give the teacher control over the flow of ideas and evaluations. Students are taught early on to ask for permission to speak, to sit still, to observe dress conventions, and to follow the regime of the school rather than an alternate. When television instruction is used in the classroom, the last possibilities of interaction are eliminated. Even computer-based instructional programs permit more interaction than do most classrooms. But interactively rich computer software is not interactively rich human discourse. Sociality is lost in such a place.

The rules of bureaucratic secrecy are designed to limit knowledge, understanding, and participation in political affairs in bureaucracies; designed to hide their functions and their flaws. Millions of documents are stamped with various levels of secrecy each year in government bureaucracies. National security is adduced to justify such action. Partisan security is a better term with which to account for such systematic distortion of the symbolic process.

While there has been some progress to put an end to the structures that distort communicative relations, recent data suggest that progress has halted and, perhaps, reversed in those domains. Optimistic forecasts that the new information technology will transform these ancient inequalities have not been validated (see Toffler, 1980). If anything, the increased concentration of wealth and class privilege within capitalist societies has been aided by differential control of or access to the media.

In television and radio programs, bland, safe, unoffensive material trumps that which might lose part of an audience—and part of the profits from the sale of that audience. Controversy, conflict, and morality are displaced by consensus and tact as Gouldner so pointedly put it. The endpoints of political thought are truncated and a narrow, safe discourse subverts the search for good answers to hard questions.

Adequate, accurate, reliable, complete, timely, and comprehensible information systems, organized in an interactively rich format, are necessary to unalienated human societies. In capitalist societies, the news media are used more to produce audiences which, in turn, are sold as commodity to help merchants dispose of surplus, high-profit, high-energy, capital-intensive products rather than for the democratic constitution of social life.

Vast power, wealth, and social honor still rest in the hands of a small percentage of persons and a shrinking number of multinational corporations. Compared to the multinational corporations (MNCs), the power and wealth of even the greatest nation-state in the capitalist bloc is small. As powerful and rich as are the Arab oil states, a few banking groups can crush them. The battle for democratic forms of communication has not been won—the gains only to be consolidated; the benefits of social justice only to be extended to a few isolated groups. There is much to be done before a strong and vital democracy can emerge in even the best society.

Information-Rich Communications

There are four kinds of knowledge that must be generated in any society if that society is to remain self-directed, self-organizing, self-repairing, and self-controlling.

In systems theoretical terms, a system has the potential for ultrastability—a moving and lasting stability—when it draws energy (negentropy, order) from the environment at a level adequate to its life processes and below the breaking point of the environment. In order to escape the second law of thermodynamics that warns that every system tends to collapse, a system must be in match with its environment while not exceeding the capacity of the environment to carry it.

These forms of knowledge essential to ultrastability include first, *positive knowledge*—knowledge about how the society actually works, about how it is related to relevant sectors of its environment, about its structural flaws, and about changes in its relevant environment.

If a society has this kind of positive knowledge, it has the beginnings of the capacity to be constituted as an ultrastable cybernetic system matched to its environment and competent to transfer order from the environment without destruction of that environment upon which the system depends.

Economics, politics, sociology, anthropology, and history are the knowledge-generating disciplines that offer positive information on how a society works. How successfully it works is another question.

A second kind of knowledge that a society must produce is *hermeneutical knowledge*. This is knowledge about how intersubjective understanding is possible, how shared social life worlds are created by intending human subjects, when misunderstandings exist and how they arise, and how to repair unconnected meaning systems, distorted cultural processes, or psychopathogenic relationships.

Epistemology, phenomenology, sociolinguistics, symbolic interaction theory, semantics, deconstruction, semiotics, and ethnomethodology are just a few of the knowledge-producing disciplines that try to provide this kind of knowledge at the level of a sociocultural system. Psychology, psychiatry, and some religious specialties offer information about inner-subjective states and distorted understanding within individual systems of thinking.

Since human beings are the most significant environment of each and all other human beings, and since social life worlds depend upon shared understandings created by symbol-using creatures we call humans—hermeneutical knowledge is absolutely essential. It is not possible to have social systems when people do not understand the meanings of each other. As George Herbert Mead so well put it, mind, self, and society are trine-born. Symbols must elicit the same meanings, feelings, and lines of behavior in each person within a society else society does not emerge from the biological base upon which it is founded. Interactionally and informationally rich symbol systems depend greatly upon hermeneutical knowledge if they are to be well built.

A third kind of knowledge necessary to reproduce existing social institutions and social relations is *ideological knowledge*. Ideological knowledge is comprised of all the ideas about what kind of social relations are appropriate to a society and what kind of culture is to be produced within those social relations. Ideological knowledge is embedded in the mores, in the realm of the sacred.

Ideas about family, religion, politics, education, or economics are all in the realm of ideology rather than in that of theory. It is true that something called "father" really exists when a male is defined as such, treated as such, and acts as a father. But the idea of a father (or a mother, or a president, or a pope) is an ideological construct; not an ontologically existing entity apart from the ideological activity of the people within a society.

Central to the constitution of such ideological constructs is uncritical belief, naïve acceptance, emotionally committed allegiance, open and ready trust, and a certain readiness to repress those who do not believe, will not trust, who are cynical or manipulative. If social reality is to be created, faith, trust, and belief are essential. When belief is subverted, faith betrayed, and trust turned back against people, their capacity to engage the self-fulfilling prophecy is defeated.

A society that uses the tactics of theatre in the service of the sociology of fraud is a society on its way to collapse.

Most liberal analysis discounts, inappropriately, the importance of ideology as a basis of a decent society. All societies must propagate such ideological sets if they are to reproduce themselves in the generations that follow. It is not an odious thing to engage in propaganda—it is odious to elevate the ideas that infuse and inform a society at the expense of those ideas about how to do society found in other societies.

The information sectors that create and distribute this kind of knowledge include parents, politicians, priests, most teachers, most psychiatrists, and university professors, as well as most workers in cultural life: musicians, singers, actors, writers, counselors, lawyers, judges, social workers, and most novelists.

Music, poetry, novels, bibles, how-to books, constitutions, bylaws, and of course law itself are the repositories of ideology. Again, the production of ideology is a noble pursuit—only if the ideology is noble.

A fourth kind of knowledge necessary to produce (rather than reproduce) society is critical, *emancipatory knowledge*. Information about the failings of a social form, alternative social relations, new ways to rear children or heal anxieties, things which do not yet exist, and about how to subvert the existing order, as well as knowledge about how to introduce new ways of doing things without destroying the best of the old, are the kinds of knowledge necessary to human emancipation.

It is not enough to a self-repairing society to have positive knowledge about how it actually works, to understanding perfectly the intentions of a master or boss, or to believe completely in one's leaders and their commands. To endure, a person and a society must produce, store, and quickly retrieve information about alternative family relations, alternative modes of sexuality, alternative food, energy, and housing sources, as well as alternative healing and helping processes.

In these times, the world changes so rapidly that new ways of organizing human life must be available. The ancient conservative view that all change is evil is now archaic. Change is permanent; so options must be expanded, transformations must be accepted, and integrations must be well done. The knowledge process is now central to the survival of a society in all four dimensions.

New language systems, new words, new institutions must be developed and tested against changes in the environment else the second law of thermodynamics wins and the society tends to entropy—as have so many before. The specialists who produce emancipatory knowledge range from the clown, the fool, and jokester to the most advanced futurologists in corporate and military think tanks.

It is an old understanding that prophets produce emancipatory knowledge while priests reproduce ideology. Teachers reproduce existing social relations while revolutionaries from Lenin to Guevara produce new ideas about how to subvert existing structures of power and institute new ones.

In a society with structural inadequacies and with bad politics, emancipatory knowledge comes more from the underground than from the established respectable knowledge-constitutive institutions. A rational and decent society would bring emancipatory knowledge up from its underground cave and honor it as positive or ideological knowledge.

The measures of alienation give us guidance on when to turn from ideological to emancipatory knowledge: crime, depression, suicide, infant mortality, divorce, and bankruptcy rates all bespeak alienated social relations in school, work, family, and politics as well as church, state, and market.

The media controlled by those who benefit from the reproduction of inequality carefully exclude emancipatory knowledge from the news and analysis. Instead, the columns and segments in newscasts are filled with social opinion. Social opinion includes any information set that tends to reproduce existing arrangements (Young, 1981).

A democratically oriented society must use its media to create public opinion. In turn, that public opinion must be incorporated in the political process in significantly consistent ways else a public sphere cannot be said to exist. The generation of post hoc consensus for policies after the fact cannot be called a democratic politics (Young, 1980).

False Politics

When the indices of social collapse grow at increasing rates, that is the time when emancipatory knowledge takes precedence over ideological knowledge. Yet it is precisely the time when the instruments of social control—army, police, press—are deployed by ideologues to suppress the production of emancipatory knowledge.

Under these conditions, the elements of "bourgeois" freedom are essential to all social formations—capitalist and socialist alike. No class or party is a repository of all social wisdom. Freedom of speech, of association, of experimentation—all traditional bourgeois freedoms—are important to the human project.

Nor do the arguments about time constraints or about advantage of position justify nondemocratic procedures in the production of political or ideological culture. While an inner circle may quickly produce a policy, unless it speaks to the ultrastability of the entire society, it is merely a false loop in the decision-making process and must be done again. The transfer of the costs for dealing with a problem to another part of the population creates a cycle of false politics that do not end until system and environment are in ultrastable and harmonious equilibrium.

As a case in point, one may consider the Reagan supply-side policies to transfer the fiscal crisis of the state to workers, the elderly, and the unemployed in order to generate funds to rebuild the economy and protect the position of U.S.-based corporations in the world economy with a strong military establishment.

Supply-side economics do transfer capital to private industry and do help obtain markets and raw materials for the transnational corporation. However, if the private sector makes investment decisions on the basis of their private interests, they may use the surplus funds to invest elsewhere. They may invest in luxury goods, they may buy other companies, or they may invest in credit instruments. There is no guarantee that private sector investors will invest in just those lines of production necessary to a good and decent society.

The loss in real disposable income to the family unit through the wage workers in a family only transfers the problem; it does not make the system any more stable. Workers must have enough income to buy back the goods they produce or warehouses fill up, factories shut down, and economic depressions engulf the land.

Such economics also erode the tax base and political legitimacy of the state while a variety of crime increases. A political process that answers to the needs of capital and systematically discounts family, community, and personal needs of a society creates long-range structural (and political) problems that can, in turn, transform into rebellion, fascism, wars of political liberation, or into destructive economic warfare.

A false politics is one that answers to the short-term needs of a privileged class but avoids responsive change on behalf of the whole society. If the fate of the 5 percent of the world that enjoys the benefits of such politics were unconnected to the fate of the unemployed, that of the Third World, or the fate of the masses, then such a politics would suffice.

However successful such politics were yesterday in a disconnected world system, they represent a false politics today. As the world grows more connected by economics, transport, electronic media, and by political treaties, the economic problems of any given society come to originate in the world economic system. Such a source of problems requires an enlarged and authentically democratic politics—every day the need for a global democracy grows more necessary.

Basic to a democratic politics is a democratically organized communication system utilizing every technical capacity of electronic, photonic, and holographic media: speed, storage, interactivity, and computational capacities in order to produce and meet the vast informational needs of a connected world society.

An information-rich society is one in which all four kinds of knowledge are continuously produced, continuously available to all sectors of the population, and continuously balanced against each other to produce a society located in its own history. Authentic politics is one that is so organized. Such a politics requires that symbol systems—the media—be used for the constitution of a public sphere. We will return to this point in the last section of the chapter.

Interaction-Rich Communication Systems

Returning to an earlier theme, one must keep in mind that social life worlds are produced by intending subjects. If a person or any set of persons are to be or become human, they must take part in the symbolic work out of which social relations emerge. Social reality does not exist apart from that symbolic work. It is the nature of symbolic work that it cannot be done by solitary individuals.

All information systems require encoding and decoding procedures. All communication requires speakers and hearers. Speaking is a subjective activity—but so is hearing. All this boils down to the fact that the construction of social life is, must be, collective. Persons excluded from such activity do not live in the same symbolic framework as those who do participate.

Such excluded persons cannot be said to be friends, parents, citizens, or Catholics. Mass print or electronics media with its unidirectional, isolated, and narrowly focused and privately controlled format do not answer to the communication needs of a society for the shared constitution of the forms of knowledge produced above or for the forms of social life patterned by that knowledge.

There is embedded in this statement a Marxist view of the knowledge process. The forms of authentic social knowledge, in this view, do not arise from objective methods of social science disseminated by lecture, books, documentaries, and journals but rather by intersubjective participation in creating social life worlds. One can learn a bit about Eskimo life or about bureaucratic life from print or from film, but creative participation in the production process is necessary for knowledge to be authentically, fully, intimately knowable and known.

An ultrastable society must organize its media as social media rather than as mass media. Mass media, mass sports, mass religion, and mass education are hostile to the human enterprise.

While media in a massified format can divert people, entertain them, persuade them to buy or vote in this way or that, massified media cannot produce the forms of social knowledge needed to reproduce and produce new social life.

The necessity for removing any structure that interferes with interaction derives from Ashby's law of requisite variety (1968). Only variety can destroy variety; only new ways of doing society can cope with irreversible changes in the environment of that society. Well-organized systems contain enough variety within their information-storage facilities (memories, plans, histories, ethnographies, and utopias) to cope with any new event in the environment that threatens to interfere with the process by which order in the environment is converted into order in the system—and thus survive.

The structure of class, racial, or gender inequality present themselves as constraints in the search for quality variety, the evaluation of various options, the incorporation of selected options, and the collective benefits from such variety.

An interactively rich communications system has such characteristics as will promote the search for quality variety since, in Ashby's words, variety is essential to ultrastability. This means that when there is a significant change in the structure of a system or in the relevant sectors of the environment from which a system draws resources, then change must occur in order to regain a balance between system and environment.

If the environment cannot be changed, the system must be. If workers cannot be pacified, factory life must change. If students will not be pacified, the university life must change. If the Third World will not tolerate exploitation, the First World must change else both collapse—since the Third World is an essential part of the environment of the First World. Some eighty-six essential minerals come to the United States from the Third World as well as a lot of goods, wealth, and profits.

We can suggest some characteristics of communications media organized to promote the quest for quality variety for the best ways to resolve issues. The first and most general characteristic is that it must be democratically organized. Any class, racial, national, or gender structure that discounts information about failings in the factory, home, classroom, or neighborhood artifically reduces the pool of options from which to form political policy.

Any knowledge process that dismisses ideas from women or workers about how to cope with failure, dangerously cripples the political process. Any decision-making system that excludes critique of existing policy programs blinds itself to knowledge about the sources of system distress.

Any program of issue resolution that excludes the very people who must implement the solution is a program that courts failure. All of the above provide an unanswerable demand for democratically organized communication in the creation of public policy.

If democracy maximizes ultrastability of a society, and if the electronic media are essential to binding large populations together, then electronic media must be democratically organized.

First, every individual in the population must have direct access to all other individuals in order to know their needs. There are several collecting formats that provide each person access to all others. Plato IV at Urbana, Minerva at Columbia, and the interaction rules of CB radio all offer prototypes of democratic access.

Second, every person must have access to those who possess relevant background knowledge. A society that withholds information from its citizens impairs democracy. In the United States, the history of women, Blacks, workers, and socialists is hidden and all the progressive ideas generated by these oppressed groups are excluded as well from the search for quality variety.

Information about the operation of a corporation doing business with the public, about foreign policy, or about quality of life variables in the society must be in the public domain else there is no public domain. Every citizen must have access to persons in business, government, and minority groups or the interaction matrix is inadequate.

Third, every citizen must have access to similarly situated persons at work, in school, in the marketplace, or in the family. Rules that restrict similarly situated persons from talking to each other impose a false consciousness upon such persons. For example, a classroom so organized that students cannot see each other's face or speak except to the professor renders students ignorant of each other's distress at a lecture point or an evaluation procedure. A medical system in which each patient is denied knowledge of the dangers of a given hospital or the failings of a given doctor places all patients in jeopardy.

The same is true of workers in a factory, clerks in a store, or consumers in a market. All must have the right to know about the distress of each. A political party provides an interactional format in which people can talk to each other but mass politics does not provide such a format.

People listening to a president speak on a radio or a televised program are isolated from each other and cannot interact sufficiently to understand each other's response—if any. Generally, there must be richer interaction and richer information across social cleavages than within a given social congery. Isolation from each other renders one division in society indifferent to the fate of another. Since the fate of each part of the population is tied to the fate of every part, such an interaction void renders each group less able to control its own destiny.

The interactional matrix between children and parents (parental surrogates) must be especially rich else the socialization process fails and a generation of savages is created. It is not enough for children to interact intensively with other children, although such interaction is important. There must be cross-generational interaction else the transmission of culture fails and the reproduction of society suffers.

In summary, a society is created by the symbolic interactivity of its members. To do the job well, the structure of interaction must provide continuous, intensive, reciprocal, and focused interaction. To do otherwise is to subvert the very process by which social reality is created.

It is well within the technical capacity of all forms of media from the voice to the holograph that they be orchestrated in an interactive format. Radio, television, newsprint can be collectively owned, collectively controlled, and intercollectively used. It is possible to organize radio as a mass medium or as a social media. Commercial radio is organized as a mass medium while CB radio is organized as an interactive social medium.

Film documentaries can be produced in an objective way with a film crew isolated from coalminers, factory workers, women, or insurgents, or they can be collectively produced with women and workers having a part in editing and screening decisions. There is nothing in the structure of a computer that says only the state, the government, or a class elite may have access to its contents. There is something in elitist politics, class control, or state preference that so shapes the format of such media. It is a mystification to label social constraints on interactive format as technical or natural constraints. Only in an interactively rich symbolic environment comprised of the appropriate mix of social knowledge is it possible for self, society, and human culture to develop.

Any symbolic system primarily devoted to the information needs of private capital for accumulation of profits or the state for political legitimization thereby detracts from the social process and is, in its own way, as subversive of a society as crime, poverty, terror, or famine. Consumerism is aided by advertising in a mass media format while advertising does produce markets from that mass of isolated viewers for the capitalist corporation, but the larger, prior question is whether consumerism takes precedence over the knowledge process and over the social forms that could emerge from a different use of such media.

Temporary consensus on political policies can be extracted from a massified set of separated viewers by means of the massified use of polls and surveys. The prior question is whether those policies speak to the whole social process or merely transfer the problem to another people or generation. If such policies do not answer to the human needs of all those in a given social complex, recourse to *prepolitical resistance and rebellion* waits in the wings, offstage, ready to do much mischief to the human process.

Some of the channel capacity of the various media can be used for advertising and some for private purpose without compromising the social process. The interesting question is how long can a society survive when its media, its best media, are preoccupied with private purposes of class, ethnic, or state privilege. The answer is found in rates of social disorganization, rates of change in the larger environment, and, more importantly, rates of production of emancipatory knowledge. In systems theory, measures of entropy foretell the end of a system.

Public Opinion, Social Opinion, and the Public Sphere

Most of the time for most societies, the various media may be usefully oriented to the production of *social opinion*—that which reproduces society and is oriented to ideological knowledge. Cherished beliefs, traditions, and folkways are—must be—reproduced. It is proper and fitting that the interactive-rich media be used in school, church, and family to inculcate a rather innocent and uncritical commitment to existing social forms.

Myths, novels, games, plays, classes, ceremonies, and sermons that produce social opinion are necessary to bind people together, transcend social cleavages, organize social labor, and reproduce existing social identities, roles, and institutions. All this is necessary to the human process. Sometimes social opinion is inadequate to the survival needs of society, and a public sphere must be constituted to produce public opinion. In times of crisis, or when there is gradual decline in the indicators of social well-being, or when the economic and political structures in a larger system following their own transformative laws produce a new international order, or when new technology offers better ways to rear children, heal the ill, or create politics—then established ways must be taken out of the social sphere where they are taken for granted and brought into a public sphere where they are subjected to a relentless critique.

It is a painful process and it always reorients privileges, duties, and rights, but for an ultrastable society—one able to survive a crisis by self-reorganization—a public sphere is essential. At those times of crisis, it is necessary for the journalists, editors, and directors of the various media to change from the production of ideological knowledge to that of emancipatory knowledge. It does not suffice that a few professors in the university lecture on alternative political and economic, religious and familial, educational and therapeutic possibilities. An entire society must be involved—a public sphere must be created.

It does not suffice that surveys, polls, and samples of a mass of individuals isolated from each other be made. Authentically public opinion requires an interactively rich format and an informationally rich load of emancipatory knowledge.

To conflate mass opinion with public opinion is as grievous a fraud as to use patriotism to discourage public discussion on war, welfare, crime, inflation, or women's rights.

Mass opinion, based on individual needs, will not lead to policies congenial to the general need. Social opinion, oriented to old ways of doing things, will not produce policies leading to new ways of doing things. Public opinion, based on emancipatory knowledge, leads to dissensus, conflict, and political jockeying, but is absolutely essential to the quest for quality variety.

The trouble and turmoil natural to the public sphere is preferable to the violence and destruction natural to rebellion, revolution, or the sullen, persistent subversion of the alienated worker, citizen, student, or bureaucrat. The cost of a poorly designed public sphere in human life, the harm to the environment, the waste of property and resources in warfare are high costs to pay for systematically distorted, poorly utilized media.

Conclusion

There is nothing in nature, in science, nor in social philosophy that requires any given society be reproduced. There have been 3,000 to 5,000 distinct social life worlds each with their own culture in human history of which several hundred now exist. Several thousand more will evolve over the long and endless life of the good Earth.

The central question is whether we can design a democratic communications that will enlarge praxis, promote community, maximize peace, advance social justice, and respect the physical environment or whether we will continue to reproduce social inequality between rich and poor nations, rich and poor businesses, rich and poor classes; whether we use the media to reproduce privileged gender, ethnic, or age groups and in the same moment reproduce the dangerous instabilities that these bring.

A decent and rational society requires the media organized for democratic communication. Communication is not democratic nor is it communication unless it is informationally and interactively rich. The technology for a democratic communication exists. The resources to assemble a democratic communication exist. The political necessity for a democratic communication increases continuously.

The orientation of the various media in a massified format dedicated to the management of image problems for state and for corporation leads toward the fraudulently dramaturgical society of which we spoke earlier. The orientation of the various media to emancipatory content and organization is the future of all media—the only interesting question is how many people must suffer or die before the media themselves are emancipated to the human project.

Only private ownership and/or party control of the media in most societies around the world interferes with democratically organized communication. To date communications technology has not lived up to its potential for democracy. Since Gutenberg, Marconi, the Luminiere brothers, Lee De-Forest, and Graham Bell—war, famine, poverty, and inequality as well as the degradation of the environment have been increased by the highly privileged use of the media.

A media revolution is necessary to reverse and repair the harm done to the human project by existing forms of media use. With or without violence, a democratic use of the media must replace the oppressive and/or private use of radio, television, and other media by the capitalist class and by the party elite—else the human condition continues to deteriorate.

London

I wander thro' each charter'd street
Near where the Charter'd Thames does flow,
And mark in every face I meet
wounds of weakness, marks of woe.

In every cry of every Man,
In every infant's cry of fear,
in every voice, in every land,
the class-forged chains I hear.

How the fact'ry workers' cry
Every praying monk appalls;
And the hapless soldier's sighs
runs with blood down banker's walls.

But most thro' midnight streets I hear
how the youthful harlot's curse
and the new born infant's tear,
runs to fill the banker's purse.

—William Blake

The People

The people will live on.
The learning and blundering people will live on.
They will be tricked and sold and sold again
and go back to the nourishing earth for roothold.
The people so peculiar in renewal and comeback
you can't laugh off their capacity to take it.
The mammoth rests between his cyclonic dramas.

—Carl Sandberg

Drama <to do; <IndoEuropean base:
dra– = to work whence darit = to do.

Theatre <L. theatrum <Gr. Theatron
<base of Theasthai, to see,
whence <Gr thauma, a wonder.

—Webster's New World Dictionary

Part II

Critical Approaches to Dramaturgy

Introduction

The dramaturgical model of social life maintains that society is drama and that social relations can be fruitfully understood as dramatic action. Within sociology, dramaturgy has generated a large number of interesting and important studies of face-to-face behavior and interaction, primarily through the work of Erving Goffman. However, this model has suffered from theoretical entropy, empirical inaccuracy, and political sterility.

The chapters in this section are concerned with delineating the various dimensions of a critical dramaturgical analysis of contemporary social life and its points of convergence and departure from orthodox dramaturgical analysis. In short, they help define a critical dramaturgy.

Chapter 4, "The Dramaturgical Society: Macroanalysis," maintains that dramaturgy can be utilized to understand broader levels of social reality than mere face-to-face interactions and that dramaturgy defines how large-scale organizations operate. We locate dramaturgy in its larger political and economic history. Thus, dramaturgy constitutes a societal form.

Understanding that dramaturgy defines macrosocial processes one soon becomes aware of a variety of ways in which human behavior is exploited, managed, and manipulated. Under such conditions it is scientifically and politically essential to adopt a critical perspective. Chapter 5, "Dramaturgical Analysis and Societal Critique," discusses how dramaturgical analysis can be transformed in order to understand better and critique the alienative and exploitive dimensions of the dramaturgical society. This is accomplished by situating dramaturgical analysis within the critical tradition in sociology.

Dance of the Dead

We loitered down the moonlit street
We caught the tread of dancing feet
And stopped below the harlot's house.

Inside, above the din and fray
we heard the loud musicians play
the 'Treues Liebes Herz' of Strauss.

Like strange mechanical grotesques,
making fantastic arabesques,
the shadows raced across the blind.

We watched the ghostly dancers spin
to sound of horn and violin,
like black leaves whirling in the wind.

They took each other by the hand
and danced a stately saraband;
their laughter echoed thin and shrill,
and slid into a slow quadrille.

Sometimes a clockwork puppet pressed
a phantom lover to her breast,
sometimes they seemed to try to sing.

Sometimes a horrible marionette
came out, and smoked its cigarette
upon the steps like a living thing.

Then, turning to my love, I said
'The dead are dancing with the dead,
the dust is whirling on the dust.'

But she . . . she heard the violin,
and left my side to enter in;
love passed into the house of lust.

Then suddenly the tune went false,
the dancers wearied of the waltz,
the shadows ceased to wheel and whirl.

And down the long and silent street,
the Dawn, with silver sandaled feet,
crept like a frightened girl.

—Oscar Wilde

4

The Dramaturgical Society: Macroanalysis

With Garth Massey

Abandoned by its good spirits,
the theatre can sink to the level
of a Prostitute.

  —Max Reinhardt

While the writings of Erving Goffman have illuminated the dramaturgical components of face-to-face interaction, the task of developing a thoroughgoing substantive and theoretical explication of the dramaturgical society remains. This chapter expands the dramaturgical analysis to the macrosocietal. The character of a dramaturgical society is discussed in the first section; the origins of a critical dramaturgy are presented in the next. The conditions of social organization that give birth to a dramaturgical society are set forth in the next sections, and the potential of dramaturgy for a self-directed society are weighed in the final section.

Dramaturgy

For our purposes, a dramaturgical society is defined as one in which the technologies of social science, mass communication, theatre, and the arts are used to manage attitudes, behaviors, and feelings of the population in modern mass society. These conjoined technologies are used in the marketplace, industry, political life, and the university to provide images of service, quality, accountability, and other images that shape the needs and understanding of individuals while bolstering the self-image of the corporation, the politician, and the administrator.

71

In a dramaturgical society as we find it today, a range of technological and artistic devices is used in the process of mass communication to project manufactured images in commercial and public service advertisements, press releases and news items, political declarations, and documentaries to audiences of millions.

There is no necessary connection between dramaturgy and the sociology of fraud produced in these times by the managers of social life. In better times, the magic of make-believe, "what if," "suppose," and "never was" could be put to enlarge and enhance the human project. We caution one to keep this analysis in perspective—most people, most of the time organize their behavior innocently and without guile. Most groups are transparent; they are pretty much what they claim to be. We limit this analysis to the more strategic efforts of large-scale organizations to manage the social environment in which they operate to the private advantage of an economic or political elite.

Throughout Western industrialized societies and especially in the United States, the services of expert technicians, research institutes doing surveys, polls, and samples, theatrical people, and mass communications are disproportionately available to large-scale organizations. Huge corporations, major universities, the military services, government bureaus and agencies, labor unions, as well as the major political parties hire specialized sets of functionaries. Their task is to use the accouterments of theatre, the findings of social science, and the facilities of mass media to generate an "informed" public—formed in the image of the purchaser of such services.

These public relations, management science, and communications professionals are the "tribal magicians [who] have come to life in urban guise as publicists" (Duncan, 1965:xxii). As with all tribal magicians, these specialists come to control the process by which social reality is constructed. However, they are paid to apply their control in the service of a class/elite organized society.

In sum, the dramaturgical society is one in which the interaction between an atomized mass of people and the major institutions and largest organizations is deliberately managed, marked by the images of service, quality, or agency, and the projection of these upon the population for whose benefit these organizations and institutions are ostensibly acting.

This cultural hegemony of organizations can be understood in terms of a *critical* dramaturgical analysis, insofar as life in mass society is increasingly taking on the trappings of theatre. It is theatre of a most serious sort. Contained within the one-sided use of dramaturgical technology is the systematic evasion of reciprocity.

The most general consequences for a social order in which this technology is used in the evasion of reciprocity is the exacerbation of political and material inequality: in social honor, in wealth, and in the forms of power. Such cultural hegemony creates, in the long run, instability, resistance, and revolution of a most serious sort.

Perhaps the most serious fault of the dramaturgical society is the attendant exacerbation of inequality that accrues with the unrestrained use of dramaturgy in business and political life. Use of dramaturgy to create markets for capital-intensive, high-profit items in the marketplace or to create a market for secondary political issues (see Mueller, 1973:94) jeopardizes the political and material well-being of society.

Large-scale organizations are capable of consolidating positions of privilege, while the general public increasingly experiences reduced participation in the creation of authentic culture. At the same time, material, ideological, and political cultural forms lose their function of constructing a situationally meaningful social-life world created by intending, reciprocating humans.

It is the position of the author that there are specific conditions of social organization in Western industrial societies, and particularly in the United States, that converge to create a dramaturgy alienated from the human project.

The impoverishment of public opinion and the lack of understanding in formulating societal goals are products of the dramaturgical society. The lack of a coherent public discourse in the general population and among its experts and leaders, fostered by the strength and resources of organizations that prefer to foist deceptive and narrowly defined images of service, accountability, and quality on the public, provides a major obstacle to a free and rational society.

A major facet of the distorted communication that Jurgen Habermas (1970b) has so skillfully begun to examine lies in the production of images by organizations that legitimize the distorted reciprocity between these organizations and the public. In such a society, the assumptions of functional analysis and functional interchange become invalid.

A conflict model replaces the functional model as the appropriate intellectual tool with which to contribute to the self-knowledge of a society. A social order requiring individuals and organizations engaged in serious fundamental interaction to deal so heavily in images and stagings is also inimical to the conditions of human freedom.

By illuminating those conditions in modern society that enable organizations to create nonreciprocal, unchallengeable images of "reality," and which concomitantly require people to adopt temporary identities having little permanent relation to the self system, one may be able to see a prelude to the political task of changing those conditions, of turning them in the direction of a rationally creative, reciprocal dramaturgy in social life.

In the 1988 election, the Bush-Quayle team defined crime, abortion, a pledge of allegiance, and military might as central issues in the presidential campaign. A better set of issues on which to spend public energy and funds might have been the continued bifurcation of the health care system; continued deterioration of housing; increased poverty among women and dependent children; the national debt and its mortgaging of the future, as well as the overspending on exotic weapons systems in a world too full of death and violence.

In the present fiscal crises, solutions to capital accumulation or political legitimacy call for more than the dramaturgical facsimile of value and accountability; they call for the most serious political and economic transformation yet considered by the general public in Western societies. The invasion of Grenada or the spectacle of national mourning over the death of astronauts does create a thin and short-term solidarity among the diverse, conflicting sectors of society, but when the troops come home or the flag is lowered for the last time, the supply of solidarity runs low.

Drama and the technology of theatre might be useful to the human condition in a number of ways. In the celebration of human events, in separating the social world from the natural, in rites of transition, in making visible the flaws of life—dramaturgy is a powerful instrument and a valuable adjunct to the construction of a social reality imbued with vitality and wisdom. A critical dramaturgical analysis always combines these functions.

Toward a Critical Dramaturgy

A dramaturgical analysis of society involves a recognition, not only of the nature of symbolic communication, but also of the class-based uses of dramaturgical devices that prevent reciprocal communication and the emergence of authentic self-structures and cultural forms, and that obstruct the collective establishment of societal goals reflecting the needs and interests of the entire population.

Many writers juxtapose the presentments and interpretations (e.g., Ichheiser's [1970] "expressions" and "impressions") of social reality to a "real" world. In doing so they do not necessarily derogate the "as-if" reality as an inferior facsimile, but generally attempt to make socially constructed reality as accurate a reflection of some objective reality as possible.

Marx and Freud explored the distance between things as they appear and as they are. Both were concerned to make visible the mystifications of life and to help create a more authentic, innocent, and human drama. Marx assumed that duality could be replaced by a unity of thought and being were social conditions right. Freud assumed that the duality between the conscious and unconscious could be minimized were psychological traumas removed.

Also in opposition to the postulate of duality, the forerunners to and early exponents of symbolic interactionism—Dewey, James, Mead, W. I. Thomas, and Cooley—made major contributions in bridging the gap between subjective social worlds and objective reality. They have pointed out and analyzed the fundamentally symbolic reality of human life, thus minimizing the duality of phenomenon on the one hand and ontological (in-itself) reality forms on the other.

On Mystification

For symbolic interactionists, reality is created through the subjective activity of the participants. Situations are defined as real by words, body talk, costumes, and runs of behavior. The sharedness of symbols helps create the social occasion and the social actor in the same moment. Thus, mind in the form of expressed thoughts, self in the form of embodied social identities, and society in the form of social others and social occasions are produced in the same instant by the acting, sharing individuals in a social frame. When dramaturgy is in the service of the sociology of fraud, that unity of self and society is rent asunder.

If the symbolic interaction processes are undistorted by power, dramaturgical deceptions, or secrecy, then the discrepancy between social reality and human understanding, between noumena and phenomena, is minimal.

An occasion defined as a family reunion becomes a *real* family reunion as people are defined as and act as cousins, brothers, grandparents, and wives. This form of reality is as real as an atom, a molecule, a rock, or a mountain. The difference is that the parts intend to be parts in social reality—and may cease to be such parts.

Dramaturgy has developed from this perspective, in both its depoliticized and critical approaches. Kenneth Burke's classic analyses of the dramaturgical nature of social life has been taken by many as an acceptance of the analogy of dramaturgy as an accurate portrayal of life. Life and politics, in this sense, are drama. People do not relate toward one another as if engaged in dramatic performances. They are caught up in a drama: They become the person they and others expect them to be.

But Burke intends no naive and unquestioned approach to the dramaturgical nature of social reality, as his analysis "The Dialectic Constitutions" in *A Grammar of Motives* makes apparent. Both Burke and Hugh Duncan have been well aware of the "mystifications" (cf. Duncan, 1962) that are created and sustained through the hierarchical control of mass communication.

Joseph Gusfield's (1963) analysis of the Temperance Movement exhibits both the managerial and emancipatory uses of dramaturgy. His work provides much insight into the process by which the symbolic meaning of temperance took on a far broader meaning than mere abstinence from alcohol. It reveals how the resulting political action pushed a broad range of conservative and reactionary interests. However, a critical analysis must go beyond the general position that groups in a democracy sometimes use symbols that mean more than their exponents openly reveal.

Murray Edelman's (1964) analysis of the manipulation of symbolic events, encounters, and identities in politics falls more within the critical tradition. He notes that such uses, rather than stimulating political debate and reasoned consensus, divert attention "from cognitive and rational analysis." Thus, "every individual [becomes] an instrument of the common interest rather than a cognitive and empirical manipulator of reality" (Combes and Mansfield, 1976:350).

Equally within the critical perspective is Mueller's (1973) analysis of the conditions promoting and facilitating constrained communication, where extraneous "noise" is systematically introduced and the audience "has little control over the selection of information or the quality of interpretations transmitted" (Mueller, 1973:100).

This research and more adds to the theoretical point that reality and human understanding need not be alien to each other. It is possible for meaning to flow clearly and cleanly between two people; between two peoples; between generations. The symbolic interactional processes can be designed to mystify or to clarify human understanding. To help create the social conditions under which such meaning processes can develop is the task of the critical social psychologist and the clinical psychologist.

Dramaturgy and Society

Under the conditions of social organization that constitute contemporary Western society, an analyst such as Goffman has special, but limited, relevance. His mode of social analysis presents a careful examination of the way individuals and organizations are trying not only to do but to be identified, in which identification is often a prerequisite to, and of equal or greater importance than, doing.

In Goffman's work the presentation of self-identity must have adequate dramaturgical direction and expression in order to be credible. These dramaturgical techniques become part of the diet of socialization in the family, in peer groups, and in the schools, as well as what one sees and incorporates from the media. In analyzing the dramaturgical society one must ask: What are the reasons that a dramaturgy is suborned to the sociology of fraud? When is such an analysis appropriate for a given society?

To extend dramaturgical analysis to macrosocietal levels, one must conceptually do two things. First, one must go beyond the boundaries of what Goffman (1961a) calls the "situated activity system" in his microanalytic focus. It is necessary to locate such microanalysis within the larger economic framework in which it is found.

The situated activity system must also be given greater temporal boundaries than is the case in intimate interaction. It must be located in its historical setting. The dimensions of time are essential to the analysis of events. A political campaign, an energy crisis, a campaign to sell a new product, the mobilization of support for war, or a public relations campaign may involve weeks or months of interaction between an organization or a group of organizations. The audience for such information sets may be subjected to the resulting symbol/product for seconds or for minutes.

Macroanalysis requires that each dramaturgic event be placed in the larger social and historical context in which it is located.

A dramaturgical creation may be located in still longer runs of time. As an economic system rises or falls on a 30- or 50-year Kondratieff wave, the use of dramaturgy to protect profits and to generate markets replaces the impetus to use quality and price to share in market. The increase or decrease in the sociology of fraud follows such economic transformations.

Magnitudes of Dramaturgy

In this historical epoch, the advent of the transnational corporation with multibillion dollar budgets produces a cataclysmic change in the fraudulent use of dramaturgy. The relative equality that may exist among individuals has no parallel vis-à-vis the corporation or the state agency using dramaturgy to their own purpose.

Control over the knowledge process by the rich and powerful means increased power disparity between organizations and the isolated individuals of mass society. In the analysis of interaction between large-scale, formal organizations and individuals this fact becomes more important, for it indicates the necessity to recognize that presentations will not be based on parity.

Assumptions of parity in the marketplace, of contracts freely made between equal parties are utterly false in a fully developed sociology of fraud. Access to dramaturgical resources by the private or public corporation, access to media, access to research findings in social science—all give the multinational corporation a position of power that even nation-states find daunting.

In societies that use dramaturgy as a marketing or managerial strategy, it is not the self-system that mediates behavior nor a set of significant others as most social psychologists teach their students. Experts from management science, from depth psychology, from public relations are employed to circumvent the self-system. Needs, urges, dispositions, fears, and prejudices are generated by effective advertising. Bits of behavioral knowledge are used to link products directly to human anxieties about sex, status, identity quest, and the like.

Such behavioral scientists and practitioners unscrupulously avoid generating specific social identities that can subject messages to personal scrutiny and group critique. When social identities (housewife, mother, doctor, male, or other) anchored in the self-system through the socialization process are the focus of advertising, it is to exploit or mobilize such "selves" to serve the corporate goal. Even religious identities can be used to expand markets. Xerox uses monks to tout its duplicating machines. The Encyclopaedia Britannica uses the voiceover of God to encourage people to find truth in its pages.

While a dramaturgical society is likely to arise in any society that contains ruling elites, dramaturgy finds its most favorable milieu in capitalist societies. The existence of surplus production, together with an ever-increasing surplus population, serves as an impetus for corporate directors to use dramaturgy to generate mass markets for ever-increasing productivity. If production were for use or followed social needs generated by a free, rather than manipulated, public discourse, there would be little need to generate a market for a commodity.

The United States has one special attribute that accounts for its being the leader in the fraudulent use of dramaturgy. Given the value it places on democratic forms as well as law and order, together with its tradition of an open society, the recourse to purely coercive technologies in public life is awkward and frequently counterproductive. Coercion has been used to generate markets, restrain workers, control minorities, and manage political unrest in this and other societies, but corporate liberalism in the United

States has found dramaturgy more advantageous than coercion. In America, the image industry is a trillion-dollar enterprise. Advertising alone rakes in more than $100 billion yearly from the sale of audiences to corporations.

In Europe, especially in Great Britain, the crown sold franchises to companies for monopolies in a wide variety of products, and used the king's law and the king's men to enforce the monopoly. In Latin America, monopolies are maintained by death squads and political torture to this day. In Japan, the government coordinates the corporate world. But in the United States, the trust busting of T. R. Roosevelt, the New Deal of F. D. R., the labor unions' struggles in Flint, Detroit, and elsewhere in the 1930s, the consumer movement lead by Ralph Nader's team "the Nader Bunch," the Environmental Protection movement, the Civil Rights movements, and the United Farmworkers lead by César Chávez—all converge to render direct physical and economic coercion outside the pale for most corporate strategies.

Dramaturgical society today is one in which large-scale organizations, employing scientific and artistic communities to create images and purchasing time on mass media with which to disseminate their images, generates power that far outweighs the ability of even moderately organized consumer organizations, public interest groups, and leftist political organizations to counter and refute such images.

Whether there will be countervailing sources of information in the dramaturgical society of the twenty-first century with which to control and constrain the mystifications of public relations, scientific management, advertising, and other dramaturgical technologies is an open question. While critical social psychology can help demystify interactional processes, still meaningful emancipation requires a social base rather larger than the academic community.

Protective Structures

While large-scale organizations, especially profit-oriented ones, try to create a mass-consumption market and to use theatre, social science, and sophisticated communication technologies to generate a receptive audience for their surplus production, there are still protective structures to counter that effort.

Societies in which social structures of tribe, kin, friends, or community exist to mediate behavior quickly neutralize the information content of messages broadcast by large-scale organizations and greatly increase the "problem of order" for those organizations.

Wherever there is friendship, kinship, or other forms of solidarity, there are significant and sensible others available to warn off the innocent buyer of goods, services, and politics.

Arnold Rose wrote of the importance of voluntary associations and other intervening structures to mediate between the managerial impulses of state and corporation. In a conflict-ridden society, that is good advice indeed. Each oppressed interest group—women, minorities, workers, the elderly, patients, and customers—needs a watchdog team acting on its behalf. There are problems with a society organized around interest groups, however.

1. There is no social agent acting on behalf of collective interests, of the common good. Each group is the enemy of all others and tries to advance special interest at the expense of those who have few or incompetent protective agencies.
2. In the competition for the services of the image specialists, the weak and the poor are left out of the game. The concept of community, the concept of brotherhood/sistership, the very web of social life is tattered and shredded.
3. The prepolitical activities of those who cannot afford to purchase the services of a dramaturgical specialist return to subvert the interests of all.
4. In a fully developed dramaturgical society oriented to private profit or to political control, the substance of service, value, and performance is replaced by the image of service, value, and performance. Image is everything; content counts for little. There is always another customer, another group of voters, another disenchanted audience still looking, still hoping, still trusting in the spoken word.
5. The prophetic vision of William Butler Yeats joins the voices of the old testament prophets to warn:

> Mere anarchy is loosed upon the world
>   the blood dimmed tide is loosed,
>   and everywhere
> the ceremony of innocence is drowned;
>   The best lack all conviction
>   while the worst
>   are full of passionate intensity.

Only in a society composed of atomized millions can such organizations succeed in generating markets with the techniques of theatre, television, and social science. Only in a society with false economics and false politics can the major institutions—school, religion, and play—become so deformed and unequal. Only in a massified, depersonalized, soliptic society can the wedge between self and society grow to such proportions that individuals are led to seek and adopt privatized sources of self.

The Norm of Anonymity

In the dramaturgical society role performances are often short, episodic, historical, and seldom bear a permanent relationship to one's own self-structure. This makes appropriate the term "short-take society" (Young, 1972) to describe a central aspect of the dramaturgical handling of one's self and of others (see also Helmer, 1970). Mall culture offers a vision of social relatedness for the 1990s. For those who want a short course in the social psychology of thoroughly dramatized society, one may observe the way in which people, businesses, schools, professionals, and politicians present themselves there.

Fairs, carnivals, holidays, and tourist spots also foretell of the structure of social relations. While these folk dramas could contribute to the logics of surprise, delight, and a sense of the holy, in their alienated form they are uncertain interludes in a strange and anonymous world.

The norm of anonymity is a necessary adjunct to this short-take society wherein one goes from one short-take role to another. Between social takes, one must be accorded civil inattention and encouraged quickly to change roles unencumbered by the need to express or the desire to sustain social relationships (cf. Gouldner, 1970:378-80).

Since Weber's (1946) analysis of the characteristics of bureaucratic organization, it has been taken as a commonplace of such social forms that personal relations shall be essentially without serious emotional or intimate involvement. This is part of the demands of the formal rationality (Israel, 1971:100-101) that now pervades relations among those persons within bureaucracies and between those contacting such organizations. This style is now to be found throughout interactions inside and outside the structure of bureaucratic organization.

Anonymity takes the bumps and distractions out of contact with others. It relieves each from the burden of responsibility for others' feelings and problems. This norm of anonymity makes strangers of us all as it comes to pervade nearly all formal social relations. Its location is not, however, in human nature but rather in the structural features of mass, bureaucratic social formations.

Anonymity requires that there be an intricate and extensive set of visual and behavioral presentations that inform us of just who is accessible and to what degree, as well as to whom we must accord and of whom we may demand civil attention in the public sector of social discourse (cf. Perinbanayagam, 1975:7). Thompson (1966) has insightfully analyzed aspects of this dramaturgical process within formalized and hierarchical role systems of bureaucracies and between subordinates and authority figures.

This norm of anonymity applies at both the individual and the societal level, as groups and organizations hide behind a shield of anonymity. They express and elicit only those cues, those images that serve their privately designed purposes and functions. The norm of anonymity affords—even requires—opportunity to manage impressions, in that an intimate understanding of persons, products, and services varies from being merely difficult to being forbidden. When one is unknown, one must quickly make others know who one is—dramatics serve to cue us on how to take and be taken in anonymous situations.

In the emptiness of social relations, the opportunities for the sociology of fraud abound at all levels of society. The need for increasing regulatory, compensatory, therapeutic services presses upon us. The resources of the state are strained to the breaking point in such a self-serving, soliptic society. The social sources of morality shrink to encompass only one's immediate family and very closest friends. Even those are in jeopardy of stagings, theatrics, and professional managements.

Social workers, police, teachers, clerks, bosses, and doctors are required to be impersonal instruments of bureaucratic rationality. When they do evil, they retreat behind the rule, the policy, the invisible arm of the boss, thus become anonymous even while looking at a hurting human being. In such societies, morality is programmed out of human interactions and preprogrammed by rules, policies, and programs. Morality loses its human face— and its social place.

Such a society is devoid of permanent, inclusive social relationships because anonymity norms, bureaucratic order, and power inequality all reduce reciprocity and accountability by reducing interaction. The social-life world produced in the polity, the marketplace, and in the university has little more authenticity than the dramas produced on television or in the cinema. At least these latter are not presented as actual instances of social life.

Structural Bases for the Evasion of Reciprocity

In complex societies the opportunities for exploitation and the evasion of reciprocity proliferate as complexity and anonymity increase, in spite of a real increase in the need for effective processes of communication and functional interdependence.

It is in a society where the only interest in the workplace is in the amount of surplus value that can be extracted from another person, that short, episodic roles replace community with its sustained, inclusive supportive social relations. And in the marketplace where the central interest is the realization of surplus value as profit, short-term social relations are preferable to life-long social identities.

The corporation makes a sale, extracts surplus value, realizes profit, and has no interest in any further social relatedness; there is a positive disinterest in further contact as long as new markets can be generated by depth psychology and a purchased media.

Guarantees and warranties are issued and then routinely circumvented. Insurance companies pay off small claims quickly and use statistics to create the dramaturgical appearance of honest actuarial accounting. Airlines change the definition of "on time" to create the semblance of punctuality. Governments change accounting categories to create the impression of frugality and fiscal probity. Mathematics and graphics become tools in the kit of profit-seeking firms.

Surveys, polls, and sampling services become ambushes behind which lurk the interests of managers, politicans, owners, and engineers of the mind. Measures of distribution and variations join the principles of psychology in the technologies of the theatre to circumvent the norm of reciprocity while staging a convincing image on the media that reciprocity is the object of interest. Where profits are counted, images are profitable.

Where there is extensive social differentiation, there is little opportunity for shared experiences to occur. Where there are large numbers of persons, the opportunity for contact between individuals as valued social others diminishes. Where there is no community, it becomes easy to advance one's own interests at the expense of another sector of society. Where exchange relations are complex and predicated on contrived rewards, the degree of reciprocity is difficult to assess.

Where important others in the exchange process are remote in time and place, the facts of exploitation are hard to establish. These features are common in class-organized societies and they are also found in bureaucratically organized "socialist" societies.

All of these class-based structural features, in addition to the racist, sexist, and age-based structures, contribute to a form of social organization in which the interests of one segment of the population may be so inimical to the interests of other segments that it becomes necessary and possible to create deceptive images of social relationships. In such conditions, a common tactic is the presentation of an event, not as it actually occurs, but in terms of arranging the manifest signs "at an inconspicuously gradual and piecemeal pace" (Boorstin, 1962:13).

In this way resistance is diffused and a predictably managed response is the outcome. Universities commonly raise tuition and fire popular faculty during the Summer and Christmas breaks. Politicians send out trial balloons. Price increases are hidden by reductions in weight of candy bars, corn flakes, or by the addition of water to hams and vegetables.

In Western industrial societies the synergy of functional interchange is being subverted by the structure of corporate capitalism. Parameters of growth, profit, and control of the environment by corporations and public institutions conflict with the parameters of service, accountability, and quality of human life.

Increasing resources go to banking, finance, luxury lodging and dining, high-tech medical procedures, while essential parts of the system—child care, public health, low-cost housing, sewage and garbage treatment, bridges and roads, as well as teaching and healing—are neglected. The flow of wealth is to the corporation with the best connections and the best dramatists; collective needs are set aside by soliptic market practices.

In the capitalist state, the policies and processes of the political apparatus provide disproportionate support for those corporations that sponsor the dramaturgical society. The dramaturgical arts and crafts readily lend themselves to masking these corporate interests in the political campaign and in the market, thereby consolidating the class structure. As the two-tiered class system is split further apart, the word *liberal* becomes a dirty word replacing *communism* as the epithet of political scorn.

As the fiscal crisis of the state continues and as the surplus population grows, the problems of political legitimacy require more and more dramaturgy in the political sphere as a technique to manage dissent. Mass media have solved many of the technical problems of constructing images favorable to dominant class interests. They provide the means to project impressions throughout the society, and as need for a more up-to-date image arises, mass media make it possible in a very short time to replace an image that is no longer serviceable.

Reciprocity is subverted by the expertise of a vast cadre of skilled artists, musicians, photographers, writers, producers, poets, editors, engineers, and publicists who substitute a world of make-believe for a world of serious social endeavor. They industriously engage in creating the dramaturgical impression of community, the image of friendship, the facsimile of democratic governance, and the illusion of academic excellence in concert with actors, musicians, cinematographers, stage managers, costumers, and make-up personnel.

In feudal society, kings and popes held a virtual monopoly on the services of the managers of illusion and pretense. In a capitalist society, every corporation can subscribe to the forms of art as well as theatre, and the monopoly of staging and drama maintained by church and state disappears.

In medieval Europe, artists and artisans were concerned with religious themes in paintings, tapestries, drama, and music. Artists and artisans created furnishings, fixtures, halls, palaces, cabinets, tables, silver, coin, and ceramics to serve, exalt, and comfort the elite of church, state, and commerce (cf. Burke, 1965: ch. 5).

Today most of the best artists, photographers, musicians, directors, and actors ply their trade in the world of advertising and public relations. A full-blown industry in commercial image making is indispensable to a dramaturgical society whose institutions are finding themselves increasingly unwilling or unable to cope with the material, political, or ideological needs of the population (see also Young, 1978).

A market strategy with which to sell imaginary or trivial differences in a commodity is created. The advent of mass production, coupled with industrial espionage, has diminished the differences between products. In the political arena there is a "winning image" as well as a salable political formula that, when shared by the directors of the major contributors, makes candidates as indistinguishable as their suits, socks, or shorts.

The artisans' task of imagery is to limit, then magnify acceptable differences between products and persons. As Gouldner (1970:381) sees it, "dramaturgy makes the transition from an older economy centered on production to a new one centered on mass marketing and promotion, including the marketing of the self." The dynamic of that transition is the profit motive. It is more profitable to create the dramaturgical semblance of quality than to support basic research by which to improve quality or to bear the real cost of improving quality in automobiles, medicines, appliances, or service.

Dramaturgy in Modern Systems Theory

When a social system makes claims of greatness, service, or quality, the images presented are not fraudulent in themselves. Images, visions, utopias, predictions, and wishes are necessary components of a self-fulfilling prophesy by which to embody cultural values.

Marked by the self-fulfilling prophesy, things defined and treated as real may come to be real. Desirable social events begin with an idea, a goal, a dream, a plan, a wish, a vision, an image.

All social realities contain ideas of social relationships, social occasions, social roles, and of community. In these respects, participation in the creation of ideological culture is necessary to the human condition. When ideological production is monopolized by a cadre of public relations experts serving the corporate interest of profit, control, and growth, ideological production becomes a technology of oppression rather than an essential part of the construction of an authentic social-life world.

When images take the place of reality, when they distort and hide the recognition of things as they are, when effort, genius, and intention go no further than the construction of the image, then society becomes subject to the sociology of fraud, and the dramaturgical society becomes the society of ideological domination.

In his examination of the role of art, literature, music, and other forms of "high culture," Marcuse (1964) expresses a position similar to the one taken here. The creative, artistic features of society have served traditionally to give societal direction by means of exposing the "negativity of society." They have indicated the truth of society as it is; its dark side and its light—not simply as it prefers to see itself.

In contemporary industrial society, this "artistic reality," this "other-dimension" is increasingly being "absorbed into the prevailing state of affairs . . . to sell, comfort, or excite" (Marcuse, 1964:64), and the critical capacity of an art and culture is lost to their commercial capacities. The creative spheres no longer provide "images of another way of life but rather . . . types of the same life, serving as an affirmation rather than negation of the established order" (Marcuse, 1964:59).

In doing so they encourage the use of a language of "deception, ignorance and submission" that becomes effective solely for the established interests. Mass communications thus "blend together harmoniously, and often unnoticeably, art, politics, sciences, religion, and philosophy with commercials. . . . [They] bring these realms of culture to their common denominator—the commodity of form" (Marcuse, 1964:57). One-dimensionality becomes a pernicious outcome of the dramaturgical society which, in turn, makes one-dimensionality even more unchallengeable.

The central theoretical position of this chapter is that fantasy, make-believe, theatre, game-playing, models, plans, and images are essential to self-directed social systems. These events from the world of make-believe constitute a major part of the variety, the options that make a social system active and adaptive to the needs of its populace.

Donald MacKay (1968:30–43) has provided an information-flow model of human behavior in which he represents the minimal requirements for goal-directed behavior. A modern systems theory approach postulates that a technology of information-flow that permits a social system to reduce mismatch between system goal-states and present states, or a means by which to change goals through use of stored information, is a self-controlled system (see also Buckley, 1968).

From this perspective, "pretense" is essential to "reality" in any self-directed system. In the paradigm of the modern systems approach, in order for a person, society, or machine to be self-directed it is necessary:

1. to establish a goal or a set of equally desirable goals. Goals are found in the realm of the not-is and what-if;
2. to have a receptor/monitoring apparatus by which any mismatch between the goal and the present state is gauged in a continuous fashion;
3. to have a control apparatus with stored variety for every contingency that may occur between the present state and the goal(s). Variety, i.e., options, is found in the realm of the possible but not-yet-is;
4. to have an effector apparatus organized to act on any option selected by the control apparatus.

Images, play, games, stories, myths, stagings, experiments, and such may provide a social system with goals not yet realized in the social institutions of a society. Good health care systems, better ways of doing marriage, low-crime relations, enlivening education—all now dwell in the world of magic and make-believe. There are no societies in the world today organized to institute these goals. Many do not even try.

At the same time, whatever the goals of a social system, successful goal attainment requires a variety of means, options all, in its control ensemble by which to deal with contingencies encountered in moving from the present to the goal state. These images, ideas, utopias are the equivalent of stored data for society as a whole. Every society must have in its repertoire of "make-believe" a possibility to transform itself into an entirely new social-life world.

Although the general point of his critique of systems theory is valid, we do have a profound point of disagreement with Jurgen Habermas (1974a:101). The point of disagreement lies in Habermas's assessment of general systems theory, condemned for its inspiration of "global interpretations" which "contest the possibility and substance of identity formation at the macrosocietal level," whereby "identity problems are eclipsed by steering problems and retain at best a parochial significance."

This is more appropriately a criticism of a managed society than systems theory per se. The modern systems perspective can readily lend itself to the understanding of distorted communication and its consequences, while in the same stroke indicating the value of pretend in organizing reality. Modern systems theory can be used to aid in the task of creating healthy self-systems as the central source of control for social behavior as readily as it lends itself to problems of social change and transformation (Young, 1977).

That a strong and stable self-system is not a major goal in capitalist societies is discussed earlier in this chapter and in more detail later. We should like to add that the development of the self-system is low-profit, labor-intensive production ill-suited to capitalism, while behavior mediated by a healthy self-system is inimical to an elitist society.

A major contradiction developing in the U.S.S.R. and elsewhere is that a genuinely socialist self-system is hostile to both party and class hegemony over the production of political and ideological culture. It may not occur in this century, but one day the logics of socialism will produce a generation of young people who will cast off the bureaucratic forms of socialism now endemic in the Communist bloc. Whether they will move toward the soliptic consumerism of the West or toward the modalities of praxis so essential to the Marxian agenda depends, in large part, on whether an emancipatory social psychology can be generated and communicated to the larger population of that world.

We agree with Habermas's (1979b) position that a normative structure established within the public sphere is the best solution to the problem of order. Our view is that a socially anchored self-system must be produced as a stable mediator of behavior and that a publicly constructed normative structure mediates behavior situationally. Alternative technologies of social control—coercion, dramaturgy, or pecuniary incentives—are poor seconds as solutions to the problems of order, inasmuch as they exclude praxis and community and, thus, authentic social-life worlds.

The need for alternative social goals—within a vision of wholeness—as well as the need for the capacity to change, inform us that dramaturgy can be put to better uses than those of profit, management of the political process, or the false self-presentments made by existentially isolated individuals in a mass society. In a transparent society in which images presented are fair representations of things as they are—in the marketplace, academia, personal intercourse, and in politics—the human spirit thrives.

We can call such a society a praxis society or we can call it the City of God—our rhetorics of motive are important but more important is that we get on with the job using the conceptual and emotional tools now available to educate, politicize, and organize against the sociology of fraud in the dramaturgical society we see developing in America today.

The alternative is one in which the sociology of fraud permeates and spreads. A society in which cynicism shrinks the human soul and one in which each person comes to look for private advantage from each other person. This is not the legacy we should leave to our children and the children of our children.

Time to Think

I wonder sometimes
if the soldiers lying
under the soil, wrapped in their coats
like beggars sleeping under an arch,
their hands filled with leaves,
would take vengeance on them who send
them. Coming back like beggars,
seeing the homes and fields that obedience
lost them, whether they would have anything
to say to sons or brothers or friends
only this: Obedience is death.

I wonder if they,
men of all nations,
hands full of twigs
stones on their eyes,
half afraid of what they've done,
but forgotten like a short wild dream,
but now themselves again:
tradesmen, farmers, students . . .
would they tell us to die also,
to be obedient?

Would they appeal
to our better nature,
our righteous indignation,
our pity for men like themselves,
and tell us to quit?

Would they call their cause a fraud,
would they say our cause is just,
would they help us discriminate
between the aggressor and
the regrettable necessity
or would they turn away?

Not fools, but men who knew the price
they paid. Would they melt like smoke
or would they speak; meet our eyes and
tell us what they think about this end?

Would they tell us each lesson is new;
that they would make room for us in
their dusty hall? Would they look in
a frosty window and listen to us talk
without saying what they thought?

Perhaps we might go to that frosty
window and look out to speak
to them and ask them what
now they think about it
now they have had
time to think.

—Alex Comfort

5

Dramaturgical Analysis
and Societal Critique

With John Welsh

The dramaturgical sociology of Erving Goffman and his followers, as it has come to be practiced, has failed the promise of sociology in that it has not provided knowledge so that individuals and groups can reflect upon the legitimacy of the society. The creation of rational, humane, and participatory societies remains the most important human project for a critical, truth-telling social science.

A critical dramaturgical sociology is indispensable in this regard. Having sketched the basic structural features of the dramaturgical society in earlier chapters, it is necessary now to consider the intellectual foundations of a critical dramaturgical analysis and to outline efforts that have been made to constitute a critical dramaturgy.

The Ruling Ideas of an Epoch

Inspiration for a critical view of the relationship between knowledge and social reality can be found in Marx's (1978) critique of Hegel's political philosophy. In his Critique of Hegel's "Philosophy of Right," Marx noted that Hegel's comprehension and presentation of social reality, when stripped from its pantheistic mysticism, was fairly accurate as a picture of capitalist society in its emergent form.

Because it was thought to be the true presentation of political reality and because it was backed up by state power, Hegel's political philosophy was an intellectual definition of the situation which served, in part, to shape social reality. Hegel's political philosophy was not merely an innocent oblation to the Prussian state and Marx did not critique it because he was interested in philosophy. Marx understood that the ruling ideas were the ideas of the ruling class which means, in part, that the dominant ideas about social relations benefit those who rule by legitimizing their power.

The emancipatory interest of science is advanced by examining the ruling ideas of a historical epoch. If dehumanizing, alienating dimensions can be shown in the ruling ideas, then these will illuminate the dehumanizing, alienating dimensions of a social formation. Critical sociology begins from the same premise of the relationship between intellectual definitions of the situation and the reality of everyday experience.

Dramaturgical Analysis and Human Knowledge

Jurgen Habermas and many others connected to the Critical School of Frankfurt have spelled out the need for three forms of scholarly knowledge that can facilitate the construction of a rational and humane social-life world. These endeavors serve and help constitute underlying human interests: prediction and control, insight and understanding, change and renewal.

As Habermas (1970b) suggests, all human societies share the need for *positive knowledge* about what is and how it works; *hermeneutical knowledge* about what is meant; and *emancipatory knowledge* about change and renewal of the human process. Dramaturgical analysis helps provide the first two kinds of knowledge in social science. It is knowledge of the third sort that is so seldom produced by practitioners of this branch of social psychology.

Positivism

Positivism is concerned with the production of general laws of society: economic, political, social, psychological laws together with knowledge of the sweep and patterns of history. The pursuit of general laws is informed by the human interest in the prediction and control of behavior. All societies need to know how its institutions are working; how its people are faring; in what direction trends are taking it; from whence the sources of human delight and human misery.

Positive . . . scientific . . . knowledge contributes to the critical analysis of society by producing knowledge of existing social relationships, their patterns, and their contradictions. Such knowledge is absolutely essential to a self-directed, self-healing, self-reorganizing society. A society without an adequate self-reflexive science is one that blinds itself to its own pathologies, pathways, and potentials.

Dramaturgical analysis—a simple description of how people stage reality, a clear presentation of the backstage mechanics, an inventory of how scripts, costumes, props, actors, audiences, and performances are made—provides positive knowledge about how social reality is constructed. In and of itself, this knowledge has little moral interest. However, when such knowledge is linked to the corporate interests of predicting and controlling workers or customers, positivism is alienated from the human project.

In its alienated form, positive science serves the interests of elites in certainty and technical control. In alienated social science, certain domain assumptions are made that mystify and distort the knowledge process. Knowledge is inherently neutral; the methods and theories of the natural sciences constitute the only appropriate model. That theory, once discovered, is eternal.

This form of science, "although it conceives itself as neutral, is actually an inquiry which has the theoretical interest and societal consequence of maintaining technical control" (Schroyer 1970:215). The major indictment set forth in these chapters is that dramaturgical analysis, as it now is organized, helps serve the technical interest in control and management more so than the substantive interest in reason and rationality. The human interest requires both.

Quantification and Mystification

The methods of contemporary social science claim that quantitative research is the essence of true science—if it exists, it can be measured. This assumption preempts a varied set of methodologies in which human genius encompasses the richness and themes of human life far better than mathematics. In a more modest sociology, a more inviting sociology, credit would be given to the poet and the prophet whose genius catches the world aborning before the research projects are conceived; who interpret the anguish of those whose existence is taken as unproblematic by the secluded scientist.

An alienated social science that searches for the immutable laws of society preempts history, preempts alternative futures, distorts reality, and preserves the existing patterns of social relations. A praxis sociology encourages human beings to imagine, to experiment, to invert existing patterns of social life in the effort to more fully participate in the process of reality constitution.

One knows, in epistemological terms, one's own society best when one builds it in cooperation with others. A theory or methodology that elides the subjectivity of human action, deletes the intersubjectivity of human intention, and inserts unchanging structures and remote knowledge systems upon a population is hostile to the human process.

While forms of crime may correlate one way in one social formation, another pattern, another casualty may obtain elsewhere. Social reality is built by human beings, not by immutable laws or social machines. Human beings can respond differently in different contexts, indeed, in the same context. Poverty may tend to encourage crime in a possessive society; it may tend to promote sharing and solidarity in a communal one.

Mathematical models are possible only by virtue of the fact that someone systematically discards information in order to make the richness of human life fit in the poverty of number systems. Words contain far more information than do numbers. Before one worships numbers systems and the ease with which numbers can be combined and rearranged, one might wonder what data are lost by conversion of human language into machine language; what meanings are lost; what variations are squeezed into homogeneous categories.

Positive science, conditional regularities, short-term trends, as well as cycles of history are essential to a rational society. They help us know what is and what is likely. But there is more to human life than soft facts made hard by a false or easy codification of human experience. Parallel to, prior to, foundational of, complementary to positive knowledge is hermeneutical knowledge.

Hermeneutics

Hermeneutics provides challenge and added dimensions to the positivistic presentation of social life by scientism. Hermeneutic approaches are concerned with the processes of the social construction of everyday life. According to Schroyer (1970:215), the hermeneutic sciences are conceived as "that mode of interpretation that yields an understanding of the social-cultural life world and that presupposes the interest of extending intersubjective understanding."

The intent of the hermeneutic enquiry is to explore the object of sociological analysis from a more human, more personal orientation by focusing on these intersubjective structures. Hermeneutical analysis picks up on social life at all its stages of construction—when its degree of facticity is low and when it approaches a closed behavioral system. Hermeneutical knowledge searches the meaning of a thing as that meaning comes to be shared by some set of human beings in such a way that things defined as true, become true in the consequence; things defined as real become real in the act of defining, believing, embodying a role, an occasion, a process, a relationship.

There is a social magic in the human labor of creating social reality lost to the objective, impersonal statements of positive science. There is an unstable equilibrium in a marriage, a church, a city that might, overnight, convert into quite a different thing; transformations not possible in the world of atoms, molecules, mice, or nuclear warheads. Hermeneutical analysis can uncover that magic; make it visible; enable human beings to do it better or do some other kind of magic.

Forms of Hermeneutical Analysis

Symbolic interactional concepts sensitize the student of human life to the shared, varying world in the act of creation by those present. Dramaturgical concepts sensitize us to the multiple realities superimposed upon and reverberating against each other in asylums, circuses, classrooms, hospitals, churches, and political campaigns. Ethnomethodological concepts help us understand social reality by challenging the underlying assumptions found in restaurants, families, and offices.

Literary criticism helps us to know the meaning of a novel, a play, a poem, or a song within the social context from whence it came—as well as their enduring lessons. With literary criticism, we can take the perspective of the narrator and share, over time and space, the depths of joy and pain of love, dissent, work, or quest.

Semiotics can teach us about the larger dimensions of meaning from which a photo, a film, or a cartoon speaks to us. Semantics can help us understand the ordinary meaning of ordinary language. Sociolinguistics helps us to make contact, to appreciate dramatically different uses of ordinary words across cultures. The Noam Chomskys of the world can help us decipher the mystifications of political and economic language.

All these scholarly activities contribute to the wondrous knowledge process by which disparate human beings share worlds of meaning with more or less accuracy and honesty. Dramaturgical analysis helps us know and reflect on the realms of meaning found in any symbolic universe. At its best, hermeneutical knowledge can bring people into communion with each other as enabling, enlarging coconspirators . . . those who breath together on the pathways of life.

Yet, while hermeneutic viewpoints are reflective by nature in an epistemological sense, since they assume the constitution of social reality by conscious, willful human agents, they, like scientism, are not reflective in an ontological sense. Those scholars who see the human labor when others construct social reality through symbolic interaction, these same analysts see his/her work as not constituting social reality but as merely and innocently apprehending and reflecting social processes.

Habermas (1970b:303) notes that the hermeneutic sciences have a "scientific consciousness" in that they share the methodological imperative of "describing a structured reality within the horizon of the theoretical attitude." However, since they do not accept the principle that scientific knowledge has a constitutive effect on social relationships, the hermeneutic sciences have become "the positivism of the cultural and social sciences."

In order to add ontological reflectivity, we must move on to a consideration of another mode of scientific effort—emancipatory or critical sociology. Critical social thought has consistently insisted on an epistemological break with the more traditional and conservative social theories. Max Horkheimer (1972) has distinguished critical theory from traditional theory by noting the critical theorist's awareness of his/her partiality.

Critical Theory

Critical theoretical approaches reject the value-neutral and objective self-understanding of the various traditional approaches by affirming the dialectical relationship between knowledge and society. Knowledge is part of the self-fulfilling—or self-defeating—processes of reality construction in a society. The existing structures shape the knowledge process in ways not immediately visible to those who think.

The knowledge produced by positivist sociological research and by hermeneutical research can be used in the process of creating social reality. The so-called information sciences become market commodities that provide corporate and state agencies with the tools with which to shape behavior, to shape society, and thus abort the dialectics of interaction so necessary to democratic and reciprocal social forms.

Social reality, as the object of cognition, can be transformed by social knowledge from a thing-in-itself into a thing-for-us. In contrast to the claims of those who argue that the sociological enterprise is an academic effort independent of social reality and with no effect upon it, the critical sociologist takes the perspective that sociological theory and research are intellectual definitions of a situation and, as such, become prescriptions for or proscriptions of social action, whether social scientists understand this or not.

Every sociologist, economist, historian, psychologist, or anthropologist who writes and publishes, who is read and understood, who is cited and referenced is a consulting engineer whether paid or not. In an information age, no one works in an ivory tower. In a managed society, no one is innocent if there is evil in the land.

From a critical standpoint, social reality is what it is to a great extent because of what social scientists say about it. Sociological, psychological, economic, and political science definitions of situations have a socially self-fulfilling character, while social theory and research must be understood as socially situated vocabularies of motive. Critical sociologists view knowledge and definitions of reality not only emerging out of specific sociohistorical milieus but also as affirming or transforming the social relationships of these sociohistorical milieus.

Political polls tend to freeze existing voting patterns in recent congressional and presidential campaigns, thus shaping electoral results in their own image. That the polls are but snapshots of an otherwise highly unstable opinion of a disconnected mass of people is lost in the rhetoric of science that presents them, falsely, as the final product of public discourse. There are industries now that use the media to shape opinion, use the research techniques of sampling to measure it, and use the elements of theatre to disseminate that opinion.

Critical sociology most fully grasps the dual lesson of the sociology of knowledge: knowledge has a social base and knowledge constitutes a social base. Emancipatory knowledge, although it finds precious little support in North American sociology, is emancipatory since it comprehends the constitutive role of social science and affirms the political position that human beings must participate in the interactional frames in the social construction of reality else these frames lose their human and social character. The hiring of specialists to subvert public discourse through a dramaturgical presentation of such opinion polling is, as Habermas (1970b) puts it, to create a systematically distorted communications process.

Emancipatory Knowledge

Following the tradition of Marx, Lukacs, Gramsci, and Marcuse, the emancipatory thrust of science must be emphasized in those situations in which obstacles to full participation have been erected. In its emancipatory modes, as Lukacs puts it, social science is the intellectual expression of revolution. In more concrete terms, the role of research and theory in opposing and transforming commodity relationships into social relationships is the political expression of critical science.

Critical sociology maintains that not only do the major orientations of social theory today serve as intellectual valets for the social classes and state authorities directing the various processes of monopoly capitalism, but they also help to constitute this reality in the consciousness of those who suffer it. One task of critical sociology is to critique the theory and research of the dominant modes of sociological endeavor and in so doing challenge the legitimacy of the social reality it constitutes. The larger task is to replace the existing knowledge system with a more democratic, flexible, creative, and informationally rich way of creating and recreating the social institutions in which people must live out their lives.

Ideological Hegemony and Dramaturgy

Antonio Gramsci (1971), whose very important work is only now being recognized as such by sociologists, developed further ideas that contribute to a critical dramaturgical sociology. Gramsci noted that power and domination in alienated society is maintained not only by material forces of coercion and repression but also within the consciousness of people.

With the concept of "ideological hegemony," Gramsci, in his *Prison Notebooks*, observed that the ruling class always seeks to legitimize its power through the creation and imposition of a worldview that stresses the need for order, authority, and discipline. Consciously the ruling class attempts to subvert and eviscerate the potential of revolutionary protest. Capitalism or other elitist formations can balance its contradictions and manage its objective crises by "taking captive" the minds of those victimized by its processes of alienation and exploitation.

Ideological hegemony depends upon the ruling class seizing and controlling the means of communication or the means of the production of culture. In earlier days, ruling classes and sectors obtained ideological hegemony with the help of the church, the authoritarian family, control over the market, and the military—used to intimidate—as well as the spectacles of coronation and county fair. Private corporations and state agencies buy or seize the means of mass communications, and in doing so, deploy vast numbers of dramatists to subvert the knowledge process in economics, politics, and in governance.

Immanent Critique

A critical dramaturgy attempts to unmask false presentations by contrasting the phenomenal appearance with the in-itself reality. To the extent that critical dramaturgy is successful, the mismatch between prophesy and performance is made visible. To the extent people have social, economic, moral, and physical power, they can reduce the variance between prophesy and performance. The task of a thoroughly emancipatory dramaturgy is to destroy the ideological hegemony of elites in capitalism and in bureaucratic socialism.

*In the logics of Marxian epistemology, one need not live in a world for-
ever dualistic, forever strange, forever different from what it appears. With
immanent critique and with good politics in science, the alienation and dualistic character of the knowledge process can be minimized.*

For most people most of the time, in the innocent creation of social life,
the variation between the noumenon (the thing in itself) and the phenomenon (the thing created by human perception, intelligence, and cultural bias)
is small and unintended. In alienated dramaturgy, the difference is large and
deliberately masked.

In the innocent work of social construction, a priest is, ontologically,
little different from what he is taken to be, epistemologically. In naïve work
there is a sustained effort, in the mutual construction of an individual as a
friend, to be and to be seen as a friend. Across an entire range of social
positions, the person occupying the position works to authenticate; to minimize the variation between the idea of a friend and the substantive activity
of friendliness.

Not so in alienated dramaturgy. There is the fraudulent presentation of
self as friend but the substance of the action is very different; more compatible with the idea of class enemy, of salesperson, of puppet theatre than
with authentic human discourse. In such work, the assumptions of dualism—and the irreconcilable differences between noumena and phenomena—are valid and alienating.

Goffman's work has sought to unravel the dualistic relationship between
self as a core entity and self as presented to others. In his observations of
people in asylums, in prisons, at circus, in office and shop, Goffman made
visible the boundary collusion between some of those present and others of
those excluded from the shared meanings of the former. For the excluded,
reality became drama without the courtesy of a program listing the actors
and the directors. Back-stagings and front-stagings became visible in Goffman's work when the inmates and guards alike tried to blur the line between them.

Just as the self is separated into a publicly presented phenotype and a
nonvisible noumenotype, the vast cadres of publicists, information officers,
spokespersons, advertising specialists, and other dramatists of the market
place can use the technology of electronics media to present convincing
impressions, service, and excellence on behalf of client retail corporations,
universities, religions such as that of Reverend Moon, as well as political
parties and the ruthless dictatorships in the "free world." Theatre can thus
shape thought, action, and budget of a society.

It is a canned and packaged social psychology not found in texts and lectures in the more genteel courses of academia. With the work of Goffman, it became clear that such dualistic presentations could be used to mystify the reality of the thing-in-itself. It is at this juncture that critical dramaturgy becomes important. The whole point of unalienated science is to make visible any such dualism.

In naïve social construction, the whole point is to eliminate dualist, multiple realities in favor of a collectively shared and shaped common social-life world. When there is a mismatch between the thing-as-presented and the thing-in-itself, a form of social fraud has occurred. Hundreds of billions are spent to engineer dualism and to present, falsely, phenomena as noumena.

Fraud serves to alienate objective and subjective reality and operates to circumvent processes of symbolic interaction and the sharedness of a social construction of reality. Critical dramaturgy attempts to expose fraud as an alienative, exploitative process and to return to human actors the full capacity to participate in the social construction of reality. As Fromm put it so well, one should become the object and agent of one's own will if one is to reach one's full potential as a moral and human being.

Transcendental Critique

The emancipatory mode of science rejects the necessity of historical modes of domination and seeks the emancipation of people. Human emancipation is, first of all, a knowledge industry—then it is a political craft. To do good politics, it is necessary to have whole realms of knowledge, whole battalions of researchers, effective research methods, democratically organized media, as well as a set of transcendent criteria upon which to found a transcendent critique. All of these are possible with the theory and technology now available to the scientific community.

Let us survey the realms of knowledge required to provide a democratic society with the basic information needed to come into reflective dialectics with its own institutions, with other societies, and with the natural world itself. Emancipatory knowledge has several interrelated forms.

Knowledge about the negativities and positivities of a social formation is basic to change and renewal of a society. A society that hides its defects while it celebrates its positivities has blinded itself to its own behavior and has celebrated its own collapse.

Knowledge about immanent and transcendent criteria with which to ground the critique of social life as-it-is is also fundamental to human emancipation. Knowledge for immanent critique comes from statements of goals and objectives of a social entity. Critical and Marxist theory centers transcendental criteria for critique around the concept of *praxis.* Others talk of transcendent human rights and human obligations. Still others speak of religious imperatives.

Knowledge about alternative ways to organize social life is also essential to human emancipation: alternative ways to do family, religion, economics, science, medicine, housing, agriculture, politics—in a word, society. Cross-cultural studies offer much in the way of helpful comparisons. History offers a treasure trove of such information.

Dramaturgy can be most useful in the production of knowledge from make-believe and just-pretend. Information about things that never were and never could be—all are possible in the realm of the theatre. One can think about utopias, fantasies, and futures in order to reflect upon them and imagine how they might affect the human process.

NASA has developed the technological base for *virtual reality;* a technology in which people—at present, military personnel—can experience nonreal space as if it were real through computer simulations of nonreal scenarios. Paraplegics could experience the sensations of limbs moving, grasping, and building. Physicians could experience the microscopic world of an organ through the eyes of a CAT scanner or magnetic resonator and use laser surgery to destroy minute bits of tissue. Students could enact plays in Elizabethan settings.

Knowledge about low-cost, effective, timely ways to change from existing to new ways to do social life is part of emancipation. Revolution is perhaps the most costly means of change and perhaps the least reliable.

Experimentation in child care, sports, and therapy are close cousins to just-pretend and what-if. It is possible for a society to treat such experiments as if they were theatrical productions of real life with real people enacting new scripts for the socialization or resocialization of real people.

Knowledge about how to retain the positivities of the existing social process while integrating the alternatives (and avoid the tendency of all living systems to absorb and neutralize variety—the tendency to equifinality in systems theoretical terms) is invaluable to a self-directed, self-transforming society. Role playing, role reversal, and role enlargement are techniques from the world of the theatre that may help realize change—make it more than merely paper policy.

Knowledge about impact and success of such changes on an ongoing basis is crucial. Evaluative processes that monitor experiments in social change without defeating them prematurely are essential to a fully emancipatory science.

Again, dramaturgy is a knowledge form that can contribute to the human interest in emancipation by generating understanding about how such changes might interact with the best of what *is*. Asking people to make-believe that a new way of teaching or healing is adopted, and pretend to use it in the classroom or hospital, helps make visible its problems and potentialities—to "debug" it, in that terrible neologism of the programmer.

Knowledge about participatory methodology helps widen the knowledge process beyond the present elitist system. Such knowledge would enable oppressed groups to identify research problems and develop policies essential to their own emancipation. A knowledge process broadly distributed throughout a human population exposes a new idea or policy to the widest possible scrutiny across the widest spectrum of social groups. Comstock (1980) has designed such a scientific method.

Also important, is knowledge of the interactions of society and nature, such that social processes maintain the integrity of the good Earth and all creatures upon it.

All these forms of knowledge and more do not presently reside within the syllabi of research methodology in the social sciences, yet they are vital to a democratically organized knowledge process in which the world of make-believe and just-pretend are linked to the human interest in change and renewal.

An alienated social science links up to oppression when dramaturgical possibilities become commodity to be purchased by multibillion dollar corporations or by elitist states. Such a use of dramaturgy in the reality construction process defeats reflexivity, judgment, and wisdom in the interest of management, profit, and the false peace of mystification.

The Metaphor of the Stage

Emancipation is grounded in systems of self-reflection. Consequently, emancipatory science seeks to mediate human behavior, but not to determine it. Critical knowledge must augment reflexivity and human intervention into social relationships, but must never be used for the managerial or exploitative purposes of one social group by another.

Dramaturgy can and has contributed to the hermeneutic interest by elaborating the mechanics through which individuals and groups create and sustain the presumption of social order through the metaphor of the theater. Dramaturgy as hermeneutic interpretation allows for the creativity of human subjects and affirms the essentially metaphorical nature of dramaturgy. In some social conditions, that which is only a metaphor of real life all too often becomes an invisible program unilaterally imposed upon workers, consumers, voters, students, sports fans, and others.

In such situations, dramaturgy transforms from a convenient shorthand way of understanding the reality process into an engineering tool by which the sociology of fraud intrudes itself into the world of seeking, trying, intending, trusting, and betrayed human beings.

In a managed society, a critical dramaturgical approach goes beyond the use of theater as metaphor and views dramaturgy as an ideology through which an actor or team can construct a repressive and/or fraudulent social reality.

Conservative dramaturgical ideologists object at this point to "blaming" impression management and its consequences on dramaturgical sociology. After all, Goffman is only a messenger who neutrally and objectively reports on social reality. Perhaps it is true that mind limps after reality. However, the objection of the conservative dramaturgist ignores the dialectical relationship between society and sociological knowledge.

Apart from what Goffman or other dramatists may have intended, their work is grist to the mill of those who are hired to generate markets from the passive mass of electronics or print media. Dramaturgical sociology itself must be understood as a commodity for use in the social world.

Noumena and Phenomena

Traditional symbolic interactionism rejected the opposition between in-itself reality and the phenomenon as it appeared to be. When Mead, Cooley, and Blumer state that human social interaction consists of subjective meaning being tied to an objective gesture, they are insisting that the presentation is an accurate reflection of that which is hidden from public view. You get what you see. In the sociology of fraud, there are systematic efforts to give one less than what is presented, to give other than what is presented, to falsify reality.

Marx's method of immanent critique is appropriate to a critical dramaturgical analysis. Immanent critique allows its user to restore authenticity and actuality to false appearances by first expressing what a social formation holds itself to be and contrasting that with what in fact it is. In his reformulation of the Hegelian dialectic, Marx (1978) was able to show that the false appearance of reciprocity, the equivalence of exchange between labor and capital, was negated by the structural tendencies of capitalist society that served only to intensify human exploitation and alienation by giving less value in wages than that produced by workers.

Added to this primal mystification was a second-order mystification that held that this extraction of surplus value could go on forever. But without sufficient wages to buy back all that workers produce, the unsold portion accumulates to throttle production activity. Capitalist economists thought they saw a perpetual motion machine that would always run without friction or failure. Marx unmasked that mystification.

Theory and Ideology

The politicized form of dramaturgy bears a very close affinity to the critique of ideology as it has come to be practiced in radical literature. Viewing dramaturgy not only as a mode of sociological analysis but also as an enterprise in the constitution of social reality, it was noted that large-scale organizations utilize various technologies to create false images of accountability, participation, and reciprocity.

In these days, ideological power of the ruling class is enhanced in schools, family, workplace, television, and generally by a communicative technology that generates the worldview of society as nature. The management of consciousness, as practiced by corporate functionaries on behalf of class privilege or by state publicists on behalf of state officials, must be terminated if society is to be transformed, the wedge between objective and subjective reality is to be removed, a praxis society made possible. Indeed, it is praxis to transform such a false social drama.

Independent of the work of Gramsci, the Hegelian Marxism of Georg Lukacs (1971) affirmed the ability of the ruling class to maintain its hegemony through the control of consciousness. The central problematic of Lukacs's *History and Class Consciousness* emphasized that the failure of socialist revolutions centered around the Marxist failure to focus attention on the processes through which the ruling class controlled its subject populace through ideas.

The concept of "reified consciousness" as the obstacle to socialist revolution bears an affinity to a critical dramaturgical analysis in that both emphasize that the consciousness of the people is managed by an elite for the purposes of capital accumulation and political legitimacy.

For Lukacs, the core, the *totality* of a social formation lies in the connection between objective and subjective dimensions that are historically synthesized in the class consciousness of the proletariat. In the interest of maintaining the status quo, a process emerges that falsely differentiates the two dimensions in that they are no longer viewed as identical. This is a false reification, a false apprehension of the humanmade world in terms that affirm its independence from humans. Thus, social relations and culture become viewed as "things" and are understood as being part of the natural world.

In terms of an authentic human agency, understood as a collective praxis, reification is a dangerous departure from the normal *objectification* of social artifacts and social bonds in that it ultimately inverts subject-object relations and is used to create a politically and socially docile proletariat. Reification must be overcome if human agents are to participate in the social construction of reality in a reflexive, reciprocal manner.

The work of Lukacs, and that of Marx and Gramsci as well, can be translated to a critical dramaturgical analysis by saying that in class and other elitist societies, regardless of technological development or the objective structures of inequality—domination and exploitation can be maintained or extended through asymmetrical prerogatives to define reality on the part of subordinate and superordinate social categories.

The use of dramaturgy, social psychology, electronics, and other peripheral technology to advance an economic or political interest, is the use of dramaturgy in the aid of ideological hegemony. When best, it aids the human project; at its very worst it creates a Kafkaesque world in which we are all strangers to each other and to ourselves. The problems of capital accumulation and political legitimacy can be solved by the ruling class by maintaining dramaturgical impressions of reciprocity, of the necessity of order, authority, and discipline, and thus reify social reality.

To the extent that dramaturgical analysis, or any theoretical content for that matter, enters back into society as a blueprint for behavior, that theoretical body, however valid, becomes ideology.

The major theoretical pardadigm used in these times to shape reality and thus convert itself into ideology is structural-functionalism. In the U.S.S.R. as in the United States, the dominant academicians teach variants of structural-functionalism as the received truth of the social reality at hand. That the structures of class privilege, gender oppression, racial degradation, or age-grade humiliation are functional necessities is a lie of astounding proportions.

Slavery and bureaucratic socialism are ideologies hostile to the human project. We lack a transcendent critique of capitalism or bureaucratic socialism to show them for the alienated social forms they are. When such social theory enters back into social institutions apart from the understanding and intentionality of the people who must live out their lives in those institutions, then theory becomes alienated ideology.

The attempt to rescue dramaturgy from such ideological work is intended as a project for the revolutionary transformation of society. Bearing in mind that the critical dramaturgy understands itself as being in opposition to the manipulative, coercive technologies utilized by the ruling class to manage its problems of capital accumulation and political legitimacy in East and West alike, it is helpful to review two significant efforts to constitute a critical dramaturgy that appeared in relatively recent sociological literature. The intention is to evaluate these efforts as adequate critiques for the revolutionary transformation of dramaturgical sociology.

Precursors

The first significant attempt to constitute a critical dramaturgical analysis was that of Alvin Gouldner in *The Coming Crisis of Western Sociology* (1970:378–90). Gouldner conceives of Goffman's dramaturgical sociology as symptomatic of the crisis of Western sociology. In this work, Gouldner equates Western sociology with Parsonian structural-functionalism, and its crisis lies primarily in the inability of structural-functionalism to provide an adequate theory of social change. This inability has undermined structural-functionalism's utility as a legitimation for the capitalist state, which must use change and planning strategies to cope with an increasing surplus population and crisis of underconsumption.

In the 1980s, the Reagan administration reversed a whole set of social programs which, in structural-functionalism, were conceived to be part of a progressive social evolution. Theory could not handle a reversal toward greater inequality, more poverty, more economic jungle war, and less neutrality of the state. More of the same did not fit with the Reagan policies bringing less and less of the same. Dramaturgy, critical theory, gender theory, and other conflict analyses were developed to move into the theoretical void left by the discredited functionalist view.

Gouldner sensed both the "critical" and conservative potential in Goffman's dramaturgy. He notes that Goffman's dramaturgical sociology, in a sense, is a rebellion against the systems level of analysis, which tends to preclude the comprehension of social reality as the result of an ongoing process of human interaction. Society is created by real human beings, not by objective laws of structure bending humans to its logics.

Goffman's dramaturgy can be viewed as a hermeneutic alternative to the naturalism and scientism of structural-functionalism. Gouldner also sees radical potential in Goffman's sociology of fraud, precisely because it legitimizes the individual's prerogative to con the system.

Dramaturgy, according to Gouldner, has "critical" dimensions because it certainly passes no negative moral judgment on tax evaders or upon asylum inmates who manipulate their jailers. On balance, Gouldner sees a greater degree of conservative potential in Goffman's dramaturgy. Gouldner worries that dramaturgy reduces humans to mere commodities, and he effectively ties the work of Goffman to the ethos of the "organization man" as a legitimization of "getting kicks" out of things as they are, since the transformation of society appears to be defined out of the realm of possibility by depoliticized dramaturgical ideologists. The inmates did not try to change the asylum, only to adapt to it and to build underground structures with which to repair the harm done to the human project and to personal desire.

The technology of dramaturgy is not equally available to all individuals throughout all social strata. Thus, at the personal level dramaturgy is a technology of pretheoretical rebellion primarily for the "new bourgeois." This generation of Yuppies can stage manage their persona; they can wear power ties, attend power lunches, frequent power night spots, drive power cars, vacation in power spas, and marry power-oriented Yuppies.

What staggers the imagination and besets the epistemological process is the huge industry that caters to the image problems of the capitalist corporation and the capitalist state. Billions upon billions of dollars together with thousands upon thousands of trained functionaries assiduously polish the image of the polluting, lying, cheating, stealing, disinvesting private corporation—while the largest single employer of such dramatists is the United States government itself. Only in societies with the starkest of conflict relations would such an enterprise develop to beggar the knowledge process. Neither Goffman nor Gouldner grasp the proportion of the problem in the knowledge industry.

In democratic capitalist societies, dramaturgy replaces the club and the boot as the preferred weapon of ideological management.

While Gouldner is to be applauded for illuminating the "rebellious" dimensions in Goffman's dramaturgy and demonstrating the link between dramaturgy and "commodity fetishism," his work must be understood by the critical dramaturgist as only a starting point. Gouldner was worried about the demise of structural-functionalism and he deals with dramaturgy in a briefly critical manner only as a stepping stone to his personal response to the crisis.

This is his "reflective" sociology, which turns out to be reflective in only an epistemological sense. The more important ontological reflectivity involves collective discourse in a public sphere; a discourse undistorted by class, status, and power; a discourse oriented to the collective creation of a praxis society.

A critical dramaturgical sociologist augments the Gouldner analysis by adding that the crisis of capitalist society and Western sociology is now being managed by the adoption of dramaturgy as a sociology and a technology for legitimizing this particular phase of capitalist domination. The significant task today for those sociologists wanting to contribute to the construction of a fully rational, humane, and participatory social reality process, an emancipatory symbolic interaction process, is the critique of dramaturgical sociology and the sociology of fraud it engineers.

In a brilliant, yet unheralded, critique of the dramaturgical sociology of Goffman, Ivan Chapman (1974:45–52) demonstrates the departures of dramaturgy from a fully social, fully participatory model of social action based on a modality of symbolic interaction in which each actor possesses the prerogative to contribute to the meaning of a socially significant symbol.

Using a Meadian framework of symbolic action at the dyadic level of social analysis, Chapman notes that both actors are free to exercise both their ''I'' and ''me'' capabilities in an ongoing process of defining the situation. Goffman's model, Chapman argues, is a model of the symbolic management of one person by another. We can see that, if Chapman is correct, in such situations the assumptions of symbolic interaction theory about the shared nature of the symbol simply do not hold.

In the case of the social dyad, the actor utilizing the tactics of dramaturgy feels no social constraint by the socially significant symbol, but feigns her/his ''I'' act of personal desire so that it appears to be based on social meaning and in so doing evokes in the other a ''me'' response based on the acceptance in good faith—the ''expression given off'' as though it were an ''expression given'' or an expression based on mutual social meaning.

The person acting in good faith is reduced to an object, a passive and betrayed ''me'' in the Meadian sense. Used, exploited, objectified, and/or taken captive by the exploiting actor, such a world ceases to be a *social*-life world and becomes an unreasonable facsimile of it. The exploiting actor only appears to shift to a ''me'' while retaining all ''I'' prerogatives to define the situation. With the loss, evasion, or circumvention of the reciprocity of symbolic processes of interaction, the dyad is destroyed as a full human, social, and participatory process of reality construction. As Chapman (1974:49) notes:

> Where deceitful and feigned appearance is accepted in good faith as conventional social meaning, there can be no conventional social meaning, but only the bond of a captive chained by his/her false expectations to an episode, act or ploy of behavior which begins with his/her captivation and ends with the exploiting actor's satisfaction, along with the losses of the exploited actor.

This way of creating society is inimical to the traditional social bond and of social functions. It renders society a hunting ground, with persons as legitimate prey for exploiters who use both society and persons for highly personal gratification. This is a point of view of society in which only parasites make out and only to the extent that the social bond of reciprocal good faith on the part of others can ensure a fraudulent dramaturgy at the personal level.

Chapman, thus, objects to Goffman's dramaturgical reduction of social life to episodic con games and he has ably demonstrated the departures of Goffman's symbolic interaction emphasizing good faith and reciprocity. Yet, as an exemplar for a fully critical dramaturgy, Chapman's opposition of "Social Interaction versus the Appearance of Social Interaction" falls short.

Because he chooses to deal with Goffman's dramaturgical sociology and not Goffman's constitution of the dramaturgical society, one gets the distinct impression that Chapman senses this contradiction as a transcendental human dilemma. He does not and cannot ground the dramaturgical departures from conventional, participatory models of symbolic interaction in relative and concrete sociohistorical circumstances. Chapman fails to pose the question: In what kinds of societies does the dramaturgical departure in everyday life appear or become significant?

From the critical standpoint, the dramaturgical exploitation of one person by another must be comprehended as situated in social formations that are historically relative. The rise of capitalism as a mode of economic production and distribution, with its elevation of secondary Gesellschaft group relations, undoubtedly contributed to the emergence and legitimization of the individual and team exercise of a dramaturgical technology. After all, the social reality of capitalist society insists that persons are to treat others and be treated as commodities.

Yet, the relationship between capitalism and its consequent elevation of Gesellschaft relations and a dramaturgical technology escapes Chapman's analysis. Therefore, he cannot conclude that dramaturgical exploitation can be overcome by the overthrow of the social formations. Ultimately, Chapman's critique of Goffman becomes more a moralistic lament than an emancipatory vision of prosocial uses of dramaturgy. Such a decontextualized critique produces little more than dread for the "social" reality of the present and certainly no hope for the future.

Chapman's failure to establish a fully critical dramaturgy must be tied to his choice of critiquing dramaturgy on solely epistemological grounds rather than on social-structural grounds. His is a noble and heroic undertaking, but can be an obstacle to the critique of the social sources of dramaturgical exploitation. The additional task of the critical drama-turgist is to contribute to the overthrow of those sociohistorical formations that permit and create a dramaturgical society together with its sociological legitimizations.

Perhaps the best single survey critique of dramaturgy at the microanalytic level is to be found in *Interactionism* by Larry Reynolds (1987). It broadens and deepens this critique. However, Reynolds does not explore the positive contributions possible by an emancipatory dramaturgy at either the micro-interactional or macrosocietal level of analysis.

Sovietologists see the interactional falsities and organizational frauds clearly through their ideological lens, Americans are so enamored of their own society that their anger at its betrayal and subversion limits their theo-retical vision and reduces the force of their analyses to an inchoate rage against a Reagan or a Madison Avenue. The Chapmans and Gouldners fail to raise their eyes to macroanalytic levels and thus miss both the history and the sociology of the dramaturgical fraud. Reynolds fails to look beyond dramaturgy as practiced at the interactional level—a grave failing indeed.

Conclusion

The critique of dramaturgical sociology serves the emancipatory interest by providing a map for the critique of dramaturgical society, which it re-flects and has helped to constitute. Beyond the presentation of the fraudu-lent and repressive character of the reality of dramaturgical society, the emancipatory task of dramaturgical sociology is the critique of this reality in order to return to human agents the capacity to fully participate in the social construction of reality. In addition to the general critique of an engi-neered dramaturgical sociology, more specific points of divergence are identified between the conservative and critical approaches to dramaturgy.

1. As a consequence of the political sterility of most of dramaturgical so-ciology, and apart from Chapman and Gouldner, there is little moral outrage on the part of those who reported on the managerial efforts to stage reality and manipulate the consciousness of human beings. Indeed, in many universities, whole courses are taught in support of the practice of fraudulent dramaturgy. However, the critical use of dramaturgy re-moralizes the scientific enterprise when responding to manipulation and deceit.
2. Conservative dramaturgy has failed to include considerations of the larger social forces that produce the dramaturgy practiced in everyday life. The analyst who asks what brought dramaturgy about will be dis-appointed by conservative dramaturgical literature. The historical per-

spective of dramaturgy would make one think that the dramaturgy employed in everyday life is a transcendental human dilemma and that either original sin, nature, or human biology is responsible for it. The critical view, on the other hand, understands dramaturgy as a phenomenon dependent upon various social and historical conditions. In the West, capitalism and the rise of predominantly Gesellschaft social relations loom as paramount in this regard. In the Socialist bloc, the rise of bureaucratic state organs and the continued use of coercion renders dramaturgy redundant. The connection between dramaturgy and its macrosocial base must be examined in any theoretical paradigm worthy of those whose labor supports its practitioners.

3. Conservative uses of dramaturgy have also failed to provide an immanent critique of dramaturgically constructed social reality from a perspective of the moral values claimed within a given social paradigm. The critical method emphasizes the discrepancy between the performance of social formations and their public prophesies of social justice, equality before the law, and democratic forms in the public sphere. The imperative in epistemology of social formations in public terms is overridden by conservative dramaturgical analysis that seeks instead to understand things on its private terms, which means the imposition of a theatrical model upon human subjects. The critical view does not seek to control human behavior by imposing an artificial mode on social life. Instead, the critical emphasis is to provide knowledge so that people can eliminate the obstacles to full participation in the social construction of reality.

4. An important difference between emancipatory and alienated dramaturgy is the absence of any coherent transcendent critique with which to give dramaturgical analysis a value context. The critical uses of dramaturgy accept that a valid distinction can be made between authentic and fraudulent social formations and presentations of self. Conservative dramaturgy either obfuscates this distinction or collapses the two into the latter so that it cannot get outside that which-is and that which could-be. Praxis and a praxis society serve as the standard by which any transcendental critique may be made. While the concept of praxis is complex, the general point is made in Marxian methodology: People know their own society best when they participate in the building of it. When law, religion, science, and morality are not ambushes behind which lie the interests of elites or other nations.

5. While dramaturgy as a social device is probably always utilized in fraudulent social formations, it is not true that it is always utilized in authentic social formations. In not understanding this distinction, conservative dramaturgy has not only mystified social relations, it has overlooked some very exciting uses of dramaturgy, for example, the dramaturgy of authentic social performances. (We will come back to this possibility in another book on the Drama of the Holy.)

6. A final difference between the two dramaturgies is the unconcern of contemporary dramaturgical analysis with a systematic explanation of how dramaturgy could amplify the human condition. Life without enlivening theatre and dramaturgy would be one without joy, pride, delight, surprise, nor enchantment. We have all experienced the sheer fun of pretending and fooling around. Caught up in a spontaneously madcap world—with a lover or friends—yet one in which innocence and trust remains true to the human condition, one feels the unlimited possibilities of collective imagination.

Earth Gods

Brute-tamer, plow-maker, earth-breaker,
Can'st hear me?
There are ages between us.
Is it praying you are as you stand there
alone in the fading sunset?

Surely our sky-born gods have nought for you,
earth-child, earth-master, earth-threat;
Surely your thoughts are of Pan, or Wotan or Dana.

Yet why give thought to these gods
Yet why give thought to them now?
Has Pan led your brutes when they stumble?
Has Dana eased pain of child birth?
Did Wotan put hands on your plow?
What matter your serving reply?
O man, standing lone in the sod:
'Your task is a day near its closing;
Give thanks to the night-giving god.'

Slowly the night-giver comes;
Slowly the darkness arrives.
The broken lands blend with the savage,
yet still the brute-breaker survives;
and still the god-dreamer drives.

The brute-tamer walks with the brutes
scarcely a head length above them;
scarcely a head thought further ahead.
Where do your sky-gods come from;
From whence do your god-thoughts arise?
Do they come from the thrones of the gods and their chariots;
come from their halls, and their purples and skies?

Do they come from out of your misery;
from out of your pain;
do they come from all of our failures;
will they come back again?

—Adapted from a poem by Padriac Colum

Part III

Social Psychology in a New Age

Introduction

Traditional symbolic interactionist views of the social process maintained that the self was an ongoing product of the reciprocal interaction of humans with significant symbols. According to the tradition of George Herbert Mead, Charles Horton Cooley, W. I. Thomas, and Herbert Blumer, the self results from and exists within interactions where the social identities attributed to an individual by others are internalized by that individual as self.

In socially appropriate occasions, the social identity that is part of the self system is called forth by definitions of a situation, used to organize situationally appropriate behaviors, and monitored by both individual and significant others. When behavior is inappropriate, inadequate, or otherwise unsatisfactory, both the individual and others react to elicit more acceptable behavior; thus self and society are twinborn.

Dramaturgical social psychology developed an important challenge to traditional symbolic interactionism. With the appearance of Goffman's *The Presentation of Self in Everyday Life* (1959), social psychology in the United States became sensitized to the difference between a public, performed self and a private, undisclosed self.

While traditional symbolic interactionism collapsed the two, dramaturgical analysis maintained that there is no necessary relationship between the two: The publicly performed self is not necessarily a reflection of the private self. The real difference between the two selves means that the public self can be falsified or the public self can be separated from the private, adumbrating the detachment of the individual self from the social order and the subversion of the social process.

In chapter 6, "Self and Social Organization in Capitalist Society," the individual self is not always anchored in the social order. While self and society are twin-born in most of human history, a case is made that in capitalist society self and society are separated. Communication is not jointly created. Role statuses belong to the corporation. Many social occasions are too brief and fleeting for a social self to be created. A great many encounters are economic in nature rather than social.

All this militates against the traditional understanding of symbolic interaction theory about the ways in which self is constituted, presented, and adjusted continuously in some negotiated order. Then, too, people may not have access to the means of production of the self or, if they do, others may own the means of production and set the terms under which one may "be" an engineer, clerk, soldier, student, customer, or professor. All this and more is developed in chapter 6.

Given the opposition between the traditional symbolic interactionist and the dramaturgical views of the self, a number of important questions are raised:

1. Which depiction of the structure of self is the more adequate from an empirical point of view?
2. If individuals in everyday interaction falsify their public presentations of self, under what social and historical circumstances does this occur?
3. If individuals in everyday interaction falsify their public presentations of self, whose social interests does this serve?
4. If individuals are caught up in a social matrix in which the sociology of fraud is engineered with the aid of the best in science and technology—What does this mean for morality and its location in the social order?

The chapters in this section address these kinds of questions. Much of the work here was done in close cooperation with John F. Welsh, whose contributions to the ideas and treatment of topics are inextricably tied up with those of the present author.

6

Self and Social Organization
in Capitalist Society

The Brain that fills the skull with Schemes
must have its humming hive of dreams
The tongue that talks, the lungs that shout
the thighs that bustle them about,
These today are proud in power
and lord it in their little hour.

Before this fire of sense decay
The smoke of thought blown clean away
They leave to ancient night alone,
And to the world their harmless bone.

—*A. E. Housman*

Symbolic interaction theory makes several assumptions about the relationships between the organization of society and the structure of self. The thesis of this chapter is that, under conditions of social organization in capitalist society, these assumptions are increasingly difficult to accept. In support of that thesis, we will critically examine several conditions that tend to invalidate symbolic interaction theory. The works of Habermas in Germany and of Markovic in Yugoslavia are used as a point of departure for this critique of symbolic interaction theory.

Origins of the Self System

A major implication of symbolic interaction theory is that, through the status-role structure, the individual self is anchored in the social order. The reasoning, valid throughout most of the history of humankind, is that an infant is born into a society; it is put through a socialization process, learns the role requirements in a configurational sort of way and then it is assigned roles on the basis of age, sex, and family status.

The central assumptions involved in the transformation of an individual into a social actor define a process that inserts a self system composed of social identities into the individual psyche. This process has several components.

1. *Socialization.* Each newly born infant, if accepted into the population base of a society, is nourished until old enough to manage the symbolic systems of the society into which it has been accepted. Many infants are discarded as imperfect, as the wrong gender, or as bastards. They are not likely to survive. At about age three to five, the child is put through caste, gender, tribal, and occupational socialization along with religious and familial socialization.

2. *Rites of passage.* After socialization, the young person goes through one or more rites of passage in which the social identity attached to a social role is internalized as part of the "me." The process is usually supervised by a religious functionary who, in the name of the god(s) of the kinship grouping, ushers the child out of the population base into the social base. The child, now an adult, is assigned to a number of role sets. The adult, now a person with social standing (*Stande*), comes to believe that s/he is really, ontologically, one of those things: a woman, a daughter, a tribal member and, perhaps, a weaver or potter. In various rites of passage, the individual is allocated status-roles.

3. *The status role set.* In this analysis, the social role is part of a role set. The role itself is a fairly stable set of duties and activities directed to involve the person in any one of many productive processes in a society. The role sets become a permanent base—anchor—for the self system; thus self and society are twin-born.

4. *The Social identity.* Each role set segment has an associated social identity. A social identity is, from the perspective of a given individual, what s/he is when s/he is performing the role in question. If the socializing process, itself a lengthy social endeavor, is successful, then one comes to believe firmly and existentially that one is "really" a social identity. The status-role is the social construct; the social identity is its psychological counterpart. Together the social character of the status-role and the psychological character of the associated social identity permits one to understand the proposition in symbolic interaction theory that self and society are twin-born.

Critique

There are many characteristics of capitalism, as a system of production, which calls into question the validity of the assumption that self and society are twin-born. We will look at a wide range of social processes in capitalist society to judge the degree to which each of the assumptions above can be said to be valid.

Except in adult professional role training, the socialization process is geared more to technical skills than to the production of specific social identities. Young persons seldom go through social identity allocation routines unless their families send them to church schools. Formal education is, rather, oriented to the inculcation of skills and techniques that are salable on the labor market. In capitalist modes of production, labor is a commodity to be sold and the function of the educational process in school and college is to produce workers to supply the market.

A stable self system is no longer the point and purpose of education but rather a stable business system or a stable factory system is the focus of schooling. Those who manage socialization under capitalist modes of production are charged with running an efficient and economic operation not with building character, with consolidating permanent and stable social relationships, nor concern about the integrity of the self system.

Socialization is moving and has been moved from the family and church into the impersonal mass educational complex—a bureaucracy—in which children are trained to be functionaries in other bureaucracies. At no time is a social identity and the associated role set the focus of education in bureaucratized schools. The concerns are different sets of job skills determined by the labor market rather than the cultural imperatives of human beingness.

Rites of Passage

In most societies, people are permanently placed in a status-role by means of a rite of passage. Such a rite occurs in the realm of the sacred and is endorsed by the local god(s). The linkage between self and social role is enjoined by religious fiat and may not be readily set aside or reversed. In confirmations, investitures, weddings, and other such rites, status-role and social actor are bonded beyond thought, beyond words, beyond actions.

There are, in most societies, disengagement routines by which, for reasons of moral delict, a person can be stripped of a social identity and cast out of the social base. But under capitalist notions of ownership and authority it is done for reasons other than serious moral failure. It is done for reasons of cost and profit, efficiency and control, personal animosity and career infighting.

Capitalist societies tend to eliminate the role of the sacred in role allocation and role disinvestiture. The rites of passage into and out of occupational identities are secularized in those social roles over which the logic of capitalism holds. When cost, profit, efficiency, or management are the operative principles of role assignment, management retains the right to use or discard the role incumbent as these imperatives dictate.

In such a secular process, one fills in a form, is interviewed, and is put on probation for some period of time after which an impersonal decision is made to keep or discard the human portion of the status-role. Religion is, by definition, too powerful a glue to serve the labor power needs of capitalism. Those labor power needs are determined by market forces. Shifting tides of international competition, of overproduction, and/or of underconsumption affect profits.

What is needed in capitalism as an employment tactic is a simple technical evaluation of skills and job description, of competence and management goals. The needs of the individual for occupational identity, for living wages, for prosocial labor in the company of other supportive human beings—all these individual needs are degraded to second place in the logic of profit and control.

The needs of the larger community for productive labor for each and every member of its social base are secondary to the profit needs of management in the private sector or the cost control needs of management in the public sector. More importantly, the need of the individual and of society for a strong and stable self system is inimical to the profit and managerial goals of advanced monopoly capital in both the productive and distributive phases of business.

Ownership of Status-Roles

Another aspect of advanced industrial capitalism that calls into question the historic linkage between self and society is the separation of the status-role on the one hand and the person on the other. In "modern" organizational principles, the status-role is the "property" of the corporation and the person is only temporarily "assigned" to that status-role.

The skills belong to the person but are rented out to the corporation on a temporary basis. The ancient linkage between skills, self, and social role are, in a moment, severed by the logic of labor hire. The corporate manager purchases the labor power of the individual via wages and, if the labor power is not profitable to the organization, the individual is discarded. The social identity, now property of the corporation, is reclaimed. The social role, also the property of the corporation, is emptied of its flesh and blood content and is listed as vacant on the job market, employment bulletins, or old boy network.

That a sentient human being is the vehicle in which labor power resides is not of interest to the manager. The status-role and the social identity associated with the role, as the property of the capitalist corporation may be, with "proper" notice, withdrawn leaving the self system of the worker bereft of the social identity that up to that time was used by the individual to organize his/her own behavior in stable, orderly, and predictable ways and that, therefore, constituted a core of the self system.

In societies in which social identity is the property of a personal self system, a manager cannot on a week's notice, repossess and dispossess the worker of a social identity or social role.

Disengagement, Onus, and Morality

The stripping process is done as a matter of routine and with very little ceremony in a capitalist labor market. People are hired and fired to suit the production and legitimacy needs of the private firm rather than the personal needs of the individual for a social identity that brings self-respect and a secure relationship to the means of production and distribution.

The disengagement of people from productive labor is seen as a technical question within the logic of capitalism. In every other society in history, such disengagement is seen as a moral question—indeed, the effort to keep jobs and thus retain the social bases for social identity is a political issue in some states. Massachusetts requires a firm to give notice that it is disinvesting in a community and that reemployment resources be made available to the disengaged. Thus moral reason is in conflict with the technical rationality of the private firm.

Yet it is an eminently rational thing to do in a competitive world market. If labor costs are higher in Boston than in El Salvador, then a rational manager would move production to El Salvador. If food prices are higher in New York than in Mexico, then rationality demands that food be shipped from Mexico to New York. Thus are moral questions concerning disemployment and hunger made hostage to the logic of a free market.

Free market theorists note that a higher morality may be built into the dynamics of a free market by virtue of the positive consequences in the future from restructuring the international market system. This may be a valid point but loss of moral agency is not discussed within the public sphere, let alone within the discipline of social psychology or symbolic interaction theorists, moral development theorists, dramaturgical analysts, still less among those who push technical rationality in the thousands of marketing and managerial courses in academia. In the latter circles, the moral basis for the stripping process is replaced by a utilitarian basis couched in terms of profit and loss and rationalized by the calculus of "overhead" and "selling costs."

In a curious reversal of onus, those who are disengaged from wage labor—and thus from the social anchor of self by the dynamics of advanced capitalism—are thought to be inferior, incompetent, undeserving creatures.

People are discarded by the logic of capitalism and are then made to feel that it is somehow their moral failure that results in their poverty, their ill health, their joblessness, their homelessness. The social origins of morality are thus distorted by profit concerns in a competitive market society. None of these dynamics finds its way into the textbooks on social psychology, still less into the work on moral development. Moral development theorists seem to view this as an entirely personal phenomenon.

Lawyers must take great care
When they cite a law;
Underneath their fine decisions
there lies a fatal flaw.

The law is very ill,
and mortals are undone;
when Rationality instill,
when it and Reason one.

Lawyers must take great care
when they deal in strife;
beneath their fine distinctions
There lies a human life.

—Inspired by Emily Dickinson

Short Takes and Self Systems

As most of the social life of a society comes to be organized by formal, large-scale bureaucracies, the role takes come to be short, episodic, and superficial. One is a customer for a half hour, a patient for forty-five minutes, or a student for fifty minutes. The ancient structures of time are greatly shortened by the logic of capitalism.

In capitalist relations, the point of social contact is to extract surplus value at the point of production or that of distribution. Surplus value is maximized at the point of production by vesting the corporation with property rights over the status role in such a manner as set forth above. The trend today is to reduce role involvement on the job to twenty hours a week or less to avoid the extra costs of health care, vacation pay, retirement funding, or child care.

Extraction of surplus value at the point of distribution requires a maximum of customer turnover, a minimum of personal attention, a maximum of return calls, a minimum of follow-up or warranty service, a maximum of price, and a minimum of value. The rapid turnover of patients, welfare clients, prisoners, shoppers, or students together with the other cost controls militates for the shortest possible contact.

While most adults still view work as central to their sense of self, under the occupational and market conditions above, the linkage between self and society diminishes to the smallest possible denominator. Such social identities do not become embedded in the self system through the majesty of a rite of passage; they do not stabilize behavior over the years of a life; they do not help a person to know and be known by a stable set of significant others; they do not carry with them a mirror reflecting the quality of participation in the status-role; nor do they give a person the existential satisfaction that comes with social identities honored and esteemed in the human process.

In terms of the basic assumptions in symbolic interaction theory about how the self system is created, patterned, and embodied, capitalism is a solvent disconnecting person from personality, self from society, action from intention, self from significant others, as well as mind from self and society.

The Politics of Social-Psychological Concepts

In a depoliticized social psychology, the harm done to the self systems of the members of those societies in which the social anchorage of the self system is under the effective control of a cadre of managers in a formal, bureaucratically organized office, shop, or factory is masked by such concepts as achieved status, career path, and role allocation. Social status is given and taken away by virtue of the standards imposed by managers who set profit, growth, and control of the corporate environment as the standards for judgment of merit, promotion, and dismissal.

Each of these concepts is central to symbolic interaction theory and to the assumptions of how behavior is organized in the course of social interaction seen on a day-to-day basis or on a more macroanalytic basis. In the neutered language of contemporary social psychology, a distinction between achieved and ascribed status is usually made.

In praise of achieved status over the "unearned" position to which one is ascribed in "primitive" societies, the textbook argument effectively forecloses critical examination of the process of status allocation. Such a bias in the language of social analysis cripples the capacity to reflect upon and to judge the impact on the self system of "modern" forms of role possession and dispossession.

If a status in a formal organization is "allocated" to an "employee," on the basis of achievement and merit, the question of forms of achievement is glossed over, the question of who defines merit is bypassed, and the enormous amount of political struggle to keep one's job (status-role) is excluded from consideration.

Waiting until merit is observed and measured in the process of role allocation reverses the ordinary social psychology of human behavior in which roles are allocated, expectations are embodied by significant others, and meritorious behavior is elicited.

The terms of meritorious achievement, themselves, are controlled by a specially trained and motivated managerial cadre whose interests are in instrumental use of human beings to a purpose far removed from the production of moral behavior or the creation of culture. In a humane society, the terms of achievement would be the central focus of attention; in a managed society (capitalist as well as bureaucratic socialist), the terms of achievement are given by the system, and what is of interest to the formal organization is the degree of achievement of those terms as registered on a five-point scale of merit.

All this is labeled management science and forcibly imposed upon students and/or workers in regimented phases. The concept of science is interpreted as physical, objectified, closed forms of systems organization and operation. That human systems are and must be different from physical systems is never effectively raised as an issue in a competent forum. It is a given to which all students and workers must submit else forego the material luxury of the "professional" career.

The Social Location of Moral Action

Habermas (1975) sees the realm of behavior mediated by the self reduced further by the intrusion of the realm of the technical into that of the cultural. All this makes more sense to a person equipped with concepts developed in classical European social philosophy (indeed, the absence of such concepts in American education is proof of Habermas's point) but still one can, with a little effort, grasp the salient point.

Habermas builds upon the distinction between the realm of the technical in which a society maintains itself vis-à-vis the natural world through instrumental activities involving fact and truth. But a society also needs a sociocultural system by which it maintains itself, since human animals stay in social harness through validity claims. In the sociocultural system, not truth but correctness/appropriateness of behavior is the subject of discourse. And symbolic interaction is the means by which the norms are generated. The norms of a role set or of a social occasion are to mediate behavior for all those who have, in a competent communication system, participated in settling normative questions.

Habermas says that the political and the economic system in capitalism (and in bureaucratic socialism, one might add) displaces the sociocultural system by asserting that rational-technical decision making prevails over symbolic interaction wherein norms are set. Capitalism requires that labor cost be minimized; capital-intensive modes of production disemploy people; the technical-rational process is used to implement capitalist policy irrespective of the harm such policy does to the self system of the disemployed—the disengaged.

Since the correctness of the capital-intensive mode of industry, agriculture, transport, or other production is exlcuded from public discourse, only technical questions remain. Which fuel to use, what priority to use is necessary, and how fast must energy development occur; where does market research place outlets; what investment policy brings highest returns; which labor market is cheapest given other cost parameters.

Low-energy, labor-intensive modes of production are not considered in the range of technical choices since moral choices are determined by the logic of high-energy, high-profit, high-tech systems of production. The few remaining moral questions are predecided at the top echelons of a bureaucracy.

In bureaucracies, in the factory, in the school, even in the church there is division of labor in which normative questions are predecided by an elite. On the basis of these predecisions, rules are made and the cadre of the bureaucracy has only the right to apply the rule in technical, mechanical fashion. The lower-echelon bureaucrat, as does the lower-level instructor in a university or foreman in a factory, feels regret and dismay over the plight of the mass-processed individual before him/her, but can do nothing about it since technical rules mediate behavior, not morally informed guides called "norms."

There are many evasions and infractions of the terminal rules that are supposed to mediate behavior, but Habermas's larger point remains. In a society in which the technical displaces the normative, one can only follow orders and the sociocultural realm tends to disappear. Moral action is trumped by technical application of predetermined policy, by technical administration of predetermined programs, by technical enforcement of the rules upon the clients and cadre alike.

It is a fundamental principle in the philosophy of morality that moral behavior is the product of interacting persons actively engaged in the sociocultural process. Moral behavior is impossible for most and difficult for many in an amoral or demoralized society.

One must ask why such a social organization continues that preempts the self system and the sociocultural in the interest of the rule and the bureau. The answer is not long in coming. In any society in which such a division of labor and such a rational-technical mode of organization benefits some, and as long as those "some" have power to maintain their benefits, bureaucracy will survive.

Disemployment and the Human Process

In folk communities, the whole point of a rational-instrumental mode of production is to provide the material resources by which a sociocultural system can be organized through competent symbolic interaction. In authentically human and humane societies, technical rationality serves human purpose. In capitalism, the point of production is for the owner and manager to accumulate wealth. As President Ford said, "The name of the American game is greed."

The anthropological point here is that people are not human beings unless they produce culture. Not just some people, but all people must produce culture; not just some of the time but all of the time; not just material culture but political and ideological culture. Capitalism interferes with the capacity to produce culture on the one hand and progressively monopolizes various lines of production on the other. One has little measure of the worth of his/her self system if one is excluded from the production of culture. One is subject to much criticism if one cannot afford to participate in the forms of culture set as normative in an affluent society.

Here is what happens. Profit consideration demands capital-intensive rather than labor-intensive production. In the production of material culture, machines can displace people. People are costly. Profits require they be eliminated as far as possible from production, packaging, shipping, storing, selling, and accounting. But without jobs, people are excluded from distribution. In capitalism, the only legitimate way to reunite production and consumption is by everyone selling one's labor power—the very process automation progressively eliminates.

There are other noncapitalist ways to reunite production and distribution. One can apply to the welfare state but one is reduced to a client whose incompetence is proved by the fact of application. One can turn to one's kinship system but one is infantilized in the moment one does. One can turn to private charity and beggary, but again one is degraded from the status of a full human being. And crime entails the coercive reunification of production and distribution for those not satisfied by the market for labor power. It also degrades both the victim and the thief.

When one is caught up in the criminal justice system, new relabeling processes are instituted to wipe out existing social identities in the self structure and to obliterate the social base for self. One is demoralized in such a system. If one finds oneself in such an economic system, one is doubly degraded. By not being able to work, one is denied the dignity of productive labor. By not being able to sell one's labor power on equitable terms, one is denied the material resources by which one can live a life of dignity and help constitute the various social relationships. Relationships one is told are essential to all respectable, estimable human beings; social relationships essential to the most important work of all: the human project. Symbolic social life worlds are meager and degraded for millions in capitalist America.

In the United States, some 20 million people profit greatly from the system—they have wealth beyond the imagination of most *sociologist*-psychologists (sociology-oriented as contrasted with psychology-oriented social psychologists). Another 8 million are securely connected to the distributive system by virtue of rents, dividends, interest, and royalties. These 30 million control the production of economic ideas, national policies, and community projects. They live lives of respect and dignity and they experience themselves as the object and agent of their own power.

Another 30 to 40 million are connected to the means of production by virtue of their professional, managerial, and organizational status. Working mostly in the monopoly sector, protected by union contracts, secured by adequate health care insurance, retirement, and vacation programs, these people have adequate access to the distributive system from college to death. The better the college, the better the lifestyle. They engineer the production of ideological, economic, and political culture on behalf of the 30 million or so capitalist owners.

Some 25 to 70 million have a very tenuous relationship to the means of production. They sell their labor power on marginal terms, they steal a little, and hustle welfare a little. They are not protected from illness, accident, or economic recession. Mostly women, minorities, and rural poor, these people work for small businesses and change jobs frequently. They float from construction site to construction site, from restaurant to restaurant, from used-car lot to used-car lot, from hustle to hustle.

They must rely on the degradations of county welfare, they must suffer the pettiness and temper of a hard-pressed owner. They must push their children to finish high school and get a job or drop out too early. They receive the contempt, anger, and fury of the Right wing, the school system, the social workers, and the police. They are the social junk of the capitalist system. They are denied access to the process by which people constitute themselves as human beings.

The assumptions of symbolic interaction theory simply do not hold for those disemployed and thus dispossessed of the work status-role by the logic of capitalist economics.

Except in church. In the churches of the lower classes, one can find status, community, religious fellowship, and redemption in an indifferent world. The symbolic environment of the churches of the lower classes is interactionally rich and informationally rich—it is a transcending joy to participate in such labor. This is at once a curse and a blessing. It redeems them as estimable human beings but it sidetracks them from effective political action to transform such a system of privilege and of misery. Such is the social anthropology of capitalism as an economic system.

Politics and Self Systems

As capital-intensive production intrudes into more and more domains (farming, teaching, policing, healing, and child rearing ordinarily thought to be labor-intensive production), the work ethic becomes superfluous to society and the leisure ethic useful. But with capital-intensive production people are not needed and, under capitalism, do not have the fiscal resources to buy the forms of leisure identified on mass media as necessary to the "good life." The surplus population grows and the political system finds itself in a legitimization crisis.

As the crises grow, the need for unreflective commitment to capitalism also grows. The exclusion of the masses, especially the surplus population, from the political process becomes necessary. A whole new industry, oriented to the generation of voting publics, has arisen.

Since 1968, when Richard Nixon hired Roger Ailes and PR firms to win the election for him, the technical world of the "professional" campaign manager has increasingly displaced the moral action of the citizen in political life. There is the dramaturgical impression of public discourse on the issues, but increasingly issues and opinions are managed and manipulated by technical advisors whose goal is a campaign victory, not a public resolution of issues. The issues will be resolved by an elite; the opinion of the public tactfully handled after the decision has been made.

As with political culture, ideological culture, increasingly, also is produced by capital-intensive modes and distributed via television and retail outlets as commodity produced for profit. Much art, music, myths, drama, sports, cinema, and science—religion as well—are not produced by situated, interacting groups as presumed in symbolic interaction theory when culture is discussed but is mass-produced. The drama of political life is controlled by corporate sponsorship rather than by interactively rich moral reasoning.

Although the technical means for an interactively rich politics—even in a large-scale society—exists, the production of political culture is preempted by an elite acting in the interest of capitalism as a system. Electronic models for democratic politics are developed and deployed in the recording and transfer of funds around a global network of automated EMT. The physical basis for interactionally rich political communication has been developed by NSA, NASA, and the Pentagon. This technology is not deployed in politics; if it were, it would replace Congress with computer networks.

The thin and brief democratic processes in place in the United States make it difficult for one to anchor one's self system within political life. Without politics in the public sphere close to the center of the self system, more personal kinds of politics preempt the self system. Public issues become remote and disconnected from the moral framework as from the motivational framework of the acting and interacting self. The dialectics of political drama shrinks to those within the family and within the world of waged labor.

Private Ownership of Communication

When the means to produce meaning is in private ownership, one does not have the technical means to communicate while the basic preconditions for symbolic interaction are absent for those who cannot pay. Access to telephone, fax, newspapers, postal service, television, radio, and telegraphy is limited by one's ability to pay and the owner's ability to extract profit from workers and customers.

In a highly mobile society, the communication required to maintain those social relations of kinship and friendship central to valued social identities is limited. The very mobility of society is determined by the needs of capital to transfer, lay off, expand, and restrict production. In the same instant that the logics of capitalism hurl members of the family or friendship group to the four corners, access to the media by which to engage in symbolic interaction is held hostage to the profit needs of the communications industry.

Much of the channel capacity of the means of production of meaning under private ownership is not put to use for cultural purposes (in the anthropolical sense) but rather put to commercial use. Commercial interests displace political issues. The concern to generate the largest possible audience requires that no one be offended—thus political issues, which offend, are avoided. From the audiences generated, markets are solicited for products. Community need for political discourse is set aside by corporate need for mass markets from which to realize profits. In service to the profit needs of private ownership, the various media are designed to eliminate as much interaction as possible. Marketing requires a short message to millions while the production of culture requires long interactive processes for hundreds, thousands, or tens of thousands.

Yet there is no technical reason television and radio could not be linked to the human interest in intersubjective understanding. The phenomenal growth of citizens band radio, fax, computer modems and mobile telephones testifies to the possibility. CB radio permits hundreds of truckers to organize an interactionally rich and informationally relevant social process in what had been a bleak and lonely industry. Without access to a microphone, electronic support of symbolic interaction is impossible in a complex society.

In the course of serving commercial interests, the various media tend to produce meaning supportive of a capitalist system. It is not necessary to look for a conspiracy or censorship to validate such a statement. The very fact that products are advertised for sale on the basis of profit rather than need sets as a given capitalist modes of exchange on television and thus reproduces, every eight minutes, the capitalist worldview. Corporations do not sponsor politically salient programs: nature shows, family shows, classical music and soap operas are safe supplies for the colonization of human desire.

Some ads are little else but essays on the virtues of capitalism. Bell telephone's ad stating that the system is the solution, or the Texaco ad with Bob Hope that concludes that Texaco is working to earn our trust is one of the many examples of the direct effort on the part of private enterprise to buy legitimacy and manufacture meaning via the media.

To the extent the means to produce meaning are privately owned, the symbolic interaction process is privately owned. To the extent that the means to produce meaning are sold as a commodity, symbolic interaction becomes a commodity. If meaning becomes a commodity, so does culture itself.

Symbolic Interaction and Social Revolution

There are many exceptions to capitalist control over social identity and role via the claim of private ownership to status-role positions. There are exceptions to the generalization that skills and techniques rather than character and self are the object of the socialization process. Voluntary organizations and social movements offer interactively rich alternatives to mass politics.

Even in the most routinized bureaucracy, workers still manage to act. Even in the best managed corporations, managed in terms of corporate goals, managers still respond to reasons of the heart rather than of the rule. In terms of the philosophy of the act, it is practically impossible to disconnect intentionality and value from social process. MacDonald's Corporation trains people to produce hamburgers exactly alike in all its franchises—they fail. The burgers are different from region to region, from country to country, from generation to generation. It is impossible to program for the mechanical reproduction of cultural resources. Yet capitalist firms and socialist bureaus are designed to do so—and thus are hostile to the human project. Politics and culture are regained by ignoring bureaucratic policies, rules, orders, and flow charts.

Doctors, lawyers, priests, and many professionals still go through a socialization that yields a fairly permanent social identity anchored in the social order. For many such professionals, work is still the center of life and a most valued center at that. However, as medicine and law become integrated into the table of organization of a giant corporation, the role position is no longer under the control of the physician or lawyer. S/he sells her/his labor power and is subject to dismissal just as are manual workers.

The professor in a university is awarded tenure that fixes the relation between social identity and social position permanently. The practice of hiring part-time faculty neatly sidesteps the reciprocity between professor and university. For those few faculty left under such labor market dynamics, tenure is assured; for the rest, an uncertain future. For the few tenured faculty, only gross incompetence and openly flaunted moral turpitude can trigger the process by which self and social position is rent asunder.

College faculty are proletarianized as college managers attack the tenure system with the practice of contract labor; with the use of nontenured track positions, with a recourse to part-time help and to "extension" faculty.

Still another exception to the divorce of self from society is to be found in church-related schools. In many Catholic, Protestant, and especially Pentecostal churches, the socialization process has not yielded to the rational-technical needs of large-scale enterprise but still is pointed toward the production of a stable and morally oriented set of social identities within the self system. The associated roles are anchored in the family, church life, and community, and not in a specialized salable skill or organizational chart of a multinational corporation.

The same is true for the sons and daughters of the upper classes. They go to universities where technical skills are not of central concern. For the children of the upper classes, political and economic issues are central to education. Their professors get them ready to enter the world of politics—both private and public. They are socialized as members of an elite. It is not technical skills and factual information for which they are held responsible but rather whole worldviews and class loyalties, class politics, class programs.

There is a social revolution going on in the United States and elsewhere but it is not noticed by capitalists nor orthodox Marxists since the battleground is not "ownership" of material property nor are the proletariat and capitalists the protagonists in the struggle. Rather the struggle is focused on the control of the means to produce meaning. It is not primarily a class struggle but a struggle against massification. It is not over the stratification of wealth but rather over the right to praxis and community.

The mass struggle (i.e., the struggle against the assault on the selfsystem by massification processes in capitalism) has two main fronts. On the one front is the exodus from the public school system toward private school, both secular and religious. The liberals, in charge of state and federal educational agencies, try to further massify, standardize, rationalize, technicize the school system while parents rebel, resist, go on strike, boycott, and form parallel structures once again pointed toward character and a stable self system for their children.

That the self system under construction in such private schools has racist, sexist, authoritarian characteristics cannot be denied. However, the important thing to note for the radical social psychologist is that a strong, stable, competent, and enduring self system is the object of labor-intensive socialization rather than the mass inculcation of commodity skills.

The second front on which the social revolution is occurring in the United States can be found in the Pentecostal movement and in the "born again" religions including Buddhism. Charles Colson, Governor Harold Hughes, Eldridge Cleaver, and some 50 million other Americans have been "reborn" in the last fifteen years. Most of these are lower middle class, working class, and those in the surplus population for whom the economic institution offers little in the way of an authentically human social identity.

The church, especially the Pentecostal church, offers an attractive alternative to Americans conditioned to respond negatively toward socialist theory and positively toward religious theory. In the Pentecostal movement there is a valued social identity, a permanent role relationship organized to permit praxis and a great deal of community. Were it not for the fact that many such religions limit their ideals of fellowship by race, gender, and age-grade discriminations, they might well serve as a model for the human project. Were it not for the fact that this revival of the human spirit often leaves the structure of capitalism intact with all its contradictions unresolved and its crisis untended, some of these religious communities would be very close to the vision of social revolution and communism envisioned by Marx.

In Latin American countries, the social revolution is informed by liberation theology. From its beginnings in Europe, liberation theology took its Latin American shape at the Medellín conference in 1968. Spreading out through the poor, the teachings of Christ about personal sin and the teachings of Marx about structural sin inspire thousands of nuns and priests to side with the poor and the oppressed in interactionally rich and politically oriented action. The murder of hundreds of priests and nuns attests to the power of this movement to recapture the economic process to the social process.

If we accept the distinction Marx made between social revolution and merely political revolution, the revolution going on in the United States is far more radical than are the palace coups in the Third World that replace one class elite with another elite or the stalled revolutions in East European nations. A transformation of self and society is involved in the Pentecostal movement and other less popular movements.

While capitalist modes of relationship are intruding into the "born again" movement—with commodity fetishism of sacred objects, hucksterism, and "find wealth through God" radio scams, still the larger meaning of the movement is to repair the damage done to self and social relationships in a commodity society that disposes of people in school, work, and market if profit cannot be made on their labor or purchasing power.

Socialism and the Structure of Self

The point of socialist revolutionary movements is to produce a socialist (i.e., communist) model of self. In this model, the capacity for praxis and for community is central to the structure of self. Self and society are to be reborn as a unit in which the collective good is dialectically balanced with the personal good.

The moments of praxis include rationality, self-determination, sociality, creativity, and intentionality (Markovic, 1974; Crocker, 1976). The interest in community includes collective ownership, collective control, as well as common access to the means to produce all forms of culture. In many socialist societies access to the means of producing ideological and political culture continue to be restricted to the top party echelons. Thus the dimensions of the self are restricted in the interest of bureaucratic control.

In Communist China, the cultural revolution was widely understood in Marxist circles to maximize praxis and collective control of the means for producing society and culture. Since the death of Mao, the Right wing is in control and the emphasis has shifted from collective access to the means of producing ideological culture back to bureaucratic control of policy. In exchange, people have the right to limited forms of private enterprise. The quest for material wealth displaces the quest for a praxis society.

Whatever the problems of capitalism, whatever the failing of socialist societies, the centrally important meaning of capitalism, socialism, and communism for a decent social-psychological base for the self system lies in the adequacy of the symbolic interaction process, the linkage between self and social order, and the human need for praxis and community. While one cannot be overly optimistic in surveying existing conditions and long-range trends, still one must agree that the tendency to couch the international struggles in and between capitalism, socialism, and communism in purely material terms must be set aside in favor of an analysis of the meaning of such struggles for the loss of self.

Much of the interest in fundamentalist religion around the world in both socialist and capitalist formations can be understood in large part as a quest in which self and society are, once again, united well inside the sacred sphere, a sphere set aside by both secular capitalism and bureaucratic socialism.

Go Spectre!

Go, Spectre! Obey my most secret desire,
Which thou knowest without my speaking
Go to these fiends of Righteousness.

Tell them to obey their humanity
and not pretend Holiness when they are
Murderers, as far as they are able to.

Go, tell them that the worship of God
is honouring his gifts in other men
and loving the best men best
each according to his own genius
which is the Holy Ghost in men;
there is no other
God than that God who is the poetic genius of Humanity.

He who envies or calumniates,
which is murder and cruelty,
Murders the Holy-one.

Go, tell them this,
and overthrow their cup,
their bread, their alter-table,
their incense and their oath,
their marriage and their baptism,
their burial and their consecration.

He who would see the Divinity
must see it in the children.

—William Blake
Excerpt from *Jerusalem*

Truth is good health
and safety and the sky.

How meagre and how vocal,
an everlasting lie.

—Emily Dickinson

7

Morality and Mass Society

The Loss of Self

In managed mass societies, it is profitable to divorce self from social organization in the productive process. It is expedient to circumvent the self structure in the marketplace and it is easy if not necessary to do so in the micropolitics of everyday life.

The old model of self, anchored firmly in the structure of social networks, is hostile to the interests of advanced monopoly capital for using and discarding workers, for playing one worker off against another, for moving factories and jobs away from communities, for using one set of workers to watch, manage, and exploit another, for the anonymity of the market place in which profits set the tone and purpose of interaction.

The old model of self, useful in caring and sharing with others within the larger structure of community, is hostile to the needs of elites to separate and fractionate blocs of people into individual units of power and wealth. Such a massified form of individualism fits excellently well the control needs of elitist societies in that the concentration of social power in the collective is prevented; in that the vast transformations possible informed by moral power are defeated; in that the democratic structures possible using modern electronic technologies are subverted; and the boundaries of social space are miniaturized thus making the corporation that much the larger.

The old model of self in which socially constructed social identities mediated moral behavior is displaced by a new structure of self in which bureaucratic rules, marketplace needs, and authoritarian orders shape the everyday decisions of workers, students, customers, and voters alike. In such a massified, individuated, and self-less society, moral behavior disappears. Shameless behavior is seen on every hand. The only rule is to avoid getting caught using other people to privatized purpose.

The old model of self useful in a society oriented to producing goods and services is hostile to the need of capital to control labor costs. The old model of self oriented to frugality, thrift, and modest levels of consumption is hostile to the need of capital to dispose of goods in the market place. The traditional model of self packed full of social identities linked to cooperative social endeavor is most certainly hostile to the market imperatives of capital or the accumulation goals of the capitalist.

Advertising, as a mythic form, suggests a new model of self while it parasitizes on traditional social identities attempting to generate publics via the family role set, ethnic identities, or sex-linked identities. The privatized self of the affluent consumer is the model pushed in a thousand commercials. One is to measure happiness and despair in terms of possession and fashion. One is to measure success in terms of wealth and portfolio. One is to gauge the worth of the self in terms of display and posture.

A structure of self in which shared values, collective values mediate human behavior is hostile to one in which private goals are to be met. A structure of self in which reciprocity in a role set informs human behavior is hostile to private success. A structure of self in which others mirror one's behavior, express approval or dissent, and thus mediate one's behavior is hostile to personal power and control of the negotiated order that ensues.

The Social Location of Morality

Most researchers, indeed most people, falsely locate morality in the person of the acting individual. That has never been the case. In a society organized to maximize the control of behavior of people by dramaturgy, electronics, psychology, and social research, it is still less true.

In every stratified society the locus of morality is at the apex of the pyramids of power, wealth, and social honor. As those structures become more stratified with more and more layers of bureaucratic offices between the apex and the effector apparatus, morality becomes diluted at each echelon; dissociated from the individual. Orders, policies, programs arbitrarily arrogate moral responsibility to the "leadership." Rules, regulations, and role specifications rob the employee of moral responsibility.

When decisions are to be made by lower-echelon employees, these decisions are limited to the *routinization* of authority to rational application to cases that come before the employee. If the employee fails to follow routine out of ignorance, mischief, or sheer human compassion, s/he is retrained or replaced. Thus does authority make cowards of us all: courage to do the right thing and to transcend rules, orders, and commands. Thus we become instruments of the moral (or immoral) will of others.

To their credit, people do transcend the instrumental rationality of bureaucratic logic and do respond to the simple human need of welfare clients, students, prisoners, patients, or migrants. Employees in a bureaucracy, still attuned to their own humanity, empathize with the corporation or university client or the welfare mother and do violate the rules. In such violation is the reunification of self and morality.

For better or for worse, the individual has engaged in moral action; has reunited self and society; has weighed the needs of the collective against those of the corporation and has come down on the side of mercy more than ratiocination. Morality has been relocated in the balancing of conflicting values by thinking, acting, compassionate human beings—and that is a human product.

Not all of us can be Prometheus and bring light to the world; argue with the gods who would destroy humans to make way for their one-eyed monsters. Not all of us can be Nikatetes and put the devil behind us. Not all of us are wise beyond the wisdom of the collective. Many of us break rules for the most banal or venal of reasons. Still, the location of morality is shifted from bureaucratic authority at the "top" of the pyramid of authority to the individual actor.

In the best of times, morality is a dialectic process in which each individual shapes the behavior of society. In the worst of times, the morality of thought and action is absorbed to the offices of power and deployed against the human project.

The concept of "praxis" assimilates the delicate and changing dialectics of morality. Praxis, as a concept in the arsenal of emancipatory writing, tries to make it possible in the shadowy world of words to relocate morality where it belongs: one foot in the soul of the individual and one foot in the ethos of a society. We return to the place of praxis in the human project in other chapters in this volume.

Mass Society and Morality

The logic of massification, the tendency to treat the individual as the only locus of social morality aborts the dialectics of morality. Treating persons as if they are the final arbitrators of their own behavior speaks against all the tenets of symbolic interaction theory, of societal reaction theory, of reference group theory—even of labeling theory.

While many disagree about the structure of mass society, in this chapter, the referent is to a society in which a large-scale organization is the typical unit of social involvement for most of us through the daily routines. The large-scale organization usually takes the form of a bureaucracy. The bureau is organized in a tripartite structure: elite governing body; two or more echelons of employed functionaries to embody the technical rationality of the bureau rule or policy; and an anonymous mass of individuals processed by the functionaries according to the rules.

This structure defines and incorporates a mass social institution. Prisons, universities, hospitals, state welfare agencies, military and police forces, schools, factories, retail stores, commercial sports enterprises, as well as many religious denominations have such a structure. These often exist side by side with much more intimate and collective social units.

In a mass institution, the ordinary rules of hermeneutics are set aside. Rather than trying to facilitate and stabilize intersubjective understanding, the rules of social exchange are designed to minimize authentic intersubjective knowledge. In such a society, the assumption from symbolic interaction theory about the role of significant others and of the generalized other must be reconsidered. It is valid, in a curiously distorted kind of way, to dismiss or evade the effect of others on one's own behavior. There are forms of social organization in which the significant other, as conceptualized by Henry Stack Sullivan, becomes insignificant. One can think of a son who thanks his mother for working as a charwoman to put him through medical school—and then releases her to work as a charwoman for her own benefit. One can think of businesspeople who have had the benefit of public education, the GI Bill, public health controls, hot lunch programs, small-business loans, and tax incentives who brag that they are self-made—mostly men.

In societies that stress a one-sided individualism, the assumptions of symbolic interaction theory, the norm of reciprocity, the collective conscious are assiduously discarded. The salesperson or publicist do not want others to know the game plan; do not want symbols to affect their own behavior in the same instant it affects that of others; do not intend to act in ways compatible with the intersubjective meanings of a speech act. The point is to maximize personal and corporate gain while maintaining the dramatic semblance of reciprocity.

In such a social formation, it is appropriate to speak of the rugged individual or of the "self-made man." But to so speak is to discount the vast heritage upon which we all build our lives. It is to dismiss the contributions others have made to the point that we are in possession of enough wealth or power to gain our own will even against that of those at whom we direct power.

In societies that collect social power, concentrate it in the office of the pope, president or first secretary, or CEO, then deploy that power to control smaller, weaker units of social organization—there it is appropriate to speak of the acting individual. Not the corporate entity wielding collective or economic power but the single individual coming before the pope, coming in front of that president, or standing against the rules of that CEO.

In such social formations, there are indeed such entities as individuals, ontologically speaking, but there are also giant bureaus who benefit from the distorted dialectics of power.

In those societies where the power of the individual is assimilated to the power of the corporation or bureau, there is a vast unfreedom. In those authoritarian societies of which Jeane Kirkpatrick speaks there is freedom of action in the nooks and crannies of society and outside of the large-scale organizations that wield collective power. But it is the most trivial kind of freedom. It is the freedom to be disconnected from the social world in which one must work, learn, heal, worship, or write.

In the United States, everyone has the freedom to purchase a television station and speak freely in support of one's own class interest. One has the right to listen to William Buckley or to George Will or to Harry Reasoner—but one does not have the right to enter the studio, sit down, and quietly speak of other viewpoints. One has the freedom to turn the channel to a football game, to a nature program, to a concert, or sitcom, but one does not have the right to enter into a genuinely public sphere and discuss the priorities of use of the media.

One has, equally, the freedom to subscribe to the *New York Times,* the *Detroit News,* the *Denver Post,* or the *Los Angeles Times* and read what those who own the media have to say. One has the right to subscribe to *In These Times, Telos,* or the *Insurgent Sociologist*— if one has heard about them and does not use them to challenge authority on the job, in the classroom, or at the pulpit.

The freedoms of a mass society are the microfreedoms of the isolated individual or group. They are not the profound, significant, strong freedoms of effective public discourse.

Theory and Ideology

Those theories of morality that speak of stages in the moral growth of the individual (Piaget, Kohlberg, and the generations of moral theorists following them) theories accept blindly the assumption that moral behavior must be located in the person of the single acting subject.

When such theories are studied, validated, taught, and used to judge people, theory becomes ideology. While it may be true that one is at stage two or stage five in moral development in every reasonable scaling device, still such findings bypass, overlook, disregard the social context in which stage three moralities develop and stage six moralities are discouraged. It is far easier in some social conditions to act on stage five morality than in other social formations. Try acting principled in a concentration camp or in a corporate office.

Those who live in abject poverty and are hurled through the portals of social space by the dynamics of the world economic system have very little control over the flow of jobs to and from their communities. Those who are detached from agrarian society and are born in the center city have very few skills with which to grow food or build lodging. Those who are subjected to the economics and ecology of pollution have very little choice in the quality of air or the quality of their lives. For them, moral action in significant realms of life is an impossible dream.

To Tell the Truth

The worthlessness of worldly things
is easy when a poet sings;
But if your child is crying then
its fine to have a thing to spend.

To rise above the madding throng
is noble in a poet's song;
but if your child is ill abed
then you stoop to bring her bread.

To tell the truth is fine indeed;
In every church we hear it spread.
But if your child has no roof,
Then truth can find a different proof.

Its fine to say that honor grow
and must, before all values, go;
But if you hear your children cry
then out the window honor fly.

If there are transcendent reasons why we, rich and poor alike, lie, steal, cheat, betray, and deceive in the micropolitics of everyday life, then the run of morality in the macropolitics of an emerging world economic system minimizes morality even further. In a mass society, few of us can be morally responsible for the crime in our cities, the pollution of our environment, the brutalization of handicapped people, or the foreign policy of our state.

The Politics of Morality

When the Ollie Norths of the National Security Agency do things in secret at the behest of the Reagans of the world, such acts do real mischief in the world. But Reagan acts outside of the Constitution, outside of the Congress, outside of the oath of office, and thus makes moral cretins of us all. We did not discuss the sale of arms to Iran; we did not discuss the use of profits from the sale of arms to Iran for the secret wars in Nicaragua, Afghanistan, or Angola. If children are murdered by mercenaries hired by the CIA, we are not responsible and yet we should be—it is our country; our Constitution; it is our soldiers who do the bombing and who engineer the murder. It is our money that pays for the death squads in Central America; it is our moral onus that children, women, soldiers are killed.

As moral agents in whatever stage of moral development, we must have national and open debate on such subjects. Things done for us in secret preempt our morality.

Most of us bend to the rules of the bureau; bend to the power of the tyrant; bend to the temptation of the wage. Those of us who do must be watched. We will use our position of trust against the general interest; we will use guile and guise in aid of privatized and asymmetrical gain; we will use the morality of those who still have it against them. We will break faith, betray trust, and exploit a capacity to believe in a thing. We are dangerous to the human project.

Formal Control Systems

The most direct consequence of all this is that the *social* self is not longer a prime mediator of behavior—and there can be no self-control oriented to prosocial activity or to the common good if there is no socially anchored self. The mediation of behavior by informal group interaction ceases to be effective as behavior comes to be mediated by private urges, wants, needs, interests, proclivities, and compulsions. Another basic assumption of symbolic interaction theory becomes invalid. The dialectics of social control set forth in such constructs as the looking-glass process, societal reaction theory, or labeling theory are missing.

Formal social control appears necessary as self-control is subverted by the structure of power and managerial tactics.

Law becomes a major source of ordered behavior as the self succumbs to assault by professional educators, scientific managers, and hapless bureaucrats. Police, surveillance, efficient court systems, "modern" prisons, and professional rehabilitation become technically mandated since authentic social control within a matrix of supportive others is not possible.

In a society where the state experiences a fiscal crisis as it tries to take care of all the low-profit services neglected by private capital, capital-intensive modes of control also become attractive: psychosurgery, mass-produced drugs for depressed adults or uncontrollable school children, electronic implants, or group counseling become nonrevolutionary ways to respond to the crises in capitalism.

All sorts of self-help programs are developed from Alcoholics Anonymous to the "born again" movement as the fiscal crisis pushes the state to *privatize* the problems of control and management. Private support groups, private therapy groups, private police groups, together with self-help books, subliminal tapes, and biofeedback kits help return the responsibility for control to the informal group. These responses all shift the onus of a poorly organized society from its institutions to the poorly organized self system—as if these two social units were unconnected. Voluntary organizations are to step in and pick up the moral debris of a managed mass society.

At the very time that the resources of those in the surplus population are cut back, the resources of those in the lower echelons of the working class are reduced by wage give-back, more taxes, and inflation. At the time that increasing behavioral problems arise for sons and daughters, brothers and sisters, mothers and fathers in the lower ranks of the economic order—the state removes resources that would enable such private forms of social control. Failing the first lines of social control, formal social control institutions seem to make sense. They fail. There are better tactics, as we shall see below in the section on postmodern morality.

At the very time the dynamics of those market and work institutions loosen the connection between self and society, more demands are put on the self to assume the task of solving the problems of capitalism. There are limits to this use of self. However, we can begin to handle these problems if we have a coherent analysis of what is happening. Bad theory produces bad policy. For those genuinely committed to dealing with social problems, the social dimensions of the self are a way to start. Beyond the self system is the sociocultural system that patterns behavior: moral and immoral behavior alike.

Self-Esteem and Mass Society

Just as there are no measures of shame or self-esteem possible in a mass society using the technics of dramaturgy to manage consciousness and thus defeat the self system, there can be no measures of crime or social honor. Where morality is usurped by the collective or the corporation, there can be no pride or honor in whatever one does since one's behavior is shaped, asymmetrically, by others.

The effort to measure self-esteem or to scale social honor becomes an exercise in futility. People who become shameless do not care about what others think. They do not reflect upon themselves, take the responses of others into account, nor feel mortification or pride in what they do. The looking-glass process is clouded by the false needs of privatized desire. We see morality dimly, through a glass darkly.

Such people are forever frozen at level two of moral development. If they are likely to get caught, they pause and reconsider hurting others. If they *are* caught, they experience chagrin and irritation that it was *they* who were caught and not some other equally unscrupulous person.

New Sources of Self-Esteem

Give us two days of your time
and we will remold you.

—Hudson's Ad

The architects of illusion sell the client without honor an illusion of honor. The public relations industry will, for a fee, create the dramaturgical impression of estimable worth. They will create a persona for one; market it on the mass, anonymous media, use surveys to measure effectiveness of the illusion, and rescript the lines and history of the customer to fit the anxieties and hopes of a mass audience—and thus gain public esteem for one without substantial cause for it.

Madison Avenue industries will, for a fee, polish the image of South Africa or Argentina or Guatemala. Hirelings who know how to measure hope and belief will redeem the scoundrel politician. All honor, esteem, and respect become market commodities along with faith and belief in an electronically based sociology of fraud.

Those who are disconnected from the social base, who lack a set of estimable social identities, who live and work in a moral vacuum, whose talents are hired to manage and manipulate masses of unknown others for unknown purpose—these moral casualties of mass society seek other measures of worth and status.

They join fitness centers to make their muscles and bodies the object of admiration. They turn to zodiac identities to find out what and who they really are. They shop at Jacobson's to get computer-based recommendations for just the right clothing. They stand before color monitors to select just the right cosmetics. They read "how-to," "what-if," and "kiss-and-tell" books to project just the right image.

There are better uses for dramaturgy. There are better uses for trust. There are better grounds for the allocation of social honor and interpersonal esteem. It takes a very special society, a very special democracy, a very special social psychology to ensure them. Praxis is possible only in a praxis society; morality is possible only in a moral society; shame is possible only in a society in which the self mediates one's own behavior. It is an exercise in mystification to try to measure praxis, morality, or moral worth in a worthless society.

Postmodern Morality

The recent work on Chaos theory has many implications for the dialectics of morality. The most important implication is that in something as complex and variable as a human society, formal control tactics aimed at individual persons do not work to promote morality. There is a better strategy for the promotion of prosocial behavior buried in the dynamics of Chaotic systems.

Modern moral philosophy grew out of a reductionistic world-view in which the behavior of the parts of a system determined in linear, in closed fashion, the behavior of the whole. In modern science it was thought that knowing the initial states of atoms, molecules, persons, and cultures, we could predict precisely the final state of the system in which those parts were found. In such a world, there was no place for surprise, change, or quantum leaps.

In moral theory, it was thought that the socialization of the child determined adult behavior. If the child acted badly as an adult, it was due to faulty parenting or faulty education. Just as one would never expect a car to fly, one would not expect the well-socialized child to rape, rob, murder, or cheat. Just as one would take a car to a shop for repair, one would send a person to a prison or to a hospital for repair. In such a moral philosophy, the solution is locked in; one must repair the part in order to get the proper behavior.

The postmodern world-view is much different. In order to get moral behavior using a postmodern understanding, we must try to pattern the whole system rather than mass-produce the individual parts. Automobiles are stable systems, predictable, mechanical systems; cultures and societies are not. Different approaches are appropriate to make sociocultural systems work well.

If we can make the jump from weather systems, biochemical systems, and mechanical systems such as automobiles to human cultures, the lesson is that it is far better to set up a program of social justice with which to attract rather than to set up programs to control masses of people. In order to do this, it is necessary to transcend modern science, the science of Newton, Laplace, and of mechanical engineering. One must understand the logics of postmodern science and take its lesson when appropriate to do so.

Post-Modern Science

Just where the postmodern analysis began is hard to say. Out of the ferment of social revolution, scientific discovery, political upheaval, critical theory, and social experiment came an awe-ful understanding. The neat and closed world of Newton and Laplace did not exist. There were no inviolable laws of nature and of society. There were no pure forms, no ideal types, no final telos toward which to steer with science and technology. There were only small windows of order in a larger run of unpredictable patterns.

Postmodern knowledge processes destroyed that symmetry, that perfection, that closed system of natural law. Space for chaos; for disorder, for unpredictability—hence uncontrollability—opened up.

Since the time of Mary Shelley, in her 1816 story of Victor Frankenstein, we could see, if we would look, the dark shadows shed by modern science and technology. Shelley was the daughter of the celebrated feminist Mary Wollstonecraft who challenged the idea that God and Nature perfected the human race in the male image, while her father, William Godwin, challenged the perfection of class privilege and aristocratic preference. In one nineteenth-century English family could be found the seedlings of postmodern critique.

After Darwin published the *Origin of the Species* in 1868, change lost its final, teleological goal. There was only adaptation to an ever-changing environment. Many of Darwin's readers brought back into Darwin's theory of evolution, the teleologics of racism, national chauvinism, patriarchy, and elitism but, for Darwin, it was the survival of the fittest; not movement toward the perfect, that fueled biological evolution. What fit one environment might not fit another environment; hence the development of a variety of adapted life forms. The turtles and birds of the Gallapagos were variants of each other; not inferior or superior, not successive approximations to perfection, not stages of change, not primitive and modern—only different. They, too, could be, but need not be, replaced by species more suited to the terrain, to the climate, to the ecology of the islands.

When Werner Heisenberg set forth the indeterminacy principle, the Einsteinian quest for a unified field theory to explain all order, harmony, and prediction in the cosmos emerging out of the interactions of the four forces: the strong force of nuclear bonding; the weak force of atomic bonding; electromagnetism and gravity failed. With quantum mechanics, developed in the 1920s, mathematical precision gave way to probabilistic statements. Probability statements, in sociology at least, still reflect an assumption that there is a precise relationship toward which better research and better theory could bring the knowledge process; quantum mechanics changed this view of probability to the view that all we could know, the best we could do was to give estimates—certainty did not exist.

We are all innocent in a fixed, God-hewn world, in a fixed, clockwork cosmos. In a chaotic world; in a world where patterns are possible but perfection not, we lose that innocence but, in return, we gain the chance to be moral actors; the chance to become responsible for our destiny if we are wise and good enough. To that possibility, a wise and decent social psychology might also strive.

In another place, I have tried to argue for the use of social justice policies with which to "attract" moral behavior (Young, 1989). I have taken the lesson that the cycle of socialization, hurtful activity, and rehabilitation of individuals is a poor way to generate a moral society. Far better are jobs, housing, health care, democratic politics, and compassionate religious opportunities. Most low-crime societies do not have a lot of laws, police, prisons, or probation officers. Most do not use punishment, chemicals, electronics or psychiatry to shape the behavior of individual persons. Most have social justice built into the fabric of social life—and that suffices for moral behavior.

All this ignores a most important question: what is to be the forum for democratic action? Some argue that the state should be the respository of political action. Others say the civil sector made up of a great variety of voluntary organizations should mediate moral action. Many point out the dangers of state monopoly of moral action. Others warn of the dangers of privatized morality of interest groups that works only for the benefit of its own members. I do not have a vision of what might be workable. Chaos theory informs us that there are many possible combinations of "strange attractors," each of which creates varying but beautiful mandelbrot sets. In practical terms, this means that a few simple structures should suffice to pattern social justice and social morality.

Conclusion

In mass societies, the social self is circumvented by the tactics of management science, by the technologies of theatre, by the deployment of social research, by the insights of psychology. In such a society, moral behavior is in jeopardy. There is a concentration of social power in the bureaucratic office, stratification of power by echelons, and enforcement of bureaucratic rules by instrumental rationality. In such societies, moral agency is stripped from the self system and appropriated by bureaucratic authority.

In market societies where possession and wealth motivate human behavior, those with money and property rights preempt the moral process to their own purpose. In stratified societies where power and wealth magnify the will of the elite, the dialectics of morality are distorted.

In dramaturgical societies one is coached to speak lines, gull audiences, manage consciousness, and modify behavior outside of the logic of discourse. In dramaturgical politics impressions given off do not necessarily coincide with intentionality. In dramaturgical religion the morality of the minister is remote from the members of the parish. In dramaturgical markets the sizzle masks the substance. In such societies, morality falls upon hard times.

Tactics of morality that assign moral authority, moral action, and moral onus to the boss, the owner, the manager, the professor, or the general— mystify and misdirect moralists. They measure the moral development of individuals rather than examine the social location of moral action. In these societies, the stage of morality at which the individual tends to operate is predecided by a logic and control tactics. One cannot be the object and the agent of one's own morality when one is disconnected from the locus of action. It is difficult for one to stand up against the power of the state and protest. It is rare that one oppose the power of the church and say, "But it does move."

Recent work in Chaos theory offers a guide to the creation of a postmodern morality. Emphasis on social justice programs together with a more democratically based morality might just work better than our present tactics to produce a good and decent society. It is impossible and undesirable to try to control all behavior with laws and with courts, prisons, and individual rehabilitation while destroying the social anchorage of the self system and, at the same time, making personal worth dependent upon wealth and display.

It might be far better and far more effective to reconnect individuals to society with permanent and valued social identities while relocating moral responsibility in an interactively rich and informationally public sphere.

The Mutable Self

We are the hollow men
we are the stuffed men
leaning together
headpiece filled with straw, alas.

Our dried voices, when
we whisper together
are quiet and meaningless
as wind in the dry grass
or rats' feet over broken glass
in our dry cellar.

The eyes are not here
There are no eyes here
in this valley of dying stars
in this hollow valley
this broken jaw of our lost kingdoms.

This is the way the world ends
This is the way the world ends
This is the way the world ends
not with a bang but a whimper.

—T. S. Eliot

8

Self in Mass Society: Against Zurcher

Self and Society

The study and theory of self has not developed much in American sociology since the work of Cooley, Mead, and, in more recent times, Erving Goffman. As the indices of personal and social disorganization continue to increase—and as the contributions of social psychology in the West continue to be irrelevant to the development of a competent self system in a decent society—it becomes more urgent to reexamine the state of social psychology, identify its failings, and move toward more adequate theories of self and society. A society moving toward more fragmented and predatory forms of self needs this self-knowledge more than it needs an army, automobiles, nuclear energy, and Monday-night football.

The writings of Louis Zurcher (1977) provide the opportunity for such a critique of Western social psychology. Zurcher provides us with an effort to make visible a model of self he sees as appropriate to the times. He locates himself within the framework of contemporary work in the field and aligns his model with the writings of the more popular and engaging theorists in the field. Zurcher relies upon and departs from the writings of David Riesman, Philip Slater, Charles Reich, Robert Lifton, Victor Ferkiss, Abraham Maslow, Alvin Toffler, and many others.

In that Zurcher has offered what he believes to be a metapsychology for modern society and in that he anchors himself within every liberal camp existing, it is particularly useful to critique his work. In as much as Zurcher does not mention the Critical School, structural Marxism, Adam Schaff, Mihailo Markovic, Jurgen Habermas, Wilhelm Reich, Mao, Herbert Marcuse, or Fidel Castro, he provides the opportunity to construct a clear dialectic in opposition to bourgeois models of self. Zurcher has committed himself to the notion of a mutable self as a solution to the problem of alienation, while radical social psychology, oriented to the writings of Marx, offers a strategy of social revolution as the appropriate approach to the question of alienation.

Zurcher says that alienation can be repaired within the structure of class and elitist society (pp. 215, 218, 237). Radical social psychology states that these structures must themselves be eliminated before a competent self system is possible. Zurcher is excessively voluntaristic. In his world, people may choose what kind of self to create and present (this expository case is found on pages 185–219). In the Marxist analysis of the alienated self, action, will, and choice are variables subverted by the structures of domination (Schroyer, 1973). The dynamics of the state, the labor market, the retail system, the credit system, the structures of racism and gender privilege, the heavy hand of bureaucrats in school, church, and shop—all bespeak an array of power not weighed in such liberal view.

In capitalist society, as in other class-based, elitist societies, the means to produce self are limited by the means of material production as well as by the modes of distribution. In capitalist societies, the huge inequalities in economic, physical, social, and even moral power are deployed against those who would challenge the boss, the professor, the priest, the police, or the banker.

The Dialectics of Self

For Zurcher, the crucial dialectic for a competent self system is one between modes of being: mode A, B, C, or D. For critical social psychology, however, I suggest the more relevant dialectic is between modes of social organization: between capitalist and democratically organized socialist societies.

Zurcher has reduced the question of human emancipation to a question of choice between jogging, working, reflecting on one's fate or meditating— modes A, B, C, and D respectively. For the Marxist, the question of human emancipation is oriented to the reunifications of production and distribution, of self and society, and of subjective and objective knowledge—topics that Zurcher does not address.

Topics such as praxis, distributive justice, mystification, objectification, coercion, monopoly, authority, power, false consciousness, and class conflict are not within the problematics of Zurcher's search for a competent self. The central problematic for Zurcher is a self system appropriate to a changing world apart from the direction of that change (p. 35).

In particular, Zurcher advocates a self able to move easily between four modes of being and able to integrate those four modes (p. 35).

The central thesis of this chapter is that Zurcher's model of self is just that model of self appropriate to a mass, depersonalized society in which the structure of bureaucracy is the central organizing institution and in which the interest of bourgeois freedom permits the continued appropriation of social labor to the benefit of class elites.

Zurcher provides just the theory and model of self that fits any massified society and therefore has an implicit political dimension. At the same time, Zurcher attempts to depoliticize social psychology and to lift the question of human emancipation from the shape and structure of the larger society. Zurcher performs the remarkable feat of stripping social psychology of its sociology.

It is against this model of self and against the effort to consider questions of self apart from those of the larger society that this chapter is directed. It is against Zurcher's concept of the self, against his use of the concept of alienation, and against his mutable self that this chapter stands.

In place of the mutable self we offer the praxical model of self. Against Zurcher's notion of alienation-as-feeling we assert that alienation involves concrete social relations. Against Zurcher's view of social change as a given with a mutable self adapting to it, we insist that social revolution is the central problematic and political struggle central to it. The better question is—What kind of social change?

Against Zurcher's running (p. 211), stock-brokering (p. 211), and Za-Zen meditation (p. 212) we offer resistance, rebellion, and revolution. Against Zurcher's four modes of being, we offer the five moments of praxis identified by Crocker (1976) and Markovic (1974) as central to the self structure of an authentically social person. Against mass society and its inevitable companions—crime, depression, exploitation, demeaning welfare, and family violence—we offer a struggle toward democratic socialist society. Against Zurcher, there is much to oppose and to critique.

Self and Mass Society: The Data

The Zurcher data as well as a number of studies cited by him suggest a shift from B mode responses on the TST toward C mode responses (p. 51). The TST is a twenty-statement test developed by Manford Kuhn at the University of Iowa in which people are asked to respond, up to twenty times, to the question—"Who am I?"

The analytic assumption is that the response pattern reveals the structure of self in that people take themselves as an object in ways that closely mirror their self-structure.

A mode replies focus on the body in time and space;

B modes reflect social relationships;

C mode responses are oriented to personal style; and

D mode reports are detached from either physical or behavioral attributes. Responses with abstract referents are coded D.

While the data are probably valid—the hundreds of TSTs administered by my students confirm the shift thesis—the interpretation of those data is politically loaded.

Zurcher's interpretation is that people are moving from B to C mode self concepts because the social structure is unacceptable or unstable (or perceived as such). The C mode self definition represents a self that tended to be more situation-free (p. 58). C-mode persons are more fluid, able to accommodate change, tolerant, open to new experiences, and reflective (p. 59). There is another interpretation.

Perhaps people are not deserting a social order that is unstable or in a "state of confusion." Perhaps the social order is more stable but less suitable as a structural basis for self system. Perhaps the four cornerstones of the self system—family, work, school, and church—no longer present a structural basis for a self system. Perhaps the individual is not "stepping back" from the social order but rather a permanent and stable self system is no longer possible in a short-take society. Episodic contacts of short duration with anonymous persons with interest inimical to one's own is not a fertile soil for stable social identity.

It may well be that large-scale organizations are better organized than ever—goodness knows they hire hundreds of experts in management science, industrial psychology, and time study. It may well be that the *way* in which society is organized is more the problem than the anomie alleged to mark contemporary life at work, play, church, school, and market.

If so, the political consequences are significant. In Zurcher's formula, the solution is a self capable of surviving such divorcement from social institutions. In opposition to Zurcher, this interpretation requires a social revolution from one kind of stability to another: from an alienating, suffocating stability toward a liberating, emancipating, solidifying stability.

My interpretation of the data (1972) is that the social order in capitalist society, or any managerial society, no longer serves as an adequate basis for the self structure. The instrumental rationality of profit, growth, and control of the social environment that guides the modern corporation renders an interest in a strong and competent self redundant. In fact, a weak and adaptable self, easily shaped to the new roles, fashions, and demands of monopoly capital is preferable.

Zurcher sees the confused individual abandoning a social order becoming more unstable. I see the social order abandoning the individual while the social order thrives.

Work and Self

The world of work is a central anchorage point for the self system across human history. In the past four centuries, especially the last fifty years, there have been profound structural changes in the institutions of work. Agriculture, which until lately provided a stable behavioral framework over all the centuries of pain we have seen, has become a giant corporation using capital-intensive means of production. Farmers are redundant.

Industrial production has undergone great change as well—in the pursuit of stability rather than away from it. Capitalists have moved their production from northern towns where wages were inadequate to southern states where wages are lower. The profit picture improved. Capitalists have moved many lines of production to Third World countries where labor conditions are "favorable" and where neofascist regimes guarantee stability (Chomsky and Herman, 1979). Capitalists involved in the production of apparel, shoes, watches, cars, television sets, computers, and food stuffs have abandoned the United States for countries with low wages. Capitalist flight is hostile to a linkage between self and society for those who want to work.

In the work setting itself, an instrumentally rationalized productive process rejects the self system as the primary mediator of behavior. Persons are not expected to organize their own behavior using a permanent occupational social identity as the mediator of any given line of activity. Instead, the worker sells his/her labor power and is required to use the order, the directive, the instruction from a supervisor as the mediator of behavior. The supervisor has effective control of workers' behavior (Braverman, 1974).

For a worker to stand on his/her rights as a competent person and mediate the boss's command violates the control rationality of a division of labor that gives a monopoly to management over the behavior of the employed worker. Imagine what would happen to an employee at Lockheed who protested openly, morally, against overcharging for military goods. Imagine what would happen to an employee at Dupont who suggested dropping napalm from the sales catalog. Imagine what would happen to an employee at Hooker Chemical who refused to dump tons of toxic chemicals into the Niagara waterway. The use of a morally informed self system to shape the production plans of profit-oriented companies would be economic suicide and most employees understand that as they understand the logics of profit itself.

Business colleges at Harvard, Michigan, Stanford, and Ohio State are busy producing managers who have "better" administrative schemes. The modern industry has little interest in a competent self system. It is interested in hydraulic systems, assembly systems, computer systems, accounting systems, electrical systems, and legal systems—not self systems.

The modern university follows mindlessly the interests of capitalist economics. The retail industry selects, uses, and discards employees even as the retail corporation expands. Fast food stores use thousands of young people who develop no permanent relationship to their place of employment. It is good business practice to avoid commitment to people: workers and customers alike.

The corporation has title to the social position upon which social identity rests, it discards people as they become unprofitable (Young, 1979). Braverman (1974) also reports how the world of work has been degraded for lower- and middle-echelon employees as considerations of profit shape the white-collar world. Ward's and General Motors have adopted a policy of using part-time employees and overtime to avoid permanent commitment to people. The modern university offers the same terms of employment for its faculty. Labor costs are reduced by hiring part-time people who become part-time, fragmentary selves in their world of work.

The industrial, business, financial, educational, and religious institutions have increasingly moved to the bureaucratic format as a mode of social organization. Both employees and clients are better controlled—and better discarded—within bureaucracy than with smaller, more intimate work systems. In our society the primary structure mediating human behavior has shifted from self to bureaucracy.

The competent, morally directed self-directing, self-organizing, self-motivating, self system is enemy to the bureaucratic-administrative echelon. It is precisely the structural features of the bureaucracy in particular and the formal organization in general that produces a mass society. It is the processes of self anchorage that disappear in mass society; not the formal organization and certainly not social organization.

As human behavior became "rationalized" in schools, shops, factories, offices, and churches, the control of behavior shifted to a managerial cadre and away from the self as a mediator of situated behavior. As the need for profit and control continue, the self system is an obstacle. Depth psychology, behavioral modification, electronic monitoring, enlarged police forces, and cash incentives come to supplement the administrative order as the mediator of behavior in mass society.

Millions of persons are surplus to the productive process as the quest for profit encourages high technology, high energy, and capital-intensive production. Millions more become surplus as markets are lost to socialist liberation movements as well as to German and Japanese competition. Millions more become surplus as capital moves to the Third World. And millions more are surplus as welfare rolls are trimmed and war on poverty programs discontinued. These persons cannot report socially anchored self attributes since they have none. They are deserted by capitalism and even by family and church.

Americans are turning to new sources of self (Young, 1972) to replace those short, episodic interactional encounters that mark social contact in mass education, mass sports, mass market, mass medicine, mass politics, and mass industry and business. Some of those identities are adequate and some less adequate.

The zodiac, Eastern religion—especially Buddhism which posits the self as the source of alienation—pop movements in psychology, personal attributes, animals, features of nature, and, very importantly, ethnic identities previously discarded are embraced once again by fourth- and fifth-generation Americans as the stuff out of which self is made and made known. It is now less shameful to be Black, Jewish, Polish, Italian, or Chicano than just thirty years ago.

The important thing to note is that the structural basis for self that is eroded—not social institutions that are evaporating or people turning away from the social order as Zurcher holds. A person could not have a self-system with a strong, permanent set of social identities anchored in work, play, school, church, and family even if s/he wanted such a self.

One does have A, C, and D modes for self structure. One can emphasize muscle, thigh, and breast as the defining character of one's persona. What is difficult and transitory in a massified society is to rely on "B" mode identities as the center of self. One can deploy clothing, car, or cosmetics as the essence of one's being. There are deviant identities available. One can identify with the cosmos, the universe, or the ineffable, but these have little behavioral meaning. A mass society is hostile to self as well as to the human process. The adjustments proposed by Zurcher are pathetically inadequate.

Alienation and Mass Society

Zurcher properly identifies social change as his problematic and erroneously pushes the mutable self as the solution. The central problematic remains that identified by Marx. It is not that people are dropping out and doping up as much as it is that people are alienated from the process by which a human being is constituted. Some turn away from so much sorrow; some turn on to less painful worlds. The problem is not social change per se but rather the use and discarding of people for profit. That problem would remain even if social change ended this moment or if everyone had a mutable self.

Knowledge Processes and Self

Central to the process by which people become human is the unification of subjective and objective knowledge (Applebaum and Chotiner, 1979). By this is meant that the acting subject knows the "truth" of the physical and social world to the extent that person participates insightfully in producing material and social reality. The acting individual must be the subject as well as the object of the productive process else knowledge is diminished.

The student must be acting subject of her/his own education rather than the object of another's purpose else the educational experience is alienating. The same is true for work, religion, and medicine.

A division of labor in which one echelon has effective control over subjective purpose while others can only act as objects of another's will constitutes alienation from the knowledge process. Yet this is precisely the format of mass education, mass medicine, mass industry, and mass sports. Without participation, the individual lives in a world s/he never made: lonely, mystified and anxious.

Others and Self

All social self theory is based on the assumption that self is constituted in the process of acting, of others responding to one and one's appraisal of the response of others. In mass society, it is not the individual who is the object of interest but rather the mass undifferentiated except in terms of profit or interest group. The very assumptions of Mead, Cooley, Blumer, and the symbolic interaction camp about how social reality occurs and continues are rendered false by the condition of interaction in mass society. It is an irony that, as persons become individuals apart from the social base, they come to be absorbed in a faceless bloc.

Unless others routinely take the individual into account and respond to him/her in validating ways, the individual, the individuating process does not occur. For mass sports, mass socialization, mass education, mass production, as well as mass medicine the individuating process cannot occur. Persons cannot take themselves as the subject of their own actions since the routines of the bureaucracy require standardized routines applied impersonally to the flow of persons through the system and since persons are often treated en bloc rather than individually.

This bloc treatment is "rational" in terms of the sad rationality of profit and efficiency but it defeats the process by which a stable, competent self emerges capable of mediating behavior across a wide variety of social occasions. If the individuating process does not occur in the context of adoption of a socially esteemed social identity, self and society are no longer twin-born and both deteriorate to the savage world of privatized survival. The technology of control required to solve the problem of order in such a society distorts all political, scientific, and therapeutic processes.

In such a society, politics, science, and medicine take a frightful path that leads to the new sciences of technological fascism.

Technofascism

Technofascism involves behavior modification, various forms of "chemotherapy," psychoelectronics, psychotherapy, guidance and "counseling," secret policing systems, wiretapping, electronic surveillance, and a wide variety of prisons, group "homes," and halfway houses controlled by the state.

These directions in fascism are justified in terms of the deterioration of behavior unmediated by a self system oriented around a fairly permanent social identity anchored in a network of productive social relations.

Fascism is the price one pays for a mass society—where profit and class advantage, bureaucratic authority, and mass processing take priority in the social allocation of resources and where retributive justice displaces distributive systems of justice.

Praxis in the *B* Mode

It does not suffice to the human project that one is able to shift between *A, B, C,* and *D* modes of self as Zurcher suggests. The *B* mode must be central if self and society are to emerge in dialectic relationship. However, not just any *B* mode is adequate. The social identities central to the self systems must be of a particular kind. They must be socially honored, they must be adult in terms of having full rights to participate in the construction of forms of social reality and in the forms of culture. They must be productive in terms of socially necessary goods and services.

To hold, as does Zurcher, that the mutable self is fully adequate as the basis for human behavior within military societies, class structure societies, or societies oriented to change, however senseless that change, bespeaks a fine indifference to the social context of self development. The self process is distorted in a wide variety of societies Zurcher accepts uncritically.

In class societies, those whose labor is exploited come to have poor self conceptions as they are mystified about the worth of their labor while being and doing. Presumably persons in a slave society need only to jog, meditate, or seek to be the perfect slave as a solution to the problem of self. The women and men who live in a society marked by the degrading gender politics of power and subservience need more than a mutable self to cure their interactional problems.

It is not a mutable self that is the answer to a good and decent society. It is a good and decent inventory of social roles, their associated social identities, supportive social relations, as well as a socialization process able to inculcate those social identities into the self system. Beyond this is the necessity that those social identities be used by the individual to mediate behavior and that the presentation of a productive social identity be honored in the course of everyday life. The growth of self requires the affirmations of self.

Time and the Man

The use of a stockbroker named "James Tempus" as an example of the mutable self underscores the uncritical character of Zurcher's effort to solve the existential problem of being in class society. A stockbroker is not a productive worker. S/he does not add value to the resources found in nature. A stockbroker is an instrument by which the wealth produced by the social power of workers is extracted by an unproductive social elite. The stockbroker contributes to all the problems that destroy the self process for lower-echelon workers and/or the surplus population in class-structured mass societies.

That Zurcher cannot make that connection does not obviate that connection. The chief function of the new middle class is to manage a variety of problems of capitalism ranging from the realization of profit to the management of alienated students, workers, and many sectors of the surplus population. The existential solution to the problem of self is to establish a social anchorage for self as well as the material resources for the self process of those sectors; not to manage that disoriented behavior after capitalism has excluded people from productive labor and from the cultural process.

Praxis and Socialist Models of Self

In opposition to the mutable self, critical social psychology is oriented around praxis and a socialist model of selfhood. Markovic (1974:64–69) has abstracted five moments of praxis central to a competent self system in an authentically socialist society. It is not required that one shift from one mode to another as Zurcher urges but rather that one incorporates all five moments in the same activity. It is not that one abandon one's social identity (*B* mode) as Zurcher recommends but rather that all praxis moments orient and constrain the embodiment of all social identities as they become situationally relevant.

Praxis behavior centers around *sociality* as its primal moment. In work and in other productive activity, people who are oriented to sociality are careful that their activity enrich the lives of others and contribute to the socially necessary production of goods and services. In contrast, in alienated labor there is only concern for wages and personal security. In capitalist society, what one produces is irrelevant as long as one has a job.

Sociality precludes the use of one's human abilities to produce harmful goods, dangerous drugs, ecological poisons, or cater to false needs. In capitalist societies, work is oriented to profit motives and encourages such insult to health, economy, and environment.

In praxis, *self-realization* is a second essential moment. It is that activity in which one realizes the full wealth of one's best potential. Self-realization fulfills the self in that one takes great pleasure in one's own activity however much energy, time, and effort is involved. Self-realization stands in contrast to motivational schemes that program behavior by external rewards: bonuses, prizes, rewards, wages, positive reinforcement, or the manifold forms of sanction and coercion.

Self-realization without sociality results in the soliptic behavior endemic in a privatized society. Men who use their wives as a homemaker while at university and then discard them to take a younger woman; women who abandon family to "find and realize" themselves; children who take from their parents only to leave them to the tender mercies of a cheap-jack welfare state; corporations which demand loyalty and dedication only to fire employees a few years before pension rights are vested—all these forms of self-realization are only too visible in this society, the America of the 1990s. It is this rough beast, lumbering toward Bethlehem now to be born of which William Butler Yeats warned.

Self-realization in conjunction with sociality means that all production and use of material culture be oriented to the affirmation of social relations. The privatized exploitation of sex, food, sports, drugs, and leisure is precluded by this conjunction with sociality. The privatized use of political office, bureau, religious office, of the trust invested in the honorable calling of teaching—all these permit and require self-realization but without the moment of sociality, humans are as balloons, "guileless oval soul-animals, taking up space, moving and rubbing on each other; drifting on silken invisible air currents," as Sylvia Plath put it.

Praxis is *rational* when people move progressively away from a world in which they are subjected to the blind forces in nature and in alienated society. Rationality in conjunction with the two previous moments requires collective knowledge and control of the means of survival. This conjunction precludes the thin rationality of bureaucratic control; precludes a division of labor in which the "top" echelon claims the right to establish rules and procedures to which students, workers, customers, prisoners, soldiers, and welfare recipients are blindly subjected.

Rationality as a moment of praxis requires a healthy public sphere in which positive knowledge of social structure and function is available, trends are publicly known, and goals and the means to satisfy them are collectively selected. Sociality precludes the selection of goals that benefit only rich or powerful sectors of a population or are harmful to health and nature.

Sociality precludes the selection of means, however efficacious, that transfer the costs of goal attainment to some sectors of the population—women, workers, and/or minority groups. Sociality precludes the crafty conniving of the Madison Avenue huckster, the cynical use of women by men, or the systematic exploitation of Blacks in South Africa by American firms. Sociality precludes the use of military simulations by the Pentagon or CIA as they engineer wars, invasions, coups, or blockades apart from public discussion and debate.

Praxis, as a socialist mode of human activity, unites intention and behavior, thought and action, theory and method. This moment, *intentionality,* is essential to the dialectics of subjectivity and objectivity. One must be part of the process by which goals are set and means adopted or one has lost subjectivity. One must be able to realize one's intentions and this implies optimal distribution of material resources as well as egalitarian access to the micro- and macro-politics of one's society.

Intentionality monopolized by authority or by office reduces people to objects. However desirable this objectification might be from the perspective of owners, managers, bosses, and social engineers, it is hostile to the human condition and precluded in authentically socialist models of self and society.

Intentionality must be dialectically related to the intentionality of others if the moment of sociality is to be respected. For the children of the rich to be able to travel anywhere, buy anything, experience anything does not answer to the moment of sociality—to do as they please; this ability does not advance the human project. For the general to be able to command thousands of soldiers into battle does not answer to the moment of intentionality. For the professor to give brilliant lectures oriented to a single-minded interest does not answer to the human condition if students are not also inspired by the topic.

Children of the lower classes also need the experience of overseas travel, the ability to purchase decent clothing, access to books, concerts, and plays in London or Bombay. Soldiers, those who are about to die, need do more than salute their senators: They must be able to question them. Students need do more than learn the content of a lecture; they must have some part in requesting it.

A fifth moment of praxis is that of *creativity*. Creativity restores history to the human enterprise. It demands that every new occasion be collectively organized to suit the special conditions of nature, persons, resources, and society at that time. Sameness, routine, standardization, repetition, and mass processing are precluded at the moment of creativity.

Every act of love, of child care, of teaching, of playing music, of games and sports, must be imbued with creativity. Each child, student, audience, and lover must be honored as a separate individual with a separate history. Advice for each legal client, each medical patient, each student must be hand-crafted to the constellation of circumstances in which each is found.

Each act of love, every act of child care, every lecture, every song, every game must be tailored to the personality and preferences of the lover, the child, the student, the audience, or the player—and this requires creativity.

Sameness, repetition, and routine may be appropriate in processes without history or in which history is two-dimensional--as with chemistry, physics, and mechanical engineering. However, for human beings and human society, history is variable and in its variation is found the possibility for creativity.

Creativity is constrained by the moments of sociality as well as the other moments of praxis. This constraint precludes creativity in designing poison gases, in designing instruments of torture or nuclear terror, and in pursuing scientific means of circumventing the self system.

To summarize, a socialist model of self incorporates a set of social identities oriented to productive work. These social identities mediate behavior and are the primary means of social control. The five moments of praxis permeate and constrain the range of social identities permitted and the embodiment of any given social identity in any concrete setting. All social identities are embedded in a praxis society.

Praxis Society

Such a model of self requires a specific kind of society. It cannot be a class society, a mass society, or a society that transfers alienation to other societies or to sectors of its own population. Socialist society is not comprised of formal organizations processing masses of faceless persons through the routines of the day. Such a society may have state ownership of the means of production of material, ideological, and political culture but it is not a praxis society and thus not authentically a socialist society—however useful and progressive it might be in certain historical periods.

Nor are the dramaturgical maneuvers of the trickster, the gamester, the salesperson, the public relations, or the advertising specialist natural to a praxis society. Only when the moments of praxis are possible for every human being on a routine basis will it be possible for a given society to claim for itself the title of socialist society.

There is much to do and many social transformations to come before a socialist society is possible. That does not preclude specific individuals from creative and progressive praxis in capitalist or bureaucratic socialist nations but it does make such work difficult. It is to the eternal credit of the human species that people can, once in a while, transcend particular nonpraxis social arrangements and move toward social revolution.

The task of social revolution is not the mutable self of a stockbroker; it is not the creation of a self system oriented to change per se. It is not jogging, meditating, or acts of petty criticism. Social revolution requires the elimination of those structural features of a society that obstruct and distort the self process. Social revolution requires the replacement of elitist modes of production and distribution with socialist modes.

The human process requires that each person have access to the material basis with which to sustain life, to the social basis with which to create social life, and to the cultural basis with which to enrich social life. These are possible. Class, racist, sexist, feudal, and elitist societies reduce those possibilities. Efforts to justify stratified societies, to promote reform of stratified societies, or efforts, such as those of Zurcher, to put forward false solutions to the problem of alienation impede social revolution and are to be opposed.

An Adequate Self System Requires An Adequate Society

The material bases for a strong and competent self system is a socialist society infused with the sort of Marxist humanism discussed so forcefully by Schaff (1970). An exploitive, crime-ridden society eternally in economic crisis and using war as a way to win markets and minds is scarcely the grounding for a good and decent self system. Zurcher fails to the extent he forgets to link the fate of self to that of the society in which one must manage.

In his book, the linkage between self and society is tenuous indeed. Zurcher has considerable talent and a commendable grasp of the literature. I would like to see him use that talent to better purpose. My suggestion is that he—and others who pursue his mission—read Schroyer, Ollman, Schaff, Habermas, Markovic, and others in the critical school. Then I would like to see his books and articles. As long as Zurcher stays within the literature of liberal capitalism, he will fail in what clearly are well-meant efforts.

Clarence Lee

Clarence Lee from Tennessee
loved the commercials on TV.
He watched with wide believing eyes
and bought everything it advertises . . .
    cream to make his skin feel better
    spray to make his hair look wetter
    bleach to make his white things whiter
    stylish jeans that fit much tighter
    toothpaste for his cavities
    powder for his doggie's fleas
    purple mouthwash for his breath
    deodorant to stop his sweath
He bought each cereal they presented,
bought each game that they invented.

So you see that money buys
anything for which one sighs:
so watch TV and buy from liars
anything your heart desires.

        —started by Shel Silverstein
          —ended by me.

9

Self-Estrangement in
Dramaturgical Society*

Well, if it's dancing you would be
There's better pipes than poetry.
Ale, man, ale's the stuff to drink
for fellows whom it hurts to think.

Look into the pewter pot
and see the world as it is not.
Pints and quarts of Ludlow beer
Then the world is not so queer.

In a lovely muck, you've lain
Happy til you woke again.
And malt does more than Milton can
to justify the world to man.

   —*adapted from A. E. Housman*

These contributions to dramaturgical sociology have emphasized the addition of a macroanalytic perspective and the necessity of more closely aligning dramaturgical analyses with the critical tradition in social psychology. In this chapter as in others, the attempt is to constitute a critical dramaturgy that adds to the more academic dramaturgy of Goffman and his followers in that it seeks to uncover and transform the unauthentic, alienative, and exploitive practices of the dramaturgical society. The fundamental issue of an alienated use of dramaturgy remains the false, fraudulent, and engineered separation of objective and subjective reality.

---

*An early draft of this article was coauthored by John Welsh, who remains an important source of ideas and critique in it.

The central question in this chapter is self-estrangement. One part of this problem is found in the dynamics that separate self from society; the other half is in the dynamics that lead the individual to distance him/herself from the social roles each embody. Most of the chapters in this book speak to the factors that tend to rend the individual from the social base of the society in which s/he is born. Yet from another point of view, individuals have good reason to use dramaturgy to communicate a distaste, a lack of enthusiasm, a repugnance for the things they do.

The Mutilated Self

The dramaturgical apprehension of self, with the work of Goffman as its exemplar, is based on the sociology of George Herbert Mead, yet it is a marked departure from the traditional sociological notion of self. Mead conceived of the self as the ongoing product of social interaction but he also conceived of it as the pretest for social action.

Using the dramatic metaphor, Lyman and Scott (1975:104) have suggested that the self, as viewed by Mead, is a playwright, a director, an actor, a cast of players, an audience, and a critic. The self is a playwright in that it determines its capacities and needs and attempts to establish the plot of an ensuing scene. The self is a director in that it rehearses a scene in the "theatre of the mind" before it is externalized as a social performance.

The self is an actor since it imaginatively performs in the prefigured scene with the imagined performance of the other actors in the scene. The self is also a cast of players since it acts out all the roles of all the other players in the scene, which is usually discussed in terms of Mead's idea of the internal conversation of the two characters, the "I" and the "me." As audience, the self watches the scene and as critic it evaluates the scene, judging the efficacy, morality, and potential of what transpires. Given a certain level of satisfaction with what is likely to happen, the self then sets out to perform in the external "theatre of reality."

Mead's view of the self thus entails a theater of the mind in that the person possesses the ability to determine a course of action and to act it out. In no way does this negate his view that the self is an outcome of social interaction. Instead, the Meadian view is that the self is a dialectical process that emerges out of the interaction between individual and society, subjective and objective reality. In Mead's view, the self is a pretest that unfolds in the theater of reality and eventually coincides with the text of the external theater.

Mead's social psychology is, of course, more involved and complex than the brief presentation paraphrased from Lyman and Scott. However, enough has been said to establish the departures from this traditional model of self that the dramaturgical apprehension poses, especially as it has been presented by Goffman (1959).

The fundamental difference between the symbolic interaction of Mead and that of Goffman is that "in Goffman's dramaturgy, the ultimate aim of the naturalistic dramas played out in the theater of reality is to uncover the hidden drama, and the real actors, in the secret theater of the mind" (Lyman and Scott 1975:107).

Lacking in Mead is sensitivity to the estrangement between mind in the "theater of the mind" and the social self as it is later played in the "theater of reality." Lacking in Lyman and Scott is a sensitivity to the social sources—the economic advantages—of such estrangement.

In Goffman's social psychology there is a difference between the essential self and the presented self, and it is the presented self that becomes the object of social response in dramaturgical society; the essential self becomes subordinated to the presented self. It is clear in Goffman's sociology of the self, that the only self that can be discussed is that which is publicly known, that which is overtly acted out in the audience of others.

In Mead's "theater of the mind," the essential self, which includes the person's intentionality and consciousness, is less relevant and must be made subordinate to the so-called theater of reality. What is important is not whether Goffman is an apologist for this view of self, but the human consequences of this form of the self in the dramaturgical society.

Those who are caught up in a social role in which the theatre of reality is hostile to the human project is, at some level of awareness, rendered shameful by the things that are done by self and partners. The shabbiness of such a drama is not lost on the actors themselves. There are a thousand small ways by which the agonizing actor can let others know of the bitter taste exploitation and manipulation leave in the mouth. There are a hundred hollow-sounding justifications that one can use to narcotize one's conscience. There are many doors left open in most social occasions through which one can depart as soon as possible to more human and humane endeavor. But until then, one must show it counts, that one is not committed to such a social encounter as a moral agent.

The self, in the alienated use of dramaturgy, ultimately requires that the inner reality of the person be estranged from the outer reality of the external theater. However, the estrangement of the self in dramaturgical society implies other assaults against a competent, nonalienated self that must be noted.

First, Goffman recognized in the dramaturgical society that it is possible for actors to deliberately stage the images or impressions the audience receives. Once the estrangement of these two theaters is made, the question of whether these staged impressions are authentic is not really important in the sociology of fraud because authenticity is a moot issue. What matters is only whether the presentations are creditable. In our dramaturgical society, the person is reduced to a mask. To mask means to disguise and to disguise means to mystify.

The dramaturgical society, in its alienated form, depends on mystification and the control of consciousness, whether the actor happens to be an individual, a corporation, or the state.

The second implication is important to self-estrangement and best summed up by Goffman himself. The self presented and the self taken is not the private self that dwells within the self system of the individual actor. That private self, known only to the actor, does not emerge out of symbolic interaction in public. At the same time, the staged self does not help create the reality, it is merely an illusion used by the private self to engineer compliance of a customer, a voter, a worker, or a client:

> While this image is entertained concerning the individual, so that a self is imputed to him, this self itself does not derive from its possessor, but from the whole scene of his action. . . . A correctly staged and performed scene leads the audience to impute a self to a performed character, but this imputation—this self—is a product of a scene that comes of, and is not a cause of it (Goffman 1959:252).

This viewpoint, and the reality of the dramaturgical society, is merely Descartes' "Cogito ergo sum" turned inside out: You think, therefore I am. Those who live in the Hollywoods of the world must deal with this false image on a daily basis. Sometimes it becomes so painful, so remote from anything that the Hollwoodized individuals feel, think, do, or are that they engage in self-destructive behavior. Their message is: "I want to be more than or different from what it is that you are thinking. I want to be more than the image of an esteemed person; I want to have some content that answers to the publicly projected image; I want the image to answer to the inner self."

Men have a very difficult time living up to the macho role assigned by a patriarchal society. They die emotionally, mentally, and physically in the effort to unite self and self-image. Some become hostile and violent to men who reject the image. Some reject the image and don other, more alienating masks. Some find a niche in society in which they can live in peace with women and in mutual respect and support.

But those who do not reflect upon the magnitude of the distance between the word and the deed live in a twilight world, a mysterious world, a Kafkaesque world of bluff and doubt. Estrangement is a complex response to such impossible worlds where the scripts contain heroes, fools, charlatans, and frauds. It is healthy enough to walk away from such theatre of reality.

The Negation of Self in Everyday Life

Nowhere is the alienation and dehumanization of the dramaturgical society more evident than in the phenomenon of role distance. Role distance (Goffman, 1961b:85–152) refers to the widespread phenomenon of individuals giving off impressions that they are not really part of the social occasion at hand. People distance themselves from the role they are playing with a wink, a nod, or a grimace. They make it clear to others present that they feel the occasion alienating but will not, dare not challenge it.

In the classroom, one student will roll his/her eyes at something the professor will say; in the clinic a nurse will shrug his/her shoulders to convey to a doctor comtempt for a mother whose baby is ill; at the high school dance, a popular boy will make a face while dancing with an unpopular girl to convince his watching friends that he is not "really" there as a serious partner to the girl—thus does the use of role distance betray the social occasion while protecting the inner self from social control or social consequence for that betrayal.

Role distance is a pretheoretical form of rebellion and resistance to alienated education, work, class relations, or sexuality. Role distance is a technique one can adopt to present oneself to others situationally present while inwardly retaining, hiding from public view, another, more cynical, less social self. There are any number of conditions in which a person would deliberately estrange self from society.

A first example here would be a woman who is wary of the traditional subordination of the feminine role but who gets married and acts out the traditional role on the objective level, in view of her husband, while subjectively retaining the self-affirmation that "this is not me; I am only acting this way; whatever I am, it is something other than my overtly submissive act." It is understandable why a woman might behave in the invidious sense of acting if the husband were a tyrant and the wife did not have the resources to oppose or leave the marriage.

Emanicipatory Dramaturgy

Although the dynamics of the cinema are often exaggerated and the events are overly dramatized, still the Robin Williams movie, *Dead Poets Society* offers a case in point by which the self is estranged from the "theater of the mind."

The action of the movie is placed in an elite prep school for boys and focuses on the experiences of four of these young men as they come of age in a dramaturgical society. The official routines of the school are oriented to preparation for one of the Ivy League colleges. The unofficial routines are well calculated to subordinate the variable interests of the students to the interests of career in a class society. The drama of this conflict is located in the new English teacher, Mr. Keating, the role played by Robin Williams.

In delightfully creative ways, Keating captures the interest of the young men in poetry and awakens them to their own moral agency. For good or for evil, all must sometime take responsibility for their own lives; they must demand of their friends, parents and teachers to be allowed to live before they die.

In one such creative encounter with poetry, Keating has one of the class read the introduction to poetry written by the editor of the book. The author's thesis is that one can rate a poem on a graph whose X axis is style and whose Y axis is importance of the topic. In a thoroughly postmodern exercise, Keating instructs the students to rip out the introduction—there can be no standard tests of good poetry. Poetry has too many dimensions, too many nuances, too many meanings to too many ages to be thus weighed, judged, ranked, and filed. Such a scene recapitulates the criticisms of Raymond Williams, Jesus College, Cambridge and F. R. Leavis, also Cambridge over the orthodoxy of prose and poetry, one that excluded Donne in favor of Milton. It was Donne who wrote:

> Language thou art too narrow, and too weake
>   to ease us now; great sorrow cannot speake;

If, rich as it is, language cannot capture the human experience, still less can one graph poetry, as weak as it is, in an alegebraic formula. Numbers crack and break under the strain.

The story line embodies the conflict between parental ambitions for youngsters and these youngsters' own emerging interests in the person of Neil, a lively and engaging young man who would prefer to be a poet and an actor to a premed student. His parents think otherwise. As usual, the father is made the heavy in the story with the mother a passive if unwilling partner in this subordination of the spirit.

After meeting Keating in class, seven of the boys resurrect the Dead Poets Society and meet in a cave to smoke, read poetry, and come into manhood. Harmless enough in its own right, the society comes to be the engine of rebellion against the discipline of the school. One of the seven writes an editorial demanding that women be admitted to the school and, incidentally, invokes the name of the society. Another learns that poetry will win women away from the star football player. All of them catch a poetic vision of life from Keating.

When Neil, the chief organizer of the Dead Poets Society, wins a role in a play as Puck, his father objects and demands that Neil drop the part. Neil is advised by Keating to talk to his father, tell him of his passion for acting and, thereby, expand his own dimensions. Neil tries and fails. He dissembles to Keating and plays the part with joy and verve. His father finds him out and enters the theatre to take Neil home. Neil is told that his parents are removing him from the prep school and sending him to a military school— where, presumably, Neil will learn some discipline. Neil uses his father's revolver to kill himself.

Keating is blamed for the tragedy and fired summarily. The social nexus of the school and the society it serves is preserved; the boys learn to subordinate their inner voice to conformity and success by betraying Keating to school authorities. Thus is the inner self estranged from the public self. The emotional costs of such estrangement for each young man are rendered visible by this, the most enlivening of dramaturgy.

In the denouement, the other young men in the class stand up in tribute to Keating as he comes to collect his personal belongings. Against the demands of the headmaster of the school to be seated, about half of the poetry class stand to show Keating, with their body language, that they know that there is another viewpoint to the official version of the suicide. It is a version in which Keating is the chief engineer of the forces of life, while the teachers and parents are engineers of narrow but important career lines endangered by a teacher who opens up Yeats, Housman, Whitman, Herrick, Shakespeare, and other dead poets to the boys. Keating nods his appreciation and departs. That is the end of the story.

As with all good drama, there are moral choices to be made and good reason to make any one of several of them. Parents know what the real world is like; dead poets tend to divert young men and women from such an alienated life. Audiences applauded the cinema in an unusual tribute to the excellence of that drama.

For our purpose here, the cinema captures the process by which each young man learns to separate an inner self from an officially presented self. Each of the six survivors is required to sign the official version that casts Keating as the satanic agent—or be expelled. Five of them sign, the sixth is expelled. Four of the five are among those who stand up in support of Keating as the play ends. As with Galileo, when forced to his knees by the Catholic church in a recantation of his observation that the earth circled the sun, Galileo muttered "still it turns." In similar fashion, the young men preserved their integrity by standing to say, "Still I am one with the truth I know."

While the play pivots around Neil, it also pivots around Anderson, his roommate. Anderson's parents render him voiceless but Keating helps him find a voice in which to speak. That voice is, of course, a poetic voice. Anderson leads the tribute in the final scene of the movie. His resistance and rebellion stands against the suicide of Neil. Thus there is both a sad and a happy ending to the movie—a rare and rapt event.

Other widely viewed movies and televised dramas offer insight into the dynamics of self-estrangement: "Masterpiece Theatre" dramatized a play by Vita Sackville-West, with the curious title *All Passion Spent,* in which a certain Lady Slane gave all the usual performances for eighty-five years: wife, hostess, patroness of the arts, mother, member of the nobility, and consort to Ambassador Slane. When the ambassador died, Lady Slane took command of her own presentments: she purchased a small house and took on a series of friends for themselves. She departed the artifices of decent society much to the dismay of her older children. When she died, her friends were there but her family was not. At some point, we all must ask whether we want to wait eighty-five years to reunite the private and the public performances we give.

There are those who live in a simple world where image and reality have some close correspondence—and then find themselves in a more mirrored world. That person may seek to assert some independence from the role. When management of a corporation promotes a worker to its administrative echelon there is a problem of the conflict between the old and the new presentments of self. The ex-worker who has left the status and solidarity of her/his fellows may come to feel uncomfortable with both management and with workers. Such a person may try to demonstrate on the objective level that nothing has really changed, that s/he is still the same person.

Subjective feelings belie the presentation as the new manager realizes that the new status and role sever the solidarity and demand that managerial and exploitive behavior replace the former human, reciprocal behavior of an equal. The new manager cannot change the logics of the labor process but can put forward an image of role distance when superiors are not around to see it. The new manager tries to have both: the pay and power of office together with the warmth and support of solidarity. S/he remains the class enemy in spite of small-scale efforts at rebellion.

A recent movie juggled modes of self-estrangement and role distancing in comedic plot. In *Big Business,* two sisters—putative twins—inherit a company. The Bette Midler character feigned unification with her public presentments when in the bucolic world of Hometown, Indiana. In New York, she loved the stage managing and role playing—self and society were twin-born in the latter setting but were estranged in the former. The reverse was dramatized by the Lily Tomlin character. For her, self and society were twin-born in Indiana but were divorced in New York. To be sure, the Lily Tomlin worldview prevails and all ends well—or does it?

Role distance may be resorted to as an attempt to present to others a self that has complete mastery over the role the person is performing. The coolness of a surgeon who tells jokes during a delicate operation tends to present a self to the audience of assistants that will inform them that all is under control and they can be at ease. In the final analysis, the doctor may be indifferent to the fate of the patient as long as the cases keep coming to help fund a portfolio or to finance a mistress but for public display, a visible effort to keep a team focused yet relaxed is good business.

Chevy Chase has played a series of roles in which the protagonist projected a competent, masterful self-image—only to be undone by the simplest task: walking downstairs, mixing a drink, or finding a criminal. This ploy is reversed in some cinema exploring self-estrangement. The Columbo character played by Peter Falk feigned simplicity in order to disarm and entrap a felon.

Role distance may be a way to protect one's career, material interests, and family obligations and yet salvage some slight measure of self-esteem by presenting the "happy consciousness" of the cheerful robot while on the job with work superiors as the audience.

A number of examples exist here but consider the case of a lower-level functionary in a corporation or a university who has a family to feed, shelter, and clothe. The overwhelming power of market relations, the work organization, and its managerial elite may intimidate the person to the extent that self-integrity may be sacrificed on the objective level so that the person and family can continue to survive in a material sense. On returning home at night, the functionary inveighs against this self-estrangement but goes to work at several levels of being the next morning.

In his discussion of "Role Distance and Serious Activity," Goffman's attempt (1959) is to establish that role distance can emerge out of the lack of challenge a task offers the person, and that people often mock their own activity by presenting the foolish dimensions of that activity by "fooling around." Goffmans' exploration of role distance in *Encounters* is also inadequate. He does present a brief paragraph on role distance and subordinate-superordinate relations. He has only three sentences on this very significant issue, the most penetrating of which is: "Sullenness, muttering, irony, joking and sarcasm may allow one to show something of oneself lies outside the role within whose jurisdiction the moment occurs" (1961b:131). That is the end of the analysis about the stratification of power in such relationships.

The Possibilities of Being

While the distance between what one thinks and feels, on the one hand, and what one says and does in the drama of social life, on the other, can never be eliminated, still it is possible to be one with oneself in one's performances. Children often say things in all innocence that an adult might withhold. People often say things in a pique of anger that, otherwise, they might not. In warm and loving friendships, there is little praxical discontinuity between feelings, thoughts, and expressed meanings. Big men are often quite open—they do not expect harmful consequences to result from what they say. Such a person is comfortable enough in his own skin to be honest. Elderly women are often forthright in their observations and judgments. The list continues.

These examples are not trivial, however rare. They are testimony to the possibility of the unification of self and social identity; to the desirability of self and society being twinborn. It is possible, in a praxis society, for such unity to be expanded beyond the opportunities found in stratified social formations. Such unification requires power. In the analysis that follows, one must read me carefully. In the use of the concept of power, I do not render it in its ordinary sense of power-over-others. I insist that power can be distributed broadly in a society, in an institution, and in a relationship. It is the inequities of power that help engineer the divorcement of self from public presentment, not power itself.

Power and Being

There are four kinds of power used in every-day politics that we can think about. When there is access to each kind of power, the distance between the publicly presented self and the self that writes and rehearses a script is minimal. One can be as one with one's self.

- Moral power.
- Social power.
- Economic power.
- Physical power.

Moral power is the power we have from sharing the basic *values* of a society. Everyone has moral power—it is the most democratic and the least susceptible to alienation. Moral power is based on the mores of a society. When we see someone violating those mores, we can call them to account.

We can shame people who are older, bigger, richer, or better educated when they violate standards for decent behavior—unless we live in a shameless society.

It is important to remember that moral power can be quite harmful to the human project. In racist, sexist, or authoritarian society, much crime is informed by the mores of a society. The lynching of blacks in the South, the beatings of women in Anglo marriages, the prostitution of children in Denver, Seattle and San Diego are all informed by moral reasoning—if one believes in racial superiority, male dominance, or market sex.

Social power is the power each of us has to control the actions, the thinking, and the feelings of someone with whom we have a social relationship. When we come together to build a social occasion, we have the power to influence the way each other thinks, feels, and behaves. This mutual ability to influence each other is social power.

Social relationships and social occasions cannot be built unless people try to adjust their ways of thinking, feeling, and acting to each other. Social power arises from undistorted symbolic interaction. We learn to respond the same way as others respond to significant symbols in our socialization in family, church, and play. Words, gestures, and activities are the repositories of social power.

Social power is often stratified in order to give some people advantages over others. It is a very important form of power in explaining both legitimate and illegal behavior. Discrimination strips women and minorities of social power and is, thus, a crime against the human process.

We respond to social power when we acknowledge the influence friends have to get us to do things that are helpful or things that are harmful to our full humanity.

Marcuse speaks of the right to say No! to friends or to the state when asked to do immoral things as "the Great Refusal."

Economic power is of course, the power of the dollar. In a society stratified by wealth and one in which material possession is important to the definition of personal worth, economic power can override both moral power and social power.

Economic power is very important in capitalist societies for several reasons.

1. Many essential resources have been *commodified.*

   When essential goods and services are commodified, it gives power to those who own them. Economic power often trumps moral power, and

social power and buys physical power when people need such goods and services. Money can prostitute every cherished relationship in a society in which personal worth is judged in terms of material possessions.
2. When people are without jobs or other sources of income, they may have to give up social and moral power to get resources.
3. Corporations can use economic power to buy up competitors and thereby form monopolies with which they can fix prices.
4. Organized crime leaders can buy politicians and their social power with money. Thus economic power can be converted to social power in public life.
5. Economic power can be used to restore balance in social power relationships. Women who work are much less likely to be subjected to violence in the home. Single women with children in the ghettos command economic power: welfare checks, food stamps, housing allotments—these give them status with men and neighbors.

Physical power. Physical power is the use of clubs, fists, guns, and bombs. It is power that people use to enforce their own will over others when moral or social power is not available.

Young men who are socialized to be macho often use physical power when they don't have social or economic power with which to express this alienated sexuality.

Physical power stripped of moral or social power informs much street crime, political crime, and more than a little organized crime. Physical power has to be used when human rights are violated—since most people refuse to comply unless there is a threat of force.

As with moral power, physical power cannot readily be alienated from people. However, women are taught early on not to develop or use muscles in resisting men or rebelling against alienated gender politics. Children, students, members of formal church groups, and others are required to sit quietly for long hours while others move, act, think, and decide.

In defining a praxis society, the forms of power above must be rearranged to eliminate the subjugation of one's own judgment and standards to those of more powerful others. In such rearrangement, the dialectics of selfhood are rearranged. The distorted dialectics of guise and guile are replaced by the more balanced dialectics of honesty and compassion. The potential of dramaturgy to renew the human process is thereby made larger. The potential of control and its shadow, falsity, thereby made small. If we wish to end the estrangement of self from its author, we must consider how power is produced and distributed in a society.

A situation in which the person must put on a happy face before a superordinate in order to keep a job and feed a family is certainly familiar and the role distancing behavior expressed is certainly understandable. However, an adequate sociological method also includes a discussion of the larger social conditions that contribute to the dehumanization of persons.

The critical approach to dramaturgy helps people question the legitimacy of social relations that provide the stage for the estrangement of self from role. If social relations demand that people sacrifice their integrity—even the authorship of their behavior—on the objective level, In what sense can the vital interconnection between self and society be said to exist? Role distance can be interpreted as evidence that the vital interconnections between self and society is severed with exploitative social relations or when powerful others are given all prerogatives to control behavior on the objective level.

There is a similarity between role distance as an adaptive strategy to oppressive external conditions and Marx's phenomenology of religion. Marx (1978:131) noted that religion was an expression of protest, though inverted, against the real material conditions of capitalist society. Role distance can be interpreted as an inverted protest against the real, material conditions of dramaturgical society. Goffman does not raise the possibililty that role distance may be the "sigh of the oppressed creature or the heart of a heartless situation."

As with religion, role distance is an opium of the people as it will enable them to be free of oppressive external conditions only within a subjective inner space and not on the objective level. Such an understanding of role distance leads us to consider other possibilities, other social relations, and, more dangerously, the means to revolutionize self and society.

It is also valuable to draw from Marx's (1964:110–12) theory of alienation a deeper insight into the dehumanizing nature of role distance. Recall from the *Economic and Philosophic Manuscripts of 1844* that Marx discussed, as one form of alienation in capitalist society, the estrangement of the worker from his/her act of production. Marx reasoned that since work in capitalist society is, for the worker, primarily a means of survival, the motivation for the activity has nothing in common with its objective content. Neither means of production nor the product belong to the worker. Consequently, the worker's activity does not belong to the self but to another.

As in the Marxist view of alienation, a critical view of role distance emphasizes that one's objective activity does not belong to the actor but to the audience. The lower-level functionary does not behave overtly as s/he covertly feels but estranges the two for the benefit of the external audience.

The dialectics of praxis are lost; the dialectics of self and society are lost in this form of dramaturgy.

The actor may benefit in some way from the degradation of the sacrifice of integrity or the estrangement of self and role. This moral adjustment is a mistake only to the extent that rebellion, resistance, and the revolutionary overthrow of the oppressive social relations exist as realistic alternatives for the person. For most people, oppressive social relations are a fact of life that offers a devil's choice (A. E. Housman):

> Be still, be still, my soul;
> it is but for a season:
> Let us endure the hour
> and see injustice done.

> We, of a certainty, are not the first
> have sat in taverns while the tempest hurled
> our hopeful plans to emptiness, and cursed
> whatever Brute or Blackguard made the world

The negation of self is scarcely a theoretically informed way to respond to the negation of praxis in the world of work. The task becomes, for the critical dramaturgist, to make the revolution possible and the negation of the negation congenial to the human condition.

Role distance represents a form of the unauthentic performance of roles in that the person employing role-distancing techniques presents an appearance of the role as the other expects or compels it to be performed. The role is performed "as it should be" from the standpoint of the other, but not from the standpoint of the actor. Intentionality, self-determination, as well as sociality are lost as moments of praxis in such a use of role distance.

Self-determination, a vital element of praxis, no longer exists as the person expressing distance between self and role does not claim them as her/his own. The person who acts cynically attempts to convince self and others that s/he is not the author of the act. Intentionality is lost since the act is not freely chosen by self, but is the result of the external conditions, the demands of the audience.

Role distance is a form of bad faith in that it results in a claim that the act does not belong to self. The atrocities committed by a Lt. Calley and Nazi functionaries are excused by appealing to role distance and the social situation producing it. ("It is not my fault; I was only obeying orders; I had no choice; I had to do these things since we were at war; if it had been me,

I would never have done such a thing.'') Such are the self-serving explanations of role distance in everyday life.

The organization man/woman who recognizes the destructive nature of a corporate product but who goes along with the system and work superiors for the privatized gains of career, salary, and promotions is not acting as an authentic person but has reduced self to an externally directed object and helps to reproduce the perfidious outcomes of such social relations. The social, human imperative for the person is that whatever benefits may accrue from the self-mutilation, the estrangement of self form role is not worth it.

If one no longer authors one's own activity, if one deliberately mutilates self for material gain, then one loses self agency and exists only at the level of an animal—a comfortable one, perhaps, but an animal nevertheless. For the person who is mutilated as such, questions of self-realization may become altogether irrelevant and the person will seek further escape from the onslaughts through drugs, religion, alcohol, soap operas, privatized sex, jogging, or any number of anodynes to psychic pain.

In confronting alienated dramaturgy in role distance there remains a clear-cut distinction between three ways in which actors can orient themselves toward repressive, alienative role requirements.

1. Actors can automatically and uncritically adapt to external conditions. In this case, the person will take on, subjectively, the reified identity that is externally imposed. One can be immersed in such a false presentation of self and earn the contempt of one's coworkers.
2. Actors can adopt the technique of role distance, retaining their subjective integrity while overtly conforming to repressive role requirements.
3. People may respond to repressive, alienating roles with modes of resistance.

The best examples of the latter are when the person attempts openly and critically to change and reinterpret the role requirements: those who attempt to band with others to build up alternative social life-worlds. This often means that one becomes part of an underground structure of resistance and rebellion.

Social workers often systematically violate bureaucratic rules in the effort to get food, clothing, health care, and medicine to their clients. Teachers often act with mercy rather than rational calculation when they find students cheating or experimenting with drugs. Workers sabotage superiors who too enthusiastically enforce the rules of bureau or factory.

These emancipatory examples are effective protests against the alienation in dramaturgical society as they affirm that actors can transcend their roles sincerely and authentically. This possibility is degraded by the dramaturgi-cal ideologists who attempt to maintain that the sincere actor is one who is "engulfed by the role" or "taken in by one's own act." To be sincere in an insincere world is to an imbecile.

From the critical standpoint, sincerity and authenticity are not to be den-igrated but encouraged as it is only with the sincere performance of roles that the wedge of power between the objective and subjective worlds can be removed. With the sincere orientation to role performance the actor acts "authentically." The role becomes a free and genuine expression of the self on an objective level. But before one praises sincerity, one must help trans-form the objective conditions that betray those who are sincere to those who are not.

Those who do perform roles authentically contribute in a very real way to the overthrow of oppressive social formations. Even in a racist, sexist, exploitive social-life work, open and energetic commitment to alienating roles helps demystify—and thus provides the grounds for critical, trans-forming analysis and, perhaps social change. Being a good Nazi or a good bureaucrat becomes increasingly appalling for those at the bottom of the stratification system. When a critical number of lower-level functionaries and the surplus population begin to present the "unhappy consciousness" rather than the cheerful robot routine, the society will be forced to change to a more humane form.

It is when the powerful can no longer rely on the internal shackles of their minions that the continuation of their power is tenuous. The flight of Marcos and Papa Doc Duvalier came at the same moment as those around them began to reunite subjective states and objective embodiments of comtempt and disgust. As we realize the effects of that moral vacuum that has come to be labeled "the Reagan era," we may see the teflon crumble and the image fade. History and insiders will not deal kindly with the Reagan era.

Praxis and Revolution

Praxis results in the reunification of the objective and subjective worlds. As such, the concept of praxis is the opposite of the alienation offered by the mutable self and role distance. Marx conceived of authentic human ac-tivity as being the unification of thought and action, of theory and practice, of self and society.

In his "Thesis on Feuerbach" (1972) Marx excoriated both the material-ists for their one-sided reduction of human activity to the unreflective re-sponse of external stimuli and the idealists for their one-sided reduction of human activity to thought that is never realized in overt, concrete action.

I have presented an overview of the moments of praxis in chapter 8. For our purposes here, praxis is a complex activity whereby persons in interaction create society and culture and constitute themselves as human beings. Praxis behavior centers around sociality as its primal moment. We have seen the privatism of dramaturgical society as illustrated in the phenomena of the mutable self and role distance. We have also seen the destructiveness of privatism for self and other.

In work, people who are oriented to sociality are careful that their activity enrich the lives of others and contribute to the socially necessary production of goods and services. In other human activity, people who are oriented to sociality are careful that their communications about self and the external environment are free and undistorted. Praxis establishes intersubjectivity and warm and supportive links with other humans. In dramaturgical mass society what is materially produced and symbolically communicated is irrelevant as long as it results in profit and political control.

Sociality precludes the use of one's abilities to produce harmful goods, dangerous goods, ecological poisons, or to create and cater to false needs. Sociality precludes to use of symbols to manipulate and control the information and consciousness of others. In a fraudulent dramaturgy, activity and interaction are oriented toward profit and manipulation, and encourage such insult to self, society, and environment.

Self-realization is a second essential moment of praxis. It is that activity in which one realizes the full wealth of one's potential. Self-realization is opposed to a mutable self which insists that the self change to suit the external situation, and to role distance, which insists that there need be no connection between the self and objective activity.

Self-realization requires a *transsituational self*. Such a self presents the same values, fidelities, and faces of self across all encounters. Mediated by concretely existing economic, political, or economic factors, the transsituational self brings to bear those values, those fidelities and embodies a line of behavior and affect that expresses the dialectics of a well-tempered life. One is faithful to one's self and, as Polonius put it,

To thine own self be true
and it follows as surely
as the night doth follow the day
that thou cans't then be false
to no man.

—Shakespeare, *Hamlet*

Persons are coerced into adopting self-effacing and self-denigrating strategies to survive in stratified and massified society. If they fail to give off impressions of enthusiasm and energy, if they fail to give the expected deference pattern, if they fail to wear the public mask of compliance, they are subject to a wide variety of sanctions including psychiatric labeling and therapy.

A fully human, social, and participatory model—that is, authentically socialist—of self is oriented toward activity that affirms, not destroys, mind, self, society, and their interconnections. Such a model of self and role requires a specific kind of society.

Praxis Society

A praxis society cannot be a class society, a mass society, or a society that transfers alienation to women, minorities, or other sectors of its own population or other societies. A society can claim for itself the title of socialist when these moments of praxis are possible for each human being in coordinated and democratically organized self-managed work groups.

Social revolution requires the elimination of those structural features of a society that obstruct, distort, or negate the self and falsify role performance. The human process requires that each person have access to the material basis with which to sustain life, the social basis with which to form social relations, and the symbolic basis with which to create self and culture.

A society in which role distance and a fraudulent self are adopted by individuals as means for survival is not a rational nor a decent society. It cannot be a society that is adequate for the grounding of a stable and competent self system. It is not a society to which individuals owe any loyalty. It is a society that depends on the mutilation, objectification, and alienation of individuals and, as such, it is an infectious, stultifying cancer deserving nothing but an expedient death and a quick burial.

With the demise of the counterfeit community of the dramaturgical society, with adequate theory and research, with a strong democracy of the sort Bernard Barber speaks, a more human and rational social formation will emerge and once again permit the unification of self and society in mutually ennobling modes.

The Man with the Hoe

> Bowed with the weight of centuries he leans
> upon his hoe and gazes at the ground,
> the emptiness of ages in his face,
> and on his back the burden of the world.

Who made him dead to rapture and despair,
a thing that grieves not and that never hopes,
stolid and stunned, a brother to the ox?

Who loosened and let down this brutal jaw?
Whose was the hand that slanted back the brow?
Whose the breath that blew out the light within his brain?

Is this the thing the Lord God made and gave
to trace the stars and search the heavens for power;
to feel the passing of eternity?

Is this the dream He dreamed who shaped the suns
and marked their ways upon the ancient deep?

O masters, lords and rulers in all lands,
is this the handiwork you give to God,
the monstrous thing distorted and soul quenched?

O masters, lords and rulers in all lands,
how will the Future reckon with this man?

How answer his brute question in the hour
when whirlwind of rebellion shake the shore?

How will it be with kingdoms and with kings;
with those who shaped him to the thing he is;
when this dumb terror shall rise to judge the world,
after the silence of the centuries?

—Edwin Markham

Before the War, the World was illusory,
Romantic Idolatry dominated Politics.
In place of illusion, we now have the idea
of revolution—not only in life,
but also on stage, above all on stage.

—*Felix Siege, German theatre critic in the 1920s*

Part IV

Politics in the Dramaturgical Society

Introduction

The Drama of False Politics

Infused in this analysis of the development and dialectics of self and society in a dramaturgical society has been an abiding interest in the forms of power and the ways that power relations are structured. Most of this analysis has been, so far, more concerned with the micropolitics of everyday life that bend, twist, circumvent, and negate the dialectics between individuals and more powerful others. I have emphasized the ways in which economic, social, moral, and physical power are used to manage women, minorities, workers, consumers, and citizens in societies stratified in such a way as to give an elite great advantage in shaping the behavior of masses of individuals, taken one at a time.

While the micropolitics of everyday life in bureaucratic offices, shops, schools, factories, prisons, hospitals, and banks is most important to a postmodern social psychology, macropolitics also limits and distorts the social self. In the effort to contribute to a postmodern morality that finds patterns between the authoritarian states of bureaucratic socialism and the false freedoms of predatory capitalism, emancipatory social psychology must fit the drama of politics into its analytic schemes. This section will enlarge the scope of dramaturgical analysis to consider the use of drama in the macropolitics of the state and the multinational corporation.

It is at all levels of politics that the critical dramaturgical perspective offers the greatest possibilities for emancipatory insight, change, and renewal in the twenty-first century. For a praxis self to emerge, the great imbalances in economic power marked by the stratification of wealth must be moderated. The sharp discontinuities in social power emerging from gender and racial politics must be smoothed. The systematic co-option of moral power in religion, science, work, and marketplace needs review and

191

reconstruction. Recourse to physical power in war, crime, rape, and work disputes needs alteration.

As we move into the twenty-first century, social psychology can add its weight to the glacial movement toward social justice by a wide-ranging study of the way in which the drama of social life is used to reproduce such inelegant power arrangements—or it can contribute by exploring the ways in which emancipatory drama empowers and enables specific human beings to come into the fullness of their morality. As the technology of information production and distribution develop, a dramaturgical social psychology can help create a knowledge process that makes visible the intricate web of power, the varying scales of power distribution, the great inequalities of power, as well as the many tools with which power is concentrated and deployed against the human project.

The sociology of politics is concerned with the social location, the forms and uses as well as the legitimization of political power. How power is socially distributed, used, and legitimated often depends upon a variety of factors, one of which is the ability of the powerful to utilize the means of communication to generate the loyalty of the mass of citizens. Thus, politics inevitably involves drama of some form.

However, the uses of drama become problematic since they are relative to the particular type of society. From a critical perspective, the problem of generating support and loyalty is intensified in those societies that have class divisions, gender oppression, racial exploitation, and a maldistribution of power.

Under such circumstances political dramaturgy tends to become oriented toward the fraudulent generation of political loyalty. As the problems of poverty, pollution, crime, and health care, of disemployment and poverty become internationalized, electronics and the media are used to fashion political consciousness that becomes frozen at the level of the nation-state. A false patriotism sets a nation-state against another in the war for markets, jobs, raw materials, and military power.

In the age of the megalithic multinational corporation that has budgets in the billions of dollars, the capacity to buy the political process, to buy the technologies of human consciousness, to stage the dramaturgical impression of benign economics—all these are possible; all these permeate the knowledge process and bend it to the interests of those ever-growing corporate conglomerates. Dramaturgy is captured to the unholy politics of corporate purpose.

False Enemies

Republicans and Democrats in the United States court the multinational corporation (MNC) mirroring the political process in Italy, France, England, Brazil, and Korea. MNCs move jobs and factories about the globe as nation-states compete with one another. MNCs dump billions of tons of waste into the air, land, and waters of the world as the nation-state invites them in to do so. MNCs decide in which lines of production they will invest, leaving the nation-state to provide low-profit goods and services as well as to deal with the fiscal crisis that comes with such a one-sided economic system.

Yet in the frozen political consciousness of national chauvinism, it is the nation-state that is seen to be the class enemy to all other nation-states. In the magic of an alienated mass media news analysis, it is the Socialist bloc that is seen to be the class enemy. In the afterglow of the golden age of capitalism, the poor and disemployed in the Third World are seen to be the class enemy by the once prosperous workers of the Northern nations. Everywhere the MNC sets the terms of political discourse by its economic power to buy the political process directly through campaign contributions and indirectly through $100 billion advertising industry.

False Politics

In every capitalist country—rich and poor alike—the technologies of drama and theatre replace the boots and clubs of the storm trooper in suppressing dissent and critical thought. Madison Avenue firms spread around the world and provide their dramaturgical services to tyrants, despots, dictators, and liberal presidents alike. Nixon, Reagan, and Bush join Mondale, Carter, and Dukakis in buying the information channels of radio, television, magazines, and newspapers, projecting images of agency, honesty, integrity, and lawfulness.

With such choices, Americans vote quickly and turn back to God and Monday-night football in an existential despair at ever setting things right through the political process. Yet to do good politics is a holy thing; and to do good religion, one must do politics well. The chapters in this section address the issues of how political loyalty is dramaturgically generated as well as the social origins of the fraudulent generation of political loyalty.

Chapter 10 attempts to set forth the conditions under which dramaturgy comes to be used in the sociology of fraud. It lays out the rapid capture of the film and electronics industry by the state and by the private corporation to dramatize and romanticize the uneasy alliance between state and capital. It is a sad story of co-option; a sorry story of artists and scientists on the make; a pathetic story of frozen, twisted politics presented as democratic politics by semi-ignorant newspeople, academics, and actors.

Chapter 11 is a qualitative analysis of the Watergate affair. For those who are too young to remember, the 1972 presidential campaign was subverted by CREEP (Committee to Reelect the President—Richard Milhous Nixon).

Members of CREEP, including the top law enforcement officer in the land, John Mitchell, organized a break-in—a burglary—of the headquarters of the Democratic National Committee in the Watergate building, an upscale apartment and office complex in Washington D.C. The team assigned to the break-in was caught. They lead to several intermediaries who lead to CREEP, which lead to Mitchell, Colson, and other "president's men."

Two reporters on the *Washington Post* were able to break the case with the aid of an insider, "Deep Throat," whose identity remains a secret to this very day. Someone in the Nixon administration did not care for its "dirty tricks." The Watergate Scandal was part of a vast effort on the part of CREEP to engineer the reelection of Nixon by subverting, bribing, compromising, and lying about Democrats. False news reports were released, prostitutes were hired to seduce candidates, phones were wiretapped, offices burglarized for campaign plans, and criminals protected by the White House.

The Nixon team, a product of California, Madison Avenue, and Hollywood, resorted to the tactics of theatre to protect the image of the Republican Party, of the President of the United States, and the inner circle of the White House, members of which engineered the far-reaching and unconstitutional use of political power. They covered up political reality as long as they could with the unreality of staged productions which themselves subverted the public understanding of political life in the United States.

The people will live on.
The learning and blundering people will live on.
They will be tricked and sold and sold again
and go back to the nourishing earth for roothold.
The people so peculiar in renewal and comeback
you can't laugh off their capacity to take it.
The mammoth rests between these cyclonic dramas.

—Carl Sandberg, "The People, Yes"

10

The Political Economy of Dramaturgy

We are the movers
and shakers of the world
forever, it seems.

—*Arthur William Edgar O'Shaunessey*

Modes of Dramaturgical Analysis

There are three general approaches one can take toward dramaturgy, dramaturgical analysis, and the dramaturgical society. Each approach yields valid analyses but each one carries its own politics. It is the third mode of analysis that yields the most fruit for the emancipatory interest in change and renewal.

This chapter presents the political, economic, and physical bases of an alienated dramaturgy at the macrosocietal level to parallel and supplement the microanalytic essay in chapter 8 on the structures of power in mass society.

First, one can simply report the stagings, adjustments, editings, and performances of the "new bourgeoisie" without any great depth of moral concern or any great breadth of structural analysis. Goffman (1959;1961b) does this excellently well. Second, one can locate dramaturgy in the micropolitics of everyday life. Here, Gouldner is much the better analyst in such a use of dramaturgy. Third, one can locate dramaturgy in the macropolitics of the world economic system; this approach to dramaturgical analysis has yet to be done and done well. Some ideas on how to fit dramaturgical politics in this larger macrosociology are offered in this and the following analysis on Nixon and on the Reagan years.

Dramaturgy without Politics

In a wide variety of analyses, Goffman dissects the stagings, posings, posturings, manipulations, and charms of a new generation of salesmen. In these analyses, there is always a bit of calculation in which the actor gauges just how much is to be said, how and to what effect the various forms of language are to be deployed. One is not open, self-disclosing, authentic in joy, pleasure, anguish, or pain; indeed anguish and pain have no place in the staging of friendship, concern, aid, or honest agency. Moral outrage loses customers, clients, prospects, or audience. Self disclosure—except that of false honesty—is closely curbed in the short and superficial encounters of market, office, and lounge.

If one has social or economic power one can be mean-spirited, sullen, or contemptuous of those around one. Employees, wives, service persons, or children can see the human side of the bourgeois personality in all its negativity as well as in its many appealing aspects. Goffman gives us the content and language of dramaturgical analysis but he fails to give us its social logics. He offers us the accouterments of stage and Hollywood with which to understand how social reality is created in a given social formation but he ignores the characteristics of that social formation which encourages, even requires, such a one-dimensional personality.

As sociology was getting more abstract, structural, mathematical, and remote from the day-to-day activities of real, sweating human beings, the dramaturgical analysis of Goffman was a welcome counterpoint. Rehearsal, lines, roles, cues, props, managers, editions and editings, performances, impressions, audiences, effects, backstages, and other components of theatre are employed with telling effect in American sociology in the years following World War II. This is the most depoliticized of the three approaches in that it ignores the social and economic context in which this micropolitics arises. It fails to lay out the political economy of a dramaturgical society.

There is another vital part to dramaturgical analysis that is only dimly visible in the writings of Goffman. The history and sociology of a dramaturgical society are missing. Without a sense of history, one has the impression that Goffman's people are forever. Goffman fails to tell us that his people are historical artifacts that came with capitalist economics and will disappear when wealth and status no longer depend on guiding others into profitable schemes, deals, contracts, and risky or illegal scams. In this first approach, it is as though Madison Avenue and mass advertising were part of nature, eternal and unchanging. And without a sociology, a macrocstructural analysis or the sort provided below, the reader has no sense of the life and logic of dramaturgy.

Morality and Dramaturgy

Gouldner (1970) has provided some of that sociology. He regards the micropolitics of dramaturgy as a moral calamity. He sees this world inhabited by anxious, other-directed, sweating, and ingratiating but cynical souls. Gouldner lays the character structure of this generation of performers in the slightly larger structure of profit-seeking, exchange-oriented financial and mercantile bureaucracies, and he does it superbly well. In the use of dramaturgy as seen by Gouldner, this second view is put forward with considerable passion and convincing indignation. He quotes Rousseau with telling effect: "The art of pleasing masks conflict and exploitation. Perfidious politeness creates unfounded esteem, insincere friendship as well as ill-founded confidence in the appearance of things." (Gouldner, 1970:174).

Gouldner sees that the old tension between utility and morality has been displaced by a false reconciliation between a utility of appearance and a merchandized morality. In this system, rewards are not based on merit of production of real value but in creating the impression of merit. Gouldner locates dramaturgical presentments and a critical dramaturgical analysis in the micropolitics of bureau, office, and market, but Gouldner fails to anchor his analysis in those larger political and economic structures mentioned above, and thus, in the end, becomes a jeremiad screaming in anger at a grotesque world in which the sacred and the profane are juxtaposed without reason.

Macro-Politics of Dramaturgy

There is a third view that adds Marxian theory to both Goffman and Gouldner (Marx 1964; 1972; 1978). As we see it, the creation of surplus value that was the central concern of the old capitalist class has been replaced by a concern on the part of the new capitalist class for the extraction of surplus value.

Only in a mode of production in which automation and datamation provides huge surpluses in the private sector, can such a society develop. In such a political economy, the central question of distribution is not social justice but rather dramaturgical impressions of quality and service projected to a mass, individuated audience.

Capitalism has improved the means of production to the extent that the central problem is how to realize profit from those with discretionary income. Those who have been disconnected from the means of production by this improvement in productivity do not have the resources with which to buy the mountains of goods in the stores, shops, and showrooms of America. Those with minimal wages do not have the resources to purchase much even on credit. Only those in the middle and upper echelons of firms in the monopoly sector—the yuppies—have discretionary income in the amounts worth pursuing with the false dramas of Madison Avenue.

The star, the hero, the celebrity, and the charming advertisement with charming actors help the corporation to extract part of the surplus value at the point of distribution. Whole layers of unproductive people can be nicely supported on this surplus. Were social justice the operative principle for distribution, quite nice systems of health care, child care, education, and recreation as well as quite nice social areas in urban areas could be supported.

Point of Production

Today it is difficult to extract surplus value from workers at the point of production. Unions and the power of collective bargaining can destroy access to markets by strikes and boycotts. Corporations cannot long survive a strike—not because the workers are so well organized that they can live without wages but because foreign competitors are so hungry that they will take markets away in a moment if given the chance. At the same time, capitalists replace workers with machines or with cheaper workers as a way to depoliticize exploitation at the point of production. The history of capitalism is one of the transformation of exploitation centering first on both productive workers and on unorganized consumers but now, with the aid of dramaturgy, focused brightly on consumers.

A Brief History

Capitalism, as a form of production, has gone through three great epochs. First, from the time of the crusaders, to the explorations of da Gama, Columbus, and Cortés, commodity capitalism thrived. Goods from all over the world were funneled into Italy, Spain, France, and England. Empire was built on the trading adventures of people who were a bit less than pirates, a bit more than brave. But dramaturgy served no useful purpose to exploitation there—always excepting the drama of the holy used to pacify and intimidate indigenous peoples.

Generally people in the far corners of the world were only too eager to get the wondrous things from the near corners. They were quick to rob, enslave, and kill each other to acquire the gold and silver, spices and sugar, sex and drugs with which to pay for traders' goods.

The goods themselves were produced by peasants, serfs, women, and slaves, all of whom had little social or moral power with which to negotiate wages or the labor process. Most were happy to get the pennies, pfennings, and stotinki paid for the goods by the trader. Most were paid nothing as husbands, slaveowners, and landed lords extracted surplus value through the microeconomics of home, plantation, and manor.

The second great epoch started in the eighteenth century in a Yorkshire village called Huddersfield (Morris, 1963). There energy, mind, and muscle were linked to machinery to turn out an endless stream of artifacts, textiles, tools, and weapons. The industrial phase of capitalism grew rapidly. Again, the utilitarian character of the manufactured good required little in the way of professional deception with which to attract customers.

On the backs of the working class, at the expense of whole cohorts of children, without concern for the pinched efforts of women to raise those children, feed those workers, and care for the broken and discarded bodies of miners, iron mongers, wrights, smiths, and carters—upon all this misery, tragedy, squalor, and pious unconcern, the great industrial empires were built.

The manufacturing company replaced the family cottage and the feudal manor as the unit of production and distribution. The corporation was developed in the spice and tea trade to accumulate and share wealth while escaping what little legal culpability a thin democracy could assess.

By the end of the nineteenth century, monopolies, cartels, and multinational conglomerates had hurried everywhere, nestled everywhere, claimed ownership everywhere to the wealth—the legacy—of the ages. Mountains of ore, layers of coal, caves of phosphates, lakes of salt, and wide-reaching runs of forests were converted from communal use to private property of companies complete with deeds, letters of credit, securities, stocks, and inventories. The earth was pillaged. The best land was set aside to grow tea, coffee, pepper, banana, cotton, sugar, and other export crops. Staple crops vanished and hunger walked abroad.

Food was shipped from the colonies to feed and clothe the bourgeoisie and their workers. The colonies became poorer and hungrier with each passing century. Wealth became more concentrated at the world level while greatly expanded in some parts of the international capitalist system. Great wars were fought for colonies, markets, and raw materials. The industrial revolution swept the world clean of tribal, feudal, and community bonds. The ancient structures of gender and age were—in a historical moment— dissolved. Marriage and friendship became obstacles to marketing and to private advantage.

The age of finance capitalism began in the warehouses of London as merchants divided up their share of the pepper trade from Ceylon (now Sri Lanka). As the cargoes varied in size and grade of peppercorn, the problem of division of profits was a constant source of bickering and dispute. The solution was shares based on stock ownership of the importing firm rather than on part ownership of cargo itself. The idea of per capita share in all grades, in all ship cargoes, in all warehouse stock began capitalism and the stock exchanges that now dominate the capitalist system. Industrialists and merchants now take a back seat to the finance capitalist.

Today we see the ascendancy of finance capital. Great banking groups come together to entail the assests of industry, the wealth of nations, the heritage of whole peoples. Master Charge and Visa take their 20 percent tithe from every transaction in the free world and many in the socialist. Citicorp, First Chemical, Chase-Manhattan, and The Bank of America skimmed the cream from the industry and entrepreneurial efforts of small and large business alike around the world.

Now Japanese banks displace American banks in gathering the riches of the world with the aid of advertising and global electronics system for the transfer of yen, dollars, shillings, drachmas, francs, and pounds. Joel Grey and Liza Minelli sang their theme in *Cabaret*: Money, Money, Money. Not only does money make the world go around, it makes the world over in its own image. International finance is the God of creation in these days. Television is it temple and drama, its religious ritual.

The World Bank, The International Monetary Fund, and the United States State Department coerce whole countries to pay their loans upon pain of dis-credit. The IMF estimates poor nations owe $1,000 billion at the end of 1988 and interest rates at around 11 percent, with additional fees for rescheduling.

Progressive and repressive governments alike squeeze workers, consumers, and taxpayers to pay the banks. National treasuries are depleted to satisfy the annual report of the financial giants. Military dictatorships hire Chicago economists to teach them the tricks of high finance. A new era is upon us.

In the Third World, dramaturgy is partnered with death squads to control unrest. Advertising is used to generate more and more demand from poorer and poorer debtors. Coercion is used to contain dissent and to control default in the world capitalist system falsely labeled the free world. Mass media and control of radio frequencies become ideological battlegrounds upon which the rich and powerful continue to suck the wealth of the world into bigger and bigger banks.

Neither Goffman nor Gouldner give us an analysis of the political economy of the world in which such uses of dramaturgy arise and are deployed. The sweep of history is lost to social psychology. The political struggles are invisible to the theories and findings of most dramaturgical analysts. This is the lost economics, the lost history of social science. In the United States, we can see part of this world drama played out in marketing, in real estate, in stock brokerage, in political campaigns, and in credit cards. It is harder to see the same dynamics on a world stage.

In the United States as in most of the world, finance capital has elbowed out of center stage its earlier partners—mercantile and industrial capital. They are now surly and sullen members of the ruling classes. Extraction of value is more profitable than creation of it or the selling of it.

General Motors builds cars but the real profit is in GMAC, its credit arm. Sears sells things but credit is more profitable than the tires, batteries, or televisions it sells. Sears pays its employees to push credit while Ward's employees are required to push charge accounts upon pain of firing.

Given the productivity of the greatest economic machine in all history and given the appropriation of this great wealth by a relatively small portion of the world population, there can be an unseemly and degrading scramble for the remaining share apart from merit and apart from need.

In the United States, where less than 1 percent of the population—i.e., fewer than 2 million persons—"own" most of the stocks, bonds, and other securities; where some 8 to 10 million "own" more property than they could ever use personally; in which some 30 to 40 million have considerable discretionary income; and where 30 to 70 million are permanently excluded from adequate relationship to the means of distribution—in such an economy there is a premium on dramaturgy as an essential tool with which corporations accumulate wealth.

Point of Distribution

One cannot use force or monopoly on the yuppies of the world as a way of squeezing profits from them—they are too important to the political process. They are the social base of electoral politics; as long as they vote, they must be managed carefully. Dramaturgy becomes a useful tool in this the latest and perhaps last phase of predatory capitalism.

The middle classes have access to the media. They are the producers, the engineers, the cartoonists, the writers, and the actors who run the media machine. They can use their access to radio, newspapers, video, journal, and magazines to embarrass and discredit corporations, nations, and policies that try to use force or direct economic coercion on them.

Middle-class functionaries belong to voluntary organizations and can organize resistance and rebellions. In order to mine the discretionary income of the middle classes, it is necessary to slip into their psyche and motivate them. Madison Avenue can use their anxieties about identity, sexuality, and solidarity in a society where these are in short supply.

In such a setting, dramaturgy comes to be the tool used to colonize desire. Desire is neatly shifted from humans and the human process to the possession of whatever brings profit.

The traditional values that emphasized productivity of essential goods, of honest value, of enduring quality, of genuine competition, of truth in disclosure—those values are deemphasized with the greater transformations in the means of production. These transformations in turn produce transformations in the structure of self.

All sorts of distortions accrue from alienated use of dramaturgy in the marketplace. Advertisements could, in principle, focus on the technical merits of a product or the social utility but industrial espionage and retail piracy eliminate all but the most trivial differences in design or fashion. The need for interchangeable units in work and home also reduces differences.

Federal laws mandate similarity. Mass production dictates common features of cars and appliances. At the same time social utility does not inform production and distribution except in so far as it is profitable. Children are taught early on to be profligate spenders enticed by charming puppets and appealing pets on Saturday morning television. Standardization, industrial espionage, and overseas branches all combine to eliminate variation in design. Everywhere MacDonald's and Colonel Saunders standardize food tastes. Everywhere General Motors and Nissan market the same car changing only color and trim.

The Micropolitics of Dramaturgy

While the great transformations of capitalism have changed the use and magnitude of dramaturgy in the political economy of the nation-state and the entire world economic system—not excluding the Socialist states—still there are good reasons to use dramaturgy in the sociology of fraud at the microlevels. A full-fledged critical dramaturgy must return to the micropolitics of advanced monopoly capitalism and make visible the dynamics that sustain a fraudulent dramaturgy today.

The changes in the means of production include a great increase in productivity, which means that a goodly percentage of the population are disemployed and thus disconnected from productive labor. More than 90 percent have only their labor power to sell. Each day fewer still can sell it. But these disemployed, marginally employed, and unproductive workers can use the techniques and technology of dramaturgy to wheedle, entice, cajole, and deceive the affluent 30 percent to part with some of that surplus wealth.

The Moral Majority

The affluent either "own" enough claims on profit, rents, or interest to secure their future and that of their children or they have sufficient job security with health insurance, retirement benefits, and supplemental incomes as to have a permanent claim on the economic system. These are, as O'Connor (1974) has said, mostly middle and upper functionaries in the monopoly sector or in the state sector. There are in addition some 2 or 3 million doctors and lawyers who have accumulated real estate, IRAs, mutual stocks, and profitable partnerships that pay off long after retirement.

These people do not have to scurry around and impress others. They do not have to sell themselves. They can be and are the moral minority who can show anger and indignation at a world from which they benefit but find repulsive in politics, market, and the arts. But millions of people on welfare have to feign compliance and agreement with rules written by mean-spirited and control-oriented middle-class males.

Still white-collar crime continues to run strong and fast among this sector of the population—and dramaturgy is a full partner in most kinds of white-collar crime from the dramaturgical enactments of the physician who wants to cut on patients to fill up an investment portfolio to the dramaturgy of advertising commercial touting investments in mutual funds and savings and loan banks.

Demoralization

Millions of employees in the competitive sector daily face bosses, foremen, managers, and customers in construction, shop, restaurant, and store who demand the unauthentic but visible language of body, dress, and voice that creates the demoralized social relations of deference and degradation.

Millions of women learn, as second nature, to act the part of the dependent and "feminine" female. Millions of school children have to feign interest and enthusiasm for dull and lifeless topics under the twin tyranny of parental pressure and job insecurity. Millions of minority people learn that they must dissemble, conceal, mask, and suppress the inchoate anger they experience at the continuing insult to their persona in a society that continues to reproduce racial exploitation, racist conflict, and racial animosity. One must wonder at the kind of society in which the use of language skills develops. Words strain, crack and break under such a heavy burden of deception.

> In order to survive, you have to lie a little, cheat
> a little and hustle your ass a little.
>
> —Paris woman in 1789;
> Chicago woman in 1989

The change in the character of work—increasing specialization and sub-divisions—destroys the value of productive labor oriented to useful goods. Some call this the degradation of work. Whatever neutral or morally laden terms one uses, when one reflects on it, one can see why a lively, creative, and intelligent human being would rather partake of the demimonde of fraud and dramaturgy than work at such a degrading job. Good and lively young people understandably would rather resort to the skills and tactics of the stage in a wide variety of fraudulent performances ranging from real estate, stock market, and auto sales all the way to their illegal cousins involving scams, frauds, and hustle.

Hollywood has given us a series of films portraying the latter sort: Burt Reynolds, Jane Fonda, Jack Nicholson, Dustin Hoffman, Robert Redford, and Paul Newman—all play the generic role of the enterprising hustler who cheats the cheater. As such they are variations on the Robin Hood theme in which the rich and powerful are done in by the smooth and clever. Why they do not play miners, factory hands, migrant farmers, or working women should give one pause.

It is hard to dramatize the routine oppression of bureaucratically organized work. The movie *Nine to Five* (Dolly Parton, Jane Fonda, Lily Tomlin) did manage to use the comedic form to satirize working conditions in a large corporation but such roles are seldom seen created by other box office stars.

Nonproductive Employees

A major change in the structure of the productive process is the growth of layer after layer of nonproductive employees in factory, shop, and store. The need on the part of management to control the labor process—as degrading as it is—requires a whole cadre of middle management on the make. Assigned to the dirty work of spying, tattling, and punishing workers, these middle-management types must adopt the skills of dissembling, feigning, and convincing.

Educated far beyond the purposes to which they are put, these white-collar workers—majors in business administration, personnel, and office management, in law, accounting, production management, and a whole panoply of even more exotic disciplines, these must create a convincing impression that they are doing useful and necessary work—that they are not spies, tattles, and pushers.

Being surplus to the production process they are disemployed for hours, days, and weeks on end until the workers grow sullen, devious, and unruly. At that time they are called in to deploy whatever management skills they enjoy. Between times, they create the dramaturgical facsimile of useful labor. Unable to find much satisfaction in the world of work, they seek status, identity, and meaning for life in compulsive consumption.

The huge surplus accruing to large corporations with product monopoly, regional marketing agreements, price-fixing arrangements, efficient mass production, and mass marketing systems enables owners and top management to insulate themselves from the dirty work of hiring, firing, transferring, and intimidating employees—as in olden days. They also hire useless ranks of middle-management drones to protect themselves from the moral onus of price fixing, regional agreements, advertising deceptions, industrial espionage, factory relocations—while ripping markets, families, and communities asunder in the process.

This diffusion of moral responsibility underwrites a good deal of the complexity and depth of tables of organizations in the modern industrial, financial, and commercial organization—especially in the multinational corporation (MNC) doing the nasty business of transferring wealth from the poorest countries in the world to the richest.

Corporate crime increases as market pressures increase in the world capitalist system. Advertising specialists, market consultants, public relations people, private security forces, whole legions of lawyers, as well as eager politicians are added to the table of organization of MNCs as it becomes necessary to control more and more of the legal environment.

All these sectors of the population are impelled to use dramaturgy in advancing their private, most personal interests in a larger social setting marked by conflict relations. At school, at work, in church, as in sociability occasions, symbolic interaction becomes symbolic counteraction—a war of each against all in the micropolitics of everyday life.

At the macropolitical level of social organization, a parallel dramaturgy arises alienated from the human project and designed to use symbolic media for corporate profit or state purpose. At the second level, the media and the organization of dramaturgy is far different. At the microlevel, the media are voice, body, clothing, and behavior—and the cast of characters limited to the small group. At the macrolevel of sociodrama, the media are the electronic, print, and cinema while the cast of characters assigned to the sociology of fraud run into the thousands—all orchestrated by professional managers in an emerging technofascism of social control.

Physical Bases of Dramaturgy

The change in information technology also has provided the material base for a dramaturgical society. Every major invention in communication since the arrival of photography in 1838 in France has been incorporated into the macrostructures of dramaturgy. The wireless, the telephone, cinematography, television, xerography, the microchip, machine languages, and holography, as well as satellite information flow systems, provide a technology by which masses of unknown others can be turned into audiences for every sort of political or economic purpose under the sun.

Automatic dialing systems using computer-based lists of persons with given economic, political, religious, familial, or age characteristics can convert the telephone from an interactive medium involving known others into a mass-marketing mechanism without the means to check the validity claims of the unknown actors reading carefully edited and preprogrammed scripts. Computer-generated mail together with a subsidized postal system produce millions of tons of junk mail aimed at extracting surplus value from the innocent and the believer via any number of deceptive tactics.

The physical base for dramaturgy today is most fully developed in the 500 major corporations that dominate the world capitalist system. It is they who buy and use the best of these technologies. Only the United States military and government agencies—NSA, NASA, IRS, CIA, and the Pentagon—have better information flow systems than do the private MNCs. The twenty-first century will see a sharp and bitter struggle over this physical equipment between the United States, its six partners in the West, and the private multibillion-dollar transnational corporations. Sooner or later, the nation-state will contest the MNC for electronic hegemony.

The nation-state will, perforce, lose that contest but out of the need to constrain MNCs, a new transnational political system will emerge encompassing both socialist and capitalist states, and we will enter an era of democratic socialism far stronger than now imagined. The physical bases of information will make possible democratic politics and economics at every scale not now imaginable.

Theoretical Basis for Alienated Dramaturgy

It is not that radio, telephony, television, and computer-based systems cannot be put to useful, nonmystifying uses. It is rather that the pressing need for profit or social control weds dramaturgy, deception, and persuasion to this technology. The great dysjuncture that grounds such a use of information technology, of dramaturgy and language, is the separation of production and distribution. To reunite the two sides of the economy, dramaturgy is deployed.

The intrusion of alienated dramaturgy into the marketplace is best understood in terms of the peculiar dysjunction between a prolific system of production and a strangulated system of distribution.

To dispose of surplus production on profitable terms, it is helpful, maybe necessary, to use the technologies of theatre, cinema, psychology, and television to create demand. Demand is artificially constrained by the central working features of capitalist modes of distribution.

Since workers do not make 100 percent of the price of what they (collectively) produce, they can not buy it all back. The shortfall averages the 5-15 percent of profit the capitalist class takes as a commission/royalty for the fact of ownership. Vast amounts of wealth pile up. Neither Goffman, Gouldner, nor many in their tradition adduce features of economics or politics in their analyses.

False Needs and Dramaturgy

In the United States, the solution to the separation of production and distribution for profit is to create layers of false needs within the population sector that does have discretionary income. Commercials on television using a skillful dramaturgy do create such needs to consume.

The best artists, actors, authors, and editors deployed in a multibillion dollar industry preempt the media to this economic purpose. Unfortunately, those with marginal incomes also watch television and commercials and reach for things they do not need at the expense of things they do need. No amount of exhortation by home economists to be careful in buying neutralizes this compulsive buying.

People, conditioned to be fulsome consumers beg, borrow, and steal what they cannot buy. Essential but low-profit lines of production are deserted by the capitalist class. The state takes over the care of the poor, the healing of the sick, the incarceration of the hapless thief. The state loses legitimacy and fiscal deficits grow. These deficits contribute to the political and economic transformations on a global scale in the twenty-first century.

Dramaturgy and Political Legitimacy

The two sides of economic life could be unified by producing for need rather than for profit but that is not the case. The ever-increasing flow of goods stored, stocked, and piled must be sold if profit is to be realized. Since the most profitable market in the United States is the 30 to 40 million with discretionary incomes (young, professional couples detached from clan and soil) earning $40 to $70 thousand between them—private capital orients the economic system to serve their real and false needs. As a result, several distortions enter into the economy.

Family, church, community organizations, child care, apprenticeship and internship positions for teenagers, recreational and medical institutions are not adequately funded since investment is restrained by profit. Wages reduce profits. Some institutions have embarrassing riches; high-profit firms in chemicals, finance, hotel lodging, air travel, as well as the military absorb the wealth of nations. Essential infrastructure needs such as dams, bridges, mass transit, housing, child care, and schools slowly atrophy.

Given such distortions in the economy, those charged with political agency must resort to rhetoric, image, and a false patriotism to gain election and to the crassest kind of pork-barrel politics serving special (and affluent) interests in order to ensure reelection. Thus dramaturgy and paid public relations become part of the democratic process, the point of which is to reduce democracy—to minimize it—to manage the dramaturgical impression of greatness in the political sphere and to subvert authentic representation of those who do bother to vote in such distorted politics.

The needs of family, community, nation, and of the Third World are held hostage to marketing efforts to produce and dispose of high-profit surplus production. Adolescents roam the streets unable to link their emerging enthusiasm and uncertain morality to socially useful labor. They learn to parasitize on friends, family, and merchants in acquisition of the clothes, records, drugs, and cars they are taught to want. Community needs are left to a patchwork privatized voluntarism. Voluntarism is declining. Playgrounds, parks, utilities, services, pollution control, planning, recreational programs, renovation and reconstruction, as well as care for the elderly and those with special needs, are left to the private sectors oriented only to profit or to state welfare oriented to a mean-spirited frugality.

The politics required to contain the legitimate needs of people in cities, states, and nation are ugly indeed. Dramaturgy and technofascism at home as well as with Right-wing dictatorship in client countries, go together in incestuous embrace. How else can one understand a Reagan at home and United States funding to every murderous regime in the Third World? Such a politics is implicit in a profit-oriented economy blind to human or social need and keyed only to private accumulation as the final test for production and distribution.

A productive system that creates more wealth than it employees can absorb must find some way to realize profit. If employees collectively are paid less than the totality of wealth produced, then markets must be found. Employees must be paid less or no profit can be realized. The special solutions to this age include crime, war, and imperialism. Crime renews and satisfies demand. War destroys and renews demand. Foreign markets for luxury goods as well as repeated purchases in the affluent home market absorb surplus production and thus realize profit—but only if other capitalist countries are excluded from home and foreign markets. War, crime, and imperialism require the ugliest politics imaginable.

The history of warfare since 1873 is one of capitalist countries trying to solve the need for markets and raw materials by dominating each other's markets at home and abroad while fighting to see which nation has exclusive rights to minerals and markets abroad.

Warfare, welfare, crime, and now dramaturgy, are economics by other means.

If the modern economy is to keep moving by these twin politics—dramaturgy at home and coercion abroad—there are other institutions that have recourse to dramaturgy as well. These include educational, religious, and medical institutions. Each has its own imperatives for employing a dramaturgy. Some reasons are socially valid; some are pure deceit. We can look at the university to see both kinds of dynamics embodied.

Dramaturgy in Other Institutions

I have been writing as if all the alienated use of dramaturgy were to be found in the political or economic life of a society. The truth is that alienated dramaturgy intrudes into all social institutions. Starting with the university and even into the most holy of human activities, a sociology of fraud is found.

The Drama of College Life

The university resorts to an authentic dramaturgy in sports, in the pomp and circumstance of graduation, in the promotion of medical surgery, or esoteric research. On its own merits this dramaturgy answers to the human interest in creating a sense of the sacred, a sense of awe and mystery, a sense of community and fellowship oriented to the general interest. But the delight, joy, and surprise of dramaturgy in the university may serve to mask a more profound alienation.

To meet the demands of a capitalist mode of production for well-trained, docile workers geared to technical work, the central mission of education is subverted. A school, college, or university, in varying degrees, could constitute a knowledge process undistorted by power, privilege, or profit. In American colleges and universities there is a process by which the critical and transforming self-knowledge of a society is put aside in favor of a mass-produced system oriented to the creation of skills and techniques.

Such an educational system must betray its mission by the profligate discarding of all those students whose sense of life or moral certitude resists such indoctrination into a depoliticized, technicized, and dehumanized educational system. Students from the improverished schools of the American ghetto are discarded by the millions left to roam the streets, exploit a cheapjack welfare system, and find refuge in the growing archipelago of prison gulags around the country.

Students are marched, en masse, through the four years of the university system in the cheapest, most mechanized way possible. Fitted into mass classes, lectured at, relentlessly tested in terms of a monolithic model of truth in marketing, politics, sociology, psychology, and physics and ruthlessly discarded by these testing procedures, students reach for the thin and ephemeral solidarity of sports, alcohol, and commodity sex.

During the recent years of declining enrollment, nearly 1,000 colleges used direct mail to stem further loss of students. Colleges scramble for students. Small liberal arts colleges, church-related colleges, renamed teacher's colleges—all hire "public information officers" to beat the bushes for students whose parents can pay part of the costs of tuition.

Seeking the dramaturgical impression of greatness, universities invest in highly visible public relations gambits. Notre Dame, Alabama, Nebraska, Oklahoma, and North Carolina use the beauty and grandeur of athletic ability from a few dozen young men to mask the degradation of thousands in the learning, knowing, and creating process so central to the authentic university.

Similar analyses can be made for religious, medical, or communications industries. Such movies as *Elmer Gantry, Hospital,* and *Network* resonate the alienated use of dramaturgy in "real" life. As fiction, these movies carry the larger truth made larger in order to be seen and heard. Such are the emancipatory uses of drama in the cinema.

The Drama of The Holy

The American church, sequestered in the corners of social time and social space, stripped of its concern for the spiritual in a land of materialism, larded with bland preachers who preach a careful sermon to their middle-class parishioners, indifferent to the fate of the poor and oriented to minipalaces in the suburbs—the churches fade and fail. In such a moral vacuum, the teleevangelists are an oasis for those who seek haven in a heartless world. Preaching a false justice and a false peace, the teleevangelists use the threat of Hell or the promise of a sweet Jesus to extort money from the 20 or so million who tune them in.

The electronic churches have grown to be a multibillion-dollar industry. They have computer-based mailing lists together with sophisticated software that teases out those who are gullible enough to send for a free offer and honorable enough to want to pay for it. Using these computer-compiled mailing lists, heart-rending appeals are made to save one's soul and the world by sending in an average of seventeen dollars per appeal to the Billies, Jimmies, and Johns of the mass, electronic church. Thus does fraud spread itself into the holy reaches of the ministry. Thus do ministers become hucksters and hucksters, ministers.

The drama of the Holy is central to a praxis society. In a praxis society, all of nature, all of humanity, all of the various cultures of the world must be treated as sacred. In the sequel to this book, I have explored at some length the problematics of post-modern religion. Modern science has destroyed the traditional view of God and the traditional bases for moral action. We have yet to develop a religion and a morality that embodies the best of post-modern understandings.

In our present age, there is a chaotic mixture of exclusionary fundamentalism, solipsism, and nihilism with which to respond to the disenchantment of the Holy by science and technology. The human project for the twenty-first century is to develop a religious sensibility that reenchants all creatures bright and beautiful; that redeems the emptiness of material possession; that sets other tests for status and honor than we now know.

There is much of promise in organized religion, in the philosophy of religion and in the post-modern understanding of science and the world that is important to such a task. This is not the place for its full development but one should understand that drama can be used to reenchant the world and its many forms of life. A post-modern understanding of religion permits this reenchantment without the alienation of gods, devils, heavens, and hells. In Liberation Theology, in the secular humanism of democratic socialism, in the churches of Buddhists, Protestants, Catholics, Jews, and Muslims, there is much to be preserved.

Whatever material resources capitalism has brought the world, still missing are the spiritual resources that unite and sanctify the human adventure. Large pockets of such spiritual resources remain, but the trend is not encouraging. More and more people are disemployed; more and more are victim of political, corporate, organized, and street crime; more and more lack good housing, good food, and good education in a time of plenty. There is much to do in social psychology and in the larger society to meet both material and spiritual needs with reason and constraint before the problems of modern society can be made minimal.

To that task, a repoliticized and humanized dramaturgy has much to offer. In cinema, stage, university, sports, church, and in politics, a healing religion is made real and visible by the drama of magic and make-believe. While these are not the worst of times, we still have yet to build the better time for most people and most societies in the world. We can do better and drama can work to resanctify the forests, oceans, wildlife, and atmosphere that predatory capitalism and crass socialism now degrade.

To that task, a theology of human rights and human obligations of the sort found in the United Nations Declaration of Universal Human Rights must be dramatized. To that task, the fullness and richness of low-crime societies must be dramatized. To that task the joy and energy of compassion and fellowship must be dramatized. An emancipatory dramaturgy is possible in all social institutions, in all cultures of the world in infinite variation. These and more are essential to an emancipatory dramaturgy that sanctifies and makes holy the human process.

The Health Care System

The American hospital system is also subject to monumental structural change by the forces of the market and the quest for profit. For-profit medical companies buy up failing hospitals and turn them into the counterpart of the Hyatt-Regency hotel. They serve the medical and gourmet appetites of the insured middle class and desert the unprofitable health needs of the poor and hungry.

Great chains of hospital franchises are put together. Each chain uses the dramaturgy of heart or liver transplant to create for itself the dramaturgical facsimile of medical science. The great heart surgeons are recruited much as great basketball players or Olympic stars are recruited to the profit needs of such medical corporations. Humana and other such chains compete for the cream of the insurance crop. The motto of such medical corporations becomes: "millions on advertising but not one cent on charity."

Summary

We have seen that there is a larger economy into which to lay the dramaturgical analysis of a Goffman as well as the critique of such analysis by a Gouldner. We can see the historical picture that has developed over the past four centuries in which dramaturgy has been preempted to meet the marketing needs of an economy increasingly geared to capital accumulation.

We see the rise of the MNC with a miltibillion-dollar budget to buy and sell beliefs, natural resources, governments, as well as the various media that comprise and create the knowledge process of a society.

In the West, the various technologies of information flow are developed and harnessed to the special interests of private property in profit, growth, and control of class enemies rather than in the general interest of a well-designed society oriented to community, praxis, and the integrity of the physical environment.

In the Communist bloc, information technology is monopolized to legitimate the failed politics of bureaucratic socialism and to keep an aging bureaucracy in power. Against the interests of the workers of the communist world, dramaturgy is deployed in cinema, radio, stage, politics, education, sports, and economics to falsify and to mystify those workers. State ownership and control of the media is not an improvement over class ownership of the media. It is of some importance who the exploiter is and to what use the surplus value of labor is deployed but, in these times, each system fails in major if different ways to amplify and to sanctify both self and society.

Movable type, the rotating printing press, the wireless and telephony, radio, television, computers, and holography could be assembled into a great national and international communication technology oriented to the collective discussion of pressing human concerns as well as the collective and undistorted creation of social policy with which to deal with these issues. Instead we are treated to an alienating deployment of these technologies using a mystifying dramaturgy and oriented to the creation of false needs in the marketplace, false politics in mass elections, as well as the creation of amoral technical abilities in the university.

It is against this use of technology, of dramaturgy, and of the knowledge process that this work is set forth. We know from history, from the margins and interstices of society, from personal experiences that interactively and informationally rich communications are possible.

We know from personal experience, from history, and from odd moments in religion, politics, and art that an authentic dramaturgy is possible. We know intuitively that a symbolic interactional format in family, friendship, recreation, and work can be constituted in interactively rich as well as with open and sharing information processes. These are possible. These are central to uniquely human labor. These are necessary to undistorted politics.

In East and West alike, control over the knowledge process must be ripped from the hands of the private corporation, the state apparatus, the managers, administrators, and superintendents of the shop and factory, the burgeoning advertising, public relations, and opinion-sampling firms who sell this precious commodity to the highest bidder. The knowledge process in all its dimensions must be put to the collective, the human, to prosocial uses essential to a rational and decent society. This is the political task of a critical dramaturgy, a critical social psychology, and a critical philosophy of knowledge.

11

Critical Dimensions in Dramaturgical Analysis: Watergate as Theater

Some could gaze and not be sick
But I could never learn the trick.

There's this to say for guile and guise
They often bring their own surprise.

—adapted from A. E. Housman

Dramatizing Social Reality

Dramaturgical analysis is an analytic framework dealing with the ways in which social reality is constructed. The major assumption of a depoliticized dramaturgical analysis is that elements from the theatre may be used as metaphor to understand the folk methods whereby social reality is constructed in everyday life. The radical approach rejects the notion of dramaturgy as metaphor and views it as ideology used, in its repressive modes, to construct a fraudulent social-life world.

The utility of the elements of theatre as analytic categories with which to do a qualitative analysis is not in dispute as between conservative and radical practitioners of the art. Costumes, roles, actors, scripts, directors, cues, rehearsals, audiences, performances, impressions given off, props, critics, editings, and dramatic moments serve us well whether we are trying to understand the funeral as theatre or the market as make-believe.

Where radical and conservative analyses do part company is in the question of whether the world of theatre is a convenient heuristic device with which to understand how social reality is constructed by intending human beings—or whether the art, craft, and skill of the artisans from the world of just-pretend are actively engaged in mediating human behavior in the marketplace, polity, welfare, and other institutions. The position advanced here is that metaphor transforms into ideology the moment a dramatist hires out to a manager to shape the behavior and consciousness of human beings in the production of social relationships.

Politics, Ideology, and the Creation of Culture

In the analysis which follows, one feature of the dramaturgical format is especially central to an understanding of the adoption of the theatrical format in the world of politics: The political mass, as a structural feature of theatre, is generated out of a mass society as a solution to the problem of legitimacy in a stratified society. In American politics, dramaturgy is used to create a mass political audience with which to garner political power and marshall political legitimacy.

Structural Sources of Political Dramaturgy

The mass political audience is a logical replacement for the interactive political party since it is a form by which a few political leaders can manage the behavior of the mass of voters as the problem of legitimacy grows. The mass audience is preferable as a mediator of political behavior in that a mass audience is even more passive in the creation of culture (art, music, drama, ideology, policies, science, and literature) than is the traditional political party.

Traditional political parties have several disadvantages: They tend to respond to local needs; they tend to be controlled by local politicians who restrict access to power in order to get advantage for self or client; they tend to make politics messy by presenting conflicting demands on national politicians; and they embody political principles that often get in the way of executive action.

A mass political audience is much less messy. It can be generated on the basis of very few unproblematic causes: patriotism, family values, crime, sexual probity, capital punishment, and God. A wealthy candidate can appeal directly for political power without connections to party or faction; can run for national office without serving time in the ranks and forging the ties so essential to nominations and support.

A mass political audience is composed of disassociated individuals who base their political opinions on privatized advantage extending not much further than the family system. In such a political system, the private viewing in the home suffices to the demands of citizenship. It is the very cheapest price one can pay for citizenship.

In a society where individualism trumps collective needs, such a system answers to the political impulse. Without a good and comprehensive health care system, retirement system, transport system, educational system, or housing programs, prudent persons must think first of themselves. Prudent persons must reduce politics to private advantage and personal issues.

In a society where most major decisions are made in the private sphere: interest rates, investment plans, pollution practices, pricing policy, job expansion, educational projects, location of medical practices, and a thousand other market decisions—where there is no effective national policy—the prudent person tries to work the system of mass politics as much as possible.

Strong Presidency/Weak Polity

Mass-mediated politics makes it much easier for power to be concentrated in the office of a president. Without the collectivity exercising power to offset that of a president, such a president can depoliticize the economic facts of life by a policy of *privatization*—yielding to the marketplace and to quasimonopolies. In such a political system, housing, health care, employment, interest rates, and educational, transportation, investment, and pollution decisions are made at state level if at all in any public forum.

Capitalism as a system requires that most production and distribution policies be made in the private sphere. Capitalists put together shifting coalitions of corporate power blocs with which to control the sector of the political economy of interest to them. Capitalists use a bit of surplus value with which to preselect congresspersons (over 95 percent of whom are reelected each term with the aid of such money), to preselect congenial presidential candidates, and to oppose tax policy, especially at the federal level.

In the United States, where the costs of capitalism are escalating with the loss of foreign markets to Japan, Germany, and the socialist "conspiracy," more and more funding of politicians by corporations places more and more politicians in the service of corporate capitalism thereby exacerbating the conflict between the public and the politician. The financial dependence of the politician upon the corporation renders the political party, even with its limitations in the creation of political culture, a liability.

At the same time, the ability of the capitalist state to fund the programs of social justice in America—mean-spirited and cheap-jack as they are—puts political legitimacy in scarce supply. Dramaturgy can help redeem the bought politician as well as the failed promises of social justice for all. The mass political audience, as a passive consumer of expertly packaged political culture prepared by a highly selective, tightly controlled advertising agency, is more manageable than a party whose members can get out of hand and respond to the crises in capitalism in ways awkward to power, wealth, and privilege.

In foreign affairs, the needs of semimonopoly capital require a very strong presidency unshackled by public opinion. Mass opinion, the opinion of persons taken one at a time, is preferable to the interactionally and informationally rich politics of a truly public opinion policy process in that such semicitizens get excited only about narrowly focused issues. Foreign policy questions are beyond the scope of concern for most persons taken one at a time. They are interested in mortgage payments, food prices, interest rates, and next year's automobile—marketplace questions outside the purview of a depoliticized polity.

With the aid of the CIA, the State Department, various special services of the military, international aid agencies, and foreign mercenaries, the strong president can supervise the welfare of the world capitalist system giving American capitalists and workers a slight edge in the international marketplace. Thus, the president of the United States abrogates that presidency, turning the country over to the capitalist class and power blocs at the state level while assuming the presidency of the world capitalist system.

Law and Theatre

Many have noted the curious mix of lawyers and public relations persons involved in the Nixon approach of governance. The mix is thought to be puzzling in that lawyers are seen to deal with serious matters while PR people are known to practice the dramaturgical arts without restraint. Lawyers deal in real life matters: crime, divorce, real estate transactions, contracts, torts, and wills. Public relations people are much closer to the world of make-believe and just-pretend. They make their clients look good and help them pretend to be something more than they are.

A closer look suggests there are formal affinities between lawyers and PR men not often aired. Both professionals deal in social paradigms whose reality quotient is problematic. Both are charged to frame a scenario of explanation favorable to their client. Both have to operate in a forum where much is at stake: life, power, limb, property, and social esteem. Both must deal with a tough jury. Both work with a fund of knowledge that is imprecise and contradictory. The natural talents of people in the law as well as in public relations lend themselves to service in a dramaturgical politics.

Both the lawyer and the PR person attempt to counter evidence that the actions of each client are in conflict with the interests of the general or special public. Both are dealing with unknown others whose position in the social order places them far enough from the backstage such that they have only limited technical competence to judge actions against visible standards of performance. The particular mix of lawyers and PR persons has a sound social rationale in terms of division of labor.

While publicists have expertise in constructing an original social paradigm in which the clients' actions are to be understood as functional, the lawyer has expertise in opposing a social paradigm in which the clients' actions are understood as harmful. The lawyer helps create an alternate, probable social paradigm in which the clients' actions are to be understood as innocent of social injury.

The interpretation made in the following analysis is that there were two social paradigms under construction by the Nixon team: an official, publicly visible paradigm in which the values of a democratic society are sustained, and a second, nonvisible social paradigm that was bracketed from and which superseded the public paradigm under construction by the PR specialists.

Much of what transpired in the various Watergate hearings may be understood as a contest between the Nixon team to enforce the first paradigm while the efforts of Judge Sirica, various congresspersons, and the special attorney were to reconstruct and make visible the second paradigm. In the end, power determined which social paradigm was adopted. (Nixon resigned before the climax occurred; a very poor show from a dramaturgical point of view.)

Backstage at the White House

The transcripts of the White House tapes of the Watergate and allied affairs provide a rich source of materials for dramaturgical analysis. At almost every meeting between Nixon and his aides, considerations about how best to manage impressions, stage events, cast persons in given roles, rewrite various events, downplay intent, upstage an investigatory body, or create diverting drama are to be found.

In this section, the central issue is to lay out, in qualitative terms, the way in which theatre is made to interface with politics in the Nixon White House. In the final section, we will account for that interface—under what social conditions does theatre come to be deployed in the sociology of political fraud.

The Watergate hearings constituted a source of great concern to the Nixon team. The tapes of White House conversations of 28 February 1973 reveal that the central concern was to stage a production that would protect Nixon's political legitimacy and, by extension, his policies at home and abroad. In the final part of this chapter I will present some estimate of how very important those policies were to the survival of the world capitalist system.

Staging Political Reality

In the first excerpt, John Dean, legal counsel to the president, is concerned with the pace of the action:*

D: Here it is. You see, the Baker theory is that he wants to have *a big slambang thing for a whole week and then he thinks interest in the whole thing will fall off.* And he is right about that. But his interest in having a big slambang for a week is that we will bring all the big shots up right away. The big shots you could bring up. They could bring up Stans. They have to put him on, and they've got to put Mitchell on. They would like, of course, to get Haldeman, Ehrlichman and Colson.

To counter the efficacy of the opposition in making the backstage paradigm visible, in the same meeting Dean suggests the Nixon team move to stage the hearing in the most boring way possible.

D: I think it would take a lot of the teeth out of the—you know—the stardom of the people are trying to build up to. If Stans has already gone to a hearing in another committee, obviously they will use everything they have at that time and it won't be a hell of a lot. *It confuses the public. The public is bored with this thing already.*

P: Yeah.

In the next excerpt, Nixon and Dean interpret the actions of the Kennedy team as also engaging in stage managing. For modern political functionaries at the federal level, all politics is a stage production directed by elected and nonelected power brokers.

D: *I am convinced that he has shown that he is merely a puppet for Kennedy in this whole thing. The fine hand of the Kennedys is behind this whole hearing.* There is no doubt about it. When they considered the resolution on the Floor of the Senate I got the record out to read it. Who asked special permission to have their staff man on the floor? Kennedy brings this man Flug out on the floor when they are debating a resolution. He is the one who did this. It has been Kennedy's push quietly, his constant investigation. His committee did the [unintelligible] subpoenas to get at Kalmbach and all these people.

*D = Dean; P = Nixon; H = Haldeman; E = Ehrlichman. All quotations come from the official transcripts of the Watergate tapes . . . i.e., those tapes made by Nixon in the Oval Office of the White House and released by him as that portion of all conversations taped in the office of the president.

The excerpt above makes it clear that the dynamics of governance in Washington is concerned as much with the politics of reality staging as with the values implicit in the democratic paradigm: undistorted communication between government and public, full participation in policy formulation, justice and honesty in the use of power. The ideology of theatre is seen to trump the ideology of democracy.

With respect to the casting of the actors: The 28 February tapes show Nixon suggesting that Kalmbach would make a good witness, Colson cast as a "presidential advisor" (in order that he might properly decline to testify on grounds of executive privilege). Nixon suggests Stans as a leading man since "Stans is very clean." In this backstage conference, the Nixon team is trying to protect the more vulnerable actors offstage. Colson can be cast as an aide to Nixon but Chapin cannot be since, as Nixon points out, it would be an obvious fraud to cast both as aides.

Managing Impressions and Studying Lines

In the 13 March meeting, Nixon and Dean were concerned about how best to manage the impression of cooperation. In the social paradigm held to be normal as between a president and the public, the president is expected to be responsible for enforcing the laws. In the course of events, the Senate Committee has taken the initiative and Mr. Nixon is faced with the difficult task of creating an appearance of cooperating with a lawful investigation without much in the way of substance offered.

The audience to be impressed with this cooperation is not the Senate Committee but rather the American public. The gambit used is a particularly happy one: not to "interfere" with the committee. The script calls for Nixon not to comment because that is the committee's responsibility. Nixon is to feign a wish not to compromise the integrity of a Senate proceeding. The next effect of these presentments is to convince the public that the normal social paradigm remains intact. In the excerpt below, Nixon goes over his lines:

P: *I am not going to comment on something being investigated by the Committee. As I have already indicated, I am just not going to comment. Do you approve such tactics? Another question?*

D: Did Mr. Chapin's departure have something to do with his involvement with Mr. Segretti?

P: [inaudible] What about Mr. Dean? My position is the same. *We have cooperated with the Justice Department, the FBI—completely tried to furnish infor-*

mation under our control in this matter. We will cooperate with the committee under the rules I have laid down in my statement on executive privilege. Now what else?

D: Well, then you will get a barrage of questions probably, on will you supply— will Mr. Haldeman and Mr. Ehrlichman and Mr. Dean go up to the committee and testify?

P: *No, absolutely not.*

D: Mr. Colson?

P: *No, absolutely not. It isn't a question of not—Ziegler or somebody had said that we in our executive privilege statement it was interpreted as meaning that we would not furnish information and all that. We said we will furnish information and all that. We said we will furnish information, but we are not going to be called to testify. That is the position. Dean and all the rest will grant you information.* Won't you?

D: Yes. Indeed I will!

Diverting "Horribles"

In the background of every administration, some events cast doubt on the degree to which that administration honors the publicly known and cherished political paradigm. Dean suggests that release of some previous "horribles" would be helpful. Not only is attention diverted from Watergate but the latter could be understood as well within the normal paradigm: Break-ins and other crimes are a routine, if unpublicized, White House practice. Nixon and Dean want to control drama and intrigue in their production of the Watergate scandals. The dramatic values of the opposing cast and crew are to be diminished and their production is to fail in Peoria.

Meeting of 13 March 1973

D: Now the other thing, if we were going to use a package like this: Let's say in the Gray hearings—where everything is cast that we are the political people and they are not—that Hoover was above reproach, which is just not accurate, total bullshit. *The person who would destroy Hoover's image is going to be this man Bill Sullivan. Also it is going to tarnish quite severely. . . .*

P: *Some of the FBI.*

D: *. . . some of the FBI. And a former president.* He is going to lay it out, and just all hell is going to break loose once he does it. It is going to ʿnange the atmosphere of the Gray hearings and it is going to change the atmosphere of the whole Watergate hearings. Now the risk. . . .

P: How will it change?

D: Because it will put them in context of where government institutes were used in the past for the most flagrant political purposes.

P: How can that help us? How does it help us? I am being the devil's advocate. . . .

D: I appreciate what you are doing. It is a red herring. It is what the public already believes. *I think the people would react: [expletive deleted] more of that stuff! They are all bad down there!* Because it is a one-way street right now. . . .

P: Do you think the press would use it? They may not play it.

D: It would be difficult not to. Ah, it would be difficult not to.

The shabby morals of Dean and Nixon are revealed in an effort to gain political advantage by pointing to others with the same shabby morals.

Meeting of 13 March 1973

   Casting bit players: (Herb) Kalmbach, Mitchell, and Stans.

P: Anyway we don't want to back off of him.

D: *No, he is solid.*

P: He will—how does he tell his story? He has a pretty hard row to hoe—he and Stans have.

D: *He will be good. Herb is the kind of guy who will check, not once or twice, on his story—not three times—but probably fifty to a hundred times. He will go over it. He will know it. There won't be a hole in it. Probably he will do his own Q & A. He will have people cross-examine him from ten ways. He will be ready as John Mitchell will be ready, as Maury Stans will be ready.*

P: Mitchell is studying, is he?

D: *He is studying. Sloan will be the worst witness. I think Magruder will be a good witness. This fellow, Bart Porter, will be a good witness. They have already been through grand jury. They have been through trial. They did well.*

Not only may one rely upon Stans, Mitchell, and others to study their lines well; some of them have had extensive experience on the witness stand and will not be likely to blow their lines.

> I'll tell you whose not informed. It's those stupid kids. They pick the rhetoric that they want to hear right off the top of an issue and never finish reading to the bottom. And the professors are just as bad if not worse. They don't know anything. Nor do these stupid bastards who are ruining our educational institutions! [Attorney General John Mitchell]

It is not apparent in these excerpts but later on in his own appearance before the Senate Select Committee, Dean reports that he coached many of the witnesses at length on how to give the semblance of credibility using information from within the Grand Jury obtained from the Justice Department. Dean himself did not follow the White House script and gave forth a story that compromised that script.

The two stories together—the official version of the Nixon production team and that of Dean—exemplify divergence between the social paradigm held forth for public accountability by the Nixon team and that paradigm of the unaccountable exercise of partisan power to subvert the democratic process, narrow as it is.

Mocking Up an Investigation

On 20 March 1973, it became clear to Nixon that executive privilege meant executive silence. Such silence did not sit well with the various audiences attending to the unfolding drama. The press was constructing an interpretation of sinister involvement by the entire White House. The friends of the administration needed some talking points. It would be difficult to speak to one public and not to another, so the idea of a spurious, well-contained investigation was proposed by Nixon.

This was to be the Dean report, but Dean later decided to protect himself. It then became the Ehrlichman investigation. These mock-ups had only short runs since other, less contrived, investigations rendered them useless. However, it is clear in this excerpt that a cover-up is in progress. At one point, Dean suggests a useful prop: a piece of paper that appears to be a legitimate exercise of executive privilege but is really part of the backstage handlings of impressions for a mass political audience. Nixon approves.

Meeting of 20 March 1973

P: You've got to have something where it doesn't appear that I am doing this in, you know, just in a—saying to hell with the Congress and to hell with the people, *we are not going to tell you anything because of executive privilege.* That they don't understand. But if you say, "No, we are willing to" and you've made a complete statement, but make it very incomplete. See, that is what I mean. I don't want a, too much in chapter and verse as you did in your letter, I just want just a general. . . .

D: An all-around statement.

P: That's right. Try just something general. Like *"I have checked into this matter; I can categorically, based on my investigation, the following: Haldeman is not involved in this, that and the other thing. Mr. Colson did not do this; Mr. so and so did not do this. Mr. Blank did not do this." Right down the line, taking the most glaring things. If there are any further questions, please let me know. See?*

D: Uh, huh. I think we can do that.

P: That is one possibility and then you could say that such. . . . It might be very salutary. You see our own people have got to have confidence or they are not going to step up and defend us. You see our problem there, don't you?

D: And I think at the same time it would be good to brief these people on what executive privilege means, so they can go out and speak about it. Some of them are floundering.

P: And why it is necessary.

D: *I thought about having someone prepare some material that can be put out by the congressional people so they can understand, people can understand. It is tremendous to have a piece of paper that they know they can talk from.*

P: *Pointing out that you are defending the Constitution; responsibility of the separation of powers; and we have to do it.*

This excerpt reveals some of the dynamics at work. Central to these is that reality compromises the political legitimacy of Nixon, that make-believe is preferable to an authentic version of Watergate, and that Nixon had departed from his role as something understood to be a president to something more akin to a playwright.

An Image of National Security

The simplistic politics of mass audiences responds very nicely to patriotic themes in such plays. The script writers include this gambit in order to make the Watergate scandal invisible.

Meeting of 21 March 1973

D: I talked to Liddy once right after the incident.

P: The point is this, that it is now time, though, that Mitchell has got to sit down, and know where the hell all this thing stands, too. You see, John is concerned, as you know, about the Ehrlichman situation. It worries him a great deal because, and this is why the Hunt problem is so serious, because it had nothing to do with the campaign. It has to do with the Ellsberg case. I don't know what the hell the [unintelligible].

H: But what I was going to say. . . .

P: What is the answer on this? How you keep it out, I don't know. You can't keep it out if Hunt talks. You can see the point is irrelevant. It has gotten to this point.

D: *You might put it on a national security grounds basis.*

H: It absolutely was.

P: *National security. We had to get information for national security grounds.*

P: With the bombing thing coming out and everything coming out, the whole thing . . . I think we could get by on that.

P: *On that one I think we should simply say this was a national security investigation that was conducted.* And on that basis, I think the same in the drug field with Krogh. Krogh could say feels he did not perjure himself. He could say it was a national security matter.

P: *Bud should just say it was a question of national security, and I was not in a position to divulge it.* Anyway, let's don't go beyond that. But I do think now there is a time when you just don't want to talk to Mitchell. But John is right. There must be a four way talk of the particular ones you can trust here. We've got to get a decision on it. It is not something—you have two ways basically. You really only have two ways to go. You either decide that the whole (expletive deleted) this is so full of problems with potential criminal liabilities, which most concern men. I don't give a damn about the publicity.

We could rock that through that if we had to let the whole damn thing hang out, and it would be a lousy story for a month. But I can take it. *The point is, that I don't want any criminal liabilities. That is the thing that I am concerned about for members of the White House staff, and I would trust for members of the Committee [to reelect the President: it was the group that engineered the break-in at Watergate]. And that means Magruder.*

Morality and Theatre

Nixon, Dean, Ehrlichman, and Haldeman were not entirely frank with Kliendienst, Ford, nor Peterson. The backstage use of these men for dramaturgical purposes underscores the extent to which *techne* triumphs over praxis. Praxis refers to conscious, self-controlled acting as contrasted to *techne,* a blind, externally motivated behavior in the classic Greek distinction. Those persons used by the stage managers become a mere technical apparatus.

Much of the criticism directed at the indicated felons by Judge Sirica has to do with their moral responsibility to transcend orders and to act autonomously or to transcend position and evaluate the moral standing of orders. Herein lies a central danger of a dramaturgical society: In the marketplace, in the classroom, in law, religion, and politics, the staging of behavior of masses of people constitutes an assault on human dignity not yet understood by the psychologists, sociologists, and PR and advertising people so enthusiastically involved in such endeavor.

Morality lodges as much in the larger structures of society as it does in the psyche of the individual. When players are the puppets of playwrights, then the morality of the play is the morality of the writer, not the players. The players yield their morality and human dignity.

The two social paradigms at conflict are seen side-by-side in the final soliloquy, above, of Nixon. He begins to say there are two ways to proceed. By the time he has finished the sentence, he has specified both ways to himself, evaluated both, and discarded one. By the time he has verbalized the one involving "criminal liabilities," to be completely open and go with the paradigm of law, order, and executive responsibility he has rejected it. The real point is that he does not want criminal liabilities irrespective of the liability incurred under the public paradigm of law and order.

If there is any place at which Nixon's decision to cover up is clear, it is in this passage. So the backstaging at the White House takes the James Bond route and scripts the events as if they were done for reasons of national security. That this is a post hoc scripting may be understood from the conditional mood of Dean's remarks and those of Nixon. The standard use of "might say" and "could say" indicates that these things were not said or even thought prior to the event but rather are adduced after the fact as plausible ways to construct the legal meaning of Colson's activity.

Staging the Investigation

Although some effort was made by the White House to stage manage the Senate hearings, no one seriously believed that Senator Ervin, Senator Weicker, the investigatory staff, and others could be "wired" completely. At the 21 March 1973 meeting, Nixon inquired as to the possibility of a special Grand Jury. The point of the Grand Jury was to establish a forum in which events could be managed and information withheld from the Senate Select Committee. Of course, Grand Jury proceedings are secret. One has a right to take the Fifth Amendment and to legal counsel, and it is much better than a hearing open to reporters and the public.

Meeting of 21 March 1973

P: *John Ehrlichman, of course, has raised the point of another grand jury. I just don't know how you could do it. On what basis. I could call for it, but I. . . .*

D: That would be out of the question.

P: I hate to leave with differences in view of all this stripped land. *I could understand this, but I think I want another grand jury proceeding and we will have the White House appear before them.* Is that right John?

D: Uh huh.

P: That is the point, see. Of course! That would make the difference. I want everybody in the White House called. And that gives you a reason not to have to go before the Ervin and Baker Committee. *It puts it in the executive session, in a sense.*

H: Right.

D: That's right.

H: *And there would be some rules of evidence, aren't there?*

D: There are rules of evidence.

P: *Rules of evidence and you have lawyers.*

H: You are in a hell of a lot better position than you are up there.

D: *No, you can't have a lawyer before the grand jury.*

P: Oh, no. That's right.

H: But you do have rules of evidence. You can refuse to talk.

D: *You can take the 5th Amendment.*

P: That's right.

H: *You can say you have forgotten too, can't you?*

D: Sure but you are chancing a very high risk for a perjury situation.

P: *But you can say, I don't remember. You can say I can't recall.* I can't give any answer to that I can recall.

H: You have the same perjury thing on the Hill don't you.

D: That's right.

P: Oh hell, yes.

H: And the Ervin Committee is a hell of a lot worse to deal with.

P: The grand jury thing has its own view of this thing. Suppose we have a grand jury thing. What would that do to the Ervin Committee? Would it go right ahead?

D: Probably. Probably.

Given the stagings of something to be entitled a Grand Jury, the question arises of casting the male lead:

P: If we do that on a grand jury, we would then have a much better cause in terms of saying, *"Look, this is a grand jury, in which the prosecutor—How about a special prosecutor? We could use Petersen, or use another one. You see he is probably suspect.* Would you call in another prosecutor?

D: *I would like to have Petersen on our side, if I did this thing.*

P: Well, Petersen is honest. There isn't anybody about to question him is there?

The script depended upon Nixon having control of the special prosecutor of the Grand Jury. Petersen's honesty together with deference to authority would be most useful to a carefully controlled Grand Jury investigation. As with other stagings, this one was counterproductive: Petersen was not installed as the star of the show, Cox proved ungovernable, Dworsky took Nixon to court to produce evidence, and the Supreme Court would not validate the social paradigm of an autonomous president unaccountable save the most extreme remedy: impeachment for high crimes.

Values of justice, legal and public accountability, and separation of the executive and judicial branches are in this setting in hostile opposition to the values of in-group loyalty, protection of agency, as well as Nixon's credibility. The solution to this conflict is a dramaturgically engineered investigation that provides the illusion that there is no such conflict in values.

Later, when this stage managing fails, Nixon attempts to obliterate the value conflict by appealing to different values—his personal relationship with the Soviet leadership and the crucial factor that relationship plays in keeping the peace, as well as the interest of the public in a strong, unsullied presidency. Nixon argues, in sum, that a social paradigm centered around national security from the Communist menace is preferable to one centered around the democratic process. One is therefore expected to accept Nixon's dramaturgy even though one knows the account has been manufactured on a post hoc basis.

A Facsimile of Bold Disclosure

One option suggested as stageworthy was the possibility of a Dean report. It would have the dramatic effect of boldness and a built-in guarantee of protection for Nixon if it collapsed as a believable performance. The "Dean report" tactic as a containing operation is discussed at several points, backstage and front stage as well. At no point was this script intended to be compatible with a social paradigm of authentic agency by the president on behalf of fair trial and equal standing before the law for all the president's men involved. It was always compatible with the social paradigm of unconstrained presidential power. Between the alternatives, the "Dean report" is preferable since it is less likely to collapse and has the FBI, together with unnamed others, as scapegoats upon whom Nixon might rely. The backstage context that their testimony was coached would not appear in the public version.

Meetings of 21 March 1973

H: After a little time, the President is accused of covering up that way.

E: Or is there another way?

P: Yeah, like. . . .

E: *The Dean statements, where the President then makes a bold disclosure of everything which he then has.* And is in a position if it does collapse at a later time to say "I had the FBI and the grand jury, and I had my own counsel. I turned over every document I could find. *I placed in my confidence young people and as is obvious now [inaudible].*

In the Ehrlichman plot, the president looks good as such since he is to appear to take the initiative in rooting out crime in the White House. There is a built-in ending in which Nixon says, sadly, "I put my trust in these young people and they betrayed that trust—whatever can one do with such scoundrels?"

The parts cast for Dean, and later Ehrlichman, were never to be part of a self-fulfilling prophecy by which later behavioral events were to match the prophesy of truth, integrity, and justice in the public statements of Nixon about the Dean "report" or the Ehrlichman report. These values were to be dramaturgically simulated while other values—in-group loyalty, a strong presidency, and a favorable verdict on the Nixon tenure in office by historians—were prime values. There was a hierarchy in the last set of values listed with Nixon's historical image accorded prime standing.

The Play's the Thing, Wherein We'll Keep the Safety of the King

The magnitude of the discrepancy between the social drama prophesied in Nixon's public statements about the meaning of the Dean report and intended action is seen when, in the same conversation in which the spurious Dean report is proposed by Nixon, there follows a discussion of:

Cutting it [off] at Liddy;

Total control and commitment over all of the [Watergate] defendants;

Giving Hunt $110,000 to get that control, avoiding criminal liability for those close to the presidency, keeping it off Herb [Kalmbach], off of Bob [Haldeman], off Chapin, and, if possible, off Strachan and off Mitchell.

For the most part it is Nixon who makes these points. The technical problem in achieving this protection of the inner circle of the White House is Magruder. In that 21 March conversation, Nixon understands that silence from the Watergate burglars can be bought for around $1,000,000; that after the Nixon team is out of office their silence becomes less of a political problem.

> As my husband has said many times, some of the liberals in this country, he'd like to take them and exchange them for Russian Communists anytime. [Martha Mitchell]

Meeting of 21 March 1973

D: That's right. Let's face it. I think Magruder is the major guy over there.

H: I think he's got the most serious problem.

P: Yeah.

H: Well, the thing we talked about yesterday. You have a question, where you cut off on this. There is a possibility of cutting it at Liddy, where you are now.

P: Yeah.

D: But to accomplish that requires a continued perjury by Magruder and requires. . . .

P: *And requires total commitment and control over all of the defendants which in other words when they are let down. . . .*

H: But we can, because they don't know anything beyond Liddy.

D: No. On the fact that Liddy they have hearsay.

H: But we don't know about Hunt. Maybe Hunt has that tied into Colson. [Charles Colson is part of the inner circle . . . he later goes to jail; gets converted to religion and goes on the Bible circuit.]

P: I think Hunt knows a hell of a lot more.

Nixon's response was to explore the possibility of Magruder's being compromised and thus unreliable, rather than the possibility of the public interest being served by such testimony. Nixon had his best shot at the "bold disclosure," the "full cooperation" of which he had made public reference. However, in the evening of 21 March, $75,000 was delivered to the lawyer for Hunt. This behavioral event invalidated the prophecy implicit in Nixon's public use of the Dean report. Nixon's instruction to Dean to keep the report general, to say that so-and-so did not do this, that so-and-so did not do that also belied the prophecy given out to the public that a president would make a thorough investigation.

The fact that the results of that investigation are scripted before it occurs—in the face of repeated statements by Dean, Gray, and others that so-and-so is most certainly culpable—only adds emphasis to the fraudulent character of Nixon's "bold" disclosures onstage.

The Sociology of Fraud: Theory and Practice

Had Nixon's audience understood that his bold disclosures were only images, and had they shared values with him (as did many conservative groups), the substantive emptiness of the image of honesty and justice would not be offensive any more than would an audience be offended by a stage presentation of *Oedipus Rex*.

We know that the character playing Oedipus does not really kill the character playing Oedipus' father in that play nor does he really have incestuous relations with his own mother. We know that the actors are only playing a role. The emptiness of images, prophesies, illusions, and semblances is not an exercise in the sociology of fraud. There is no discrepancy of values, no systematic distortion of the knowledge process. When both discrepancies occur together, value discrepancy and empty prophesy in the context of a social paradigm, then the sociology of fraud obtains.

The dualistic nature of subjective knowledge and objective reality is, in the sociology of fraud, a human artifact.

The theoretical speculations of the symbolic interaction school relating to the necessary role of prophesies in the construction of social reality no longer hold. The theoretical speculations of the dramaturgists with respect to the role of play, games, and simulations in the construction of social reality no longer hold. The value discrepancy destroys the very social paradigm under construction rather than sustains it as would be the case in a "real" stage play.

Make-Believe and Social Facticity

There are interesting exceptions to the destructive potential of images in social life, not relevant to the White House actions. In the opening phase of face-to-face social encounters, one often must simulate interest, concern, understanding, as well as pleasure in states of copresence. This simulation of reality ordinarily fades as, through ongoing symbolic interaction, shared interests and meanings and states of emotional orientation are indeed constructed. One gradually comes to be glad to know another person.

In this exception, however, this is no great value discrepancy. People do share the same values and can check out subsequent actions of social others for compatibility with those values in routine social life. Deception often is prelude to authenticity. However, backstage at the White House, it is unrelieved treason to democratic values and Constitutional protections. Nixon knew this. He resigned rather than risk being held accountable for his part in the subversion of democratic politics.

A Dean Masquerade

Dean has several roles in the Nixon team paradigm. If Nixon is the producer, Dean is the director in the Watergate cover-up. He is also cast as a special presidential investigator. In the former role, he needs political protection; in the latter, he needs credibility. In order to serve these values, a third role is cast for him: presidential counsel. He has been, in name and in deed, presidential counsel. Now he is to be presidential counsel for public purposes and the director for private purposes. Thus are reality and make-believe conflated.

In the public paradigm, the social value of privileged communication between lawyer (Dean) and client (Nixon) is to be used to advance the private values of self-protection for those close to Nixon with some degree of criminal liability including Dean.

Masquerading as a lawyer enables Dean to continue in his role in the cover-up without jeopardy by giving off the impression of having no operational role in dealing with the key figures in the cover-up rather than the impression of coaching, instructing, deciding, and executing a cover-up of a crime as previous White House tapes indicate.

Dean was especially active in organizing the money to pay for Hunt's silence and in using the president's name to extract advance information from the Justice Department. By means of quick change artistry, Dean is to act the part of the president's man in the cover-up but to switch to the role of presidential counsel in any forum in which he is asked to testify.

In this masquerade is found a subversion of the intent of lawyer-client confidentiality. Such confidentiality is not intended to mask the culpable involvement of a lawyer in one setting by reference to his status as lawyer in another—and yet precisely this is scripted by Nixon.

D: One issue may come up as the hearings go along is the fact that the focus on this book is that Dean knew—as you all know I was all over this thing like a wet blanket. I was everywhere—everywhere they look they are going to find Dean.

P: Sure.

H: Well, I don't think that is bad.

E: I don't either. You were supposed to be.

P: *You were our investigator. You were directed by the President to get me all the facts. Second, as White House counsel you were on it to assist people in the Executive Branch who were being questioned. Say you were there for the purpose of getting information. That was your job.*

D: That's right.

P: But the main point certainly is that Dean had absolutely no operational activity. *The wonderful thing about your position is that as far as they are concerned—your position has never been as operative.*

H: That is true—even in the private sessions then—you volunteered to give them a statement on the whole question of your recommendation of Liddy which is the only point of possible kind of substantive culpability that you could have and now you can satisfy all of those actions—that is if you want to.

P: At the President's direction you have never done anything operational, you have always acted as counsel. We've got to keep our eye on the Dean thing.

Presumably, society values lawyer-client confidentiality as a means to provide due process and full legal protection to the client, not to the lawyer acting as culpable agent for the client in a series of criminal actions. On 27 March 1973, Ziegler, press secretary at the White House, was instructed to present Dean-the-presidential-lawyer rather than Dean-the-presidential-aide at the daily press briefing—the President's men were to use the nightly news broadcast as a stage.

Z:*   Then if I am asked a question about whether or not Dean would appear before the grand jury, if I am asked that question. . . .

---

*Z = Ron Ziegler, White House press secretary

P: Why don't we just say, "well, this is a matter that is not before us." *Point out that he is counsel to the President, counsel to the White House—use the White House.* Say, *"He is the White House counsel and, therefore, his appearance before any judicial group therefore, is on a different basis from anybody else,"* which is basically what I, you know when I flatly said Dean would not appear but others would. You know, I did say that, and of course. . . .

In any authentic news program, it is incumbent on reporters to give enough background so viewers can make sense of it in epistemological terms. In the American media and other news media distorted by wealth and power, the media become part of the structure of mystification. Rather than minimize the alienation of subjective understanding, such use of news increases it. The quality of a *public sphere* depends on a news media oriented to the correspondence of objective reality and subjective understanding. Democracy, in turn, depends on a well-designed, well-operating public sphere. In Watergate, the *Washington Post* reporters set a precedent not yet well met in the news media.

Upstaging the Senate Hearing

Two goals were in serious jeopardy by the Senate investigations: the elections of 1974 and protection of the participants involved in criminal conspiracy to subvert the political process in the 1972 presidential election. Haldeman proposed a Dean extravaganza that would neutralize the Senate hearings, drag out the investigation until after 1974, and give Nixon the "final stroke" of pardon on his last day in office.

The official line is that no one is above the law, but the value of a fair hearing trumps all other considerations. A nice thought, but one that would carry more weight were the president's men equally concerned with a fair hearing for those Democrats whose reputation and fortune were subverted by secret things done in the night at their direction. The scenario below lays out the concept of a "superpanel" with which to upstage the only forum in which anyone hurt by the Nixon team could possibly get a fair hearing. Haldeman first gives Nixon his lines:

H: Now, no man is above the law and that is a basic principle we must operate on, but under these circumstances there's no possibility of a fair hearing and every man is entitled to the protection of the law and the public is entitled to the facts in this matter. But the people who are in charge and are involved are entitled to fair treatment. People who are involved, well wasn't any [unintelligible] in being involved. *So, I've created a super panel which will have the cooperation of all investigative agencies. All the people who have been charged in this matter have volunteered to submit their entire—their facts—to this panel.*

P: Be questioned by it.

H: And be questioned by it. They've agreed to waive their right to trial by jury.

P: What [unintelligible]. . . .

H: And the panel is empowered to act to remove anybody that it sees fit because of involvement, to level fines and to impose criminal sanctions. The defendants in the Watergate trial, the men who have already been—can also submit any information that they want.

P: *Right.*

H: Will be faced with the fact that all information developed by the committee and all other sources will be turned over to the Justice Department for criminal prosecution. There will be no judgment until all the facts are received by the commission and then the commission will make public all of its findings and the reasons for all actions taken. *They will proceed in secret and their decisions will be final and not subject to appeal.* And the people appearing before them will voluntarily submit to that. What [unintelligible] is appeal.

P: Wonder if the President has the power to set up such a thing. Can he do that sort of thing? You know, that's the whole point. I don't think so.

E: Executive process.

H: By voluntary. . . .

H: He feels that there are a lot of advantages on this and two major internal ones. It will take the panel a long time to get set up, get its processes worked out, get its hearings done and make the findings and *then you'll probably be past the '74 elections which'll be desirable. Secondly, the President maintains the ultimate stroke on it, because he always has the option on January 19 to pardon anybody who [unintelligible] a pardon.* So the potential ultimate penalty anybody would get hit in this process could be about two years. His view could be to put—you need to get someone on the panel who knows politics.

Again, the proposal is to use the powers invested in the presidency for dramaturgical presentations not in consonance with the social paradigm in which those powers are delegated from the people to a person to act as its agent. Nixon and his team exhibit a fine indifference to the public trust implicit in that paradigm. Someone has said in the Judiciary Committee hearings that, in all the thousands of pages of testimony, not once has Nixon asked what his constitutional duties and limits are.

That is not precisely true. In this meeting he does ask the question and apparently, not as a "devil's advocate." However, Ehrlichman and Haldeman respond as though Nixon has not asked whether a president has such power but rather, how a president might create a plausible basis for arrogating such power unto his office. They immediately suggest two ways.

Casting a Villain as Innocent

In stage life, prophecies are made that are not taken to be models of seriously intended events to come. In social life, prophecies are prelude to a series of behavioral events that validate the prophecy on the one hand and are given meaning by the prophecy on the other.

In the offstage dealings of the Nixon team, there are many prophecies of cooperation, of thorough investigation, of valid assignment of criminal responsibility for those involved. At no time are these prophecies held to be seriously intended paradigms for mediating the team's own behavior. There is one case in which a future state of affairs is envisioned whereby Mitchell is to be the "big enchilada" to quiet the appetites of the Watergate investigators. He is high in the administration, not a direct part of the White House team, and was thought to have agreed (signed off) on the Liddy package of political subversion.

The problem was to get him to admit culpability and resign in order to protect against further inroads of the high-echelon officers in the Nixon administration. Nixon fully intended that later performance match the prophecy if possible.

Meeting of 27 March 1973

P: Well, what is Mitchell's opinion though? You mean to say—let's see what he could do. Does Mitchell come in and say, "My memory was faulty. I lied?"

E: No. He can't say that. He says—"ah, ah."

P: *"That without intending to, I may have been responsible for this, and I regret it very much but I did not realize what they were up to. They were—we were—talking about apples and oranges." That's what I think he would say. Don't you agree?*

H: I think so. He authorized apples and they bought oranges. Yeah.

P: Mitchell, you see, is never going to go in and admit perjury. I mean he may say he forgot about Hunt-Liddy and all the rest, but he is never going to do that.

H: They won't give him that convenience, I wouldn't think, unless they figure they are going to get you. He is as high up as they've got.

E: He's the Big Enchilada.

H: And he's the one the magazines zeroed in on this weekend.

P: They did? What grounds?

H: Yeah. [Unintelligible] has a quote that they maybe have a big fish on the hook.

P: *I think Mitchell should come down.*

A Venture into Reality

Haldeman is instructed by Nixon to call Mitchell to Washington from New York. The meeting with Mitchell is set up for the next morning. The tape of that meeting was not released to the public. Later conversations indicate a decided preference for Mitchell to accept full responsibility thereby exculpating Nixon and tuning down interest in more investigation.

At this point the private White House script comes as close to the social paradigm presumed to hold between a president and a citizenry as any of the backstage deliberations. From the behavioral events to this point, it seems a reasonable interpretation that Mitchell bore central responsibility for the Watergate intrusion and that Nixon had no prior knowledge. A good case could be made that the values implicit in the paradigm used in American political activity would be satisfied by Mitchell's assumption of responsibility and penance.

Even if this were standard operating procedure in the Nixon administration, with Ehrlichman and Haldeman knowing the full measure of the Nixon enchantment with power as well as understanding the license they had to advance that interest, still, the central effect of Mitchell's fall from grace would be a serious constraint on the extension of presidential power. In the realpolitik of American life, this result would have been satisfactory to all but the purest conservatives and liberals.

In another place, the final act scripted by the White House dramatic group is set forth and discussed, but at this point, an ending sacrificing Mitchell but salvaging others appeared to be given serious consideration.

Belief and Betrayal

The social construction of reality is not possible without belief, innocence, and faith. In real life, disbelief is suspended to help each other act on the level of innocent and uncritical discourse. Social reality does not exist ontologically, apart from the thoughts and actions of believing human beings. When people believe in the social presentments of each other, believe in the situation as defined collectively, believe in their right to act as a party to such an occasion—when all this happens, the reality quotient of social forms is as high as that of physical realities that do exist ontologically.

Social reality is more complex than physical reality in that it has both ontological and epistemological dimensions that determine its facticity.

If we go into a restaurant and someone presents herself as a waitress, we suspend our disbelief that she is not. Were we to disbelieve, we would ask for identification and references. Our insistence that the waitress prove her identity would cause consternation and incredulity. Whenever grounds for disbelief enter into the real world, the reality process must stop; those concerned must move to a metadiscourse and evaluate the validity of those grounds for belief. It takes time to sort out truth claims. It tends to stigmatize those who are so challenged. In such a case, a restaurant manager would simply ask the disbeliever to leave. But the facticity of the relationship between two people as "customer" and "waitress" would not have emerged as a social entity. No belief, no reality.

One must take a great many things on faith in building social-life worlds. Those who have ever had reason to lose belief in a spouse will recall what an existential shock it is to innocent belief and will remember the great damage done to the process by which marriage is constructed. In such a case, the reality quotient of marriage bottoms out. The same is true of politics, therapy, teaching, and preaching when the suspension of disbelief is no longer possible.

Disbelief in the social presentments of others must be suspended in order to treat them as though they were really doctors, mechanics, mothers, or whatever social role they now stand ready to embody. Disbelief in picnics, parties, classes, courts, and hospitals would subvert the reality process. In the sociology of fraud, repeated insults on belief lead to cynicism—a sort of holding back on naïve commitment.

In the world of make-believe, the suspension of disbelief is achieved by an understanding on the part of the viewers that they do not thereby lose anything—they are not any the more gullible nor any the less competent adults by a voluntary suspension of disbelief. It is not a great fault to laugh and weep at a movie or play, but it does imply a bit higher reality quotient than full and competent adults should give—more belief in the authenticity of the events in the play that the situation calls for—and certainly an inability to see clearly the larger framework in which the activity occurs, that of make-believe.

In the sociology of fraud the capacity of an audience for suspension of disbelief is utilized to gull an audience into a social paradigm hostile to the value structure assumed to be mutually pursued. A good con artist gives attention to details that otherwise would be of small consequence. Some small slip can trigger recourse to reality checks not usually made when faith obtains.

Reality checks call for more stringent standards of internal coherence than are usually demanded. Nixon, being a practiced liar, knows how tangled a web of lies can become when one practices to deceive. In the excerpt below, Nixon double-checks to determine whether a false story would seem plausible. He does the basic research into whether the polity will suspend disbelief of the explanation of why money was given to the burglars by the inner circle.

The use to which this basic research was put did not contribute to a social paradigm of mutually shared values as between Nixon and his audience, but rather led to a dramaturgical presentation in which the audience was not to understand that it was only "just-pretend" but rather that the script as written had been "for real" as far as the parties involved at the time were concerned. They really believed that they were given money as charity rather than as bribe. In a "real" play, factual events can be at odds with each other and one is not greatly distressed. We know the "nongame" event to be a mistake, an error, or a Freudian slip. These we can overlook and get on with our reality.

Nixon, in this excerpt, was betraying the belief in him-as-president acting, instead, as Nixon-as-coconspirator in a crime. The articles of impeachment were a true indictment of Nixon who had, in sociological terms, departed from the role of president to embody that of crook. Later, I will explain why Nixon and his team could, "in good conscience," do such things.

When the sociology of fraud may be suspected, basic research is even more crucial to the generation of naïve trust. Note that, among themselves, the men accept that the money transferred was a *payoff* for silence, rather than humanitarian aid to their families as would be staged for mass consumption.

Meeting of 30 March 1973

P: All right. Let me just take a minute further and run out the Hunt thing, and then the grand jury. I want to get all the pieces in my mind if I can.

E: Sure.

P: Hunt's testimony on *payoff*, of course, would be very important.

E: Right.

P: Is he prepared to testify on that?

E: Apparently so, that's what they say, that he will, and that he will implicate O'Brien and Parkinson. And then, of course. . . .

P: O'Brien and Parkinson? [Lawyers for the burglars who got the money from the inner circle for legal fees and living expenses]

E: The lawyers.

P: Were they the ones that talked to Hunt?

E: Well, he says they were and that they handed him the money. He in turn handed it to his wife and she was the go-between for the Cubans.

P: Yeh. For what purpose?

[Later in the tapes there is concern for Kalmbach who provided the payoff funds. Hunt organized the break-in and had a direct connection to the inner circle.]

P: Hunt then is going to go [public]. Now that raises the problem on Hunt with regard to Kalmbach. *He [Kalmbach] has possible vulnerability as to whether he was aware, in other words, the motive, the motive* [the motive for giving the crooks tens of thousands of dollars, donated illegally as it turns out— more crimes in the White House].

E: This doesn't add anything to do with Kalmbach's problem at all.

P: What happened on that? Dean called Kalmbach? And what did Dean call Kalmbach about?

E: He said we have to raise some money in connection with the aftermath, and I don't know how he described it. *Herb said how much do you need, and . . .*

P: It was never discussed then?

E: *Presumably Dean told him, and Herb went to a couple of donors and got some money and sent it back.*

H: Dean says very flatly that Kalmbach did not know the purpose of the money and has no problem.

P: Dean did know the purpose? Hunt testifies—so basically then Hunt will testify that it was *so-called hush money*. Right?

P: Would it reduce his sentence?

E: Have his sentence reduced.

H: He'd be served the same purpose by not saying it was hush money, by saying he gave it to these guys I [Hunt] had recruited for this job and I . . . was concerned about their family. . . .

P: *That's right, that's what it ought to be and that's got to be the story that . . .*

P: Will be the defense of these people, right?

E: Only defense they have [unintelligible] and so forth.

H: That was the line they used around here.

P: What?

H: *That was the line they used around here. That we've got to have money for their legal fees and family.*

P: Support. Well, I heard something about that at a much later time.

H: Yeah.

P: And, frankly, not knowing much about obstruction of justice, I thought it was perfectly proper [rehearsing lines].

Dramatic License

The excerpt above, perhaps more than others, reveals the dramatic license that will be used to place a context around the transfer of funds to Hunt. One such feature is in the ambiguity of meaning of events themselves. The transfer of money has no intrinsic meaning; not even that the item transferred was money or that it was in fact transferred.

Bills of the kind manufactured by the mint lose their standing as money when withdrawn from circulation; it is the social meaning assigned to the bills that makes them money. Without competent testimony by someone sociologically there, the meaning of the money as payoff is problematic. And, without a receipt, it is unclear whether money has been transferred or merely stored. Given the power of the presidency, it will be presented as if it were really humanitarian aid.

In authentic, demystified construction of social reality, there is considerable dramatic license to invent and experiment. This license to venture outside the normal modes of acting in order to clarify and illuminate, to highlight and improve insight, is testimony to human genius. It is a surprise and a delight to be party to such a use of drama. However, put to the sociology of fraud, it is depressing and generates cynicism.

Truth is good health
and safety and the sky.

How meager and how vocal,
an everlasting lie.
                    —Emily Dickinson

But Congress, the courts, and the media also have social power vested in them. In this instance, they define the money as hush money, their definition of the situation holds, and thus is history writ. Nixon does the basic research in order to gauge the credibility of a public story that the money paid to the Watergate burglars was for family support and legal fees in the context of sympathy and concern for wives, children, and adequate legal aid rather than bribes or hush money purchasing silence in the obstruction of justice. He appears to be satisfied that this interpretation has sufficient credibility to gull the audience and instructs his team to advertise it.

The Boundaries of Social Space

A most significant technical feature in the determination of criminal culpability for the cover-up has to do with the boundaries of the event sequence. Whether or not someone is inside the inner circle that engineered the cover-up of the burglary (it is called misprision of a felony and *is* a felony), is problematic when it comes to social space.

The boundaries of social space are quite different from those of physical space. One can be physically present and sociologically outside; one can be physically remote from the scene of a crime and be fully present in socio logical terms. There is sufficient connectedness of this event with other behavioral acts to construct a meaning (one of several possible) of presidential involvement in a suborning of a witness—E. Howard Hunt and misprision of a felony. There is also sufficient looseness to argue that Nixon's behavioral events lay outside the boundaries of any event sequence prophesied and carried out as bribery.

Then there is the question of prophecy itself. In order to be in social space, one must be party to the process by which a situation is defined—prophesied—as a crime or a cover-up. Nixon has sufficient basis for arguing that he never understood the social prophecy about to be staged was anything meant to be bribery. One could, however, argue that the correspondence of that prophecy was close enough to the subsequent events as well as the overall context to support inference of a bribery prophecy even if it were explicitly not the verbal meanings assigned to it by Nixon. Else why talk of the possibility of culpability for Kalmbach?

Social Time

It is a peculiarity of social reality that one can be involved in a social event outside the ordinary run of time. In the case of the bribery, Nixon joins the act of crime after it has been committed.

The boundaries of social space are not coincident with the boundaries of social time.

By joining the conspiracy some days after it started, the boundaries of social time were stretched to include Nixon. In the social forensics of criminology, one must pay attention to the elastic boundaries of social space and social time. Who said that physics and chemistry are the hard sciences?

The Social Magic of Social Power

Heretofore, Dean has been one of the principal authors, stage managers, directors, producers, and actors performing before the public on behalf of a White House ensemble. In the excerpt that follows, the shifting boundary between actors and audiences is illuminated. Dean ceases to be, epistemologically, a co-conspirator and becomes a prop to be used by the inner–inner circle which uses the power of the office of the president to reconstitute Dean.

Dean follows Mitchell as a prop to be used in furtherance of the Nixon paradigm. As with Mitchell, he ceases to be part of the acting ensemble and stands in the uncertain zone between actors and audience—he is neither one nor the other. Later, he will clearly be used as a prop and thus become part of a hostile audience to be managed, played to, impressed upon, and contained.

There is a fascinating point to be made here. All social reality is constructed. There is a sort of social magic involved in its construction. In this instance, Dean, an ontological entity, was transformed from an insider in partnership with the president's team to an outsider. Nixon had the social power—delegated to him for more honorable purpose—to make such magic. He used it against Dean.

Dean however, was later given social power of a different sort. He was called before the hearing, named a witness, and, in that social life, was able to do Nixon great harm. He was a key sorcerer in the transformation of Nixon from president into an ex-president. Social magic requires social power. Whose magic is greater depends on whose social, economic, and moral power is greater. One can shift levels and use physical power to dispel social magic. But as long as people define something as real, it has a good possibility of becoming real—with enough social power.

Meeting of 30 March 1973

P: No. Bob, the point that I make is let's suppose they get Mitchell. They're going to say now what about Haldeman, what about Chapin, and what about Colson and the rest? I've got to have a report indicating—you've got all those Segretti projects. I want somebody to say, now look, here are the facts. Of the White House people [unintelligible]. There are no other higher-up. The White House [unintelligible]. Put a cap on it. And second, then face the Segretti crap.

E: *In forcing this out, Dean remains a problem and here's—let me just read you what I've come to on that.* "John Dean has not involved himself in this matter as your counsel for several months and properly so. I should not continue to fill in for him," meaning me, "for several reasons, including the impermissible demands on my time that were involved. You need a full-time special counsel to follow these related problems who can advise you of the legal niceties from his experience in constitutional criminal and [unintelligible] law practice. I'll be happy to continue to consult with him, etc. I do not recommend that Dean take a leave. That is neither in nor out. He has involved himself to the extent described above. Either that requires dismissal, or it does not. And that choice should be made at once. If he is discharged, the U.S. attorney and the grand jury should be [unintelligible]." But I think you've got to bite the bullet on Dean, one way or the other, and pretty quick.

H: *All right, but recognize that that kills him. Dean's reaction basically he says that that kills him.*

P: Well, let's see what does Dean say when you tell him that?

E: He doesn't agree with that. [Dean doesn't agree that he should be mur-
        dered—sociologically speaking.]

Changing Paradigms and Fair Notice

The same external conditions that decided the Nixon team to write Dean
and Mitchell out of the play, led Magruder to decide to testify before the
grand jury. Magruder was putting the White House on fair notice that he
was changing from the officially given paradigm (dishonest) of the White
House to the officially given paradigm (honest) of the Justice Department.

It is important to note that Ehrlichman did not serve fair notice to Mitchell, Dean, nor Magruder when the White House team changed the way in
which they related to the ensemble. Some measure of the dishonesty of the
Nixon team is available from this duplicity.

In social life, one is expected to advise others who are within the same
social paradigm whether one is in or out and whether the paradigm has
changed. When the paradigm is changed, the values implicit in a given
structure of action are changed. Failure to notify significant others of such a
paradigmatic change has the effect of misleading them as to the values
pursued.

In analyzing the White House practices in constructing stage life and
social life, there is frequent mismatch between actors and directors, ensemble on the one hand and audience on the other about the paradigm utilized.
On the occasions such as the one in the excerpt below, when one party fails
to inform another of a change, social betrayal exists. Yet it is possible, as
we shall see in the last section, for belief to be subverted without betrayal—a case all too frequent in conflict relations.

In the micropolitics of social life, those parties commanding more power
can defend themselves if the switch is discovered; those less powerful, more
dependent cannot and thus are more likely to give fair notice in order to
deflect anger or to retain support. Such imbalance of power explains why
Magruder warns the president's men but Nixon does not bother to warn
those whom his team will throw to the investigating committees.

Meeting of 14 April 1973

P: Magruder.

H: He has had him in there for 45 minutes, but he still [unintelligible]. I called
        Magruder—it took a long time to get him—he was not available—and I was

trying to get him through his office but his lawyer said he could reach him in about an hour which he did and had him call me. Jeb [Magruder] said—I started out by saying now there have been some developments and we have reviewed this whole thing with the President and he thought it was important to have you and your lawyer meet with John Ehrlichman right away and get up-to-date on where things stand from this side. He said—fine, I can do that, I can't make it until about four o'clock. That was the way it was left—but he then said—you know this whole thing—I don't know the situation but it is all done now. I said, what do you mean? *He said I decided late last night with my lawyers that I am going to go ahead—you told me to do what my lawyers told me to do.* You said you couldn't advise me.

P: Is that what you told him?

Improvising

In the repertoire of every great ensemble, the ability to respond to the exigencies of the moment is manifest. From many sources, the White House is aware that the "egg is becoming unscrambled." In the excerpt that follows, Ehrlichman and Nixon discuss another mock investigation to take to the new attorney general by five PM in order to give the appearance of their breaking the case.

Meeting of 14 April 1973

P: The purpose in doing this is what?

E: The purpose of doing it is . . .

P: The White House has conducted an investigation and has turned it over to the grand jury.

E: Turned it over to the Justice Department.

P: Before the indictments.

E: Right.

P: How much are you going to put out?

E: *I think I would let them drag it out of me in a way. I don't know, I just really haven't thought that part through.*

P: Because if they say why did the White House wait for Justice Department to do all this . . .

E: Did the White House know, is probably the way this would, in turn, come.

P: Yes, as a matter of fact.

E: We have been at work on this for some time. President first ordered it.

P: Independent investigation.

E: Needed it known.

P: *I had ordered an independent investigation at the time McCord had something to say. Right.*

E: All right.

P: At that time you conducted an investigation.

E: *And that—at the time I was ready to report to you my tentative conclusions, and they were no more than that, you felt that they were sufficiently serious— well, you felt that one overriding aspect of the report was that some people evidently were hanging back feeling that they were somehow doing the President a favor. That the President had me personally transmit to them his views that this ought to be a complete open thing; that may or may not have played some part in . . .*

P: Jeb Magruder's subsequent disclosures to the grand jury?

E: In any event, rather than for us simply to hold the information in the White House, we turned it over to the Justice Department for whatever disposition they wanted to make of it.

Moral Contamination

Dean had originally been cast as the "presidential investigator," but he became contaminated by involvement in a social-life role that would impair his performance in the part. Ehrlichman has learned enough to improvise and has sufficient talent and backstage information to know how to replace Dean in that role. The scenario of a special presidential investigator had been previously worked out, but the time seemed more propitious for prompt recourse to it than any previous time.

In stage life, the moral standing of an actor has no great bearing on his acceptability in a given part. In social life, moral standing has great bearing on the sorts of roles in which one may properly be cast. In the former instance, there is public knowledge of psychological distance between actor and role; in social life, one assumes no such distance—the performer has some moral commitment to the role and that brooks no moral contamination if the presentment is to be taken seriously.

There is a sociological school that argues that bureaucracies and other large-scale organizations convert moral actors into mere technicians. Under that analysis, moral commitment to a role is irrelevant. Such involvement replaces technical expertise for the moral dimension of social life. The same replacement attends a stage presentation: technical competency in a performance rather than moral commitment to it. The merit of this approach, explicit in the writings of the Frankfurt School and others, is that one has a sociological framework in which to understand moral collapse rather than a religious or psychological framework.

The larger question to ponder in the White House dealing as in all merely technical discourse is whether social life can survive in any social mode without a set of fairly explicit value orientations based on distinctly *human* values. There seems little doubt but that patterned activity can be sustained without relating back to human values but whether that patterned behavior sustains social life is another question.

Suicide rates, rates of infant mortality, crime, dropout rates, rates of psychological depression may be the quantitative indicators of the collapse of life to purely technical modes unattached to a framework of human values. When theatre overlaps politics, when that theatre is oriented to the management of human beings rather than the celebration of the human project, then the moral bases in politics are lacking.

The sources of human morality are to be found in the character of the social forms available as much as in childhood training or in privatized modes of worship.

Rehearsal and Performance

One of the few occasions in which a dramaturgical event is available to us in both the form rehearsed and performed side by side occurs on the evening of 14 April. In the performance, Ehrlichman gives a superb presentation of the main points scripted earlier in the day. The performance was played to Attorney General Kleindienst. It is based on the 27 March scripting.

In this performance, Ehrlichman enacts the role of a special presidential investigator for the benefit of Attorney General Richard Kleindienst (Kleindienst replaced Mitchell who quit under fire). Recall that it was in the office of the attorney general that much of the larger plan to destabilize the campaign of the Democratic presidential candidate took place. Kleindienst is really an attorney general while Ehrlichman is a stand-in for Dean who had been playing the part of the president's investigator until he defected to the world of seriously intended social reality from the world of make-believe and just-pretend.

Telephone conversation

K: Hi, John.

E: Hi, General. How are you?

K: Pretty good, how are you?

E: How was the golf?

K: Half good and half bad.

E: First half good?

K: Well, the middle was good and . . .

E: I want to bring you up to date on what I have been doing. For about the last three weeks—well, since I saw you, before I saw you in San Clemente—*the President has had me trying to gather together, as you know, a certain amount of law and facts to be in a position to kind of substitute for Dean, and to advise him on the White House involvement, in this whole transaction.* Yesterday, I gave him my summary and, admittedly, it was hearsay, but some of it pretty reliable. And the whole thing fit together pretty well as, at least, a working hypothesis. One of the things that I told him what that I had encountered people who appeared to be reticent to come forward because they somehow felt that the presidency was served by their not coming forward. *So he had me today, in a series of conversations with people, to straighten them around on that point.* The first one I talked to was your predecessor. Then I talked to Magruder, and . . .

K: It's pretty hard to talk to those two when they have testified under oath before a grand jury.

E: Well, as it turns out, I was just a little late in talking to Magruder, because he was just coming back from telling everything to the U.S. attorney. He has decided to come clean.

---

*Ehrlichman and Kleindienst, 14 April 1983, approximately 6:00 PM.

K: No kidding? Magruder?

E: Yep. He had his informal conference minutes before he came in to see me.

K: Would that be inconsistent with his testimony before the grand jury?

E: Dramatically inconsistent.

K: [Expletive removed]

E: *And he implicates everybody in all directions up and down in the Committee to Re-Elect.*

K: Mitchell?

E: Yep, cold turkey. My instructions after I had completed—well, I might say I also talked to a couple of other people who are around here just to pass the word to encourage them to testify, if the only reason they were not testifying was some concern about the presidency. Also, being very careful to say that I recognized everybody had rights, and that I didn't mean in any way to indicate that they should not avail themselves of their full rights. Now, Magruder then . . .

K: Let me ask one thing . . .

E: Yep.

K: As a result of what you just told me, it would indicate there is a substantial case of perjury against Mitchell and Magruder in the first instance.

E: Yep. No question.

K: So, complicity in the overall conspiracy?

E: More than just a participation in a conspiracy, Dick.

K: They would be principals?

E: Yes, they are principals.

K: Uh, I can't believe John Mitchell would have ever known that and let it go on.

E: Well, I must say that my conversation with him was reassuring in that regard. He is very steadfast in his protestations of innocence. Well, the Magruder case is not only testamentary, but is circumstantial—is persuasive to me.

K: But Mitchell denied it?

E: I saw Mitchell first. I didn't have all of this Magruder business. *Now, here I am a citizen of the United States and the designated inquirer of a body of information.* My purpose and intent is to advise you of this when I got finished with this process and tender this information for whatever purpose it would serve, recognizing that up until just a few minutes ago it was almost entirely hearsay. Magruder has just unloaded on me the substance of his conversation with the U.S. attorney—informal conversation. And I find that I now have very little to add to what Magruder had already given to the U.S. attorney.

K: That's not good.

E: I felt that I should go forward and at least advise you of this and to . . .

K: John, at this point, it seems to me that you are going to have to be very careful.

E: Let me spoil your afternoon completely, will you? One of the things Magruder told me was—and his attorney who was with him corroborated—*was that they are very concerned about Dean's facility for advising people at the committee of the proceedings of the grand jury* [treason to Dean].

K: [Unintelligible]

E: Well, he was apparently informing Magruder and others of what the grand jury was saying and doing.

E: And Silbert or someone else said to his attorney, well, we know the source of Dean's information and it was from higher up.

K: That is pretty speculative, because I don't think Henry Petersen would have told him.

Impressions Given Off

In the foregoing excerpt, Ehrlichman contrived several dramaturgical images that do not correspond to the behavioral events of which they purport to give an account. Central to every dramaturgical performance in real life and onstage is the success with which impressions are given off and the degree to which they succeed in creating a given social paradigm. Among these nonsupported images are the following:

1. The impression of a presidential summary. There was summing up but not the result of a charge designed to help Nixon act as president.
2. The dramaturgical impression of presidential antipathy for reticence on the part of the involved. The actual events suggest that freedom to testify or not was carefully adjusted to protect Nixon. The impression given off by Ehrlichman to Kleindienst was quite the reverse.
3. The impression of concern for civil rights. An earlier passage suggests that the script would call for prejudicing rights as a tactic for ensuring "you don't get anybody in jail." In this case testimony by Magruder was a fait accompli and testimony by Mitchell unlikely.
4. The impression that Mitchell was a principal in the case. This impression had the effect of minimizing Haldeman, Ehrlichman, and Nixon as principals—the dramaturgical effect central to all the staging of the past few days.
5. The impression that Ehrlichman is acting as a *bona fide* citizen doing his duty rather than as an actor merely giving forth lines.
6. The impression that Ehrlichman has nothing of substance (even if hearsay) to add to the Magruder account.
7. The impression of routine concern about Dean's access to privileged information from the Grand Jury. The fact was that Dean, knowing the drama to be produced, leaked information as directed by Nixon.

All in all it was an admirable performance by a skilled performer using a minimum of words to construct several useful impressions. Part of the usefulness of the impressions above is Kleindienst's response to them in the social paradigm thought to obtain between himself and the White House. He did not have direct knowledge he was being treated to a performance from the world of theatre. He, believing and trusting in Ehrlichman's performance, would later be reluctant to prosecute others in the course of duty as chief law enforcement officer of the United States. By virtue of this naïve (and necessary) trust, a subtle conversion of staged life occurs and enters into social life as "the real thing."

To engineer a convincing impression for the benefit of Mr. Kleindienst is a political act. Anytime one party engineers the beliefs, understandings, and behavior of another, a political act has transpired. If the engineering does not involve a mutual awareness on the part of all parties, then political fraud has transpired. When Ehrlichman was rehearsing and being auditioned by Nixon earlier in the day, there was mutual awareness of the social paradigm out of which both were operating. This was not the case in the Ehrlichman/Kleindienst conversation.

Mystifications in Mass Media

Immediately after the Kleindienst call, attention turned to how best to play to a wider audience the vignette that went so well before an audience of one. The solution is to plant a question with a reporter for Ziegler's press briefing the next day.

Meeting 14 April 1973

P: *Ehrlichman should get out the facts that he has made this investigation, that we weren't drug kicking and screaming into this thing.* I don't know.

E: I may have a legal problem. I'll talk to Dick tomorrow.

P: Yeah—it may be a real problem.

E: And if it's not a legal problem, *I'll have a question Monday for Ziegler on what Mitchell was doing at the White House.* "Just say he was here talking to me."

P: "The whole matter has been referred to the proper authorities."

E: Yeah, he'll have to.

P: And he'll say, "Oh that's been given to the proper authorities." That's what I would think.

News, reporters, networks, and press conferences are part of the "real" world of prophecies meant to be taken seriously even if fraudulent. In this instance, the more obvious use of "news" in the politics of reality construction is manifest. Someone who purports to be a reporter is to ask something that purports to be a question in something that purports to be a press briefing.

Those who are "sophisticated" will immediately know that much in the way of new is manufactured—much of it bearing little relationship to prior or forthcoming events. The point here is not to rehash a cynical view of news conferences but rather to stress the theoretical point that mass media provide a structural link between stage managers and their audiences. The dramaturgy of fraud depends on the fact that what is presented is defined as "news" by reporters rather than exposed—and thus deconstructed as "plants" by those same reporters.

A theory of reportage that discourages such background information, the so-called objective school of reportage, is a political instrument of fraud rather than a neutral party to information flow. Such reporters themselves create the dramaturgical semblance of reporting rather than its substance. All democratic societies need a practice of reportage that enables citizens to see through the mystifications of those who produce and direct the sociology of fraud in order that they may use their social power to defeat the fraud. The Washington press, oriented as it is to private profit and personal career, seldom meets the standards of emancipatory reportage.

The political advantage available to those who permit themselves to be converted from reporters into press agents is primarily one of access to inside information. This patronage is valuable to the career of one working the media but is hostile to the public values proclaimed by a free press.

A press that subscribes to a principle of reportage so objective that careerists need not appraise the reader-viewer of the managerial meaning of news plants is not really a free press but rather irresponsible to its public. It is more accurate to call it a "kept press" (for a devastating analysis see Bagdikian, 1983).

Self and Society: Constructing the President

In the process of constructing social reality, a first step is to establish what Goffman refers to as "copresence": a state of mutual sensitivity and shared orientations to runs of thought, emotion, and actions of each party. The political effect of copresence, once established, is that each party is partner in constructing the social self of others situationally present. Thus, mind, self, and society can be trine-born.

In this excerpt, one can see that "President Nixon" is really a collective product. Mead's point that social psychology is a social product is well supported. Even presidents are a complex and ever-changing process. Presumably the acting self is the chief author, director, and actor in such a production—but again, power is an intervening variable. Nixon has more power than most and in greater variety but still he is an amalgam of different elements.

Social roles, when embodied in the behavior of the parties concerned, constitute a coherent and existentially real part of the shared self structure of each of the actors. In this respect it is valid to state that self (the social identity embodied) and society (the social role programmed) are twin-born.

More to the point, it is valid to state that mind is social, i.e., a joint product of two or more persons. That is the sense in which Mead held that mind and self were something more than that residing inside the skin of a given social being. When the linkage between self and society is strong, the fact and forms of power become increasingly important in the transactions wherein self is constructed.

In Nixon's case there is an extensive use of power to construct the social role, hence the self structure of those who extend copresence to him. And with Nixon, those who participate in the construction of the social role of "the president" and thereby in the construction of his social identity, have considerable social power. At each point in the presentment of self, Nixon believes that he is the president but in the question of protecting Dean, Haldeman, and Mitchell—Nixon understands at some nonverbal level that he is protecting himself in quite the technical meaning of "himself." He and they are one as long as they share a role set.

Insofar as Mitchell and Dean have been crucial to the construction of the role of the president, they have shared in the personal esteem of Nixon for "himself." Nixon also realizes that his own personal esteem is a variable that is linked to the public esteem of Dean, Haldeman, Mitchell, and others of "our fellows." In almost any passage selected, one can see Ehrlichman and Haldeman tailoring Nixon's thoughts, responses, feelings, and understanding. Inasmuch as Nixon is in the role of president, Ehrlichman is tailoring the behavior set linked to that role—and in more coherent fashion than if the task were solely Nixon's.

This is not a put-down of Nixon as a person—the same point can be made in every shared construction of self and society. However, in the excerpt selected, it is particularly easy to observe the tailoring process: sometimes with Haldeman and Ehrlichman shaping Nixon on what to say, think, and feel; sometimes Nixon shaping Ehrlichman and Haldeman.

Meeting of 16 April 1973

P: Incidentally, I don't think it will gain us anything by dumping on the Dean Report as such.

E: No.

P: What I mean is I would say I was not satisfied that the Dean Report was complete and also I thought it was my obligation to go beyond that to people other than the White House.

E: Ron has an interesting point. Remember you had John Dean go to Camp David to write it up. He came down and said, "I can't . . . "

P: Right.

E: That is the tip off and right then you started to move.

P: That's right. He said he could not write it.

H: *Then you realized that there was more to this than you had been led to believe.* [Unintelligible]

P: How do I get credit for getting Magruder to the stand?

E: *Well it is very simple. You took Dean off of the case right then.*

H: Two weeks ago, the end of March.

P: I want the dates of all those . . .

E: I've got those.

P: Go ahead. And then . . .

E: And then it culminated last week . . .

P: Right.

E: *In your decision that Mitchell should be brought down here; Magruder should be brought in; Strachan should be brought in.*

P: Shall I say that we brought them all in?

E: I don't think you can. I don't think you can.

H: *I wouldn't name them by name. Just say I brought a group of people in.*

E: Personally come to the White House.

P: I will not tell you who because I don't want to prejudice their rights before [unintelligible].

E: *But you should say, "I heard enough that I was satisfied that it was time to precipitously move. I called the attorney general over, in turn Petersen."*

P: The attorney general. Actually you made the call to him on Saturday.

E: Yes.

P: But this was after you heard about the Magruder strategy.

E: No, before.

P: Oh.

The Reviews

The press and television journalists were consistent in the poor reviews given to all of Nixon's performances, formal and semiformal. Generally reviews varied with party politics—conservative and very conservative partisans giving Nixon credit for his presentments at face value, even lauding his tenure in office. The liberal/radical elements in politics were very critical of Nixon's cover stories and refused to honor any performance irrespective of its dramatic quality, internal coherence, or its polish as a staged event.

Each audience responded differently to the staging of the meaning of Watergate and in that difference is a point of intellectual leverage for understanding the dramaturgical construction of social reality. The central question is how to understand the variation in response between these three audiences. The thesis advanced here has to do with the social paradigm; especially the interest sets and value sets for which each audience worked to construct and to implement as a self-fulfilling prophecy.

The conservative Republicans and Democrats responded to the Nixon dramaturgy out of one set of values. This social paradigm was one of the "new federalism" which dismantles the power of the federal government to police and restrain the activities of other power centers. The values implicit in the new federalism appealed to Southern conservatives in returning control of racial policy to the states, especially in the area of education; appealed to the small entrepreneur so hard-pressed by federal bureaucracies; and especially to monopoly capital in abandoning the efforts to constrain corporate capitalism on profit rates, ecology matters, truth in lending and advertising, product standards, labor policies, as well as the delicate transactions between business and political candidates. From the point of view of this set of values Nixon is a "good" president.

Both liberal and most radical audiences accorded a negative review to Nixon's presentments. For the liberals, if Nixon were not vulnerable on the point of economic policy, foreign policy, fiscal policy, and welfare policy, he certainly was vulnerable on Watergate and his performances were critically evaluated out of an opposite social paradigm. In neither paradigm, that of the conservatives nor that of the liberals, did values associated with constitutional procedures, legal accountability, and "free" elections play a central part.

The liberal politicians were also vulnerable on the point of contrived elections. They did not pursue legal accountability once Nixon was out of office nor were they moved to insist on significant reform in these areas— they simply wanted Nixon out, assuming that control of the political apparatus would come to them in 1976 and they could use the power of the state to redress the worst effects of monopoly capital and thus save it.

For the liberals, Watergate proved how well the system works; for conservatives, it proved how unfair the critics were; for radicals, it showed how superficial politics and justice are in America.

The far Left operated out of a social paradigm in which the coming and going of Nixon was of small moment. In a system of corporate capitalism, the fate of this president or that does not matter much. If anything, the continuation of Nixon in office was preferable in a social paradigm that required an unweakened Nixon acting effectively with his programs of fiscal policy which advanced the historical moment of dramatic collapse of capitalism from its internal contradictions.

In the socialist paradigm, the more the Nixon administration transferred the social costs of corporate capitalism to the working and white-collar classes, the sooner would these classes rebel against higher prices, higher unemployment, higher taxes, larger welfare rolls, larger and more serious unemployment, and the closing off of opportunity. This audience maintained a discrete silence. The open support of Nixon by the Soviet leadership is understood, in part, by reference to this paradigm.

Ringing Down the Curtain

Consistent with his performance from about 1967 on, Nixon exerted much effort to construct the meaning of his departure from the White House in ways supportive of an image of himself as a "great American statesman" interested in peace, prosperity, justice, and opportunity. In hostile contrast to that image is one drawn by Nixon's most persistent critics as a cynical opportunist who presided over a state apparatus dedicated to the welfare of monopoly capitalism.

In the formal business of constructing social facticity, the truth value of any given number of variables converges to produce the final product. Epistemologically, there is no truth other than that collectively adopted as the official meaning for a given social paradigm. Since there are an infinite number of social paradigms by which to interpret events, there can be an infinite number of social "truths."

In Nixon's case, the power variable was almost sufficient by itself to establish the official meaning of his presidency. Now that he is out of office, most of the power is gone and his meaning will be constructed by other power groups. In the excerpt to follow taken from the resignation address before one of the largest live television audiences in history, Nixon proposed this image of his meaning in public office:

Good evening. This will be the 37th time I will have spoken to you from this office where so many decisions have been made that shaped the history of this nation. Each time I have done so to discuss with you some matters which I believed affected the national interest. In all the decisions I have made in my public life I have always tried to do what was best for the nation.

Throughout the long and difficult period of Watergate, I have felt it was my duty to persevere, to make every possible effort to complete the kind of office to which you elected me. In the past few days, however, *it has become evident to me that I no longer have a strong enough political base in the Congress to justify continuing that effort.* I would have preferred to carry through to the finish no matter the personal agony that would have been involved. And my family unanimously urged me to do so. *But the interest of the nation must always come before any personal consideration.*

From the discussions I have had with congressional and other leaders, I have concluded that because of the Watergate matter I might not have the support of the Congress that I would consider necessary to back the very difficult decisions and carry out the duties of this office in the way the interests of the nation would require.

I have never been a quitter. To leave office before my term is completed is abhorrent to every instinct in my body. As President I must put the interests of America first. America needs a full-time president and a full-time Congress, particularly at this time with problems we face at home and abroad.

To continue the fight through the months ahead for my personal vindication would almost totally absorb the time and attention of both the President and the Congress in a period when *our entire focus should be on the great issues of peace abroad and prosperity without inflation at home.*

Therefore, I shall resign the presidency effective at noon tomorrow. By taking this action, I hope that I will have hastened the start of that process of healing which is so desperately needed in America.

In this address, Nixon practices with consummate skill and under considerable stress the performer's art of structuring meaning. In defining his departure from office, he emphasizes the withdrawal of support by Congress. Another analyst constructing the meaning of that departure might have said that the resignation was forced by his participation in the obstruction of justice. In the offering of a personal motive, Nixon creates the impression that his central concern is for the national interest rather than any concern to avoid being the first president removed by impeachment proceedings.

In the act of quitting office, Nixon asserts that he has never been a quitter. In evaluating his administration, Nixon suggests that we can all be proud of that administration. In listing his achievements, he neglects to mention inflation, unemployment, decline in health and medical care, the use of Madison Avenue tactics in his campaigns, or the effect of his policies on the structure of opportunity for minority groups. Still less does he mention the increased support for repressive regimes in the Third World.

There are other events of his presidency that could be assembled in support of a dramatic reading giving still other interpretations of that presidency. In the everyday methods of constructing social reality, there are any number of events that are omitted or defined as not occurring: belches, burps, bumps, false starts, poor gambits, unacceptable lines, inadvertent acts, as well as many other events within any given social paradigm. In order to compose just that set of events out of all possible events occurring, we say, "excuse me," "pardon me," "I'm sorry," "I misspoke myself," "I mean," "you know," and the like—or perhaps we simply behave as though a given act had not happened at all.

If the persons involved are operating out of a common paradigm with shared values, such deletions are accepted routinely. If there is a suspicion of differing value sets, the deletions are challenged. In such challenges, the use of power is invoked. Power is seldom used where a shared paradigm obtains.

Conflict Methodology and Critical Dramaturgy

Conflict methodology entails the search for quality information under conditions of conflict between classes, genders, age cohorts, nations, and other social entities. When social solidarity is high, the knowledge process is transparent; the need for a formal research process is of limited utility. It is when there are barriers to information flow between people that a special methodology is required.

It is when there are skilled efforts to mask or to dissemble that the communication process needs the help of more formal research methods.

As a technique in conflict methodology, critical dramaturgical analysis helps to clarify the role of power in the construction of social meanings, social identities, social roles, as well as social processes. In every series of events, there are several technical features that permit the intrusion of political power in the reality construction process.

We have looked at many technical features of the reality constituting process using the Watergate tapes as a source of data. The tapes clearly demonstrate a skillful and sustained effort to subvert the knowledge process as it focused on the break-in of the Watergate complex and its cover-up. We have seen that the Nixon inner–inner circle used the elements of theatre to mock up the dramaturgical image of a variety of social facts with which to mystify their various audiences.

Now comes judgment time. It is necessary to go beyond the facts of alienated theatre and politics to understand the conditions under which the interface between theatre and politics comes to be distorted so. The key to such an understanding has to do with whether the use of the powers of office of the president of a nation can fairly be used to link politics and theatre in such a fashion.

Political power, when deployed legitimately, helps make the knowledge field more transparent to those with social standing. When it is used to cloud the knowledge field, to mystify the parties concerned with constructing what is, putatively, a shared symbolic environment, when power is used to force a set of policies inimical to their objective interests upon others— then the use of political power is illegitimate. It is illegitimate within the framework of democratic politics, international peace, and social justice considerations.

In the case of Watergate, the use of political power by Nixon to deceive the American polity was legitimate—within the context of capitalist relations. Remember the passage: "Our entire focus should be on the great issues of peace abroad and prosperity without inflation at home."

It is, objectively and without qualification, in the interest of a capitalist society to have peace abroad, prosperity at home, and a low inflation rate. Peace is necessary to move vast amounts of goods and raw materials from the Third World to the capitalist countries. Think of what tomorrow would be like were access to cheap oil to be cut off from Europe, North America, or Japan. The economic machine would stop.

Prosperity at home is necessary—indeed, the rationale—for capitalism. Without prosperity, political legitimacy would dissolve; the social base of the capitalist state would shrink; domestic markets would be unable to absorb the goods produced at home and abroad.

Control of inflation is necessary to stabilize the world capitalist system which uses the dollar as its medium of exchange. It is necessary to keep political faith and political legitimacy with a growing bloc of senior citizens who are on fixed incomes and who have direct access to members of Congress. Control of inflation is necessary to keep competitive with foreign corporations that grow more competitive every year.

Richard Milhous Nixon and his central advisors, especially Henry Kissinger, knew exactly what must be done to maintain the hegemony of the United States in the world capitalist system and to maintain the system itself. Richard Nixon was the first president of the world capitalist system. His first duty was to preserve it. His loyalties to the American voter and to the democratic process ran a dismal, distant second. The Nixon-Kissinger team were very astute players on the world stage. They came to power just as American capital needed them to deal with enemies at home and reorganize the world in its own image abroad.

The United States was and is under many economic pressures at home and abroad that tend to destabilize American capitalism. Demanding workers, civil rights advocates, ecology advocates, senior citizens, a very spoiled leisure class demanding more profits, overloaded managerial staffs, increasing demand for police and prisons, a growing load of welfare recipients, the consumer movement—all these sectors of the population made demands on an economic system that was dependent on outdated equipment.

Abroad there was the loss of markets to industrialized Europe, to the emerging Asian nations, to the Socialist bloc, and to local capitalists in the Third World. Foreign markets are essential to capitalism since the workers in a given nation are not paid 100 percent of the value of what they produce. The rest must be sold overseas in order to realize profits.

There were the Third World producers cartels that threatened to reverse the flow of wealth from the poor countries to the rich. There were multinational corporations that would move vast amounts of capital and millions of jobs out of North America. There were the socialist liberation movements in Southeast Asia, Latin America, and Africa to be dealt with.

With all these conflicting interest groups at work, there was a need for restabilizing the world capitalist system before it went into depression or before it moved toward socialism. Nixon and Kissinger engineered a new world order with the United States securely on top. It was, objectively, in the interest of American workers and consumers for Nixon to continue in office. Nixon knew this; Kissinger knew this; and Mitchell, Ehrlichman, and the other president's men knew it.

Watergate was but the tip of the iceberg. Stealing campaign plans and getting evidence against democrats from their office in the Watergate complex was but one small part of the much larger effort to make sure that Nixon was reelected. He won handily but he and his team had to deal with the aftermath while he and Kissinger were attending to the larger job of American hegemony in the world.

Power and Theatre

As president of a nation, Nixon occupies an office from which several different kinds of power can be deployed with which to deal with the aftermath of Watergate. Given these technical features that undergird all intersubjective understanding presented in the analyses above, it is readily understood that differences in power enter into the construction of social reality to resolve any problems with the "real" meaning of events. There is much justification to a theory of power stratification that states that all power differences function to resolve conflicts in the definition of a situation, social interpretation of events, as well as conflicts in the selection of behavioral events said to be compatible with a given social prophecy.

Ordinarily, the conflict is between parties with a grasp of the sociocultural paradigm at hand and those without a good grasp. In such a case, power is said to be legitimate since it keys off the value set implicit in the paradigm. Sometimes the conflict is between two parties each of which has a good grasp of the social values implicit in two different coherent paradigms and the same standing as regards legitimacy. In both cases power is used to impose a social definition taken to be the official history of the social group. In the former instance power is used more gently and with due process. In the second, power is wielded ruthlessly and under the assumption that there is no shared social paradigm. Such is the nature of politics.

Much in the way of Nixon's use of power with respect to the Congress, to the "enemies" on his enemy list, to the courts, and the media operated as though there was no common social paradigm that embraced all parties. In this case, dramaturgical analysis permits us to understand why the House Judiciary Committee voted out articles of impeachment on the Watergate affair but not on the illegal bombing of Cambodia by Nixon.

We can infer in the latter instance that there was a consensus about the social paradigm out of which sufficient numbers of congressmen acted that permitted Cambodians to be bombed without formal specification of the social prophecy at hand as "war," as required by the Constitution. Both Nixon and Congress interpreted the war in Southeast Asia as being against the "Communist threat." That justified the use of physical power, since social power seldom runs beyond the boundaries of the social unit that uses it.

In the case of the Watergate affair, there was no sharing of paradigm and so power entered into the resolution process. The Democrats did not understand the need to cut back on programs of social justice, to neutralize the socialist revolutions and the Soviet Union, to discipline workers and consumers at home, to keep the world capitalist system free from nationalism, to support repressive regimes in the Third World, or to use China against the Soviet Union. Nixon, Kissinger, and most "free world" leaders from Margaret Thatcher to Helmut Kohl understood the need for Nixon to "lead the free world."

But since the power base of both parties had keyed off the compatibility of actions and values, Nixon was in a precarious situation. He had to subvert democracy while making it appear that it was embodied in the national election. Apparently he and his men thought he might lose. His power collapsed quickly as Congress used its power to oppose his constructions and impose its own. As Simmel has said, power implies compliance by others; when others do not accept, power disappears. Dean, Magruder, Haig, and other Washingtonians gradually withdrew their support. Exit Nixon.

The millions of viewers who respond to the use of power in constructing meanings had come to believe that what had been put together by the Nixon team was a state of peace, justice, opportunity, honest brokerage, and quality service by the White House. Millions of persons who struggled on a subsistence diet, whose taxes supported the infrastructure of corporate capitalism, whose children were school dropouts or the marginally employed, whose private lives were bland and imbued with a sense of quiet despair, were mystified when a person they respected in an office they still esteemed abused their trust with deception.

Yet for millions of Americans, the good life they and their children enjoyed depended on something like a Nixon as president of the world capitalist system. Carter was elected in 1976. He failed to follow Nixon policies and the fiscal crisis of American capitalism returned with a vengeance. Then Reagan was elected. He was the second president of the world capitalist system and once again stabilized it at home and abroad. For the 5 percent of the world who benefit from capitalism—mostly in Europe and North America—Nixon and Reagan look good.

For the workers and peasants in the Third World whose labor enriches that 5 percent; for the growing numbers in the underclass at home; for the millions of small businesses and farms abandoned to their fate by Nixon; for the young men and women murdered by the death squads and mercenaries run by the CIA—the prosperity of a handful of White workers and capitalists is far too high a price to pay for the loss of democracy and socialism.

And the final word on Nixon: his recourse to allusions to his mother, to his dead brothers, to the larger causes of peace and welfare; the recourse to allusions of great sorrow and great joy, to the gods of his viewers—these are cheap and theatrical ploys that contradict whatever dignity and grace he may have mustered in other presentments. Nixon is off stage and the nation is better for it. In speaking of the social conditions of the United States in the 1972 election, Nixon had this to say:

As far as this kind of activity is concerned, we expect it. However, under no circumstances will I be affected whatever by it.

Part V

Emancipatory Uses of Dramaturgy

Introduction

In scientific terms, critical dramaturgy emphasizes the historical relativity of forms of social drama. In political terms, critical dramaturgy facilitates understanding and participation by all competent adults in social processes of human emancipation and societal development. The chapters in this section attempt to address the analytical and political interests of critical dramaturgy by suggesting how dramaturgy might be put to emancipatory uses.

Beyond the boundaries of this book lay the forms of human drama that help constitute the most holy forms of social life. I return to explore the realm of the Holy in the sequel to this book as part of an effort to help fashion a postmodern social psychology for the twenty-first century. Its major dimensions are sketched out in this chapter; however, each person must, one day, write his or her own chapter that extends and improves the few simple points made here.

In "Emancipatory Dimensions in Dramaturgy," I discuss what is necessary in the theater and in human drama if these are to contribute to emancipatory knowledge. First, theater and drama must point to the limitations of life as it is; there must be a descriptive dimension. Second, drama must give us a vision of life as it is not; it must have a critical dimension. Third, it must motivate or push people to realize their human potential; that is, it must have a revolutionary dimension.

Against the background of these three elements of emancipatory dramaturgy, there is an analysis of the emancipatory potential embedded in three popular films—*Casablanca, Cabaret,* and *The Wizard of Oz*—to show how theater and drama might contribute to emancipatory knowledge. Each of the films reviewed here help specify (1) a critique of society in its alienated forms, (2) a vision of drama more closely allied with human interests and the human spirit, together with (3) a discussion of how processes of opposition can be organized.

There are chapters on the use of the drama of religion and sport as well. These are offered as antidote to those who would use their genius, talent, and energy to create an alienated dramaturgy in the world. Then finally, there is a chapter on how young people unite magic and make-believe with the world of seriously intended reality in which they live, love, adapt, struggle, doubt, and die. Each young person searches for a voice with which to tell her/his own story and that is the way it should be.

12

Emancipatory Dimensions in Dramaturgy

There is an inertia that tends to defeat hope,
but there are also melodramatic
confrontations which
renew it.

—*Laud Humphries*

There are three tests of dramaturgy and theatre that one can apply to gauge the degree to which such uses of make-believe are emancipatory. In this chapter I would like to present these tests and apply them to several forms of dramaturgical presentations.

Content

The first test criterion that one may apply has to do with the content of the dramatic event. One may say a dramatic event is emancipatory if the play, film, novel, painting, or poem reflects upon the quality of social life, evaluates it against some standard of collective and personal good, and offers, as well, an alternative vision of social life.

There is an analysis of the emancipatory content of three well-received movies below that will help flesh out this most important moment of liberation.

Medium

A second test has to do with the originality and creativity of the staging of the event: new and creative forms of costuming, set design, scenic organization, and scenario development may have emancipatory moments. New

ways to use color, line, form, texture, materials, or combinations thereof
provide a radical dimension in art and drama.

The theatre of Andrew Lloyd Webber offers a rich lode of creative gold.
Cats is one of the most imaginative plays ever to be staged in London or
New York. In the New York version, an alley complete with the soft grays
of dusk offered a stage upon which the cats could frolic and reflect on a
cat's life. Whoever would think of doing a musical in the 1980s about Evita
and Che? Whoever would think to write a song about Argentina that would
become an international hit? In the London staging, *Starlight Express* required that Victoria theatre be rebuilt as never before, with train tracks running high into the balcony. The staging of *Song and Dance* in London was
original, with a full orchestra backstage yet visible as a woman sang of the
vicissitudes of love. "Tell Me on a Sunday, Please," is one of the most
touching acceptances of love lost to be found in a genre known for its
melancholy.

Creativity in this second dimension without the first and third comprises
a false emancipation however original it might be.

Mummenschanz, a delightfully creative mime, magic, and puppet show,
has almost no emancipatory values at all. Still it is well worth the time and
effort used to stage it. On their own terms, a vast possibility for surprise
and delight, genius and insight, is opened up by such artistic work. Most
modern art and drama has a narrow, limited, and depoliticized form of
radicality and, as such, scarcely deserves the name "radical" even though
fully deserving of the larger term "art."

Expressionism, cubism, abstract art, realism surpassing reality, impres-
sionism, and other schools of art are best understood as a desperate effort
to create something new, while they also absorb some of the surplus capital
of the owning classes, provide something of a portable treasury, offer a way
to acquire status outside of the traditional forms of status allocation, or
break through the tiny parochial network of established art.

Mode of Production

Third, the modes of production and distribution are most important factors in a determination of the emancipatory potential of stage, cinema, television, or radio drama. Modes of production in which the artistic function
is widely dispersed among workers, actors, authors, musicians, and editors;
where the line between artists and audience is scarcely visible; and where
the art form is widely available apart from tests of class, status, or power
may be called emancipatory. This third variable, in combination with the
first two above, interacts in a wide variety of ways to enhance emancipation. In some instances, content alone suffices to stimulate emancipatory

action, but to be fully emancipatory, theatre must merge with life and with the people who live it. We can look at each test factor in detail, but first a note on emancipatory knowledge in all its forms: science, art, prose and poetry, cinema, the healing arts, as well as critical theory.

Emancipatory Knowledge

Emancipatory knowledge judges all existing social forms in terms of some coherent set of values. For critical theory, these values include praxis, community, democratic self-management, social justice, and the integrity of the natural and human environment. Other value systems that emphasize property rights, individualism, capital accumulation, competition, and elitist forms of production in art, music, science, and theatre are not intrinsically emancipatory. In the latter, emancipation does not extend to all persons but only those selected by chance, talent, or position. Central to all questions of emancipation is a judgment about how broadly an emancipatory critique is to be drawn.

It was rightly said by Donne that the death and degradation of any one person tolls the death knell of us all. In degrading others, we degrade ourselves. Studies of guards and prisoners, slaves and slavemasters, authoritarian leaders and their sycophants, passive wives and rigid husbands—all these bespeak the truth: Self and society are twin-born. For weal or for woe, the mean-spirited things we do to others are registered as a mean spirit in the deep structures of our soul.

Then too, the carrying capacity of the earth is finite. Without wideranging social justice in production and distribution, economics and politics become a smash-and-grab operation that reduces the possibilities of future generations. Each time we rip a ton of minerals from the good earth, each time we pour a ton of poison into the air, each time we drain a swamp or cut a forest we do inestimable harm to all creatures large and small, and to the most dangerous creature of all—ourselves.

It is part of the human condition that each generation must consider the legacy it gets and the legacy it leaves for each successive generation inasmuch as each generation benefited from that principle as it was observed by still earlier generations. In the solipsistic generation that now rules everywhere, the vast treasury of invention and idea given freely to it is taken without thought of thanks. In this generation, the central existential question is how one might get more, faster, with less effort, and keep more of it; how one might take more and share less with the people whose labor produced it.

Life is a seamless whole; human life is part of that whole. A school of art criticism that severs itself from a comprehensive approach to the human conditions constitutes itself as an exercise in technical appraisal rather than one of social judgment. In this modality, art criticism strips art of its sociology, politics, economics, and history. Such a technicized art criticism has all the merits of a well-tended cemetery.

> As flow the rivers to the sea
> down from rocky rill or plain,
> a thousand ages toiled for thee
> and gave thee harvest of their pain.
>
> The ancient toilers for thee wrought
> chaos from primeval clay; and for thee sought
> a thousand tools for thee to build
> upon the harvest that now they yield.
>
> Just as you, wise and strong,
> to other ages, shall pass along.
> And of their debt, they will rest,
> if as yet, you make the same bequest.

Drama and Democracy

There is an epistemological and philosophical point worth mentioning in any discussion that tries to erase the boundaries between drama and real life, actor and audience, politics and pretend—in the interest of praxis. The orthodox view of human alienation from the knowledge process is that objective reality exists and the human being is limited in his/her capacity to subjectively grasp objective truth. Alienation thus is found in and measured by the size of the gap between the objectively existing laws of nature and laws of society on the one hand and subjective human understanding of those objectively existing laws on the other.

In this mode of alienated knowledge, science is the solution to alienation while the publication of scientific law is the means by which the knowledge process is socialized.

In the Marxist view, alienation and its solution are a bit more complex. Elsewhere in this book I have listed a dozen or so varieties of emancipatory knowledge; all of these are pointed toward making possible the collective politics of change and renewal. Drama is radical in the third dimension when it offers one or more of these forms of knowledge about how to make the revolution.

Reality, especially social reality, is infinitely variable and profoundly complex. However, alienation is not separation between objective reality and subjective understanding. It is rather separation from the productive process by which truth is constituted. One knows accurately the meaning of work, family, church, or school by participating actively in their constitution. One knows, accurately, the laws of nature by actively working to appropriate nature. One knows, intimately, the laws of society by actively creating and changing them.

Any system of cultural production that excludes people from producing their own realities also alienates people from the knowledge of those realities. Any way of staging drama that freezes people into a passive audience thereby alienates them from full understanding of the play, movie, or game to which their time and attention is given.

If we accept the broader role of critique, then the structures of class privilege, of racial and ethnic oppression, of gender preference, and of age discrimination are subject to critique in terms of alienated knowledge processes. Elitist forms of theatre tend to reproduce those forms of privilege.

Critical theatre examines the negativities of such social relationships and offers alternative visions of egalitarian relations in work, family, play, and politics. Critical theatre satisfies the human interest in emancipatory knowledge by, in the first instance, making visible those negativities and opening up those possibilities.

Good radical art provides the social magic by which people come to a theoretical understanding of the social sources of misery and oppression and, inspired by this insight, act collectively to change social life.

More than radical content is necessary for human emancipation, however. Radical theatre must show how an oppressed population might get from one set of relationships to another. Emancipatory theatre offers a vision of life as it might be rather than as it must be.

Pretheoretical Theatre

Pretheoretical theatre shows only the negativities of that which exists. Pretheoretical theatre offers one flight or temporary refuge from the degradations of class, gender, or racial oppression. Pretheoretical theatre glorifies the ugliness of power, privilege, and exploitation.

The drama of Punk life with its creative use of clothing, hair style, face decorations, and language is overtly pretheoretical art. In the screaming rage of Punk life, its violence and its sexuality, there is a inchoate rejection of middle-class values and middle-class programs. But beyond withdrawing and screaming contempt, Punk life has little to offer.

The drama of terrorism creates a collage of misery, surprise, wonder, and fear. It also dramatizes the inadequacies of existing politics and economics. In Ireland, Palestine, South Africa, and Central America the work of terrorists can suspend ordinary taken-for-granted social activity. In its nihilism, terror can tear down that-which-exists but has no direction and no positive moment. Other than extending oppression and thus building a social base for resistance, the politics of terror are of little value.

The drama of crime is also pretheoretical theater. The rape of a woman, theft from the rich, excrement and vandalism in school, murder and assault of the oppressor all constitute a certain drama of resistance but, again without a program and without mercy and compassion, such theater does not survive the moment of its performance.

Exhibition of a pile of manure in a Chicago art show or the decoration of an island with pink plastic falls far below the emancipatory potential of art. The performance of atonal compositions, unrhythmic brass, discordant piano, or unmusical song may be creative enough and help define a postmodern critique of the assumptions in modern music about what is natural and good, but such performance reduces to noise in the system without a theory and a politics to give emancipatory direction to art.

Emancipatory art in all its forms motivates, mobilizes, transforms, evaluates those transformations and leads the way toward further progress in the human condition. It leads law and politics, science and economics; it leads religion and revolution toward social justice. Radical art inspires its artists and actors to unite drama and grace with the forms of social life. It destroys the artificial boundaries between art and the kitchen, art and the classroom, art and the workplace, art and the bedroom. Radical art suffuses each moment of life, each trajectory of life, each realm of life with its transcending beauty, grace, wit, joy, and wisdom. Radical art makes it good to be a student, a worker, a lover, or a cook.

Drama and Revolution

Emancipatory theatre must have a theory of social revolution—implicit or explicit who is going to make the revolution and how it is to be made. In many forms of theatre, justice triumphs and evil is defeated by impersonal agencies: history, chance, fate, God, or accident. A theoretically informed theatre invests the revolutionary impulse in people organized and informed by their own historically located (and self-created) understanding of what may and should be done.

The most significant way in which a relationship to the mode of production is changed is in terms of the way in which radical theatre is related to the means of producing political culture. Ordinarily politics is produced within the narrow limits of institutional governance. Very often, when institutional politics serve the interests of a class, party, or tribal elite, social movements arise to create an ad hoc politics. Street politics with its drama of anger and rebellion, with its signs, slogans, curses, rocks, and martyrs all offer a revivifying politics.

The drama of street politics with its dances, marches, parades, balloons, flowers, and costumes mocking the oppressors all infuse politics with fun, humor, sarcasm, wit, and surprise. In such moments, the artificial (and alienating) line between elite politics and collective art is erased. In the same fashion, the line between theatre and real life, theatre and politics, audience and actors vanishes. An authentically radical dramaturgy reunites the separated parts of life and society while it informs the political process.

Radical dramaturgy stimulates praxis broadly understood as good theory oriented to collective interests.

The Braided Circle Theater in Colorado is an instance of radical dramaturgy. Comprised mostly of women, it offers theatre that asks the audience to take the emancipatory message embodied in a play into community political activity. In a play about sexual violence, the players read stories from current news stories about violence done to women in that town. Players walk about reading excerpts from local papers or from local shelters for battered women.

The play dramatizes several points of policy to be taken by men and women from the theatre into city council, county, and state governance and into the home by which women and men can create more supportive and affirmative relationships. Resistance to gender oppression is a central theme.

There is of course a radical dramaturgy oriented to the creation and recreation of the structures of domination. The mass rallies in Germany during the 1930s, the cinema of D. W. Griffith, the sexual violence in Alfred Hitchcock, the ugly politics in Jimmy Swaggart religious revivals, as well as the anti-Communist propaganda of Hollywood in the 1950s all tend to reinforce existing structures of class, race, ethnic, or gender privilege or else produce new structures in which one elite supplants another.

In order for dramaturgy to be emancipatory, it must identify false politics and make known those authentically tied to the human project.

The human project is infinitely variable. There have been 3,000 to 5,000 cultures in the history of the world so far and there will certainly be more. What does not vary widely, however, is the necessary dialectic between individual creativity and repression; between the collective good and the energizing effect of personal autonomy; between generational sacrifice and generational enjoyment; between the natural world and social consumption; between the heritage of the past and the conditions of the future.

The role of critical dramaturgy is to explore these dialectics, weigh them, and suggest alternative resolutions of the tension between contesting goods. Those alternatives must be real dilemmas else theatre is merely propaganda and the dialectical process is aborted.

The central defect of pretheoretical theatre, poetry, prose and play is that it leads to false politics. Theatre that focuses on individual evil suggests that evil ends with the death (or salvation) of the individual. Poetry that suggests a group or race is at the source of human distress diverts attention from social relationships. Religious prose that calls one toward personal salvation only while it accepts the structural evil of class and racial exploitation leaves these larger evils intact. Justice after death is a thin comfort to those who suffer injustice in this world. While this life is but a small fragment of eternity, it may be the only portion of eternity that we have.

Drama and History

The writing of emancipatory drama entails the danger of reification. Whether a given social form is oppressive or emancipatory varies in time and place. While it is proper to assign an emancipatory role to this or that agent in a given historical situation, it is improper to set that agent as emancipatory for all time and all places.

The working-class struggles of the thirties may have been progressive; by the sixties, it was clear that working-class politics was reactionary. The liberative potential of science and technology appropriately may be celebrated in the Sherlock Holmes novels and movies, in the World War II movies, or in any number of movies having to do with doctors and disease. But the negativities of science and technology are rightly condemned in the Frankenstein movies, in the *Star Wars* series, or in the catastrophic movies of nuclear holocaust.

Violence and street justice may be the correct political path to take in opposing villainy in Robin Hood movies, in anti-Nazi movies, or in movies about liberation in Algeria, Kenya, or South Africa. But there are other politics suitable for revolutionary social change in other social formations. Marx and Engels (1972) in the "Manifesto," preferred the voting franchise, union organizing, tax policies, and land reform.

A given play or movie must always be judged and used historically, in terms of the special historically existing condition in a special time and place. To do otherwise is to act blindly—without knowledge. What is good theory and politics in one setting may well be bad theory and politics in another.

It is a structural characteristic—and a serious limitation of the written novel, play, or cinema—that once written or filmed, history is frozen. Alternative endings, interpretations, and internal dynamics are set as general form for all time.

While it is significantly true that situations arise time and again in history rending some plays, novels, songs, and movies of lasting value; and that shadings of performance give a new and unexpected yet apt insight to such plays as *Hamlet, Faust,* or *Bitter Rice*—still our esteem and sense of propriety forbids any great change. One may always use the topics and themes from old plays in new ones, but still the old plays remain as ideological tools that preempt history.

Emancipatory drama must give us a vision of history as change; an understanding of the unnecessary limitations of life as they are; as well as a push to move us toward our human potential. This is the core of emancipatory knowledge. It leads toward change and renewal; it stands against power and privilege; it affirms our right to act collectively on values that transcend and yet resonate with our present interests as living human beings.

Commodity Art and Drama

Any art form packaged and distributed so that it can be appropriated by a private individual or corporation is not emancipatory. Books, movies, cassettes, and other copyright drama falsely assert private ownership of plays, dramas, and tales.

The material and ideological base from which all communication derives is the collective product of countless generations of unknown authors, inventors, improvers, or reusers. For one to claim ownership of a play or novel is as false as a private claim on a language or alphabet, a printing press or a camera. These are social inventions that are the common heritage of humans as are the ideas contained in politics, religion, sexuality, or economics. Ninety-nine percent plus of any product is in the common realm else it would be inexplicable and worthless.

What makes something worthwhile is that it speaks to the common need, to the general interest, and in the common language. While the author deserves the resources to create art and drama, the right to exclude significant portions of society from using, sharing, and enjoying the dramatic experience until a profit is extracted from each and every consumer greatly magnifies the small contribution made by the author and greatly minimizes the collective portion of the created thing.

Art and Ethics

Worthwhile art examines and illuminates the contradictions in love, marriage, politics, religion, or play. Art worthy of the name gives dimension and dilemma to the events depicted or delineated. Such art becomes the seedbed of wisdom and insight. One-dimensional art is mere propaganda however beautifully done; in the end it is boring or irrelevant.

Art and drama without dilemma; art or drama that portrays life only through the eyes of a class, elite, or ethnic interest and tends to reproduce that interest at the expense of a more general, more human interest; art in any format—painting, music, ballet, theatre, cinema, novel, poetry, or lecture that does not give honest weight to other views, interests, hopes, and troubles is self-serving opinion that loses its appeal as its client audience disappears from history. Those who survive create and are recreated by newly emerging social groupings as time goes by.

Three Films and a Play

The most popular film among children of any age in the English-speaking world is, most probably, *The Wizard of Oz.* Among adults inclined to be romantic, *Casablanca* carries a continuing fascination. For those who know theatre and its political uses, *Cabaret* is a classic. Probably the least known of any play in America, at least, is *The Resistible Rise of Arturo Ui,* a play by Bertolt Brecht.

We will look at each of these films and the play in terms of the three dimensions of a critical dramaturgy set forth above. Being romantic, I will start with *Casablanca,* a town in North Africa under the control of Vichy France (the Nazi collaborators) and to which many French came for reasons set forth in the film.

Casablanca

The continuing attraction in the content of *Casablanca* lies in the dilemma of the Ingrid Bergman character in choosing between two loves honestly held. There is a real dilemma, in social terms, in choosing between the Paul Henreid and the Humphrey Bogart characters. Both are admirable and both have human failings in their own way.

The Bergman character came by the love of each in honest ways. She has a valid social obligation and a valid personal attraction for both. She is not an evil woman for accepting the love of either and would not be deemed dishonorable whichever love she chose. That is an honest dilemma and not a situation in which illicit love can be condemned while social probity upheld. It is not propaganda but rather discourse that the film presents us.

The overdone and unmitigated evil of Nazism in the movie is not as universal as the theme of tyranny opposed and invincible power defeated. It is not the various petty defeats to which the Nazis are subject that have enduring appeal, rather these defeats resonate with the petty victories at work and in school in which the tyranny of boss or teacher is embarrassed. It is the satisfaction we draw from the frustration of arbitrary power that elicits our applause.

A more honest portrayal would have given the Nazi officers some human attributes and the Nazi cause some better grounding. After all, millions did find such grounds and millions still do. It is propaganda—not enlightenment—to draw such lines of unmitigated evil.

Casablanca is radical in the first dimension mentioned earlier. It offers a case for nontraditional sexuality. A married woman accepts love of a man outside of marriage and we approve. Another married woman offers herself to a venal policeman to obtain a needed visa in order that the husband may get to America, we understand her offer. She is saved by Rick, the Bogart character from this degradation—the traditional sexual monopoly values are upheld.

Casablanca also offers a case for a more international view of politics. Against the isolationist politics of American pacifism, the film pushes for intervention at a time when sentiment for American involvement was problematic (the film was made in 1941 and released in 1942). And, in terms of content, the sympathetic treatment of Jews and the dignity permitted a Black pianist (Dooley Wilson) contribute to the human project. Only the Nazis were presented without human redemption.

As to the other two dimensions, *Casablanca* failed as radical art: It offers no great creativity in the use of the camera, lighting, or casting. It did use song as effectively as any previous cinema, maybe more so. The closing scene in which Rick and the captain walk away to their destiny was effective but not original. They strolled into the fog toward an unknown fate. The camera rose above the two men so we could see them as but two small creatures caught up in a big war. The personal tragedy of a Bogart or Bergman was reduced to its proper scale—just another incident in a savage convulsion of the world at war.

Casablanca was produced with the usual stratified system of production and the usual commodity form of distribution. For all that, *Casablanca* has radical and transforming merit. (Another picture, *The Overlanders,* made in Australia the same year, was made with three professionals, eager amateurs, internment camp personnel, and people off the street. It was radical in the third dimension but pure propaganda beautifully done in the first dimension.) *Casablanca* will continue to draw audiences as long as love is lost, found again, and as long as sacrifice and choice of love is difficult. *Casablanca* will facilitate renewal wherever and whenever the insolence of power is flaunted and good people stand against it, since both speak to the universal needs for dignity and of commitment.

Cabaret

Cabaret focuses on quite different dilemmas and themes. In that movie, the central story line is the changing role of theatre. As with all media, *Cabaret* holds up a mirror in which a society can see itself. Critical dramaturgy requires that, however distorted the glass, however darkly tinted, the medium must present both the positivities and negativities of the life upon which it reflects.

In the beginning, *Cabaret* does illuminate and mock the negativities of bourgeois mentality, of distorted sexuality, and of politics in pre-war Germany. As the months go by, the cabaret loses its voice as a social critic and becomes a propaganda tool for Nazism. The Nazis cease being the target of emancipatory humor in the cabaret; Jews and communists become the target of humor as Nazi street thugs beat those who rebel and resist them.

Cabaret is thus a statement about the role of drama in society and accepts its inconstant success.

A subsidiary theme is the temptation and fall from grace of Brian, a young student played by Michael York. There is a Faustian theme that we all remember in the deep structure of our morality. In this version, there is an Eve who tempts an Adam and a Lucifer who offers Adam the usual temptations of gold and sex.

Led into temptation by the Liza Minelli character, Sally Bowles, the student succumbs to a variety of sexual and social pleasures. The evil of such degradation is embodied by the charming and likable count—a vestige of the feudal aristocracy whose only valid social role is exploration of the far corners of human delight. In such a scenario, anyone who might be tempted must accept that they, too, would respond to the beauty, charm, sensuality, and sexuality of Sally Bowles and the count. Thus a real dilemma is posed.

A third confounding theme of *Cabaret* is the dilemma of the Minelli character who must choose between the alienated role of a wife to Brian or the more lively and autonomous life in the demimonde of Berlin. She chooses life and sexuality. A Faustian bargain is made when she aborts the child fathered by Brian. She sells her child in order to live more fully.

We can accept this even though in other circumstances, such a bargain speaks against our values.

Cabaret is the universal art of the universal artist. It demands that the artist—in the Minelli and Joel Grey roles—make a choice between the forces of life and death. All great artists must at some time so choose.

Cabaret is radical in two of the three dimensions. In content, it explores the negativities of middle-class morality as well as Nazi claims of superiority. It explores the positivities of that which is ordinarily viewed as negative. It offers an open and varied sexuality but not without the complexities and consequences of such sexuality. Sally does get pregnant; the count does walk away and does cheapen Sally and Brian by giving them money—but the money is helpful and that is, in part, why it is given.

The emcee part played by Joel Grey warrants special mention. At a different level, Grey plays the Luciferian part—he welcomes one into the world of magic and make-believe, sexual fantasy and tawdry love, overweening wealth and perversions of power—"welcome, stranger." And we all are strangers to the view of society and sexuality found mirrored in a cabaret of one of the most decadent cities in the world—Berlin.

As he offers tarts and slatterns to the bourgeois men who frequent the club, the emcee purrs that each one is a virgin, bringing lewd laughter from the customers who have phones on their tables with which to bid the sexual services of well-worn women. With his white, clown face, his formal attire, his plastered-down hair, and his slurring, burring voice, Joel Grey offers each client—and then Brian—knowledge of the forbidden. His duet with Minelli on money is definitive as a critique of bourgeois morality: If it exists, one can buy it, if it does not exist, one will manufacture it.

In that role, Grey embodies the fool and the clown in history, who have always had a special license to ridicule and deflate kings and popes. That character, in its negativity, is a Lucifer; in its positivity, a Prometheus. Both bring light; both shed light. Both reveal that which is unknown and maybe unknowable. Both are dangers to that which exists since they both show that which is not supposed to exist. Each in his own way is often admirable; both are always interesting.

Cabaret is also an exercise in creative cinematography and editing and thus satisfies the second element of a truly radical theatre. Directed by Bob Fosse, it uses the distorted mirrors in the cabaret to reflect the distorted sexuality and politics in bourgeois and Nazi Germany. It uses song and dance to mount a savage parody on both. "Money Makes the World Go Around" is a classic critique of bourgeois values comparable in its own way to Shakespeare's soliloquy on gold in *Timon of Athens*.

But *Cabaret* was produced and distributed as a profit-making commodity. Actors and audiences are forever separated. There is no discussion permitted or encouraged by members of the audience among themselves. They come as isolated pairs and singles, watch as insulated individuals, and depart as lonely as they arrived. It is simply a mass-produced and -distributed commodity. It fails in the third and most important measure of emancipation: People do not leave the theatre, taking the liberating content with them, and infuse it in creative and prosocial ways at work, church, or classroom. Instead, they are amused for a moment, distracted for a minute, disturbed for an hour. Then they go home to the dark corners of a drab, debilitating life—the light goes out. Without connection to the other side of make-believe, *Cabaret* is little more than divertissement.

Off to See the Wizard

Perhaps the most enduring American film is *The Wizard of Oz*. It has been shown on television each March for more than twenty-five years. The book was written by L. Frank Baum and published in Chicago in time for Christmas season in 1899. Baum was a reporter who had lived among farmers in the Dakotas and who watched the workers in Chicago set upon by their enemies. He fashioned the story for the children of the neighborhood from those experiences and told it for years before setting pen to paper.

Set in the form of a child's tale and painted in bright colors, the story identifies four universal needs and gives them flesh and soul in the four main characters of the story. For kinship and solidarity there is the Dorothy part; for love and compassion there is the role of the Tinman; for brains, competence, and praxis, the part of the Strawman; and for courage, properly used, there is a very un-Cowardly Lion.

A very complex and subtle story, *The Wizard* embodies class struggle (the Wicked Witch from the East represents finance capital, while the Strawman stands for all powerless farmers, as the Tinman stands for all alienated workers) in which a revolution (the tornado) overturns the state (the farmhouse) and destroys the enemy of workers and farmers (the Wicked Witch) by crushing her. There is a summary of the major elements of the story at the end of this chapter.

In the book if not in the movie, Baum offered the populist theme of gold against silver in his imagery of the yellow brick road and the silver slippers (not ruby). This theme reiterates the class struggle motif: hard money, high interest vs. easy, low-interest money. (In these days we recognize this theme in demand-side vs. supply-side economics.) Only those wearing silver slippers can safely negotiate the yellow brick road which deteriorates as one travels it—an allusion to the recurrent fiscal crises of capitalism.

There is, too, the theme of alienated power in the form of the Wizard in the Emerald City. The Emerald City stands for Washington, D.C. (where green is the color of power), while the Wizard stands for any humbug of a politician who can give people only what they already have.

In the case of the Strawman, long before he met the Wizard, he already had used his brain to save the little troupe on several of their adventures. In the case of the Tinman, he had already wept for all humanity when he wept for the ants upon which he stepped; he had felt anger on behalf of the Mouse Queen such that he slew the wildcat chasing her. The Cowardly Lion had already stood bravely against the Kalidahs and other assorted monsters met on their journey. Dorothy, too, had found family and friends on the journey as must we all.

Even the Hollywood distortions, omissions, and simplifications would not destroy the universal and particular interests embodied in the play. Taken as a whole, *The Wizard* recapitulates the life of a person who grows from innocence and passivity toward knowledge and praxis. The quests in life are for brains, love, courage, and friendship.

In the play, Dorothy is told by the Wizard she must destroy the Wicked Witch from the West. She says, "I really don't want to kill anyone, but if I must, I must." She comes far from the little girl in Kansas who stands innocently in the grey and grim life of rural docility. She becomes a significant actress in the drama of life. She leads, she understands, she acts, and she triumphs.

In the cinema as in the story, Dorothy's life is transformed from the monochrome shades of gray to the bright colors of Oz through struggle and sacrifice. The original story held many adventures, each of which posed a problem common to humanity and each episode set forth a solution embodying brains, courage, love, and community in one combination or another. The Mouse Queen, the China people, the Hammerheads, the poppy field, the dark forest, the great ditches, as well as the wide river—all posed problems that could only be solved by each of the characters acting collectively to surmount the obstacles posed.

Once it is interpreted and located in the history of class struggle in the 1880s and 1890s, the rich and varied content of the story is most emancipatory. At some level in American political life, the story continues to work toward populist politics in the deep structures of public opinion.

The movie is also radical in terms of the creative use of the medium. The switch from black-and-white film before the tornado to color after the house landed recapitulates the qualitative change in life before and after progressive social change. The use of midgets to encompass the idea of alienated workers made small by the oppression of the Wicked Witch from the East is a stroke of genius. And so is the use of the Strawman to represent the brainless farmers who fail to vote for William Jennings Bryan and for populist politics.

The Tinman, under the spell of the same Witch, is an embodiment of the factory worker chained to and made machine-like. The yellow brick road symbolizes the gold standard while the silver slippers liberate one economically by allowing one to travel safely, through dangerous places. The songs in the movie added enormously to the story line of the book. Although Samuel Goldwyn at one point had ordered the deletion of the rainbow song, it was retained and captures the promise of a better life sometime after the revolution.

Hollywood managed to divest the story of its socialist content by two devices. First, there was the introduction of amnesia: Dorothy was presented as dreaming while in a coma after hitting her head; not so in the book. In the book, Dorothy finds she can really go home if she has silver slippers, i.e., a good relationship to the means of production. As any woman can tell you, a job brings one more respect from husbands and fathers than makeup and coy flirting.

The second copy change made by Hollywood involved the transformation of the Winged Monkeys into Cossacks marching in lock step into the fortress of the Witch to the tune of "The Volga Boatman." The Monkeys were not Russians in the book, they were anthropoids made captive by the theft of a golden cap. Whoever owned the cap could demand three wishes from the winged troupe. The days of slavery in America had just ended to give Baum this theme. Such an analysis also resonates with the alienation of students held hostage by the golden cap of knowledge—and who must give their schoolmasters three wishes before being freed to disport themselves as full human beings.

The Wizard is distinctly bourgeois in its mode of production. The actors were hired, paid, then discarded except for those who had some fiscal potential at the box office. The only relationship most of us have to the movie is as passive viewers. That relationship is changed, of course, the moment we explain to our children, our students, and our friends how to interpret the movie. By so doing, we make the movie our own work.

It is possible for Blacks to appropriate the story line to their own theoretical understanding of racism as was the case in *The Wiz*. It is possible for each of us to sing the song "If I Only Had a Brain" and then to get one. It is possible for all of us to make a journey of discovery in which we realize our own powers to think, love, and be brave. In this fashion the third dimension of radical art is realized. After all, we need not remain midgets, morons, cowards, or cold to the human project.

Brief Summary of the Book

The *Wizard* is, above all, an Easter story that embodies the theme of change and renewal. It teaches a lesson of which we never tire: with love, intelligence, courage, and a sense of community, people could, somewhere over the rainbow, build quite a nice society. The *Wizard of Oz* is a child's history of the quest for Utopia. Down through the long white centuries of winter, people have met the new spring with hope and energy.

1. Dorothy represents a quest for community. She personifies those who are still young enough to hope and to act. Dorothy is Dorothy Everybody— even you. On the other hand, alienated social life is symbolized by—

2. Aunt Em and Uncle Henry: Hard times have taken the sparkle from their eyes and the color from their life. They live in a grey house in a grey land; and they are sober grey. They do not smile.

3. Kansas and the farm on which Uncle Henry and Aunt Em live represent the economic conditions of the country after the depressions of 1873 and 1893. A great grey plain without trees, flowers, or water, it is hard-baked by the pitiless sun.

4. Toto is the one bright spot in Dorothy's life. Toto represents history's clown/jokester who unmasks pretense and deception. Baum is Toto and so is everyone who laughs at a king or tyrant.

5. The cyclone represents the power of the people to overturn alienating social conditions. It is comprised of the North and South winds in the story. Baum lived through the aftermath of the Civil War.

6. Oz is Utopia. With bright colors, happy people, and a brook that bubbles nearby, Oz is the possibility of a good and decent society. But things weren't always good in Oz—until the house crushed one of them, there were two evil witches who oppressed the people.

7. The Wicked Witch of the East represents finance capital that keeps the country on a gold standard with high interest rates while the Wicked Witch of the West represents business barons who exploited the farmers of the Midwest. The farmers had to pay high interest rates, high prices for manufactured goods, and high prices to ship their beef and grain to Eastern markets as a result of monopolies.

8. There were four regions of Oz in the original story. Dorothy came down in the Land of Munchkins. They once were full-sized people but were made small by the working conditions imposed upon them by the Wicked Witches. The munchkins are very happy that Dorothy killed the Eastern Witch and want her to stay and be their Queen, but Dorothy is determined to go home to Uncle Henry and Aunt Em.

9. Dorothy is helped by the Good Witch of the North (Jocasta) who symbolizes abstract good. She gives Dorothy the kiss of Goodness which protects her from the many dangers that she meets on—

10. The Yellow Brick Road. The gold bricks of the road stand for the gold bricks of the finance world, which insisted upon the gold standard, itself a symbol of the tight money policy that was ruining farmers and small

businesses. You may have heard of the famous speech by William Jennings Bryan, who said that America was being crucified on a Cross of Gold. Vachel Lindsay wrote a poem about it:

> Then we stood where we could see
> every band,
> and the speaker's stand.
> And Bryan took the platform.
> And he was introduced.
> And he lifted his hand
> and cast a new spell.
> Progressive silence fell
> in Springfield,
> in Illinois,
> around the world.
> Then we heard these glacial boulders across the prairie rolled;
> 'The people have a right to make their own mistakes . . .
> You shall not crucify mankind
> Upon a cross of Gold.'
>
> Election night at midnight:
> Boy Bryan's defeat.
> Defeat of silver.
> Defeat of the wheat.
> Victory of letterfiles
> and plutocrats in miles
> with dollar signs upon their coats
> diamond watchchains on their vests
> and spats on their feet.
>
> Victory of custodians,
> Plymouth Rock,
> and all that inbred landlord stock.
>
> Victory of the neat.
>
> Defeat of the aspen groves of Colorado valleys,
> the blue bells of the Rockies,
> and blue bonnets of old Texas,
> by the Pittsburgh alleys.

—Vachel Lindsay (1920)

11. The Silver Slippers (not ruby) embody the demand for the silver standard. In the book, whoever wore the silver slippers was safe when walking on the Yellow Brick Road—that is why the Wicked Witch of the West demanded that Dorothy give them to her later on. The populist poli

tics of the time demanded low interest rates, good wages, and fair prices for farm products as against the high interest rates and high prices of the "great malefactors of wealth" who organized the monopolies and cartels.

12. The Strawman was a takeoff on the farmers who, in the 1896 election, didn't have enough brains to vote Democratic. The Strawman embodies the quest for good theory and good understanding. We all would be better off if we only had a brain. You may recall that the Strawman was first seen hung on a cross in the cornfield. Again there is that crucifixion theme.

13. The Tinman embodies a quest for things of the heart; he was in love with a girl but he worked for the Wicked Witch from the East. She made him work so fast that he cut off first an arm, then a leg, then split himself down the middle with his ax. Each time a tinsmith repaired him, but after it was all over, the Tinman didn't have a heart. He wanted a heart so he could, once again, love his sweetheart. His is a search for the authentic sexuality of sharing and giving love.

14. The Cowardly Lion was a putdown of William Jennings Bryan, who was too cowardly to enter the race for president after being defeated. Bryan raved and roared, but he was too cowardly to attack the big tycoons of industry and finance. But in the book, the Lion drew courage from his friends and protected them from the giant Kalidahs—two fearsome beasts not used in the movie.

15. The Wizard of Oz symbolizes alienated politics. People assign their power to politicians then go back to them, hat in hand asking for help. He also represents politicians who don't want to see the people because they can't give them what they don't have in the first place or what they already have. His real name was Oscar Z. Phadrig Isaac Norman Hinkle Emmanuel Ambroise Diggs.

16. Washington D.C. inspired the Emerald City concept. It was green because green is the color of money, and in Washington, money is the name of the game. Washington represents any false solution to any social problem. It takes more than money to solve problems; it takes heart, brains, courage, and community.

17. The flying monkeys represent the newly freed slaves. Whoever had the golden cap could make the monkeys do anything they wanted. Dorothy uses the third wish she had to get them to fly her and her three companions back to the Emerald City after she killed the wicked witch from the West. Then she frees them. MGM was having labor troubles in the 1930s, so Samuel Goldwyn turned the monkeys into villainous Cossacks. Goldwyn also ordered the song, "Somewhere Over the Rainbow" to be cut from the movie; he thought it too radical given the times.

18. The Poppy Field represents anything that puts people to sleep—that immobilizes them. Drugs, Monday Night Football, HBO, whatever turns people into couch potatoes.

There is a lot more to the book that didn't make Hollywood; the Hammerheads who were rooted in one spot and knocked down anyone who tried to go beyond them; the China people who were broken by vandals; the Octospider, which devoured all creatures it reached; the wildcat who chased the Queen of the mice who rescued Dorothy and her friends from the Poppy Field; the trees that grabbed and caught at all who passed by them represented the various branches of science used against the people. Lots of good stuff left to make another movie.

The story ends when Dorothy demands that the Wizard give the people what he promised them. So he gives the Strawman a "brain"—new brain complete with pins and needles so he would be sharp. He gives the Tinman a heart-shaped watch that is guaranteed to go on ticking. He pulls out a bottle of green liquid and gives the Lion a big drink—as the Wizard says, lots of people get courage from a bottle (there are a lot of horrible puns in the book). But he cannot help Dorothy get back home—later the Good Witch of the South tells her that she always had the power to go home; she was wearing the silver slippers. Dorothy does go home. She finds Uncle Henry and Aunt Em smiling; the house is newly painted; the grass, fields, and trees are green, and once again the promise of spring is fulfilled. The Tinman and the Strawman stay behind to help govern the other lands of Oz.

Conclusion

Each of the three dramas discussed above represent emancipatory forms of theatre and cinema in one or more of the tests one might use. They speak a language understood across ages, age-grades and cultures. The content of all three films resonates with the lived difficulties of each viewer. They are the problems of life made visible.

There are honest dilemmas posed—especially in *Casablanca* and *Cabaret*. *The Wizard of Oz* is less problematic except in the scene where the Wizard validates each character by certifying as to their brains, courage, and heart. In that instance, a politician is not an unmitigated fraud. There are alternatives posed; some realistic and some Utopian. Other forms of politics, of love, of sexuality, of economics, and of social roles are shown to be worthy of consideration. The thrust of each movie is toward collective praxis founded on authentic human values.

All three movies are creative in staging, in the use of props, costumes, cinematographic devices, casting, and events. The change from black-and-white film to color in *The Wizard of Oz* is particularly apt. The use of music in all three films was memorable. The "Rainbow" song in *Oz*; the two songs in *Casablanca*—"As Time Goes By," and the counterpoint singing of the "Marseillaise"—were soul stirring. And in *Cabaret,* who can forget the "Money" duet by Grey and Minelli or the young German lad singing "Tomorrow the World"?

On the third test, the mode of production variable, all three fail. All three end up simply as commodity produced by an elite and distributed in mass format by commercial organizations for private profit. *South Pacific, Oklahoma, The Music Man,* and *Porgy* can be appropriated by high-school students, community acting troupes, amateur theatrical ensembles, or by church groups to their own purposes and talents. Of the three above, we are left only with snatches of songs and fragments of dialogue to appropriate to our own purposes. I expect every male over forty has said at one time or another to a beautiful lady, "Here's looking at you, sweetheart."

The Resistible Rise of Arturo Ui

As I read Marx, I understood my dreams.
I discovered that I had not written
a whole collection of Marxist Dramas
without knowing it;
But that Marx was the only audience
I had come across for the dramas.
A man of his interests
would have been interested in them;
Not because they are brilliant,
But because he was. . . .
                                —Bertolt Brecht

This play contains vintage dramaturgy à la Brecht. There were three reinforcing dramas going on at the same time in the production I saw at Central Michigan University Theatre. First there was the apparent play in which some Chicago gangsters used bribes and violence to control the cauliflower market there—and then expanded to Cicero. The head gangster was Arturo Ui. Upon the back of this thin plot, there was superimposed a heavy-handed critique of the rise of Adolf Hitler. Some of the characters had names that echoed those of Hitler's assistant dictators: The notorious Rhoemer became Roma in the play and met a similar death when betrayed by Hitler/Ui. Upon both and within both plays within plays was a critique of capitalism (the cauliflower trust/Prussian Junkers).

Arturo Ui is emancipatory in all three dimensions. It is a very creative play in its content critiquing the Cauliflower Trust of Greater Chicago—and by extension, all monopolies. It is one of the few plays that do not have a hero or heroine into whose persona we may be inserted—thus the play does not set up a false politics within its cast or audience with which to deflect understanding.

The play is also very creative in staging. The Central Michigan University Theatre presentation used slides and music from the Nazi era to make the connection more closely to the actors and events set in Chicago in the 1920s. The semiotics of the play say that the Nazis are a bunch of gangsters—not very radical given the fact that the Allies won the war. However, at the time it was radical to say such things.

The play is designed to be radical in the third dimension as well—as are all of Brecht's plays. In *Arturo Ui*, a woman enters from the last row of seats in the audience and screams for someone to help. Her plea is directed to the audience; the audience is to move out of the realm of make-believe and help defeat fascism after they leave the play. At CMU, of course, the plea fell on deaf ears—even if the members of the audience knew how to understand what was transpiring, they would not know how and what to do given the genteel technofascism of the dramaturgical society.

All of Brecht's plays try to erase the boundary between audience and actor; between play and real life; between history and philosophy. As such, Bertolt Brecht is a truly radical playwright in the best sense of the word even if the plots are thin, the characters one-dimensional and the moral philosophy without dialectics.

Living Theatre

There are plays in which the false line between actors and audience is obliterated; in which the audience stands and sings, has lines to say, and takes the action out of the theatre and into the street. Living theatre, street theatre, guerrilla theatre, and some working-class plays do so. The British play *Can't Pay, Won't Pay* sets shoplifting as a social practice for workers disemployed by advanced monopoly capital.

The art of Christos involves whole communities and whole states in draping plastic or building screens. Christmas pageants involve whole congregations. Sports events such as marathons and walkathons involve thousands. Art, drama, music, and dance need not be organized in a mass format with a set of stars, a set of owners, and a set of passive customers. This is not the natural or the only possible mode of production in any art form. It is a form special to profit and to control purposes and, as such, constitutes an alienating knowledge process. There are more emancipatory forms of theatre, film, science, and television. They exist; they can be expanded.

13

The Sociology of Sport: Structural and Cultural Approaches

In every class organized society,
Sport served a political function.
Capitalism supports a division of sports
into "theirs" and "ours."
Into workers sports and bourgeois sports.
The Working class must use sports
to bring back people from their
lonely, tortured and shattered worlds
to their rightful human dignity.

> —*Fritz Wildung,* Arbeitsports

A Marxian theory of sport has two major dimensions: a political economy in which one weighs the degree to which sport serves the accumulation problems of advanced monopoly capital and a cultural Marxist dimension in which one examines the ways in which sport solves the problems of legitimacy and helps produce alienated consciousness in self and society. This chapter provides insight to both uses to which commodity sport is put. In brief, advanced monopoly capitalism uses the advertising industry to colonize desire and myth in sport as an envelope in which to insert commercial messages. The human desire for good and enlivening social relations is transferred to the lifeless commodity. A better use of sport is to locate desire within community and interpersonal concerns rather than profit and a false solidarity.

The sociology of sport is increasingly disputed ideological territory in American social science. On the one hand is the uncritical descriptive and statistical examination of sport activity created by an admiring journalism. In the same camp is the celebratory history of sport and sport figures that redeems its ugly aspects by enlarging the heroic efforts of individual players and teams. Joining with these extensive statistical presentations and their selected historical forays is a safe and bland sociology of sport that trivializes and depoliticizes sport in particular and leisure-time pursuits generally.

Among the major introductory textbooks of the past twenty years, very little attention is paid to the sociology of sport. Babbie (1983) does not mention sport or leisure as an institutional form. Wilson (1971) treats leisure activities as a subsection of work containing no theory or analysis. McGee (1980) does not mention sport and treats leisure activities as a problem that may arise in the future as people work less. Again no analysis. Ritzer et al. (1982) have a very decent section on sport although it is primarily descriptive of organization and variety. It does have some mildly critical dimensions about sport as corporate business as well as the disturbing influence of mass media.

Opposed to this happy, marginalized view of sport is a new genre of Marxian work embodied in the works of Paul Hoch (1972), Jean Marie Brohm (1975), Richard Gruneau (1981), Jon Sewart (1981), Leon Chorbajian (1984), and Thomas Keil (1984). A Marxian perspective when viewing sport has two major approaches: The first and more orthodox approach centers on the political economy of sport while the second focuses on its ideological meaning for socialization as well as for legitimacy within a strife-ridden nation.

Structural Analysis

Central to the first approach are the concepts of profit, capital accumulation, concentration of wealth, extraction of surplus value, externalization of costs, as well as the exploitation, objectification, and commodification of athletes, games, leagues, and seasons of play. This approach is concerned with the ways in which the mode of production of sport is organized to socialize the costs of production while the profits are privatized.

Economic benefits of commodity sport includes profits, tax write-offs for losses, residuals, stock and real estate appreciation, as well as copyrights and commercial spinoffs. Profits from financing, construction, and auxiliary services to sport all rebound to the private owner, while the costs of production are transferred to the taxpayer, workers, and fans through player training programs in school, college, and community, public stadium building, low wages and benefits for nonathletes, and ticket and television revenue.

Modern American society invests a great deal of resources in commodity sport. This political economy critique of sport shows how it accumulates and concentrates capital for ownership, how it manages player unrest, how it has developed to a labor aristocracy that joins with management to exploit other sectors of the working class, and how it commodifies every element of sport from intermissions of play, to grand moments in play, to the very reputation and esteem of players.

There is also an economic analysis of mass sport made of the ways and means by which banks and monopolies have taken over the financial side of sports; the interconnections between ownership within and between differing sports; between sport and other economic activities such as publishing, cinema, advertising, as well as gambling and politics.

There is the mapping of the subsidiary businesses to sport: transport, food, hostelry, equipment manufacture, construction, sport medicine, development schemes, as well as insurance and investment. There is a critical history of sport as well. Brohm (1975) notes that world sport paralleled the rise of colonial imperialism. Sport is modeled upon capitalist modes of production and the accumulation ethic, and is assimilated by the state in such a fashion as to socialize the costs of producing athletes, stadia, and injury while privatizing the profits of mass sports.

There are forms of crime, of policing, of justice, and of control to be studied—a sort of microcriminology. There are frauds, tax evasion, blacklisting, spurious bankruptcies, bribes, medical crime, illegal transfers, and point fixing to be analyzed. These analyses are made in the traditional structural analysis of the political economy.

Cultural Marxism

The second major approach in Marxian analysis is cultural Marxist analysis. It involves the concepts of legitimization, ideological culture, alienation, false consciousness, solidarity, massification, character, structure, eros, surplus production, and the realization problem. Cultural Marxism studies how commodity sport creates a false solidarity between workers and owners, Blacks and Anglos, rich and poor, East and West, North and South, as well as between nations within the world capitalist system and the Socialist bloc. In Brazil and Argentina, revolutionary groups stop the revolution for the world soccer finals.

Commodity sport colonizes the beauty, elegance, joy, and despair of physical performance. Thus it bends eros to the accumulation and legitimization needs of capitalism in crisis (as well as bureaucratic socialism, feudal relations in the Mid-East, or fascist relations in the poor capitalist countries). Eros is colonized in order to transfer desire from essential social and community needs to privatized consumer goods. In advanced monopoly capitalism, the entire sport ensemble becomes a product sold to major corporations that need to dispose of surplus production in order to realize profit.

Commodity sport legitimizes the false separation of social life into the world of work which is said to be necessarily alienating on the one hand and the world of play in which one finds delight and joy on the other hand; in which the forces of life may be expressed in exhilarating play and thus redeem the bitter imperfection of alienated relations at work, in school, in family, or in church. The possibility that eros, conceived as the forces of life, could be expressed at work, school, in family, or in religious practice is falsely excluded from the consciousness of the worker, the student, the husband, or the somnolent church-goer.

These two approaches together—use of sport for capital accumulation and for the mystification of conflict relations in class, racist, sexist, or national chauvinistic societies—combines to provide the emancipatory knowledge basic to the transformation of society in general and sport in particular to more human and humane purpose. The critical project is always to advance the radical anthropological project of Marx in which individuals constitute themselves as human by the appropriation of nature including their own athletic abilities in building a just, harmonious, and egalitarian social-life world in concert with others. It is to that end that this chapter is written.

Before I develop both approaches a bit, I would like to set forth the contemporary but depoliticized ways in which athletes and fans falsely understand the meaning of sport. There is some truth value in each approach. It is not that these other approaches are false but rather that, in their limited truth, they provide a false consciousness of sport in capitalist societies that deflects the authentic self-knowledge of sport and society and thus defuses and deflects political control over the very institution so many give so much of the body and loyalty.

The False Self-Understanding of Sports

The officially given uses to which sport and other athletic activity are put center around physical health and character building. The vast resources laid on for physical education in high school, college, and city league programs are justified by appeal to the presumed increase in quality of life or in moral character for participants. There are several features of modern sport activity that bespeak this rationale. The incidence of injuries to professional ball teams subverts the claim of better physical condition as a result of participation.

The use of drugs to train and repair players as well as for controlling pain so one can play while injured also calls such a rationale into question. The kind of muscles used and their development may have no real lasting effect on quality of health. And the physical deterioration of players after they cease playing suggests that this philosophy of sport is much more gloss than substance.

As far as the moral character, in commercial sport in particular and competitive sport in general, one must wonder whether that particular character is indeed an ideal to be adopted. The widespread cheating by coaches and players, the envy, disappointment, cynicism, and hypocrisy entailed in commercialized competitive sport, as well as the abusive and profane behavior of the fans, leave one in doubt about the psychological benefits accruing from and calling for such social investments.

Finally, the minuscule differences in performance of runners, throwers, catchers, batters, and jumpers need critical analysis. With electronic timing and measurement, the differences between "winners" and "losers" in races, series, and games may be magnified far beyond any sensible proportion. If two runners finish within a tenth of a second in a four-minute mile—How is one declared a winner and the other a loser when both are superior examples of athletic excellence? If two teams are tied in the last minute of play after a long season and the "winner" depends upon the last basket in the last second, the last pass on the last down, or the last kick in overtime—all this is exhilarating drama but rests more comfortably in an analysis that places sport in a dramatic framework about endurance, persistence, or national superiority than in one centered on superiority or merit.

The view taken here is that these physical activities are central to the human project if organized adequately; that these aesthetically pleasing capabilities are and should be expressed in the world of work, family life, politics, and, indeed, sport, theatre, dance, and the plastic arts.

Solidarity

Perhaps the most visible and pervasive understanding of sport activity is a solidarity use. High schools, small towns, large cities, entire nations, friendship groups, male associations, father-son relationships, as well as whole economic systems make use of the aesthetic, dramatic, mysterious, and strategic responses in sport, games, and play to define, celebrate, expand, and reaffirm a special solidarity status for those assembled to participate or observe.

As a solidarity device in conjunction with a variety of other solidarity supplies—food, alcohol, violence, risk, song, sexual display, chants, special clothing, and physical ecstasy—such sports as football, basketball, soccer, hockey, and baseball bind people together.

The solidarity function is central to a sociological understanding of sport, games, and play. We do act, feel, and think as one as we cheer, chant, despair, and rejoice together at the turns of events in the game. There can be no greater solidarity than dozens, thousands, millions thinking, doing, and feeling the same things in the same place at the same moment. These are the precious, rare moments of perfect harmony and collective exuberance in a world all too short on such moments.

But this is a narrow solidarity limited in time and place and confined to the world of make-believe and not-for-real. When the game is over, the enthusiasm dies, the solidarity runs short, and disharmony in other relations reasserts itself. Much as one hour a week cannot answer to the religious impulse, one game a week cannot answer to the solidarity needs of a racist, sexist, or elitist society. In this respect more radical structural solutions are preferred.

In a conflict-ridden society where each is the natural enemy of similarly situated competitors for jobs, land and resources, sexual access, and for other scarce items, where there are class antagonists and ethnic opponents, where ever more people are impoverished—such solidarity activity is important to the masking of these antagonisms. When the home team beats the putative enemy with skill, genius, heroic acts, deceit or trickery, and guile—great delight, joy, and enthusiasm emerges and can be shared with those present on our side. Class antagonisms, ethnic hatred, as well as gender and national hostilities with real conflicting interests can be assimilated to the harmless competition in sport. The structures of privilege, inequality, and oppression are left intact by use of solidarity in sport.

Alienated Sexuality

Perhaps the most simple-minded view of the current way sport is organized centers around sex and violence. This view reduces the analysis of sport to some universal psychological drive/anxiety about sexual and violent behavior. The depth analyses made in this kind of understanding is that the equipment and events in football, basketball, baseball, golf, and other sport events lend themselves to sexual interpretation.

The pitcher throwing the ball to the catcher to deceive the hitter readily lends itself to this interpretation if we regard the bat as a phallic symbol, the ball as a sperm, the catcher and the mitt as earth-mother and her genital organ, the pitcher as the castrating father, and the home run as the symbolic murder of the primitive father.

In like fashion, football action may be so reconstructed as to evoke the primal scene. If the goal line is the hymen and the ballcarrier the phallus while the ball itself is a primitive womb to be delivered in triumph to earth-mother, then a touchdown is a symbolic rape uniting sex and violence in a series of downs in which the underdog team (the symbolic son) pushes away the defenses of the favored team (the primitive father) to penetrate the sacred opening of that mother.

Golf also takes on sexual meaning if we convert the golf club into a phallus, the white ball into sperm, and the drive itself into an ejaculatory orgasm aimed at a hole-in-one. Basketball with its inaccessible hoop, its oversized balls, and its slam-dunk could create an image of the primal scene in the violence of rape. And so on. In these analyses a horse is a phallic symbol as is a car, motorbike, bicycle, rifle, or running back. In sport, one side represents the father and the other side the adolescent son reaching for incestuous control of the primitive mother embodied in the win, the bucket, the touchdown, the hole-in-one, the home run.

In this perspective, sport is seen as a form of sublimated sexuality that makes the world safer for decent women.

A variation on this theme is that sport and the deep involvement of Americans and people everywhere with it is an expressive outlet for undesirable and/or unusable emotional drives or psychological imperatives. Rage, anger, antic genius, violence, sexuality, phantasy, foolishness, and humor (eros generally) are said to be "safely" channeled into harmless pursuits through sport, games, reading novels, watching plays, and dreaming. It is not that these are central to all forms of human activity but that they have a very limited place in "real" life and must be rendered neutral by expressing them in nonserious endeavor. Sport is, here as before, a safety valve to discharge "naturally" occurring and "dangerous" emotion.

Divertissement

Another well-received view of sport is as a diversion from serious matters. In this analysis, ordinary work, politics, and family are adult matters. One who seeks escape into trivial, nonserious activity is immature. More generally, the social world is split into two components: seriously intended social reality on the one hand and make-believe, just-pretend, and just-for-fun on the other. It may be all right for children and students to engage in such frivolity, but the sober citizen works hard and remains joyless.

In this view, eros is not to be linked with work, still less is it to be colonized to encourage consumerism—eros is to be denied. This view sees life as necessarily involving suffering—joy being unnatural. In a marginally efficient mode of production the Protestant ethic of hard work and self-denial has a certain social utility. In an affluent society, this approach makes sense only to those whose relationship to the means of production is so precarious that the least indulgence would be a serious matter.

A great many people, including some Marxists, hold a differing view. They accept that life is alienating and that people inappropriately escape that alienation by fleeing the family, onerous work, dull/mean-spirited religion, as well as massified educational forms to the lively world of play and sport. Alienated workers escape the boredom, drudgery, and humiliation of work in the ever-expanding weekend of commercial sport, drinking, bowling, jogging, hunting, or swinging sex. People give up on local, state, and national politics, surrender elitist control over politics to the politicians in exchange for the private freedoms of sports, games, and play.

The difficulties with this analysis are many, including the unjustified assumption that work and sexual life within institutional marriage forms or institutional politics necessarily are alienating. It simply does not follow that since these are alienated in this social formation they must be alienated everywhere, eternally for all people. There is the prior question about the relationship between reality and make-believe.

Sport, games, theatre, fiction, rehearsal, are, have been, and must be integrally linked to the human project. As we shall see a bit later, the realm of make-believe and magic can be alienated from the human project—the salient political question is how to forestall alienation. The short answer lies in the democratic modes of production for make-believe and just-pretend including sports.

The Political Economy of Sports

There are several structural characteristics of a political economy approach upon which I touched earlier and would like to develop a bit here. The first and most general point I want to emphasize is that the character of sport varies with the mode of production of the society in which it appears. The history of sports parallels that of human society.

In each of the five great modes of organization for social production, sport, and the world of serious activity have been mutually interdependent. In primitive communal societies, in slave, feudal, capitalist, or socialist society, sport has been shaped by the dominant mode of production.

Modern football, basketball, soccer, track-and-field events have their origins in intertribal, interfeudal, and intercapitalist warfare. Football probably started out as a predator villager kicked the heads of conquered neighbors around. Baseball is little else but the skilled use of the bludgeon. Field events such as shot put, javelin, hammer throw, and archery—all come out of the weaponry of feudal warfare.

Such events as the marathon, hurdles, obstacle course, the dash, and the relay recapitulate the structure of field communication in the various military encounters between low-tech armies from the wars between city-states in ancient Greece to the crusades through the feudal conquests of France, Britain, Scandinavia, and the African nations.

The modern assimilation of sport to military goals came in 1811 when the Germans were occupied by the armies of Napoleon. The mass calisthenics that later came to be associated with the *Jugendschaften* of the Hitler era were encouraged as prelude to the overthrow of the French oppressors by German patriots.

In our times, sport is shaped more by the commercial needs of advance monopoly capital. There are several points at which its needs shape the structure and development of sport. The most significant structural change in modern sport is its gradual and continuing commodification. This means that the social, psychological, physical, and cultural uses of sport are assimilated to the commercial needs of advanced monopoly capital.

The major problem of advanced capitalism to which sports are put is the solution to the "realization problem." Given the profit motive, capitalist firms produce more than their workers can buy. This happens for three reasons. First, workers collectively do not get paid 100 percent of the price set by the market. For any given firm labor costs are about 25–35 percent of the price set. Across all workers who share in the division of the profits, the wages are less than 100 percent of the price available with which to purchase the goods they produce.

In low-profit lines, workers may have 95 percent of the value produced; in high-profit lines of production, they may have less than 50 percent of the value of the wealth they produce. Whatever the case they cannot buy it all. In such a case, the economy tends to slow down to recession or depression levels. There are several ways to renew demand, each with other problems—warfare destroys wealth and renews demand. A prolonged recession renews demand. Price wars dispose of surplus production but benefit big competitors. Crime requires replacement of items stolen.

The welfare state redistributes wealth. Credit and deficit spending can keep the system going a while longer. Capitalists compete for foreign markets and try to capture surplus value from foreign economies with which to renew demand but a major way to dispose of "surplus" goods and realize profit is to transfer desire for the world of cultural events: sport, theatre, religion, or patriotism to the world of commodity production via advertising.

The inability of a capitalist firm to dispose of "surplus" production leads corporations to purchase sport programming as a commodity to generate demand by using the beauty and elegance of athletics as an envelope in which to insert a commercial message. A second structural feature of advanced monopoly capitalism that besets the accumulation process is the inequality of income distribution among those who do work for wage labor.

The yuppie portion of the population has discretionary income as do most elements of the capital class, but in the capitalist system today a few million people get around 40 percent of that wealth and hundreds of millions share less than 50 percent of the wealth. In America, the bottom 20 percent of the population share only 5 percent of the gross national product. A lot of money, to be sure, but far less than is required to purchase all the cars, beer, refrigerators, cigarettes, and other items produced.

The few million who do have surplus income and could purchase the surplus production do not need the fourth car, the fifth television set, nor the tenth toaster. This distortion in income means, again, that capitalists cannot realize profit. A third reason that there is a surplus of goods is the tendency in capitalist systems to disemploy workers by the use of new technology or by increased productivity from each worker.

These disemployed workers join the surplus population. Their material needs may be met by the state in its welfare system, by family members, by private charity, or by friends. Many turn to crime as a way to reunite production and distribution. So, in order to dispose of the surplus production on profitable terms, capitalist firms turn to advertising to create an ever-expanding layer of false needs and wants among those who may have discretionary income. Or they try to expand markets overseas to the disadvantage of capitalists in other countries who also have the same realization problem.

Since sport events generate large audiences and participants (for any or all of the reasons mentioned earlier: the alienated solidarity, the alienated sexuality, or the alienated aesthetics of play), advertising firms buy the audiences and sell them to capitalist firms that are large enough to have national markets and wealthy enough to pay the costs of the audience, the commercials, the media time, and the teams involved. Apart from the fact that this solution to the problem of capitalist production greatly inflates costs of distribution and apart from the fact that small firms tend to fail, the real problem of this growing alliance between sport and capitalism is the linkage between mythic concerns of a society and profit concerns of private capital.

Cultural Marxist Analysis of Sports

In brief, the argument is that sport has absorbed some of the religious needs of a secular society for solidarity and for a metaphysic. The analysis of sport presented here is that it embodies elements of the four great founding myths of society—especially that of a moral metaphysic that instructs players and fans alike about how to approach the problem of interpersonal interaction, how to relate oneself to the social unit, and how to confront the imponderables of nature and other groups.

This moral metaphysic intrigues and engrosses fans in the actions and outcomes of a sport event. This moral metaphysic can be used as an envelope in which to insert advertisements. To understand the rise of commodity sport in America, we need to connect the political economy of capitalism to alienated social life.

Every society has four general myths that help reproduce it across generations. The first is the creation myth. The second and the one used here is the morality myth—one that instructs us on how we are to deal with the ordinary contingencies of life, how we are to relate to others inside and outside our group. Morality myths instruct us about the forms of evil, the sources of evil, the agents of evil, and the solutions for evil. The third great myth form tells us how to understand and survive the inevitable tragedies that are the common lot of all people—what to do about death, love gone wrong, children gone wrong, and the imponderables of life. The fourth great mythic form speaks to the future and to the failings of the past in that social formation itself. This fourth mythic form usually says that times were good before, they turn bad through no fault of the system, and they will be good again if one has faith.

A myth is a line of symbolic activity—in music, in mime, or in words—that grasps the basic concerns of a society and resolves the conflicts and contradictions inherent in social life in its chronology and in the logic of its action (Silverstone, 1983:138). The simplicity of the sport event is especially amenable to mythic use. In the play, the protagonist must overcome adversity in society and in nature. Each play and player must, to be successful as a mythic element, transcend everyday activity. The game is transparent in its play and unlike written or narrated myths has no foregone conclusion. Every fan has the same standing as do all others. In those crucial moments of play, a satisfactory event is anticipated and recognized by all present. One does not need a priestly functionary to interpret the mysteries as in religious myths. In that respect, sport may be experienced directly for its aesthetic and mythic meanings.

The structure of sport as a mythic form is about socialization under conditions of conflict. In feudal society, in competitive capitalist societies with class as well as ethic conflict, in the world capitalist system with its nationalistic antagonisms—the mythic structure of modern adversary sport resonates with the lived experiences of workers, Blacks, Third World patriots, as well as partisans of geographic animosity. All stress the need for the individual to accept and to work within the existing structure of social conflict and "friendly" competition.

Commodity capital, with its internal crises and contradictions, has assimilated the mythic form to its own needs for survival, for profit, for socialization to competitive, aggressive, privatized character as well as for legitimacy with workers, consumers, and citizens who are its natural antagonists. I raise the question about whether American sport in its commodity form—however excellent and appealing—should be harnessed to the ideological needs of a given class or elite in any society. The view advanced here is that sport, indeed all cultural activities, might better be oriented to the general social interest in authentic solidarity and prosocial cooperation rather than the special character and consumer morality of monopoly capital.

Every social group needs to use the awe and mystery of myth, magic, pretend, rehearsal, play, and the world of imagination and make-believe to the reproduction of cultural forms.

All sport activities are mythic endeavors in which the forces of life are pitted against those of nature. In the case of football, basketball, baseball, and, more intensely, tennis, the effort to control a ball pushes the player to the limits of psychobiological capacity and endurance. The catch takes on added drama if it occurs in a strategic moment of play. Still more dramatic impact arises should the moment of play be located in a strategic game or even in a moment of note in the entire history of a league or nation.

Conflict is to be resolved by means of excellent individual performance within the logic of team goals. In a recent (18 July 1983) Monday night baseball game, the shortstop of the Toronto Blue Jays made four such plays in that single game. Few persons on earth could have made the moves as swiftly, as gracefully, or as accurately and with the panache displayed. The grace, beauty, and art possible from the human body was shown forth clearly in that game.

In like fashion, the extension of the physical capacity of the human body in making spectacular catches in football is even more remarkable taking place as it does in the face of expert defensive play by the opposing team. Most of those who watch football know and appreciate those catches, the moves for which match in grace and timing the finest of ballet. By itself, this physical excellence is only of passing interest—observed only for the purest of aesthetic reasons as indeed one may appreciate ballet. But unlike most ballet today, sport games are located in significant social frames within which they take on mythic force.

In a world series, with the bases loaded and two out, and with the score tied in the ninth, a long fly ball is immediately anticipated as a dramatic event. As the center fielder races back, gauges the flight, lifts off the ground in every effort, whether the catch is made or whether the ball clears the 430-foot marker, the partisan crowd is on its feet as one, explodes in a cheer of delight as one, and appreciates that all others present share the grand moment. The soaring grace of the fielder's catch or the perfect timing and power of the batsman testify to the possibility of human success in everyday life. That is what the myth—and the game—is all about.

As noted, the sport event teaches us four things: it tells us what the sources of evil are, it tells us who the agent of evil is (often conceived as the enemy), it instructs us in the forms of evil, and it instructs us in the means by which evil is to be overcome.

In the case of baseball, the source of travail is to be found in the physical forces of nature: time, space, gravity, weather, and light. The sources of evil are found as well in the individual imperfections of the players: the lazy player, the inept player, the foolish player, the cheating player, the selfish player, and the indifferent player. Evil is to betray one's teammates to sloth, greed, envy, pride, anger, and hate.

If not the unproductive team member, the agent of evil is the outsider. For most major sports, it is the visiting team. High school and college sport set as enemy the opposing team much more than do the professional teams although in baseball everyone hates the Yankees, in football for years it was the Chicago Bears, and in basketball the Boston Celtics embodied adversity. The particular forms of evil embodied in these teams entailed unfair tactics, dirty play, illegal recruiting, purchasing of pennants and players, as well as architectural innovations of the field of play that gave unfair advantage to the other team.

When combined, the forms and agents of evil as embodied in the mythic structure of sport teaches a lesson. It says the tribe is the paramount unit of social order and the enemy is other neighboring tribes; they cheat and thus are less than human. This default renders the home tribe the embodiment of the human being in its highest, most principled form. However, since the opposing team violates the rules of social life found in the sport event, it excludes itself from the normal courtesies of social conduct. Such self-exclusion in turn justifies less than social treatment of the enemy. By this practical logic, the home tribe at once justifies noncompliance with social rules and at the same time preserves the home tribe myth of superior moral standing.

If the Yankees buy up all the best players, they default on the rules and may be subjected to tactics otherwise inconceivable. Since the Chicago Bears hit, gouge, kick, and pile on, they disqualify themselves as equals and may be hit, gouged, and kicked without culpable wrong imputed to the home team. Since the Celtics use picks, fast breaks, double-teaming, presses, and platoon substitution tactics, since they grab the superstars from college ranks and use the home court advantage in extremis, they also are the embodiment of evil for all other home teams—and ceteris paribus, the Celtics, Bears, and Yankees view the Philadelphia Warriors, the Green Bay Packers, and the Dodgers as less than human.

In the Marxian analysis presented here, sports have been commodified and massified in response to some of the structural problems of advanced monopoly capitalism. A separate but parallel analysis is possible for bureaucratic socialist economies or the semifeudalities in the Mid-East and Far-East.

Sport solves the problems of accumulation and legitimacy in the ways mentioned above. Sport in its present form presents us with a modern metaphysic for daily life. It redeems, in a false and trivial manner, alienated conditions of work. It provides alienated solidarity in a conflict-ridden society. Its supermasculine model of play offers to redeem an alienated sexuality. And its aesthetics and metaphysics provide an envelope into which to insert a message vesting desire into possession of material goods rather than in primary social relations. In a final section, I would like to add to this cultural analysis of sports a structural analysis of advertising, since the advertising industry is the enterprise that uses the metaphysics and aesthetics of sport to colonize social desire in the interest of private profit.

This analysis is part of a larger analysis of the use of dramaturgy in society to manage the political and economic problems of class cleavages, racial conflict, gender preference, and bureaucratic authority in mass society. The major thesis of this work is that the technologies of electronics, theatre, and the social sciences—sociology, as well as psychology—are used conjointly to mystify consciousness and subvert democratic and collective political possibilities in the interest of class elites as well as other elites within the world capitalist system (and in bureaucratic socialist societies).

This technology provides a slick, smooth, scientific way to preserve privilege in a putatively democratic society. The crude and disruptive politics of fascism is replaced by an $110 billion industry of dramaturgical practitioners in the advertising industry whose only productive labor is to serve elites in the extraction of surplus value and creation of false consciousness.

Commodity sport is but one expression of the alienation of the lively arts to the managerial needs of capitalism. Commodity politics, theatric commercials, electronic religion, as well as the spectacles of space and war— all converge to use dramaturgy in the sociology of fraud to serve power, privilege, and the great wealth of multinational corporations.

Advertising and Commodity Sport

We have suggested that commodity sport embodies a myth that serves as a metaphysic. Located within the problems of commodity capitalism, the increasing use of sport lends itself as a particularly effective tool for advertising. If the morality myth embedded in sport resonates with the lived experience of fans, advertising resonates with the structural features of advanced monopoly capital.

In an automated, productive economic system the main problem of the capitalist is to realize profit. The shift is from the exploitation of the working class to the extraction of surplus value from the consumer. To do this it is necessary to use science and guile rather than coercion and discipline. The modern corporation cannot force the consumer as readily as it can coerce the employee. It turns to depth psychology and social science to generate demand. Monopoly capital uses advertising to solve the problem of accumulation and legitimacy. Advertising uses the drama and mythic power of sport to generate demand and to realize profit for advanced monopoly capital.

There is also the shift from price and quality to generate demand. It is not possible to use pricing to generate demand in a stable monopoly system (Baran and Sweezy, 1976:115). Were one of the ten or so giants that dominate a product line to resort to price as a demand mechanism, it would destabilize the entire industry with devastating results for many. Quality cannot be used to generate demand for several reasons. There are the additional costs of quality; there is industrial espionage that quickly ends any advantage a new improvement might bring; there is the profitable parts and repair industry; and most of all there is the advantage of built-in obsolescence for future demand—all of which militates against quality—and for advertising. The products advertised nationally are products from the monopoly sector. Products from the competitive sector of the state sector are seldom advertised on mass media.

A third thesis on advertising relates more directly to the realization problem. A capitalist economy can only realize profit if all products are sold. But since workers do not have 100 percent of the price of a product paid to them directly or indirectly, capitalist economies tend to have surpluses that are not readily absorbed by workers taken collectively—and the tiny handful of capitalists could not use all the gas, beer, autos, chain saws, and sanitary napkins produced—so they must create a neurotic need for such surplus purchasing.

Commodity sport with its morality lessons provides an envelope in which to hide the compulsion to consume apart from need, merit, thought, and words. Advertising cannot increase demand for all commodities but can shift demand from commodity *A* to commodity *B*. Fourth, advertising is the cheapest way to reach millions of people. Commission sales only work in very special circumstances. In cons or swindles, in real estate and other superhigh profit, high-growth lines, face-to-face sales can be used, but not in mass sales with low-profit margins.

In the United States, it is by the structural needs of advanced monopoly capital that one can best understand the growth in broadcast sport. And it is the morality myth embedded in sport that connects compulsive needs of the consumer with the compulsive needs for profit. Other myths may also be used to create demand. On day-time television, oriented to the alienated housewife, a differing myth is used to envelop demand—that of the competent woman, still attractive and able to cope with the many failings of husband, children, and neighbors. Such women use the household budget (about 60 percent of family income) to marshall the supplies to sustain their social skills.

Advertising capital furnished by monopoly industries at once encourages the production of cherished cultural supplies such as sports and transforms these in the same moment into their alienated form. A whole host of unproductive labor is used to reunite production and distribution on profitable terms for the monopoly capitalist beset by increasing costs or production, increasing legal restraints on dangerous practices, increasing foreign competition, decreasing markets in the unfree world, and decreasing freedom to control Third World supplies. Advertising is a necessity in this time of crisis for monopoly capital. Sport is a happy cultural activity upon which capitalism may parasitize—for a while.

Conclusion

There are many ways to understand the huge investment a society allocates to sport and other athletic activity. At any given level of analysis there are significant and important validities on which to focus depending on the interests and concerns of the critical scholar. In the previous section of this chapter the focus has been the mythic character of the rules and lines of play in contemporary American sport culture. In the earlier section, the focus was on the political economy in which sport is located.

A political-economy approach to sport examines how and why it has been commodified. The Marxian view is that commodity sport is used by advertising to generate demand in an economic system in which demand is restricted by profit considerations, monopoly practices, and a continuing discrepancy between aggregate wage and aggregate price across all capitalist lines of production. The need for profit in advanced monopoly capitalism results in every possible good or service being commodified. Sport is commodified and sold to the largest corporations in order to add dimensions of desire and false need to products without intrinsic value to those with discretionary income.

That so many people invest so much time, emotion, and money in these pursuits instructs us that something important is happening. Sport has gradually absorbed the religious impulse of a secular society, commodified it in capitalist societies, and is in the process of assimilating that impulse to the economic and legitimacy needs of capitalism. Perhaps there are better ways to understand sport but I know no better for the present organization of American sport.

The analysis here presents a given sport event as an instance of one or more of the four great myths found in a society with which to instruct its young people in the metaphysics of human life as it is constructed in that culture. The four myths are: the creation myth, the morality myth, the tragic myth, and the destiny myth. All interesting novels, plays, poems, and sport events incorporate the structures of one or more of these myths into their story line.

The morality myth of advanced capitalist society suffuses the structure and chronology of contemporary sport events in the United States. Competition, the resultant system of individual stars and individual viewers, the emphasis on playing within the rules set by a small nonplaying elite, the constant push by coaches and managers for greater productivity, for personal excellence, and for uncritical acceptance of the authority system—all resonate with the issues of capitalist production in shop, office, school, and factory: competition, discipline, creativity, teamwork, victory, and alienated joy.

As an embodiment of a mythic form that instructs all persons concerned, fans and players alike, on how to live out their life in a laudable and praiseworthy style—sports supplements, complements, and in some instances displaces the sacred writings of the Bible and the Church Fathers. In a secular society, the drama of sport events absorbs and bends the quest for the sacred to the profit concerns, to the control needs of the rich and the powerful.

It is this concern with the morality myth that so intrigues and captures the fan and the player. We all need a metaphysic for the shaping of our everyday behavior. Professional football, baseball, basketball, volleyball, and soccer, each in its differing format, provides us with such a morality. There is a basic incompatibility between commercial sport and the longer historical interests of a society. A society that permits its mythic forms in sport to be purchased as a commodity, mortgages its future to the rich and powerful. In this case, it is the private capitalist firm that has absorbed sport to its ideological, political, and economic needs.

Such commodification of sports ceases to serve the general social interest in morality, solidarity, and excellence of individual effort when these interests are confined within the special interests of the capitalist firm for profit, legitimacy, growth, control of markets and material, and a complacent labor force.

There is much of social value found in sport and in other mythic carriers. Given the social utility of morality myths and the great investment of time, talent, and concern with sport in America, the significant question is whether a society should so organize the talent and time of athletes, artists, and actors to serve interests of private profit. Corollary to that question is whether other forms of sport, other modalities of morality, other structures of myths might not better serve the social interest or the human project.

In this respect, the sociology of sport fits within a larger framework of the political economy in which it is found. The usual approach to the study of sport sociology surgically isolates sport from the society in which it is found and form the content and outcomes of the cultural activities. One should keep in mind that it is the cultural activities—ranging from family life to religious life and embracing art, music, science, games, leisure time activities, as well as politics and parties—that give life its distinctly human character. Work, food, shelter, health care, and survival skills are basic to life but the creation of culture in all its forms is basic to human life.

The propensity is to trivialize the sociology of music, theatre, sports, folk arts, and their economic and political meaning. A Marxian theory reclaims these cultural activities and locates them in a research endeavor that emancipates them once again to celebrate distinctly social and collective endeavors.

In history and in theory, there are cooperative, communitarian, and creative forms of play, game, and sport. Since these do not help create competitive workers, ambitious professionals, authoritarian functionaries, or compulsive consumers, these forms of games, sport, and play are selected out of sport history while more competitive games and sport are selected into the social experience of the child, the adult, and the senior citizen by a complex institution of sport board members, owners, sponsors, coaches, fans, and editors.

Dance is the unity of force,
time and space,
bound and unbound by inner rhythm.
Dancing can be done by anyone
who has desire and love.

—Mary Wigman, Philosophy of the Dance

14

The Typifications of Christ at Christmas and Easter: Critical Explorations of Religious Dramaturgy

Who is the Wise man?
And who knows the Interpretation of a Thing?
A man's Wisdom makes his face to shine,
And the hardness of his Countenance is Changed.

—*Words of the Preacher in Ecclesiastes.*

A post-modern approach to enlivening and sustaining religion requires a systematic critique of the ways in which the drama of the holy are used to advance or impair human endeavor. The categories of cultural Marxism are used to explore the major ideological fields in which in this chapter the Jesus symbol is located. The typifications that surround the Christ figure define two quite different ideological fields: the one at Christmas lending itself to the social and commercial needs of advanced monopoly capital, while the Easter ideological field and the significations surrounding *that* Jesus lend themselves more to a radical revolutionary movement. While commercial capitalism in crisis may prefer the Christmas Jesus, the Easter Jesus has more appeal to oppressed people and resonates with their lived experience.

Durkheim rightly said that when we celebrate the gods, we celebrate our own society. Marx rightly said that when we speak to the gods we cry out, in anguish, for a better society—a futile, misdirected, pathetic, fruitless cry for help. For Durkheim, the sociology of religion was to save society from revolution; for Marx, it was to help make the revolution. For Durkheim, religion heals, binds, consolidates, and transcends social cleavages; that can be very true. For Marx, religion is a fraudulent institution, a

315

false healer, a patent medicine itself oriented to private, not social ends. Too often, Marx is right.

In the United States the Durkheimian view is the received truth for most American sociologists. For those who look at national and international structures and see widening faults glossed over by established religion, the Marxian view has considerable appeal. The truth value of a theoretical explanation is always grounded in the shifting, complex whole of a society, the boundaries of which may go far beyond the area in which particular gods are constituted by the worshipping activities of the religious practitioners.

Fictive Realities

The analysis that follows applies some recent developments of Macherey's (1978) explanation of the *literary subject*. Macherey holds that the irreconcilable cleavages in society can be expressed in concrete terms in the written/spoken/sung text. In the novel, in the story, in the song, and in the religious myth, these cleavages are transformed from the ungraspable richness of everyday life into a graspable, solvable symbol. These cleavages are realized in a form that offers a solution on a fictive plane.

All the varied, shifting complexities of the "signifying practices" of people are reformulated in language alone—in the text of song, poem, novel, play, or myth. By nature, the symbolic representations we create to represent the fullness, the seamless experience of living creatures—these are caught but partially with the words we use.

As we go from the complexities of reality into the limitations of language, into the emptiness of numbers, into the skeletal systems of statistics, we systematically lose information and ruthlessly rob reality of its richness and contrariness. Yet it is through language that people are inserted into life and literature as subject. The form of language is such that an "I," a "me," or a "we" is constituted as subject perforce—even if that is not the case in the lived experience. One cannot, of course, literally *be* inserted as a subject in a novel, song, movie, or television program. But in every case of fictive literary art—and in most nonfiction—there are characters with which one identifies.

In most novels, plays, or poems the *point of view* of the central character becomes that of the reader, auditor, or viewer. The subjectivity of that character is presented as the proper, natural, normal way to experience life. To develop the analysis here we must shift, as Macherey does, from the subjective experience of the central character—as well as from our identification with it—to the larger social context in which the author writes. Bertolt Brecht tried to do this when he omitted fictive persons with whom we could identify in such plays as the *Three Penny Opera* or *The Resistible Rise of Arturo Ui*. Those plays in which such a sympathetic figure is found become more an exercise in mystification than emancipation.

All authors who create a work of art work out of an ideological structure. This ideological structure is grounded in the material interests of a given social group. Depending upon the author and the text at hand, the group is connected to another by the larger structures of social life. In American society, the structures that the author connects are class, ethnic group (race), gender, age, and nationality.

In the class structure, capitalists and proletariat are related and each has an ideology that helps interpret, justify, and sanctify the lived experience of each group to the other. It is always a political question which ideological field will prevail in those fictive connections. The same is true of gender, ethnic, and other social divisions. Out of all possible ideologies, the author of the song, movie, or novel creates a fictive subject whose lived experience helps interpret, justify, and sanctify a solution to the divisions of social life brought into focus by the story line of the novel or song.

Macherey adopts Althusser's view in which the role of ideology is to dispel the contradictions of people's lived experience by offering a solution that is framed within the logic of some privileged group. An ideology is always a closed system. In order to stay within its boundaries, the ideas that contain the solutions to life's difficulties must remain silent on problems that call into question the relationship as lived. In order to free oneself (and society) of the ideological work going forth in song, novel, and ceremony, it is necessary to step outside the social group whose interests are celebrated.

The novel, song, myth, or movie, then, enables us to experience a given problem and a putative solution as understanding subject. In the case at hand—Christian plays, programs, songs, and pageants create a fictive subject from whose point of view we can grasp the fundamental issues of an age from the perspective of the group through the symbol of the Jesus figure. The content of that symbol is mediated by the social forms in which the author/artist arises and lives.

The defining quality of great art is that it cannot be reduced simply to those interests. If it is, it is merely bad or mediocre and strikes us as dull. But Christmas and Easter are seldom dull—nor are the stories that grasp the fullness of the contradictions experienced at Christmas or Easter. Irreconcilable positions are delineated in play or song at Christmas and Easter.

In each story a fictive solution emerges. For Macherey, the appeal of literature and language is the illusion of reconciliation of that which is, within the existing structures of society, irreconcilable. However, the one must add to Macherey that such fictive symbols can show the way to new radically different social arrangements. This is the emancipatory dimension of every authentic work of art whether it be Goya, Gershwin, or Brecht.

It is the particular appeal of the Christ figure that it allows one to experience, in differing typifications, alternate reconciliations of one's own experienced unsolvable fears. However, Christmas and Easter offer two quite different problematics and two quite different solutions in our culture to these private fears and collective conflicts.

Our Experience of Christ at Christmas

At Christmas, those in the Christian tradition experience life from the perspective of the Holy Child and of the Holy Family. In song, in cinema, on television, in the novel, as well as in the news story, the perspective we are expected to take is that of the child, helpless in a hostile world but embraced by a living, protecting mother and a more distant but dependable father.

At Christmas time in the United States at the turn to the 21st century, the themes of Christmas center around the family. The plight of the family as experienced in these times includes the problem of homelessness, inflation, crime, employment insecurity, divorce, child abuse, and disintegrating kinship structures.

The story line at Christmas time in song, play, and pageant suggests how these may be repaired within the structure of commodity consumption. We are offered a solution that does not take up questions about the larger structures that strain and crack the family. In fact, the mythic solution offered on commercial television is a warm, strong, caring family circle made holy by the delight we take in each other's joy in gifts—toys, cameras, perfumes, wines, watches, as well as kitchen appliances, video games, and power tools.

In its commercial moments, television offers a wide variety of fictive Christmases. Children can learn through Raggedy Ann that Alexander Graham Wolf can ruin Christmas by sealing toys in unbreakable, transparent boxes. The (Christ) child experiences life thusly as visible but untouchable—and within the context of gifts as a central typification of Christmas. Peanuts, Bugs Bunny, and the songs of Perry Como interpret, justify, and sanctify Christ as the collective child and justifies the family as the receptacle of alienated consumption. Parental love, abstractly embodied in the gift, is sanctified. The sources of inflation, unemployment, family violence, and juvenile delinquency run far beyond the boundaries of the family in the first instance and gift-giving cannot repair the structure of alienated familial, class, gender, or ethnic relations in the second instance.

The use of Christmas and the Christ figure in American society to interpret the structure of alienation and to sanctify family gift-giving as the solution warrants critical reflection. For six weeks out of the year, beginning the day after Thanksgiving, amid great excitement and effort, Christmas is made to embody the full range of these structural distortions. No other institution—not even the American presidency or the American state—is so celebrated. Consumption of unnecessary products comes to preempt the meaning of Christmas, while its meaning as communal activity as in some European or South American villages is progressively lost.

The notion of the religious experience as a binding, incorporating experience oriented to the widest possible social solidarity is passed over. The notion of the church as an encompassing fellowship in which each person stands in unshakable supportive relationships to all is quietly displaced by the notion of Christmas as a mass of isolated families engaged in a great shopping spree attended by ringing bells, electronically broadcast street carols, special town decorations, and cheerful clerks ringing up record sales until after the New Year.

Religion itself, so precious to the human enterprise, is reduced to the tinsel and wrappings of Christmas, soft lights and festive decorations, and bumper stickers and slogans of Christmas cheer.

Such an organization of the Christmas experience represents a response to the needs of industrial capital to produce and dispose of high-profit, capital-intensive products; of commercial capital to merchandise such products to uncritical, vulnerable customers; and to the needs of finance to loan out the high reserves of capital it has accumulated at the highest possible rates of interest. The ineffable joy of Christmas and the promise of surcease from alienated work, politics, and sex are thus shifted neatly from serving the need for community and intergenerational accord to increasing sales on favorable terms in the market place.

The mass electronic media and the mass print media are preempted by the corporation to the task of constituting this typification of Christmas as a marketplace and Christ as supersalesman. The solution to alienation for the capitalist system is consumption and the redemptive act is shopping. Visa, Mastercard, and Carte Blanche replace the three wise men as the givers of gifts.

Easter, on the other hand, receives considerably less attention in the mass media. It is located mostly in the social media, i.e., home and church. Easter receives but two or three days' attention in the media. In earlier times, Easter had to do with change and renewal of the seasons. In Christian times, the death of the old social order is symbolized by the crucifixion while the birth of the new social order (Heaven on Earth) is symbolized by the resurrection of Jesus.

On television, this change-and-renewal motif is reduced to clothing and fashion and the Easter Parade on Main Street. While Christmas is a $10 billion economic bonanza, fashion is a $5 billion market spread out over the year and only marginally connected to Easter. Merchants make up to 50 percent of their profits in the two-month Christmas shopping season.

Easter does not lend itself to the economic and political needs of advanced monopoly capitalism as does the fictive Christmas. Easter stories are far less often presented on mass media, slotted outside of prime time and presented as a public (religious) service. Inserted into Easter through the symbol of the crucified Jesus, the agony of the individual and the anguish of the grieving Christian community attracts few sponsors and fewer playwrights. What can one learn from Disney or Dr. Seuss about an Easter that meets the needs of commodity capitalism?

The viewing audience, then, can be inserted in the Christmas story through the protected Christ child in ways that help reconcile (fictively) the cleavages of family and society in modern capitalism. The viewing audience, when inserted in the Easter myth through the symbol of the suffering adult Christ, does not heal the cleavages of the existing social order but would, rather, call it into doubt, cast it aside, and move to a qualitatively new social order—the Kingdom of God on Earth.

The Easter message, founded in Christian understanding, especially in Revelations, calls forth a Utopian vision of Satan thrown into a bottomless pit and of Christian martyrs reigning on Earth with the resurrected Christ for a millennium. Then there is to be peace on earth, freedom from evil, as well as the rule of righteousness realized by faith in Jesus and the power of God. The advent of the millennium is concerned with the prospects of a human community on Earth. This vision is not a subjective experience useful to the sponsors of the American Christmas on mass media. Insertion of the alienated person in such a fictive vision creates trouble rather than a happy consumer whose compulsive shopping helps (1) reunite production and distribution, (2) realize profit, (3) dispose of surplus production, (4) accumulate capital for further expansion of the economy, and (5) displace pressing, macrostructural questions.

Easter brings these macrostructural distortions into focus for the understanding subject. Authentic Easters, with the suffering Christ paying penance for the institutionalized evil of throne and temple, do not resonate with the compelling consumption of the capitalist marketplace. And so, bland middle-class ministers appropriate the Christ figure to the false needs of their middle-class parishioners. Out of all this comes an Easter that is dull and lifeless; given a false flash of color by hats, frocks, scarves, and shoes.

The Structure of Christmas Song

There is a semiotic approach that helps us understand singing: voices without information. Semiology is an effort largely stimulated by Barthes (1971) that tries to place a given message—photo, text, or art form—in the ideological field that helps define its meaning and in the same instance reproduces that ideological field.

The search in semiology is for the "significations" preferred in any message and that give an ideological field meaning as a totality (Weedon et al., 1980). At the level of pure semantics, Christmas songs are nonsense. In terms of semiology, they are important events in renewing an ideology field. The structural features of these songs are significations that constitute the ideological field.

The Structure of Gender Domination

Almost all the popular Christmas songs are sung by an older male. Bing Crosby, Perry Como, Mel Tormé, Johnny Cash, Glenn Campbell, Mac Davis, and Dean Martin have a virtual monopoly on Christmas singing in the mass media and in the mall. The use of a male voice is a structural device that signifies the gender division and reasserts the superior status of the male in celebrating the sacred.

Female voices, as in the family setting, back up the baritone male voice. This emphasizes the male quality of the voice lead and, in the same moment, reasserts the power relationship between male and female in the family. The politics of gender is an important part of the total ideological field in the United States. Such song formats, even when they do not say so specifically, linguistically, do say so structurally. Power—this time sacred power—gives a male monopoly in song, in family, and in society.

The Nuclear Family as the Significant Social Unit

The structural arrangement of voices often reproduces the structure of a small kinship network called the family. The male voice backed up by two or three lighter voices in the background reproduces the family structure of Mom and Dad and Bud and Sis.

The choral group typifies, in its form, the structure of the gender-differentiated extended kinship system. The choral group is more often-found at Easter than Christmas. In the United States there are about 65 million such kinship units. The trend is changing toward singles, childless couples and to single-parent families. The ideological content of this male-dominated song structure is to deny and discourage this trend. Get married, have children, let the male dominate the family structure—this is the un-voiced message of this format.

Jesus, the Sacred Child

The fictive subject in Christmas songs is the sacred child represented by the real person of the infant Jesus. Every child who is old enough to grasp the ideological system of its own culture understands itself as the object of the lived experience of the Christ child as it is depicted in song. The child inserted into the song as object of all of Christ's experiences—as a pre-cious, loved, and cherished object. Sweet little Jesus child, infant so tender and mild, son of God, love's pure light. All these typifications tend to use the Christ figure to sanctify the child.

As the lived experience of the child deteriorates, the fictive expectations incorporated in Jesus-as-child songs become all the more urgent. A loving mother, a protective father, a warm, strong family setting, the touch of a benevolent God, the unending flow of gifts and food astonish and sanctify the child—especially those who, as in Dickens's *Christmas Carol,* find their lived experience far different.

The vision and image of life presented in this voiced music is at once a prophecy and a command—and, in modern times, an impossibility. On the one hand the songs command solidarity; on the other, they sing of an im-possible dream since such a Christmas, even if joyous to a few million parents and a great many million children for a few hours, is not the lived experience of most people, most of the time, in Christendom in our time. It is no accident that suicide, alcoholic excesses, depression, and family vio-lence increase in the Christmas season.

The Gift Structure

The structure of Christmas that validates the sacred character of the child is the gift structure. In most societies, gift giving is a noncommercial prac-tice that demonstrates beyond question the social character of a relationship (Mauss, 1955). Gift-giving when it is irrational, painful, and troublesome, when it serves no productive purpose, is the generic form of the practice and the highest test of the social nature of a relationship. At Christmas, the child is sanctified and brought into a social relation by being identified as the subject of gift-giving. When kings, princes, and saints bear the gift, all the more special is the child. Saint Nicholas brings the gift; not the more mundane (profane) parent. Christmas is the peculiarly modern expression of the potlatch. The gift structure is, in most communal societies, an embod-iment of the social unity of the entire clan or tribe with another clan or tribe

(Mauss: 32). In our gift-giving system, the boundaries of solidarity stop at the margin of the nuclear family, with but few ties between third-generation or second-degree kinship.

In the American Northwest, the potlatch is at once a system for the allocation of social honor based on giving rather than upon accumulating—and at the same time a most important way of redistributing wealth. In New Guinea, the pit roast accomplishes the same two communal goals: the reward of status for sharing and the fact of redistribution of scarce goods—protein in the New Guinea version. In our system, the central question is, What did you get for Christmas rather than how much honor did you earn by giving. Such a change in the ideological field of the gift better fits a privatized commodity system than a socialized need system.

Society as Harmonious, Orchestrated Object

The form of the music is of special interest. Music produced by choral groups, orchestras, and in programs has the idealized structure of bourgeois society. Christmas carols in concert, for example the Mormon Tabernacle Choir, have all the idealized characteristics of a well-ordered society. Everyone has a part, is part of a social division, everything is prescheduled, coordinated, and contributes to the emergent whole.

At the level of lived society, Christmas music often takes the formal characteristics of a well-ordered society with a single dominant male orchestrating everything. At the level of abstract theory, the use of the orchestra format resonates with the structural-functional theory of Parsons, Merton, Radcliffe-Brown and other consensus-oriented theorists.

In contrast to jazz which is idiographic, concerts are nomothetic. Jazz is unpredictable; in choral concerts everything is predictable, since they are planned and rehearsed. In jazz there is no ordered division of labor, no leader and led as in the case of the orchestra or choral group. Jazz could, of course, be used in Christmas song but it would not have the structural characteristics of the present form. It would not contribute to an ideological map of Christmas that sanctifies a special, bourgeois form of social organization: control, predictability, profitability, and commercial transformation of gift-giving into gift-buying. In these times, a jazz version of "Holy Night," or "Little Town of Bethlehem" would be seen as profane.

The Structure of Belief, Faith, Innocence, Awe, and Mystery

The tone of the songs at Christmas about the Jesus child are full of the awe and wonder of the ineffable. This emphasis on belief and faith, innocence and magic stands in sharp contrast to the profane world of physical reality in which cause and effect are mechanical and mundane. The important thing to note is that social reality requires faith, belief, and innocence in the process of constituting it while physical reality does not. And the effect of Christmas song, taken innocently, preserves the ability to create social reality even as this ability is eroded by secularization trends in the production of culture in politics, marketplace, factory, shop, office, and classroom.

The Structure of Peace

A conflict-ridden world requires peace to suppress the aspirations of the oppressed. Class elites need labor peace to keep the factories going. Transnational corporations need peace to keep the traffic in wealth and food flowing out of the poor countries toward the rich ones. Merchants need safe, peaceful streets to keep customers coming. Politicians need peace to maintain their continued political legitimacy. A central message of Christmas is unreflective, unqualified peace.

The ideological utility of peace arises when class and national interests are threatened. The use of Christmas as an ideological instrument for peace is made possible by the conflation of the special interests of class elites with the general interest in a peaceful society. The experience of the various revolutions in history often demonstrates that the general interest is better served by the violent overthrow of feudal, slave, and despotic elites than by peace *per se*. Song, pageant, and television programming separating peace from social justice is part of the ideological field of contemporary Christmas.

The Structure of Action

The structure of staging the drama of Christmas song tells us we are not to respond at any action level to any given information bit of any word in any lyric of any given Christmas carol. When such songs are sung, it is not within the structure of work or sport, where one might move; one understands that one is to do nothing during or after the singing of the song.

The whole ideological field, as it is constituted in Christian churches today, is to listen to a choir sing and to be still and silent as the night while doing so. In the marketplace, however, the music is played without words— they take too much attention away from price tags and "buy" signs to be used. The context of recorded music permits us to stroll around from one department to another but not to come together as a glee club and sing with power and majesty.

The Structure of Sin

The typifications of sin in Christmas and Christmas carols tend to help reproduce existing structures of social order by locating the source of sin inthe failing individual. One receives Christmas gifts because one is good; presumably those who don't get what they want are bad.

In like fashion, Christmas is the season for sinners to be reconciled with God, as the carol goes. Sin has a human face. "Joyful, all ye Nations rise; join the triumph of the skies" is another line in the same carol that implies that it is up to all nations, that is, all peoples, to rise to join God. The fault lies in the people; not in their social arrangements. After all, those arrangements were set in place by God and God wants all peoples to be humble and to walk in peace all the days of their life.

Postmodern religion locates sin in both the actions of specific individuals and in the structures of domination that require people to be sinful in the embodiment of them. There is no popular Christmas carol that encourages the transformation of the social order; only the transformation of the individual. Liberation Theology teachers that both must be freed of sin; that structural sin is the other half of redemption.

The forms of sin are of interest in the Christmas carol; what is condemned and what is neglected. Peace is an enduring theme but the exploitation of nations by stronger nations is not at issue. Giving and sharing are important themes, but the international banking system that pours wealth into the seven richest nations and that leaves dozens of poor nations beggared is not mentioned in the structure of Christmas song or Christmas story. Greed, envy, sloth, lust, avarice, and the other mortal sins seldom find expression in songs of Christmas. The structural sins of class, racial, gender, or colonial oppression have no home in the present stories of Christmas.

The dominant structural sin is, of course, the temporary homelessness of the Holy family. Yet as visible as it is, the manger scene is not the subject of the Christmas pageant but rather the birth of the Holy child and the homage paid him by the three Kings who traveled far to bring him gifts.

It is worth noting that the solution to sin is, as the song goes, mercy mild. There is much to be said for mercy as against retribution as a way to deal with sin. Mercy encompasses the outcast while retribution excludes those who sin. Mercy elicits mercy and redemptive response from the sinner while retribution elicits bitterness and ever-widening circles of sin. Mercy transcends the narrow logic of technical ratiocination while retribution exacts a mathematical precision. But the solution to structural sin requires more than mercy; it requires the change and renewal that is the central theme of Easter. While mercy is most helpful at the level of the individual, it has little effect on the impersonal processes of economic and political exploitation.

If we are to use the drama of the Holy to identify and thus take action against our personal and structural sins, then the stories and songs at this most holy time in Christendom might well focus upon them.

Only when we enlarge the analysis and place it in the totality of which it is a part can we make out its meaning. Its structural characteristics provide the significations—how we are to take these songs—that shape out consciousness and guide our overt behavior. We will make the interpretations on the semiologic meaning of Christmas, Jesus, and the carols as we explore and make visible some of the structures of these songs. Generally, songs are a form of social opinion and help reproduce existing social structures.

The structures above abstracted from Christmas songs together with other structures, synergistically, define the ideological field in which the figure of Christ is situated at Christmas. Since these are the stressed features in Christmas songs they are the typifications by which the ideological field is made visible.

That ideological field posits as sacred a social form in which a male-dominated family structure uses gifts to celebrate the position of the child. This family of three generic roles—mother, child, and the commanding father—is the basic building block of a highly orchestrated, stable, and peaceful social-life world. Other possible building blocks are foreclosed in this ideological field. The community, the individual, extensive friendship, the cohabiting couple, the homosexual couple, the extended family, the clan, or other historically viable building blocks are excluded from the ideology emergent from this structural combination. Excluded as well are democratic societal forms, spontaneity, rotas, and unique, idiographic permutations.

The transformation of Christ into a revolutionary who heaped scorn upon the scribes and Pharisees (Matt. 23:25)—symbolized by his crucifixion—can be seen in the treatment of Christ by Weber (in Lash, 1980:7). Weber notes that transforming social change (diachronic change) became embodied in the Christ figure as he became the vehicle of natural law (*Wertrational-ität*). While the priests preempted legal rationality (*Zweckrationalität*), Christ had to resort to charismatic reason (nonrationality) as his source of authority.

It is possible to understand that the *wertrationnal* Christ of biblical times has been replaced at Christmas by the *zweckrational* Christ of advanced capitalism. The Christ of Easter is altogether a different story.

There remain elements of Wertrationalität *in the Christ of Easter among many Latin Americans associated with the Liberation Theology movement.*

In interpreting the selection of typification in Christmas song, the first point is that the structures selected are of significance (and thus worthy of selection) only when they are problematic. One does not have to create a special ideological field for structures that are not undergoing change; that are not threatened by still deeper, unexamined contradictions.

Only when structures are undergoing dereification is the social labor of reification and deification necessary. Out of the thousands of structures taken for granted whose production is necessary for a given social-life world—a culture—only a few are problematic enough to burden the Christmas season with them.

The status of the family is made more problematic as the need for more labor from both males and females increases. Christmas carols and caroling formats that reproduce the family structure (e.g., the Osmond family, the old Crosby shows, the Johnny Cash, Glenn Campbell, and Lawrence Welk television programs of the Christmas season) vary in popularity over the years. By "problematic," I mean that some processes in society depend upon the family while other processes tend to change it.

A large number of highly mobile and easily fragmented family units with highly productive members blessed with a lot of disposable income for consumption is just the family structure best suited to capitalism. It supplies the highly trained labor force so necessary to produce profit. Family units with disposable income help realize profit. The structure of gift-giving absorbs that disposable income.

But family and other structures in late capitalism must be reproduced if they are to absorb the costs of supplying trained labor, help to realize profit by absorbing surplus production, and help provide the dramaturgical facsimile of a solution to the problem of alienation. The use of Jesus as Christ child helps the family—on a yearly basis—to make the sacrifice for twenty years or so to rear and train a child to be a punctual, conscientious, productive worker and dedicated consumer. By the time the child is twelve, he or she has learned that the good life, obedience, and consumption are ineluctably tied together through the sacred Christ of Christmas.

The American Christmas, in its television, radio, and newspaper version, orients the family to absorb billions of dollars worth of surplus production. In a Marcusian analysis, the Christ of Christmas helps sanctify to parent and child alike an ever-expanding layer of false needs. The economic dynamics of Christmas are such that high profit is realized and, to some extent, the accumulation crisis of advanced monopoly capitalism is moderated.

Buying at Christmas time is especially irrational. The ordinary canons of caution, calculation, and utility are set aside—indeed they must be set aside if the spirit of Christmas is to be captured. And the control over media accorded to commercial capitalism by virtue of the advertising format of television sponsorship provides the industry with a virtual monopoly over the defining process. What is defined as a suitable gift is controlled by the sponsor. It is in the fiscal interest of such private sponsors to define high profit/capital-intensive items as the appropriate gift.

A full analysis of this control is a long treatise itself but suffice to say that such control over the defining process creates a long-term trend to economic distortions among which is the movement of private capital to cheap labor countries as well as the movement of investment capital to high-profit lines of production. The essential lines of production are thereby deprived of capital investment. Housing, health care, child care, education, pollution control, and other labor-intensive, low-profit lines of production are deprived of resources.

The ideological field created by commodity capitalism at Christmas contributes in some small but important degree to this institutional distortion. It is difficult for parents and others to define labor-intensive necessities as suitable gifts in the face of this multimillion-dollar campaign by commercial capital at Christmas to dispose of high-energy, high-technology, high-profit forms of production.

Profit considerations tend to push the marginal capitalist firm toward Third World countries with cheap labor and lax pollution laws as sources for Christmas items. This contributes to the continuing disemployment of American workers who are expected to absorb the production from both the United States, Taiwan, Korea, Hong Kong, and Malaysia. The capitalist version of Christmas is an economic morass. It is not unimportant that most Christmas decorations are now made in Asia and imported to North America.

However, the aspects of Christmas and of Christ selected by sponsors of television, radio, and municipal pageants are also mediated by tradition, family needs, and religious functionaries. Needs for love, affirmation, selfless giving, surprise-oriented to affection and to the warmth of the extended kinship-friendship complex, are not false to the human process—these are central to it.

The Christ of the American Christmas also endorses and elevates these out of ordinary time and ordinary experience. The American version of Christ at Christmas is not entirely alien to the human project. There is a whole universe of experience at Christmas which, although not the focus of this analysis, deserves to be included and weighed against the mystifications of Christmas.

The Jesus of the Easter Ceremony

Once again, it is central to a critical dramaturgy to identify the ideological field from which this dramatization of Christ is created and helps recreate. The immediate observation that presents itself is that the Jesus of Easter does not lend itself to the capitalist venture to the same extent as the Christ child of Christmas. The centrally important significations of the Easter Child are far different from those of the Christmas Christ.

A structural analysis of the Easter Christ provides us with these typifications: The Christ at Easter is an adult, not a child. He embodies suffering and the accumulated sins of the whole society rather than the joy of the hearth and home. The Easter Christ stands as a voiceless critic of the established institutions of society—the marketplace, the occupying army, alienated governance, personal greed, and collective indifference to justice. Church, state, police, and ordinary life are the targets of the protesting Christ figure.

The suffering Christ carries far too heavy an ideological burden for a happy holiday. A child could not carry the burdens of sin and redemption at Easter time.

Easter can be depoliticized and, as is the hoar leper, refreshed once again to the April day. Easter can be trivialized by egg-rolls on the White House lawn, by tiny chicks squeezed tightly by tiny hands, and by melting chocolate rabbits. These are not the central features of Easter in the lived experience of many Christians, especially those in the poor capitalist countries of the Third World. For these people, the typifications of Easter are more oriented to Christ and to his crucifixion. A structural analysis of the Easter Christ provides us with these ideological typifications:

1. The suffering of Christ and rejection of a sinful world. On the cross, Christ looks at the world through the eyes of the poor and those forsaken by God, not through the eyes of the merchant, the money lender, nor the arrogant state official.
2. The symbol of the egg and the spring colors used to decorate it are both typifications of rebirth brought over from the pagan spring rituals that predate the Easter service. Change and renewal are the significant meanings.

3. The renewal of the human spirit and the reconstitution of a moral order oriented to community embodied in the resurrection myth. Christ did not die, in this drama, for the individual; he died to redeem all humanity and to move the world closer to the City of God.
4. The emphasis upon the Holy Mother Mary and her despair at the sacrifice of her child. This typification reverberates through the very soul of the Third World mother who loses 20, 30, 50 percent of her precious children to hunger, disease, migration, crime, and prostitution.
5. The association of Christ with the outcast and the thief on the cross. In a world where millions of workers are discarded; where the elderly are abandoned; where the mentally ill are made ill and then pushed into the street; in a world where crime is a way to feed children, pay rent, buy Christmas presents, or to pay fuel and doctor bills—one responds with all of one's soul to the promise of salvation in Christ if one is a believer.
6. The redemption of sin through the death of Christ. There must be a way out of such an impoverished life. The drama of death and rebirth tells us that we must destroy and rebuild—that is a revolutionary message. It does not bring the false peace of the grave since Christ rises. The message is that the people, too, must one day rise.
7. The emphasis of the church (as congregation) as the social unit rather than the family as in Christmas. One does not stay home on Easter morning. One joins the larger community in pain and penance.
8. The displacement of redemption from the present to the future; from this world to the heavenly city; from the gift to the sacrifice of human beings.

The pain, anguish, suffering, sacrifice, and rebirth of the Jesus symbol does not lend itself to a safe resolution of the defects of advanced monopoly capitalism. Compared to Christmas, sponsored radio ignores Easter. Sponsored newspapers stress clothing and Easter parades. Television finds few sponsors for Easter specials.

In the face of the suffering Christ, one cannot create false needs for electronic toys, automobiles, or such solidarity supplies as beer, candy, and food. The simple, unadorned, seminude body of Christ on the cross is not conducive to the realization of profit. The generation of false needs so vital to consumerism cannot be supported by the real grief of Mary at the loss of her son. Buying high-profit items cannot be made to assuage the grief one feels at the death of Christ.

The Christ of Easter reflects the alienation of humanity in a world defective in significant ways. The resurrection of Christ is a promise for transcendence of the humiliation, indignity, and suffering of the oppressed. It is precisely the same promise of a critical and revolutionary Marxism. It would be a distortion to say that the typification that infuses the crucifixion drama leads toward the radical transformation of life in this world.

Such an ideological field often leads to mysticism and self-flagellation; not explicitly toward emancipation. However, it would be equally a distortion to state that the Jesus of Easter is indifferent to human suffering and does not, cannot, speak to an authentic emancipation. The ideological field in which the Easter Christ dwells defines an apocalyptic view of redemption. It is an ideological field fundamentally critical of injustice, oppression, and the suffering produced by an exploitive and privileged society (Quinney:67). The figure of the crucified Jesus continues to rage against the corruption of every society in which a Christian suffers from structural sin—the institutional distortions of war, profit, privilege, or denial of a common human part.

This is the grounding of every revolutionary faith—Muslim, Marxian, and Christian alike. Every social movement that teaches the irreformability of the present system, that teaches the radical transformation on a new and more communal basis is apocalyptic in its typification and emancipatory in purpose whether it couches its argument in scientific or in sacred language.

Liberation Theologies

It is the ideological map of Easter typified by anguish, suffering, and rejection of corruption in this world that informs the liberation theology of the Third World poor, especially in Latin America. In the capitalist Third World each suffering Christian is inserted as subject in the crucifixion of the Christ figure. In the liberation of minority groups at home, the message of the martyred Christ speaks a powerful message. In the liberation of women, the asexual Christ holds open his arms.

The Christian is not inserted as subject in the ideological field of the Jesus child comforted, plied with gifts, nor defined as bringer of joy to the world. The subjective experience of that Jesus speaks to the middle-class children in the fourteen rich capitalist countries more so than the increasing desperation of poor children in the 115 deteriorating capitalist countries.

For the unemployed, the ill, the elderly, or the lower-echelon employee, as well as in the wealthy European and North American countries, it is the Jesus of Easter that answers to the lived experience of the alienated Christian. In a society accustomed to better things, to responsive action in this world, the Easter Christ poses more danger than in other, more docile times.

There are ugly directions toward which that Christ might to be taken. The 50 million born-again Christians in the United States turn to Right-wing politics and toward that ideological camp for responsive action. Confined to the ideological needs of White, Anglo-Saxon males, the Easter

TABLE 14.1   Ideological Fields at Christmas and Easter

Structural Typification	Christmas	Easter
Anthropomorphic subject	Jesus as Child	Jesus as adult
Subjective ontology	joy and comfort	suffering and sin
Redemptive action	buying	death of the old (resurrection)
Social unit in focus	the family	society (the church)
Location of Sin	Individual	Social Order
Social action required	peace-goodwill-mercy	sacrifice-struggle
Medium (U.S. 1990s)	mass media: television, radio, magazines, papers	social media: congregation, community, family
Media controlled by:	corporations or state	father, church, and community
Political message	enjoy the present	change and renewal
Acting agent	parents	community
Economic meaning	privatized consumption	sharing, rebuilding

Christ foreshadows a different drama, a drama once played out in Europe in a thousand concentration camps.

As the contradictions of capitalism exacerbate rather than transcend the situation for these millions, the ideological field of the apostolic church, the social gospel, and liberation theology stand by close at hand as a revolutionary alternate for alienated Christians.

Conclusion

There are at least two generalizations to be made in light of the foregoing analysis. One is germane to the sociology of religion while the other speaks more to the sociology of knowledge.

The nature of the ideological field in which a religious figure is placed depends upon the political economy of an epoch. The contradictions now existent create two contesting fields in which to insert the Christ figure.

Which of the two ideological fields now contesting over which Jesus figure takes precedence in the religious practices of the Christian world is a historical question related to quality of life variables—including those of a spiritual nature. By "spiritual" I mean here those attributes relating to *joie de vivre*, enthusiasm for work, self-esteem, social anchorage, confidence, easy interpersonal support, and boundless affection for life and for living peoples.

The final judgment we must make at this historical juncture is that the Christ child of Christmas takes precedence in the media as well as in the social-life world over that of the crucified Jesus in the United States and Europe. It is organized to repair exploitive cleavages and so works to some degree. Religion, in the present Christmas mode, preserves defects in the structure of society and thus stands against human emancipation. However, the efficacy of Christmas to help bind together a given society varies over time. Such efficacy varies with the material conditions of a society, as Marx would have said.

Richard Quinney (1980) is correct in his insistence that the spiritual and the sacred are important to humans and must be accommodated within critical, socialist analysis and practice. An open cultural Marxism must examine the Quinney thesis unblinded by a dogmatic antireligious bias.

Quinney argues that it is wrong to dismiss the revolutionary and human character of a religion even if the capitalist version is particularly subversive of community and in many ways hostile to social justice. Neither Marx nor Durkheim can tell us whether religion is always and in all ways hostile or conducive to the human process—that is an empirical question.

In South America, a different finding might be appropriate. There is an open invitation for competent research on the South American situation. The future will reveal any social and ideological changes in the way the Christ figure is mediated and constituted in the capitalist complex. I expect a shift in the importance accorded to the two ideological fields. I should think that Easter will gradually displace Christmas as the significant way to experience the Christ figure as the crises in capitalist societies continue. Along with Quinney, I am willing to concede an emancipatory dimension to a religious ideological field, especially as it is developing in liberation theology.

To fully understand how ideological fields are constituted and used, one must go beyond semantics, information theory, and the spoken language to include typifications and semiotics. An understanding of the ideological field of Christmas cannot be acquired by listening to the words of the Christmas song, by following the line of meaning of a Christmas play, by attending to the words of the announcers, nor by reading the listings in television guides and sections.

The meaning of any cultural event comes from the totality of the social-life world in which it appears. It does not have a universal, eternally stable meaning.

The meaning of Christmas, Easter, Veterans Day, Halloween, or any collective cultural production must be located in the social totality. Such meaning arises out of nonverbal typifications and significations. Sometimes these meanings are located in deep structures—in the very form and sequence of patterned activity. The work of Macherey, Barthes, and other cultural Marxists helps provide the analytic tools with which to extract those meanings and contribute to the authentic self-knowledge of a society in its quest for social justice.

Those who believe all religion to be alien to the human condition must pause and ask themselves what other ideological field speaks clearly and deeply to the oppressed masses in Latin America. Surely it is not a scientized Marxism any more than a scientized capitalism. Whatever one's views on the reality of God, Christ, and the religious doxology, the oppressed of the world act upon their own beliefs, understanding, and interpretations. I agree with Quinney that it is necessary to solve problems of integration, unification, coordination, and solidarity in every social philosophy.

A postmodern morality needs to do more than dismiss such religious teachers as Jesus, the Buddha, Mohammed or Lao Tze as the dust of history. At the same time, the postmodern use of these figures for the colonization and channeling of desire in commercial advertisement needs more than impatient expressions of disgust. In this chapter, the dramatization of Christ in his two major embodiments is contrasted that we may recover the best of his teachings to the human process.

In the face of all this, the redemptive power of Christ is a more realistic instrument of social justice than the sanitized structural analysis of orthodox Marxism for most of those people who will have to finally act on their own understanding.

Apart from Cuba and perhaps China, the socialist world has little to offer the Third World other than the model of a dispirited bureaucratic socialism. That the socialist block outperforms the capitalist block in measures of social justice counts little, and in fact these data are not even available to the peasant in the Third World. They are not even available to the highly educated worker in the information-rich societies of Europe and North America. Still less is the Marxist vision of authentic democratic socialism celebrated and sanctified in the West.

In the short run, it matters little what Marxist theorists prefer—what counts is commitment to emancipatory ideologies. In that arena, the Easter Christ has a present advantage. Another century or two may alter that fact but right now, the student of revolution, of social justice, of moral development, and of spiritual renewal might well focus on the Jesus of liberation theology—the crucified Jesus of Easter rather than the helpless child of Christmas.

The drama of the holy offers much to the human project. At its best that drama, in all its cultural variations, enables people to transcend the thousand private ills to which the flesh is heir; to put away for the moment, the hundred petty hurts that each inflicts on those around each; to hold out a hand to those whose burden is too heavy to carry alone. Such a sense of the holy expands the soul; makes the hair stand on end; warms the heart of those who have grown callous to the pain of others.

It is always true that people need bread, shelter, and protection from the elements. They also need the drama of the wafer, the mystery of the wine, and the arching canopy of the sacred—else the ordinary world of the profane, the biological world of the animal, the mechanical world of mere survival comes upon the land.

Nicaragua's Revolutionary Easter

By Alma Guillermoprieto in Managua

It could be an ordinary Easter, except that it is the second time Jesus has risen again in Nicaragua since the Revolution. The difference shows most inside the churches.

At the Church of Mercy, Father Antonio Castro is proud to show the new alter, built in the shape of a barricade, out of the same paving stones local children used to build barricades with against the National Guard of the late dictator, Anastasio Somoza.

"The congregation wanted it that way," he said. There was popular enthusiasm as well for the new Stations of the Cross. The First one—Jesus condemned to death—shows a young man being pushed in the back of a lorry by the National Guard. "At first some people objected to that," said Father Antonio, "but I explained that the old paintings we used to see were of old people, who painted a thousand years ago what they thought happened two thousand years ago. We have to do that again today."

The initiative to make Christ a contemporary figure is transforming the Nicaraguan Church and the way it is perceived by the faithful—and creating some internal friction. What a local observer calls "the great battle for Jesus Christ" is on between the prorevolutionary clergy and the traditional Church.

In the name of Jesus, the "popular Church," as it is sometimes known, is actively collaborating with the revolutionary regime. In the name of Christ, the religious hierarchy is warning against excessive Church involvement and cautiously siding with the Opposition.

The Sandinista National Liberation Front (FSLN) could not be happier with its success in capturing the imagination and loyalty of so many of the clergy. Four priests serve in cabinet-level positions. Ernesto Cardenal, the poet-priest, is minister of culture. His brother, Fernando Cardenal, a Jesuit, headed the literacy campaign. He is now executive director of the Sandinista youth organization.

Miguel D'Escoto is in charge of foreign relations. Edgar Parrales is minister of social welfare, and like his colleague in culture, a lay priest. In addition, many of the country's 300 or so priests are serving in government.

The alliance of a left-wing revolutionary organization with the radicalized propounders of "liberation theology" is not a Nicaraguan phenomenon. In the early 1960s, Father Famillo Torres of Colombia was one of several priests to exchange his vows for a guerrilla rifle. The difference in Nicaragua and the rest of Central America is that the clergy does not give up its vows, but preaches liberation from the pulpits.

Many revolutionaries are no longer ashamed to call themselves Christians. Among the Sandinistas, many of the leaders—among them the National Directorate member, Louis Carrion, and the army's second-in-command, Joaquin Cuadra—began as members of the Christian communities.

The FSLN's statement on the role of religion in the Revolution last November made the new alliance explicit: "Our experience shows that one can be a believer and a committed revolutionary at the same time, and that there is no insurmountable contradiction between the two."

The Nicaragua Church hierarchy disagrees at least with the interpretation of the statement, and a year ago it asked clergy serving in government positions to resign. The priests asked the Vatican to mediate. The Church softened its position to say that those priests who could be replaced in their government tasks should resign. The Vatican said the affair should be settled in Nicaragua and to date, no priest has withdrawn from the government and more have joined.

The Opposition here is as intent as the clergy in claiming the certificate of Christian authenticity. The Catholic radio station and the Opposition daily, La Prensa, use the Christian vocabulary to voice their attacks on the Government. The Archbishop of Managua's homilies are regularly reprinted in La Prensa and the Opposition and the FSLN think that the sermons are subtle attacks on the Government. The archbishop claims neutrality.

"The hierarchy is growing isolated, and it is concerned about that," said Father Antonio Castro, as he prepared for an austere celebration of Good Friday.

Is "Christian" Just a Code Word?

Here is what the spokesmen for the Religious New Right say:

We've already taken control of the conservative movement. And conservatives have taken control of the Republican Party. The remaining thing is to see if we can take control of the country. [Richard Viguerie, key fundraiser and strategist for the Religious New Right.]

Groups like ours are potentially very dangerous to the political process—a group like ours could lie through its teeth and the candidate it helps stays clean. [Terry Dolan, chairman, National Political Action Committee.]

We're radicals working to overturn the present structure in this country—we're talking about Christianizing America. [Paul Weyrich, director, Committee for the Survival of a Free Congress.]

If necessary, God would raise up a tyrant, a man who might not have the best ethics, to protect the freedom and the interests of the ethical and the Godly. [Rev. James Robison, TV evangelist.]

You can't be a good Christian and a liberal at the same time. [Rev. Jerry Falwell, TV evangelist, president of Moral Majority, Inc.]

15

Dress, Drama and Self:
The Tee Shirt as Text

Sex is better than drugs
If you have the right pusher

    —Mope's Tee Shirt

    This chapter interprets the results of a three-day observation of the dress of students at a college event. Categories for the analysis of tee shirts were generated by participant observation. The analysis of clothing is located in the larger process by which social reality is constructed. Clothing is one of four information media over which a young person still has control. As students are processed through the routines of mass bureaucracies, voice, body, and behavior are repressed as language media. As young people fail to find an institutionalized medium which expresses their concerns and their responses to the contingencies of life, they invent one.

    The tee shirt is the uniquely postmodern medium that young people have found to speak out. We can read these tee shirts as text, deconstruct them and thus, help reconstruct a world in which young people can give voice to those concerns.

    To deconstruct a discourse is to think about how it fails its own project and interferes with the competent practice of social life. While this seems unnecessarily negative, one assumes that its positivities are registered in the knowledge process, in the sociocultural process, and will survive such a critique. Deconstruction of a topic requires that all its privileged assumptions are desanctified, returned to the human hand, and the human mind that gave them birth and thus repoliticized—made part of a radical democracy of ideas and a rich democracy of decision.

In deconstructing, one illuminates the inconsistencies, the omissions, the easy assumptions and the failings of a theory, a practice or a concept, not in order to prove it false but rather to remind its practitioners and its users that the truth value of a statement is variable while the utility of it fades as conditions change—that in social science, there are no finalities, no boundaries, no iron laws; nor are there eternal truths. Life is always larger than theory and always richer; always more connected; always messier and more chaotic. Deconstruction opposes itself to all claims of permanence, objectivity, or authoritative finality.

As Leitch suggests, deconstruction challenges every boundary, every frame, every margin, every inscription, every border in order to reconnect a topic to its rich social past and its wide-ranging consequence (1983:261). As Culler asserts, deconstruction holds a discourse responsible for the philosophy it asserts (1982:86). As Derrida proclaims in the *Gaze of Oedipus,* the self-knowledge of a science, of a critique, of a theoretical tradition is always disqualified as a final arbitrator of its own worth and validity. As Derrida asserts in *La Verité en peinture,* deconstruction always meddles with solid structure, with "material" institutions; it always goes beyond mere discourse and into the social dynamics that call forth and give form to discourse.

All this is part of a knowledge process that contributes to the self-reflexivity of an academic discipline, a political economy or a social relationship. The point is not to *destruct* such a theory or concept; such an institution or social formation, but rather to set it in its sociohistorical context and to reconnect it to its history. As such, deconstructionism is part of the postmodern methodology that abdjures all talk of value-free theory; all talk of objectivity; all pretensions to grand, unified concepts and theories as well as all claims to modernity with its implications of finality and of perfected social relations.

What is done with such an analysis is, of course, dependent upon how good the political process might be; how well such knowledge is produced and how widely it is distributed; how well it is connected to an interactively rich and democratically oriented public sphere. At its best, deconstruction sets the stage for a patterning of social life oriented to the human project—it is part of *praxis,* a reconstructive process. At its worst, deconstruction is endless, petty, defeating self-doubt. The first leads to the dialectics of life; the latter to isolating nihilism or simply cynical withdrawal.

The foreclosure of linguistic capacities alienates young people from the process by which social reality is constituted through symbolic interaction. Students regain control over that process, sometimes in pretheoretical and privatized ways, by the political, sexual, status, and economic messages on display to anonymous others in mass recreational events. Some theoretical foundations for the alienated use of clothing are suggested.

Speaking Out

All over the world young people collect and display tee shirts. In the United States, the wearing of tee shirts is a national phenomenon. The typical middle-class youngster has from five to ten such tee shirts with which to communicate his or her special message of style, gender, affinities, politics, status, interests, beliefs, and value preferences. Mope, an employee of the Copy Center Service at Central Michigan University, has about a hundred such tee shirts that he wears on appropriate occasions—that is to say, everyday.

Symbolic Systems

In the constitution of shared social-life worlds, each individual has four language systems available with which to interact symbolically. There is first and foremost, the voice. The voice is a complex modulation of sounded plosives used to create variations of meaning. With control of pitch, tone, volume, sequence, and color of sound, an infinite number of voicings can be used to create an infinitely complex symbolic universe in which to live.

In mass societies, the voice is stilled. The structure of mass media is such that most information flow is not communication—i.e., the interactively-rich product of two or more persons creating a special shared social event. Rather the flow of information is one-way. Symbols are generated, edited, and transmitted unilaterally from a few persons interested in the unilateral shaping of ideas, attitudes, and activities of a set of minimally known others.

Where there is face-to-face exchange of voiced plosives, the rules of mass organization are such that a set of lower-echelon functionaries elicit information from a set of anonymous persons processed uniformly by those rules. Information other than that required by the functionary to know how to apply the rules is defined as *noise in the system* and excluded from the final social product. Thus, in mass society, is the voice stilled as an instrument of symbolic interaction.

In the long years of education, young people are taught to repress their vocal abilities. They are to sit silently through the long hours of the school day. They are to speak only when called upon to speak. They are to talk only about that which the teacher sets as a topic. They are to suppress that which is of passing or pressing importance to them; divorce at home, new love and recent rejections, money problems, animosities, and other private concerns. Still less may they speak about the injustices, animosities, and contradictions that abound in the classroom. The metaphysics of discourse are out of bounds to the student—they may not criticize teacher, topic, or administrative policy.

Employees in business, science, school, and hospital are required to flatten out their linguistic capacities and to use a mode of speech that mimics the deadness of mathematics, the lifelessness of machine. Tee shirts reawaken the capacity to speak in the chromatic shades of life—Why should a computer monitor have 12,000 colors and the human voice but one? The human voice can speak with rage, compassion, or tenderness. Mass institutions are oriented toward profit, control, efficiency, and productivity—they are not oriented to the human forms of culture.

In mass politics, mass media, mass welfare, mass marketing, mass education, mass sport, mass religion as in mass communications, the individual is alienated from a very important means by which social life could be created. That leaves the other three media by which social reality could be constituted.

The second language system is the body itself. There are two ways in which the body can be used as a speech act: by body adornment and by movement of body parts. For most of history, for most societies, the body is adorned with jewelry, hairstyle, is painted, scarred, twisted and deformed, clothed or left bare to inform all present as to the gender of a person, to denote age grade, political place, sexual availability, religious character, or occupation.

In mass societies, the body is hidden behind the standard identity kits of the mass occasion. The scars, cosmetics, shapes, or hair arrangements of the human body are information-poor carriers, but even those few bits of information the body could carry to signal social identities, social meanings other than those officially prescribed by the rules of the mass organization, are forbidden.

In the army, the hospital, the school, or in business, body adornment is demoted as an informational carrier. Employees whose body speaks a various language risk firing and certainly pay a price in denial of wages, salaries, or promotions. There are important qualifiers to this point, of course. In those employment situations where the body cannot be seem—or if seen, is irrelevant to corporate goals—then one can recapture one's body and adorn it as one wishes.

Body talk is a system of speech that complements and augments voiced speech. The meaning of a vocal act is amplified, modified, or neutered by the body act that accompanies it. The face itself has some 100,000 information bits that can be used to help convey meaning. The arm position, hand gesture, turn of the body, upturn of the mouth, the tone of large muscles—all tell us what is happening in the drama of social life, how to interpret the voiced sounds, the degree to which the other is engrossed in the social occasion at hand. The twist of a hand, the tilt of an eyebrow, the lift of a step, the slump of a shoulder, the curl of a smile, or the tapping of a foot—all are read by others and responded to in the delicate endeavor of shaping each other's activity.

The use of body talk is carefully controlled in mass institutions. The soldier is trained to hold eyes, mouth, hands, and feet still while the officer speaks. The clerk is trained to use eyes, face, and head to attend to the task at hand. The student is taught to sit quietly and demurely, to watch closely, and to nod attentively to the voiced interpretations of the teacher. In other alienated social occasions, women would have been taught to do the same in the company of men.

When body and voice say the same thing, we know the meaning of a thing. When voice and body say different things, we are put in a double bind—we do not know which language system to read. In mass institutions, body talk is also silenced. In the class, in the army, in the church, or in the office, the wonderful power and grace of the body to dance, gesture, punctuate, scoff, or to embrace life is deadened. That leaves two other symbol systems.

Behavior is a third language system merging subtly and powerfully with the other three to create a shared symbolic environment. The larger cycles of behavior have meaning that may be read by the skillful, intimate others who build and embody social reality.

In Africa, princes walk with a gait and demeanor that tells all who watch that they are princes, proud warriors who yield to none. In Kansas, men walk with their hands in their back pocket to tell strangers that they are reserved, cautious, secure in their own skin without the need to reach too soon for connection. In Tibet, women stride along with a sword in their belt telling men that they hold up half the sky.

When a hostess wants to signal the end of a dinner to lounging guests, she may begin to remove dishes. When a friend wishes to signal danger to another, s/he may become very quiet. When a young man wishes to communicate extreme displeasure with a parent, he may engage in destructive behavior, the message of which is that something is wrong and must be remedied.

Psychiatrists become adept at reading the meaning of long cycles of behavior in a patient—repeated shopping binges, alcoholic and other addictive behaviors, cycles of love and disenchantment—tell of their own private compulsions in their own private configurations.

Mass medical establishments, mass educational institutions, mass political organizations, large corporate entities, vast public bureaus, mass electronic churches have no capacity nor have they any interest in reading out the meaning of these cycles of behavior so important to the health and joy of life.

A fourth language system available to a person with which to create the infinitely rich and varied social-life worlds found in authentic social action is clothing. Every society in history has used clothing for more than mere physiological function. Clothing has, for most of human history, been used in infinite permutation with voice and body to help define a situation, to help sanctify it, to help keep it going within its own logic, and to help end it. Each special social occasion demands a separate costuming. If a person is involved in many special occasions, s/he will have a closet full of meaningful clothes.

People who have five different kinds of shoes, jackets, hats, trousers, ties, or belts have transcended the physiological meaning of clothing and have entered into the symbolic world of clothing. For each set of clothing there is a separate and distinct social-life world that is to be constructed somewhere sometime. There are clothes for sport, clothes for work, clothes that speak of romance, and there are clothes to wear in the quiet and holy places of the world.

Fashion and style further expand the closets of the world. Those without secure and significant social anchorage for their self system can buy instant identities from a fashion boutique. Many shopping malls include stores that sell an identity to those who have none in which they can take pride. Young men and women, disconnected from the society in which they find themselves, buy, steal, and borrow clothing with which to project an image of status, of human worth.

Superefficient textile factories, superproductive sweat shop industries, superaesthetic advertising firms combine to colonize the desire of young men and women for social honor. They create and recreate fashion with which to do so—and thus garner superprofits.

In mass education, mass marketing, mass religion, mass sports, mass medicine, and mass politics, clothing comes under the control of a clothing police and loses its vocabulary. Dress codes for the patient, physician, and nurse are set by the singular logic of mass medicine, not by therapeutic logic. If a patient and a doctor knew each other as distinct human beings, there would be no need for white jackets or blue pants. Mass hospitals process masses of patients through the fragmented routines of mechanized medicine. In such a way, hundreds of patients can be mass-produced by the deskilled labor of unknown others.

Dress codes for the military or for the police are set by the logic of partisan conflict, not by the logic of law or justice. Dress codes for children in school or their teachers are set by the logic of social power, not by that of pedagogy. In business, dress codes are set in such a manner as to submerge alternate—and human—potentialities of clerk and customer alike. Even in the factory, field, and mine, some of the codes of clothing are set more by the administrative interests of management than by the logic of safety or task.

Mass institutions subvert the individuality of language systems, of meaning construction, the individual contribution to the social occasion at hand even as mass societies proclaim the ascendancy of individualism. What is meant by individuality in that context is that each individual should come before the bureaucracy one at a time rather than in organized collectives, and that any activity to act autonomously should occur outside the mass occasion at hand. Dress codes subvert the capacity of human beings to embody personal desire and to focus on distinctly human beings and human endeavor. Tee shirts recapture and express this alienated desire to their own purpose.

Clothing, voicings, body decor, and behavior are the four symbol systems used, in manifold and subtle variation, to create meaning by the participating individual within a collective enterprise. These four information flow systems are used by the individual in informationally-rich and interactively-rich social occasions with which to share in the creation of social reality. In mass society, the speech-carrying capacity of voice, body, clothing, and behavior is sharply reduced. The means of producing meaning are alienated by the rules of mass society.

Mass society itself arises from the interests of a few persons consolidated in an elite to preprogram the behavior of a mass enlarged as much as possible, in ways compatible with the interests of that elite. A special set of persons, hired and trained by the elite, process the mass through the routines of the mass institution in ways compatible with the rules of the organization.

The mass is processed as individuals in questions of power and as standardized blocs in questions of status. Historically, the structures of mass organization arose with bureaucracy in prehistoric hydraulic societies, of which China and Egypt may be the prototypes. In modern history, the mass armies of France in Napoleonic times are perhaps the prototypic form of mass organization.

For our purposes here, we are interested in the ways in which students reclaim control over their own clothing as part of an interest in how media are alienated and liberated in given social occasions. In the study at hand, we will find that students use the tee shirt not as a physiological device by which to help regulate body temperature but rather as a political device by which to give voice to their anguish, ambitions, and needs in a world where their voice counts for little in the process by which social reality is created.

The Structure of Mass Society

Mass societies are comprised of organizations controlled by a few persons, managed by a few more, to control the activity of large numbers of people. The name we give to most of these organizations is *bureaucracy*. A bureaucracy is a stratified system of power in which an *elite* employs a *cadre* to process masses of people through standardized routines. The structure of a mass society serves as the social background and the theoretical soil out of which comes the growing interest in the tee shirt as a medium of discourse.

The rules by which people are processed—in education, medicine, sport, theatre, politics, industry, the marketplace, or in religion—are ordinarily set by the elite. And ordinarily the elite set the rules for their own convenience or purpose. The convenience or advantage of those persons processed may be considerable but is incidental to the purposes of the elite. The rules themselves are set forth and enforced without the rich dialectics of symbolic interaction. Interaction is reduced to the voicing of the rules and the control of deviation from the rule.

The one-sided nature of these rules requires considerable political effort on the part of the cadre. They organize the lines of action to reduce to a bare minimum the use of symbol systems by the individuals processed en masse. Modern policing arose to accommodate the interests of the few in controlling the activity of the many. Modern administrative science arose as a scientific alternative to the use of force in the shaping of behavior.

Unfree Speech

In the classroom, students must raise their hand to be permitted to speak. In the hospital, the use of body adornment with which one signals status, gender, sexual availability, or age grade is sharply curtailed. In the fast-food shop, clerks are instructed to use their voice in friendly manner and to say only the words set forth at headquarters by industrial psychologists. In the military, the complex wardrobe of the civilian used to create a dozen different social occasions is removed and a uniform set of clothing issued. This clothing says but one thing: "I am to give orders; you are to obey my orders." In the professional sport endeavor, the use of behavior to say something to the crowd or to the other team not previously set forth by coaches or by management is forbidden. Five yards for dancing in delight.

Bureaucracy destroys the use by the individual of one's own personal language systems. And yet one cannot be alienated from one's own voice, one's own body, one's own clothing, or one's own behavior easily. In the back of the classroom, students whisper; on the factory floor, bets are made; in the fast-food restaurant, youngsters giggle; in the prison, inmates tap out messages.

Unfree Media

There are information flow systems that more readily lend themselves to alienation than those under the direct control of the individual. Electronically based systems designed to put only a cadre in control of the switch, the mike, the speaker, the copier, the printer, or the modulated electronic impulse do so and in so doing, alienate the mass from the wondrous ability of the human to create, in cooperative process with others, the incredibly complex and varied social occasions reported by ethnographers from around the world and throughout history. In a bureaucracy, mass production of meaning replaces the art and craft of human interaction.

The advent of mechanized media in elitist societies gave control over symbolic interaction to elites. In capitalist societies, the costs of access to magazines, television, radio, or newspapers give the rich a louder voice in which to shape the economic environment than the poor. In bureaucratic organizations, access to the media give the bureaucratic officer control over the symbolic environment in which the faceless client, supplicant, inmate, student, or patient must live.

Free Speech

Outside of mass-produced social endeavors voice, clothing, body, and behavior remain the private property of the individual to use as he/she sees fit. When there is no organized, mass-mediated occasion that requires the political control of symbol sets, and when young people are left to their own devices, shut out of the organized world of the adult and cast adrift from the more private arenas of social life, symbol sets may be used in quite idiosyncratic ways.

Out of the politics of mass society, come the privatized use of the graffiti that young people put on their bodies, upon walls, trains, clothing and, in particular, tee shirts.

More generally, when existing communication systems are used for purposes alien to the human project, parallel and underground structures of communication arise (Young, 1983). The phenomenon of the tee shirt, as with other graffiti, is a parallel symbolic system by which people, usually young people, attempt to create a social-life world that resonates with their own preferences and affinities. Often these same symbol systems are used to express rage, contempt, rebellion, or are used to plea for redress of grievance.

What is said here about the structure and use of symbols and interactions does not hold for the fully open and collective creation of social life. The rules are very different for interaction and so are the results. For the shared creation of social life, each person defined as situationally present has a turn at shaping the activity of others present and, generally, the benefits of such a social life occasion are shared on the basis of need. Collective needs especially are served in social life. Massified forms of organization benefit first the elite, then the cadre, and only incidently, the mass.

Tee Shirts as Text

This section reports the results of a three-day observation of the wearing of tee shirts over a school holiday called "College Days," at Colorado State University. The holiday, incidently, received considerable national news coverage as a "riot." The riot is not, in the first instance, the subject matter of this study, but passing comment will be made in the analysis here. Riots, too, are a form of language in which the voiceless get the attention of those who are "hard of listening."

The study of tee shirt display arose out of a class in sociology entitled Public Opinion and Mass Society. The point of the course was to think about and explain the differences in symbolic interactions between mass society on the one hand and interactively rich social occasions rich in information on the other. The point of the assignment was to locate the tee shirt culture in the larger social context in which it appears; to deconstruct the origins of the tee shirt so that we may reconstruct the larger meaning of their popularity. If we are to read tee shirts for the full meaning they carry, we must read them as a collective event in a sociohistorical process.

The research team reported to the class that the students observed at the parties, concerts, and later at the riot wore tee shirts that bore a wide variety of messages. One of the students took slide photos of the tee shirts to add visual depth to the report. The observations of the research team were first put into a classificatory scheme. The categories generated included:

brand names, exotic vacation places, morality messages including religious sentiments, sexual concerns and action, and youth culture themes oriented to music.

Commodity Fetishism

Most were brand-name shirts; little more than walking advertisements for shoes, beverages, beers, and sporting equipment—all high-profit consumer items. Stroh's, Henry Weinhard, Dos Equis, and other beers showed up on the chests of young men. The Banana Republic is, I was informed, a clothing chain. Sole Suckers was, it seems, a shoe advertisement. One person advertised Camel cigarettes on his chest.

The naturalness of wearing brand names implies a naïve commodity fetishism that for many would be distasteful. Materialism and possession has permeated the consciousness of these young people without the shame it might bring in other settings.

It is the intent of the 300,000 ads seen by preschoolers that they become walking commercials for cereals, toys, burgers, clothes, electronics, and other high-profit, mass-produced goods. The adornment of one's body by commercials is testimony to the success of the advertising industry to colonize the very bodies of their victims.

Status Quests and Proclamations

A second most popular motif was the display of exotic foreign place names. Many students are widely traveled. Central America, Europe, and Asia were represented in the tee shirt parade. A shirt with the logo of Bear Surf Boards not only indicates one's hobby, one's socioeconomic status, but also one's choice of vacation place (we were told that shirt came from Hawaii).

As with commodity fetishism above, the display of vacation place names bespeaks a social status and serves as an opening device for similarly traveled persons. In a mass of unknown others, one can dramatize one's potential affinities and thus invite overture from those unknown others.

Only in those societies where the social self is cut loose from social identity would such pathetic efforts to proclaim status be found. The social identities available in mass sports, mass education, mass religion, and mass markets are too fragile, too flimsy, too short, and too narrowly focused a social take upon which to ground the richness and complexity of a whole human being. Young people as do older people understand this and do not ground their social standing on mass institutions.

One would not say, "I am a K-Mart shopper," or "I am a Channel 7 viewer," in answer to Kuhn's Twenty Statements Test about the social anchorage of self-identity. Sad enough to adorn one's car with bumper stickers saying, "I 'heart' New York," or "I 'heart' Shelties," or "I 'heart' my VW." Sad commentary on the locations of love in mass society.

Morality Lives

The third most commonly observed tee shirt messages were a wide assortment of morality statements. The environment, religious values, friendships, comments on peace and war, as well as social-philosophical comments were displayed. For the most part, a profound concern with brotherhood, sisterhood, and fellowship across social boundaries was, to their credit, dramatized on youths' bodies. Communion with the forms of nature spoke loudly, publicly, and dramatically of concern with pollution and ecological integrity.

"Life is a beach," was perhaps the most cynical philosophy noted. There was a tee shirt that suggested that one partied until one died—a particularly nihilistic philosophy. One understands that the message is not to be taken literally but, at the same time, there is the question of the quality of life in school or at home that makes such a shirt wearable.

A particularly innocent shirt said simply, "Señor Frog." We assumed the allusion was to Kermit and to the delights of magic and make-believe put forward in the Muppets. I was reminded that, after all, the people who wear such shirts were, only yesterday, children.

There were several shirts among the hundreds seen telling unknown others of the benefits of a life dedicated to Jesus. On a young woman was a cross encircled by a wreath and printed words informing the world that she was a "national member." Such tee shirts are close cousins to the bumper stickers that say, "Jesus Saves," "Honk if you love Jesus," "God is coming—and is She pissed."

One wonders if one will ever see such bumper stickers or such shirts used by Muslim youngsters, Jewish youngsters, Buddhist or Shinto devotees, or those still practicing animistic religions. There must be something different about the ways young people are fitted into religion in Christianity and the ways they fit into other religions that they would have to say such a thing on a tee shirt.

In other, more devout societies, such membership would be a background assumption. Only in secularized, technicized, and atomized societies would such tee shirts make sense.

Other morality statements had to do with touching one another, smiling at each other, helping each other, or showing concern for others at home or abroad. One particularly effective shirt for making contact in a friendly sort of a way was called the "ten questions" shirt. The students explained to me that shirt had ten questions on it one was invited to answer: "How old are you?" "What is your major?" "Where is your home?" and such. There was also a tee shirt from Copirg, a public interest research group, advising students to "take it to the streets," presumably because institutional politics were closed to the voice of the student or to the public interest.

In mass society, morality is programmed out of the grasp of the individual. An elite claims control over moral questions in factory, shop, stadium, school, marketplace, and church. The location of morality is so remote from the worker, the guard, the soldier, the student, or the professor that each is reduced to the tee shirt as a feeble cry for a just and decent world.

Just coming into the fullness of their morality, young people find no social role, no social occasion, no social institution in which morality can mediate their situated behavior. Rules, orders, policies, programs, commands, as well as reified social relations preprogram behavior and reduce the self system to the mechanical robot that embodies those rules, orders, or commands.

Sexuality Lives

There were a few shirts with sexual content. Most were of a good-natured sort but one was distinctly chauvinist. The front of the shirt had two cherries over which was superimposed the international symbol of negation. It took us about two seconds to figure out what it meant—then came a chorus of groans. The next slide showed the back of the same shirt. It said, "Busting makes me feel good." The classroom became very quiet.

The group reported that the young man who wore that shirt was observing the norm that one wore such outrageous shirts only in the company of friends. In this case, the shirt was worn at a fraternity party. The party members were all from the same frat or their dates together with a smattering of friends. Even in that company, the person who wore the shirt was made uncomfortable. He was made to understand that few if any of even his close friends appreciated the humor of the message. We were told that he did go in and change shirts after bearing for a while his discomfort.

I have mentioned the practice of commercial advertising to colonize desire and to relocate it in a beverage, a car, a CD, or other commodity. In our society, sexuality becomes a highly privatized activity disconnected from family, community, or gender solidarity concerns as was the case in all previous history.

As a mass society displaces community, human sexuality is liberated to be used for quite personal or commercial purpose. This idiosyncratic use of sexuality offends those who think such a thing as sexuality is too valuable a solidarity tool to discard; who think that community is too valuable a social form to discard. However, the logic of mass society is that solidarity is too strong a social glue to use, and all such solidarity supplies need be made private property.

The privatization of human sexuality permits it to be vested in commodities while the outrage at privatized sexuality by those still oriented to solidarity concerns means that one must avoid an open, honest display of one's sexuality. But that part of the population still too lively or too unsocialized will proclaim that their desire still aims at living human beings—or parts of them at any rate.

Against Mass Culture

A great many tee shirts proclaimed the merits of musical groups. "Bruce Springsteen and the E Street Band" as well as other popular and/or exotic musical groups were promoted. In an earlier report, the students noted the rich interaction between musicians and audiences at rock concerts, jazz festivals, and blue-grass affairs. These cultural events contrast with the highly organized, formalized, and ritualized behavior of the musicians and audience in musical concert out of the eighteenth century, where attire is formal and the conventions of applause and response well regulated by convention.

Such cultural events also stand against the deadness of mass education, mass religion, or mass sport. When young people are given a choice between watching and doing, they opt for the forms of living. When not given that choice, they feign interest and involvement—then find parallel or underground cultural events in which to embody the forces of life. They will act as zombies, as vegetables in the classroom, but in the halls, in the game room, at parties, or in riots, they act in more human ways.

Discussion

The class as a whole reflected upon the semiotics of tee shirts. We wondered how one was to understand the place they had in the overall organization of the lives of young people. We agreed that the major way to understand the wearing of tee shirts was a way to find voice in a mass society.

We agreed that one tried to tell unknown others what one believed, what one liked to do, what another person could talk to one about if one wanted to make human contact, and told others as well what one was worried about at a college event at which most people did not know most others. The anonymity of mass events strips one of most of the language systems one could use. Of the four unalienable symbol systems mentioned earlier, clothing has the particular virtue of speaking when the other media—voice, body, and behavior—are silenced.

The tee shirt can be seen from afar. It can speak over the din of a concert, a party, or a sport event. It can carry a concise and lucid message in ways body and behavior cannot. It is fairly inexpensive and can address a comment to a faceless mass without the expensive electronics or printing equipment ordinarily used in such situations. The tee shirt is the modern equivalent of the poster in prerevolutionary France, wall graffiti in Latin America, or the flaming cross in antebellum South. It is a billboard for those struck dumb by the alienation of mass media in mass society.

We agreed that in a society in which status is based upon one's labor power as a commodity, and at a stage in one's life cycle in which one could not easily sell one's labor power in a way that reflected an acceptable presenting identity, some young people sought other foundations upon which to base status.

In a mass society, the structure of self is freed from the ancient social anchorages of tribe, gender, occupation, religion, or age grade. Those who have no social base for their identity outside of the mass institution turn to other sources of self. Astrology, electronic as well as exotic religions, exclusive clothing, body building, and such cultural semiworlds as punk, hippie, yuppie, country-Western, and college tee shirts provide the structural basis for a quite privatized self system as the social sources found in mass institutions become too alienated and trivial a foundation upon which to build one's life.

The wearing of brand names, of exotic place names, of expensive tee shirts—all resonate with the materialism of a consumer society. Such shirts say to all who will look that the wearer is well located in the class system. There is the discretionary income available to the wearer—that clearly the wearer did not earn—that permits travel in style to far away places. One can say, "If it is money that gets your attention and enlists your company, I have it."

The tee shirt says to anyone who will look, "I am a person worthy of notice; you are to orient your approach to me upon the clues given off by my shirt." By extension, the shirt informs others that the person will be hard to approach if these basic interests are not respected. The possibility of

impromptu formation of affinity groups—dyads, triads, and quartets—
arose out of such artful presentments.

Morality shirts say to all who will listen that the wearer is an estimable
person of moral worth. Concern for the good earth, for the oppressed of the
world, for the morality of others, for the fellowship and love of each other
is a central value in the life of the bearer. One may expect something of real
value in a relationship with such a person.

Shirts carrying sexual messages carry an invitation to embark upon a
short-term, impersonal sexual venture. They say: "In my life, my essential
sexuality is a matter of great concern; I am in the process of developing my
sexuality and I invite you to consider the possibility of exploration together."

Tee shirts that bear the name of a musical group, the marijuana leaf, or
death's head say to their age group that they are angry at the stupidities of
the adult world, that they join with others in a protest that cannot be lightly
ignored and that they fully intend to stay in the youth culture until the
message is heard. One might agree that such a protest is pretheoretical in
its self-destructiveness, that young people should engage in more construc-
tive forms of resistance and rebellion, but such a view asks that children be
wiser than the adults who criticize them.

At the same time, one wonders about the need to use the information-
deficient tee shirt as an opening gambit. Given the mass, anonymous character of state universities in general and "College Days" in particular, one
can understand that more traditional sources of information about how to
respond to another are lacking. One cannot be certain that one will have a
common friend who will provide the necessary opening clues. One appreciates that one misses out on meeting others whom one might like to meet
and get to know. The living graffiti of the tee shirt helps bridge the social
distance between unknown others when more traditional bridges are
missing.

We talked about the curious fact that young people feel the need to make
contact with unknown others. Most people for most of history felt no such
need. Even today, many strangers will walk away from casual openings and
most will make little effort to initiate them. But here are a large number of
young people, mostly Americans, Europeans, and Canadians who will
make the effort and take the risk. It is easy to say that Americans are
friendly or that they are open or that they are assertive. The more interesting question is why they feel the urge to be friendly.

The short answer lies in the systematic displacement of young people by
their society. They are displaced persons trying to make the most of the
cultural resources available in the effort to build a parallel social-life world
that resonates with some of the best of human hope and some of the worst

of human avarice. The society that discards its young will find cause to regret it. The society that values profits and budgets above persons and work will find the costs very high—both in human waste and in dollars.

*Mope's Tee Shirts**

I think you're cute
But then I think I'm cute.

My idea of camping out is when
room service is late

Stupidity should be Painful

Yesterday was the Deadline
For all Complaints

The difference between dark and hard
is that it stays dark all night

Sticks and Stones Break My Bones
but whips and chains excite me

All Extremists should be Killed

Joan of Arc is Alive and
Medium Well

Not everything that sucks
is necessarily bad

The older the wood
The hotter the fire

Built for Comfort
Not for Speed

Ready, Willing & Still Able

---

*Mope runs the Copy Center Service at Central Michigan University. On the day after Bush was elected in 1988, Mope wore the following tee shirt message:

When I was young
They told me anyone
Could be President.
They were right.

Where there's a Will
I want to be part of it

Valley Girls

Valley boys and valley girls
lips of gloss and hair of curls
loins of fire and kisses sweet
give us pause when in the street:
Teased hair and fitted jeans
lots of "you knows" or "I means";
"fucking" this and "fucking" that;
not much mind below their hat.

Read their shirts and read their cars
you can read of their desires.
In the space between their breasts
you discover where each invests
all their wants and all their hopes
voices for a million Mopes;
you can read their primal curse
written in some simple verse.

Salt in coffee
sand in tea
these were never meant to be.
Was it this for which we planned,
Adam delved and Eve had spanned?

References & Bibliography

Amin, Samir. 1977. *Imperialism and Unequal Development.* New York: Monthly Review.

Antonio, Robert J. 1983. "The Origin, Development, and Contemporary Status of Critical Theory." *Sociological Quarterly* 24 (3) :325–51.

———. 1981. "Immanent Critique as the Core of Critical Theory: Its Origins and Developments in Hegel, Marx, and Contemporary Thought." *British Journal of Sociology* 32 (3) :330–45.

Applebaum, R., and Harry Chotiner. 1979. "Science, Critique, and Praxis." *Socialist Review* 46:71–108.

Ashby, H. R. 1968. "Variety, Constraint, and the Law of Requisite Variety." In Buckley, *Modern Systems Research for the Behavioral Scientist.* Chicago: Aldine.

Babbie, E. R. 1983. *Sociology.* Belmont: Wadsworth.

Bagdikian, Ben. 1983. *The Media Monopoly.* Boston: Beacon.

Baran, P., and L. Sweezy. 1976. *Monopoly Capital.* New York: Monthly Review.

Barber, B. J. 1984. *Strong Democracy: Participatory Politics for a New Age.* Berkeley: University of California Press.

Barthes, Roland. 1977. *Image, Music, Text.* Ed. Stephen Heath. London: Fontana.

———. 1971. "The Rhetoric of the Image." *Working Papers in Cultural Studies*, Centre for Contemporary Cultural Studies at the University of Birmingham.

Basham, A. L. 1954. *The Wonder That Was India.* New York: Grove.

Baxandall, Lee. 1970. "Spectacles and Scenarios: A Dramaturgy of Radical Activity." In M. Goodman (ed.), *The Movement toward a New America.* Philadelphia: Pilgrim.

Berger, Peter, and Luckmann, T. 1966. *The Social Construction of Reality.* Garden City: Doubleday.

Boorstin, Daniel. 1962. *The Image.* New York: Athenaeum.

Boskoff, Alvin. 1972. *The Mosaic of Sociological Theory.* New York: Thomas Crowell.

Boulding, Kenneth. 1956. "General Systems Theory." In *Management Science*, II.

Bourdieu, Pierre. 1979. "Public Opinion Does Not Exist." In Mattlelart and Siegelaub (eds.), *Communication and Class Struggle.* New York: International General.

Braverman, Harry. 1974. *Labor and Monopoly Capitalism*. New York: Monthly Review.

Brenner, H. 1976. "Estimating the Social Costs of National Economic Policy." *Joint Economic Committee, U.S. Congress Report*. Washington, D.C.: U.S. Government Printing Office.

Brillouin, L. 1968. "Life, Thermodynamics, and Cybernetics." In W. Buckley (ed.), *Modern Systems Research for the Behavioral Scientist*. Chicago: Aldine.

Brissett, Dennis, and Charles Edgley. 1975. *Life as Theater: A Dramaturgical Sourcebook*. Chicago: Aldine.

Brohm, Jean-Marie. 1975. "Twenty Theses on Sports." *Quel Corps?* no. 1 (April-May).

Brooks, John. 1979. *Showing Off in America: From Conspicuous Consumption to Parody Display*. Boston: Little, Brown.

Buckley, Walter. 1968. "Society as a Complex Adaptive System." In Walter Buckley, *Modern Systems Research for the Behavioral Scientist*. Chicago: Aldine.

Cuzzort, R. P. 1969. *Humanity and Modern Sociological Thought*. New York: Holt, Rinehart, & Winston.

Burke, Kenneth. 1955. *A Rhetoric of Motives*. New York: G. Braziller.

——— . 1945. *A Grammar of Motives*. 1855 New York: G. Braziller.

——— . 1935. *Permanence and Change: An Anatomy of Purpose*. 1965 New York: Bobbs-Merrill.

Burneston and Weedon. 1978. "Ideology, Subjectivity, and the Artistic Text." In Bill Schwartz (ed.) *On Ideology*. London: Hutchinson.

Cackowski, Z. 1983. "Human Work: Its Creative Power and the Conditions of Its Destruction." *Dialectics and Humanism*, no. 2: 47–59.

Cadwallader, M. 1968. "The Cybernetic Analysis of Change in Complex Social Organizations." In W. Buckley (ed.), *Modern Systems Research for the Behavioral Scientist*. Chicago: Aldine.

Chapman, Ivan. 1974. "Social Interaction versus the Appearance of Social Interaction." *International Review of History and Political Science* 11 (2) :45–52.

Chomsky, N., and Edward Herman. 1979. *The Washington Connection and Third World Fascism*. Boston: South End.

Chorbajian, Leon. 1984. "Toward a Marxist Sociology of Sport." *Arena* 8, no. 3.

Clawson, Daniel. 1978. "Class Struggle and the Rise of Bureaucracy." Ph.D. dissertation, State University of New York at Stony Brook.

Combes, James E., and Michael W. Mansfield (eds.). 1976. *Drama in Life*. New York: Hastings House.

Comstock, Donald. 1980. "A Method for Critical Research: Investigating the World to Change It." Red Feather: Red Feather Institute.

Cox, Harvey. 1984. *Religion in the Secular City*. New York: Simon & Schuster.

Crocker, David. 1977. "Markovic's Concept of Praxis." *As. Norm. Inquiry* 20: 1–43.

——— . 1976. "Markovic on Marxian Methodology." Red Feather: Red Feather Institute.

Crook, Steve, and Laurie Taylor. 1980. "Goffman's Version of Reality." In Jason Ditton (ed.), *The View from Goffman*. New York: St. Martin's.

Culler, Jonathan. 1982. *On Deconstruction*. Ithaca: Cornell Press.

Dreitzel, Hans Peter. 1976. "Social Roles and Political Emancipation." *International Journal of Sociology* 5:117–45.

Duncan, Hugh D. 1968. *Symbols in Society.* New York: Oxford University Press.
_____. 1963. *Communication and Social Order.* New York: Bedminister.
_____. 1953. *Language and Literature in Society.* Chicago: University of Chicago Press.
Edelman, Murray. 1964. *The Symbolic Uses of Politics.* Urbana: University of Illinois Press.
Edgley, Charles, and Ronny Turner. 1975. "Masks and Social Relations: An Essay on the Sources and Assumptions of Dramaturgical Social Psychology. *Humboldt Journal of Social Relations.* (Fall-Winter):1–12.
Edwards, Harry. 1973. *Sociology of Sport.* Homewood, Ill.: Dorsey.
Eitzen, D. S. 1984. "Conflict Theory and the Sociology of Sport." *Arena* 8, no. 3.
Fiorenza, Francis Schussler. 1977. "Work and Critical Theology." In *A Matter of Dignity: Inquiries into the Humanization of Work.* Notre Dame: University of Notre Dame Press.
Foote, Nelson. 1975. "Concept and Method in the Study of Human Development." In Dennis Brissett and Charles Edgley (eds.), *Life as Theater: A Dramaturgical Sourcebook.* Chicago: Aldine.
Gelles, Richard J. 1971. "The TV News Interview: A Case Study in the Construction and Presentation of Social Reality." ASA Meeting, session 3.
Gleick, James. 1987. *Chaos: Making a New Science.* New York: Penguin Books.
Goffman, Erving. 1951. "Symbols of Class Status." *British Journal of Sociology* 2:294–304.
_____. 1956. *The Presentation of Self in Everyday Life.* Edinburgh, (Scotland Social Sciences Research Center.
_____. 1959. *The Presentation of Self in Everyday Life.* Garden City, N.Y.: Doubleday Anchor.
_____. 1961a. *Asylums: Essays on the Social Situations of Mental Patients and Other Inmates.* Garden City, N.Y.: Anchor.
_____. 1961b. *Encounters.* Indianapolis: Bobbs-Merrill.
_____. 1963a. *Stigma.* Englewood Cliffs, N.J.: Prentice-Hall.
_____. 1963b. *Behavior in Public Places.* New York: Free Press.
_____. 1967. *Interaction Ritual.* Garden City, N.Y.: Doubleday.
_____. 1974. *Frame Analysis: An Essay on the Organization of Experience.* New York: Harper Colophon.
_____. 1976. *Gender Advertisements.* New York: Harper Colophon.
_____. 1981. *Forms of Talk.* Philadelphia: University of Pennsylvania Press.
Gonos, George. 1980. "The Class Position of Goffman's Sociology: Social Origins of an American Structuralism." In Jason Ditton (ed.), *The View from Goffman.* New York: St. Martin's.
_____. 1977. "'Situation' versus 'Frame': The 'Interactionist' and the 'Structuralist' Analyses of Everyday Life." *American Sociological Review* 42:854–67.
Gouldner, Alvin. 1970. *The Coming Crisis of Western Sociology.* New York: Basic Books.
Gramsci, Antonio. 1911. *Prison Notebooks.* New York: International Publishers.
Gruneau, Richard. 1981. "Elites, Class, and Corporate Power in Canadian Sport." In John W. Loy, Jr., Gerald S. Kenyon, and Barry D. McPherson (eds.), Sport, Culture, and Society, 2nd ed. Philadelphia: Lea & Febiger.
Gusfield, Joseph. 1963. *Symbolic Crusade.* Urbana: University of Illinois Press.
Habermas, Jurgen. 1979a. *Communication and the Evolution of Human Society.* Boston: Beacon.

_____. 1979b. "The public sphere." In Mattelart and Siegelaub (eds.), *Communication and Class Struggle*, vol. 1. New York: International General Press.

_____. 1974a. *Legitimation Crisis*. Boston: Beacon.

_____. 1974b. "On social interest." *Telos* 19 (Spring):91–103.

_____. 1971. *Knowledge and Human Interests*. Boston: Beacon.

_____. 1970a. "On Systematically Distorted Communication." *Inquiry* 13: 205–18.

_____. 1970b. *Toward a Rational Society*. Boston: Beacon.

_____. 1970c. "Toward a Theory of Communicative Competence." *In Recent Sociology*, no. 2, ed. Hans Peter Dreitzel. Toronto: MacMillan.

Harblin, Thomas. 1971. Lecture series at Colorado State University. Fall quarter.

Helmer, John. 1970. "The Face of the Man without Qualities." *Social Research* 37 (Winter):547–79.

Henry, Jules. 1963. *Culture against Man*. New York: Vintage.

Hoch, Paul. 1972. *Rip Off the Big Game*. Garden City. N.Y.: Doubleday.

Horkheimer, Max. 1972. *Critical Theory*. New York: Seabury.

Horton, John. 1966. "Order and Conflict Theories of Social Problems as Creating Ideologies." *American Journal of Sociology* 71(6).

Ichheiser, Gustav. 1970. *Appearances and Reality*. San Francisco: Jossey-Bass.

Israel, Joachim. 1971. *Alienation: From Marx to Modern Sociology*. Boston: Allyn & Bacon.

Jacobson, Nolan Pliny. 1986. *Understanding Buddhism*. Carbondale: Southern Illinois University Press.

Keil, T. 1984. "The Sociology of Sport in Advanced Capitalist Society." *Arena* 8, no. 3.

Klapp, Orrin. 1976. "Dramatic Encounters." In Combes and Mansfield, (eds.), *Drama in Life*. New York: Hastings.

Lash, Scott. 1980. "Right and Liberalism in the Thought of Weber." Paper is presented at the Conference of the American Sociological Association, New York.

Leitch, Vincent B. 1983. *Deconstructive Criticism*. New York: Columbia University Press.

Lévi-Strauss, C. 1969. "The Raw and the Cooked." *Introduction to a Science of Mythology*, vol. 1. London: Jonathan Cape.

Lukács, Georg. 1971. *History and Class Consciousness: Studies in Marxist Dialectics*. Cambridge, Mass. MIT.

Lyman, Stanford, and Marvin B. Scott. 1975. *The Drama of Social Reality*. New York: Oxford University Press.

Macherey, P. 1978. *A Theory of Literary Production*. London: Routledge.

MacKay, Donald M. 1968. "Towards an Information-Flow Model of Human Behavior." In *Modern Systems Research for the Behavioral Scientist*, ed. Walter Buckley. Chicago: Aldine.

Mannheim, Karl. 1936. *Ideology and Utopia*. New York: Harcourt, Brace, & World.

Manning, Peter. 1980. "Goffman's Framing Order: Style as Structure." In Jason Ditton (ed.), *The View from Goffman*. New York: St. Martin's.

Marcuse, Herbert. 1964. *One-Dimensional Man: Studies in the Ideology of Advanced Industrial Society*. Boston: Beacon.

Markovic, Mihailo. 1974. *From Affluence to Praxis*. Boston: Beacon.

Maruyama, Magoroh. 1963. "The Second Cybernetics: Deviation Amplifying Mutual Causal Processes," *American Scientist* 51:164–79.

Marx, Karl. 1978. *Critique of Hegel's Philosophy of Right*, ed. Joseph O'Malley. Cambridge: Cambridge University Press.

———. 1972a. "Capital: Selections." In R. Tucker (ed.), *The Marx-Engels Reader.* New York: W. W. Norton.

———. 1972b. "Thesis on Feuerbach." In Robert Tucker (ed.), *The Marx-Engels Reader.* New York: W. W. Norton.

———. 1972c. *Grundrisse.* New York: Harper Torchbooks.

———. 1964. *Economic and Philosophic Manuscripts of 1844.* New York: International Publishers.

——— and F. Engels. 1972. "Manifesto of the Communist Party." In R. Tucker (ed.), *The Marx-Engels Reader.* New York: W. W. Norton.

Mauss, Marcel. 1955. *The Gift,* tr. I. Gunnison. Glencoe: Free Press.

McCarthy, Thomas. 1978. *The Critical Theory of Jurgen Habermas.* Cambridge, Mass. SIT.

McClelland, David. *The Thought of Karl Marx.* New York: Harper Torchbooks.

McGee, R. 1980. *Sociology:* New York: Holt-Rinehart.

McGinniss, J. 1969. *The Selling of the President, 1968.* New York: Trident.

Merelman, Richard. 1969. "The Dramaturgy of Politics." *Sociological Quarterly* 10 (2) :216–24.

Mills, C. Wright. 1959. The *Sociological Imagination.* New York: Oxford University Press.

———. 1940. "Situated Actions and Vocabularies of Motive." *American Sociological Review* 5:904–13.

Monod, J. 1972. *Chance and Necessity.* New York: Vintage Books.

Mueller, Claus. 1973. *Politics of Communication.* New York: Oxford University Press.

Nimmo, Dan. 1976. "The Drama, Illusion, and Reality of Political Images." In J. Combes and M. Mansfield (eds.), *Drama in Life.* New York: Hastings.

Norris, Christopher. 1982. *Deconstruction: Theory and Practice.* London: Methuen Press.

O'Connor, James, 1973. *The Fiscal Crisis of the State.* New York: St. Martin's.

Ollman, Bertell. 1979. *Social and Sexual Revolution: Essays on Marx and Reich.* Boston: South End.

Perinbanayagam, R. 1982. *The Karmic Theater: Self, Society, and Astrology in Jaffna.* Amherst: University of Massachusetts Press.

———. 1975. "The Reality of Drama." Paper presented at the Annual Meeting of Midwest Sociological Society, Chicago.

Prigogine, Ilya., and Isabelle Stengers. 1984. *Order Out of Chaos.* New York: Bantam Books.

Quinney, Richard. 1980. *Providence: The Reconstruction of Moral and Social Order.* New York: Longman.

Rahula, Walpola. 1974. *What the Buddha Taught.* New York: Grove.

Ritzer, George. 1975. *Sociology: A Multiple Paradigm Science.* Boston: Allyn & Bacon.

Ritzer, G., K. Kammeyer, and N. Yetman. 1982. *Sociology:* Boston: Bacon & Allyn.

Sax, Joseph,1971. *Defending the Environment.* New York: Knopf.

Scaff, Adam. 1970. *Marxism and the Human Individual.* New York: McGraw-Hill.

Schumacher, E. F. 1973. *Small Is Beautiful*. New York: Harper & Row.

Schrodinger, E. 1968. "Order, Disorder, and Entropy." In W. Buckley (ed.), *Modern Systems Research for the Behavioral Scientist*. Chicago: Aldine.

Schroyer, Trent. 1973. *The Critique of Domination*. New York: Brazillier.

———. 1970. "Towards a Critical Theory of Advanced Industrial Society." In Hans Peter Dreitzel (ed.), *Recent Sociology*, no. 2. New York: MacMillan.

Sewart, John J. 1981. "The Rationalization of Modern Sport: The Case of Professional Football." *Arena Review* 5 (September):45–51.

Silverstone, R. 1981. *The Message of Television: Myth and Narrative in Contemporary Cultures*. London: Heineman.

Smelser, N. 1981. *Sociology*. New York: Wiley.

Soelle, Dorothee. 1984. *To Work and to Love*. Philadelphia: Fortress.

Stebbens, Robert, 1969. "Role Distance, Role Distance Behavior, and Jazz Musicians." *British Journal of Sociology* 20:406–15.

Sumner, Colin. 1979. "The Semiology of Roland Barthes." In *Reading Ideologies*. New York: Academic Press.

Tawney, R. H. 1961. *Religion and the Rise of Capitalism*. New York: Mentor.

Tedeschi, J. (ed.). 1981. *Impression Management Theory and Social Psychological Research*. New York: Academic Press.

Thompson, Victor. 1966. *Modern Organization*. New York: Knopf.

Toennies, F. 1957. *Community and Society*. East Lansing: Michigan State University Press.

Troeltsch, Ernst. 1960. *The Social Teaching of the Christian Churches*, vol. 2. New York: Harper & Row.

Veblen, Thorstein. 1979. *The Theory of the Leisure Class*. New York: Penguin.

Wardell, Mark L., and J. Kenneth Benson. 1979. "A Dialectical View: Foundations for an Alternative Sociological Method." In Scott McNall (ed.), *Theoretical Perspectives in Sociology*. New York: St. Martin's.

Weber, Max. 1968. *Economy and Society: An Outline of Interpretive Sociology*, 3 vols., ed. Guenther Roth and Claus Wittch. New York: Bedminster.

———. 1958. *The Protestant Ethic and the Spirit of Capitalism*. New York: Scribner's.

———. 1946. *From Max Weber: Essays in Sociology*, ed. Hans Gerth and C. Wright Mills. New York: Oxford University Press.

Weedon, Chris, et al. 1980. "Introduction to Language Studies at the Center." In *Culture, Media, and Language*. London: Hutchinson.

Weiner, N. 1968. "Cybernetics In History." In W. Buckley (ed.), *Modern Systems Research for the Behavioral Scientist*. Chicago: Aldine.

Williams, Raymond. 1976. *Keywords*. Glasgow: Collins & Sons.

Wilson, E. 1983. *Sociology*. Homewood: Dorsey.

Woodward, F. L. (trans.). 1965. *The Book of the Kindred Sayings*. London: Luzac.

Young, T. R. 1989. "Chaos and Crime." Circulated by the Red Feather Institute as part of the Transforming Sociology Series.

———. 1987. "Information, Ideology, and Political Reality: Against Toffler." In *The Ideology of the Information age*, ed. J. D. Slack and F. Fejes. Norwood, N.J.: Ablex.

———. 1983a. "Underground Structures of the Democratic State." *Mid-America Review of Sociology* 7 VII, no. 2 (Winter).

———. 1983b. "Symbolic Interactional Theory: Assumptions and Social Reality." Paper presented at the Pacific Sociological Meetings, San Jose, Calif. (April).

_____ . 1982. "The Structure of Self in Mass Society." Transforming Sociology Series, Red Feather Institute.

_____ . 1982. "Folk Methods vs. Scientific Methods of Reality Construction." American Sociologist.

_____ . 1982. "Information, Ideology, and Political Reality." Paper presented at the PSA meetings in San Diego.

_____ . 1981. "Public Opinion, Social Opinion, and Mass Opinion." Red Feather: Red Feather Institute.

_____ . 1980. "The Division of Labor in the Construction of Social Reality." Urban Life 9 (2) :135–62.

_____ . 1980. "Social Opinion, Public Opinion, and Mass Opinion." Red Feather: Red Feather Institute.

_____ . 1979. "A Theory of Underground Structures." Transforming Sociology Series, Red Feather Institute.

_____ . 1979. "Self and Social Organization in Capitalist Societies." Red Feather: Red Feather Institute.

_____ . 1977. "Radical Dimensions in Modern Systems Theory: A General Theory of Social Order and a Special Theory of Social Change." Western Sociological Review. V. 8: No. 2.

_____ . 1976. "Critical Dimensions in Dramaturgical Analysis: Backstage at the Whitehouse." Presented at the annual American Sociological Association meetings in New York.

_____ . 1974. "Radical Dimensions in Modern Systems Theory." Red Feather: Feather Institute.

_____ . 1972. New Sources of Self. London: Pergamon.

_____ . 1971. "The Cybernetics of Stratification." Sociology and Social Research 55 (April).

_____ . and J. Brouillette. 1976. "Bureaucracy and Mass Society." Paper prepared for the Southern Sociological Meetings at Miami.

_____ . and Gordon Schwartzman. 1974. "Public Opinion Tradition and Information half-life." International Journal of Systems Theory (1):259.

Zurcher, Louis. 1977. The Mutable Self: A Self Concept for Social Change. Beverley Hills: Sage.

Index